THE WORLD OF
YESTERDAY

STEFAN ZWEIG

THE WORLD OF YESTERDAY

Newly translated by Anthea Bell

University of Nebraska Press
Lincoln

Die Welt von Gestern © 1942 by Williams Verlag, Zurich
English translation © 2009 by Anthea Bell and Pushkin Press
All rights reserved
Manufactured in the United States of America

First Nebraska paperback printing: 2013

Frontispiece: Stefan Zweig. © Roger-Viollet/The Image Works.

Library of Congress Cataloging-in-Publication Data
Zweig, Stefan, 1881–1942.
[Welt von gestern. English]
The world of yesterday / Stefan Zweig; newly translated by
Anthea Bell.
pages cm
Translation of Die Welt von Gestern ©1942 published by
Williams Verlag, Zurich.
Includes bibliographical references and index.
ISBN 978-0-8032-2661-6 (pbk.: alk. paper) 1. Zweig, Stefan,
1881–1942. 2. Authors, Austrian—20th century—Biography.
I. Bell, Anthea, translator. II. Title.
PT2653.W42Z46 2013
838'.91209—dc23
[B]   2012050218

This edition follows the original in beginning the main text
on arabic page 23; no material has been omitted.

TRANSLATOR'S NOTE

It should be remembered in reading this memoir by Stefan Zweig, first published in the original German in 1942, the year of his death, that the Second World War was still going on while he was completing it. That in itself explains why its place of first publication was Stockholm rather than anywhere in Germany or Austria, because as a Jewish writer he had already been banned in those countries under the National Socialist regime, as he tells his readers in the later chapters of his book. In translating, I was often brought up with a jolt of automatic if momentary surprise by comments reminding me that the war was in progress as he wrote. When, for instance, he says: "Inevitably, the dimensions of the present day have changed our point of view", he is referring to the Nazi regime from 1933 on, culminating in full-scale hostilities from 1939. He never knew the end of the story; he and his second wife committed suicide together in February 1942.

Their double suicide raises another point: there has been discussion of the reason for it, since at that date, when the United States had just entered the war after the Japanese attack on Pearl Harbor in late 1941, there were clear signs that the tide was turning against Hitler. Talk of final victory and a 'wonder weapon' may have sounded persuasive in Germany and Austria, where a heavy propaganda system was brought to bear, less so outside those countries. One surmise, with which I concur, is that Zweig's underlying reason may have been a sense that whether the war was won or lost, the world of civilised culture

v

in which he had lived and worked was gone for ever. I concur merely on the grounds that the close work of translation brings one close to an author's mind—as Zweig, who often worked as a translator himself early in his literary career, and knew what translation sets out to do (see several passages in this book), might, I think, have agreed. He delivered *The World of Yesterday* to his publishers not long before his suicide. It was not all written in consecutive order as published, but even the closing chapters, leading up to the declaration of war on Germany by Britain and France in 1939, while Zweig was living in England, simply do not leave me with the impression that the book was a long suicide note. Close to the end of it, Zweig mentions years still unlived ahead of him and books yet to be written, with the evident intention of writing them if he can, and his final sentence is an affirmation of the value of life lived to the full. The suicide note that he did write is reasoned and lucid, but who knows, maybe an element of sudden desperation was also involved. One can only speculate.

Gloomy as Zweig felt about the lives of Jews under Hitler—and he describes their predicament in detail in his closing chapter—it is also a shock to the modern reader to realise that at the time of his death he did not know the full horror of what was still in store. The Wannsee Conference, which discussed the infamous Final Solution policy, the brainchild of Reinhard Heydrich, was held in December 1941. Details of the death camps and the Holocaust did not leak out to the Western media instantly by any means, in many cases not until after the war. When Zweig was writing, he describes the fate facing a Jew under Hitler in 1939—deprived of all his possessions, he would be expelled from the country with only the clothes he stood up in and ten marks in his pocket. It was certainly bad enough, but there was worse to come.

What Stefan Zweig would have thought of the Holocaust one can only imagine. But his memoir, a quintessentially humane document and a record of European culture in the late nineteenth and early twentieth centuries, stands as a sane, civilised counterblast to the horrors of war as he already knew it, and as a well-informed and sometimes quirkily individual account of the cultural life of his time.

ANTHEA BELL 2009

Let's withdraw
And meet the time as it seeks us.

Shakespeare *Cymbeline*

FOREWORD

I NEVER CONSIDERED myself important enough to feel tempted to tell others the story of my life. Much had to happen, far more in the shape of terrible events, disasters and trials than any other single generation has known, before I found the courage to embark on a book in which I feature as the main or, more accurately, the central character. Nothing is further from my mind than to bring myself to the fore, unless in the sense of being the presenter of a lecture illustrated by slides. The times provide the pictures, I merely speak the words to go with them, and it will not be so much my own story I tell as that of an entire generation—our unique generation, carrying a heavier burden of fate than almost any other in the course of history. We have all, even the least of us, known the turmoil of almost constant volcanic shocks suffered by our native continent of Europe, and the only precedence I can claim for myself among a countless multitude is that as an Austrian, a Jew, a writer, a humanist and a pacifist I have always stood where those volcanic eruptions were at their most violent. Three times they have wreaked havoc with my home and my way of life, cutting me off from the past and all that it once comprised, and flinging me with dramatic force into a void where I soon became familiar with the feeling that there was nowhere to turn. But that in itself was no great cause for complaint; the homeless, more than anyone, are free in a new way, and only those with no more ties can afford to cast consideration to the winds. So I hope that I can fulfil at least one of the main requirements of every proper account of a certain era, and look at it with honest impartiality.

For I have indeed been torn from all my roots, even from the earth that nourished them, more entirely than most in our times. I was born in 1881 in the great and mighty empire of the Habsburg Monarchy, but you would look for it in vain on the map today; it has vanished without trace. I grew up in Vienna, an international metropolis for two thousand years, and had to steal away from it like a thief in the night before it was demoted to the status of a provincial German town. My literary work, in the language in which I wrote it, has been burnt to ashes in the country where my books made millions of readers their friends. So I belong nowhere now, I am a stranger or at the most a guest everywhere. Even the true home of my heart's desire, Europe, is lost to me after twice tearing itself suicidally to pieces in fratricidal wars. Against my will, I have witnessed the most terrible defeat of reason and the most savage triumph of brutality in the chronicles of time. Never—and I say so not with pride but with shame—has a generation fallen from such intellectual heights as ours to such moral depths. In the brief interval between the time when I first began to grow a beard and today, when it is beginning to turn grey, more radical changes and transformations have taken place than in ten normal human generations, and we all feel: this is too much! My today is so different from all my yesterdays; I have risen and fallen so often, that I sometimes feel as if I had lived not just one but several completely different lives. When I say, without thinking, 'my life', I often find myself instinctively wondering *which* life. My life before the world wars, before the First or the Second World War, or my life today? Then again I catch myself saying, 'my house', and I am not sure which of my former homes I mean: my house in Bath, my house in Salzburg, my parental home in Vienna? Or I find myself saying that 'at home' we do this or that, by 'we' meaning Austrians, and remember, with a shock, that for some time I have been no more of an Austrian than I am an Englishman or an American; I am no longer organically bound to my native land and I never really fit into any other. I feel that the world in which I grew up and the world of today, not to mention the world in between them, are drawing further and further apart and becoming entirely different places. Whenever, in conversation with younger friends, I mention something that happened before the First World War, their startled questions make me realise how much of what I still take for granted as reality has become either past history or unimaginable to them. And a lurking instinct in me says that they are right; all the bridges are broken between today, yesterday and the day before yesterday. I can only marvel at the wealth and variety of events that we have compressed into the brief span of a single lifetime—admittedly a very uncomfortable and dangerous lifetime—especially when I compare it with the life my forebears led. Both my father and my grandfather lived their lives in a single, direct way—it was one and the same life from beginning to end, without many vicissitudes, without upheaval and danger, a life of small tensions, imperceptible transitions, always lived in the same easy, comfortable rhythm as the wave of time carried them from the cradle to the grave. They spent all their days in the same country, the same city, usually even in the same house. As for what went on in the outside world, fundamentally that was only something they read in the newspaper, it did not come knocking at their doors. There was probably a war of some kind in progress somewhere in their time, but only a little one compared to the dimensions of modern warfare, and waged far away from their borders. They did not hear the cannon, it was all over and forgotten after six months, a dry-as-dust page in a history book, and the same old life began again. But we have lived through everything without ever returning to our former lives, nothing was left of them, nothing was restored. It was for our generation to experience, to the highest degree, events that history usually bestows sparingly on a single land over a whole century. One generation might see revolution, the next a coup, the third a war, the fourth famine, the fifth national bankruptcy—and many lucky countries and lucky generations never knew any of that. But as for those of us who are now sixty years old, and *de jure* should still have a little time left ahead of us, what have we *not* seen, *not* suffered, *not* experienced? We have made our way through the catalogue of all imaginable catastrophes from beginning to end, and we have not reached the last page of it yet. I myself have lived at the time of the two greatest wars known to mankind, even experiencing each on a different side—the first on the German side and the second among Germany's enemies. Before those wars I saw individual freedom at its zenith, after them I saw liberty at its lowest point in hundreds of years; I have been acclaimed and despised, free and not free, rich and poor. All the pale horses of the apocalypse have stormed through my life: revolution and famine, currency depreciation and terror, epidemics and emigration; I have seen great mass ideologies grow before my eyes and spread, Fascism in Italy, National Socialism in Germany, Bolshevism in Russia, and above all the ultimate pestilence that has poisoned the flower of our European culture, nationalism in general. I have been a defenceless, helpless witness of the unimaginable relapse of mankind into what was believed to be long-forgotten barbarism, with its deliberate programme of inhuman dogma. It was for our generation, after hundreds of years, to see again wars without actual declarations of war, concentration camps, torture, mass theft and the bombing of defenceless cities, bestiality unknown for the last fifty generations, and it is to be hoped that future generations will not see them again. Yet paradoxically, at the same time as our world was turning the moral clock back a thousand years, I have also seen mankind achieve unheard-of feats in the spheres of technology and the intellect, instantly outdoing everything previously achieved in millions of years: the conquest of the air with the aeroplane, words travelling all over the world at the moment when they are spoken, the conquest of space, the splitting of the atom, the defeat of even the most insidious diseases. Almost daily, things still impossible yesterday have become possible. Never until our time has mankind as a whole acted so diabolically, or made such almost divine progress.

It seems to me a duty to bear witness to our lifetime, which has been fraught with such dramatic events, for we have all, I repeat, witnessed these vast transformations—we have been forced to witness them. For our generation, there was no other option, no chance such as earlier generations had of standing aside. Thanks to our new methods of spreading news as soon as it happens, we have been constantly drawn into the events of our time. When bombers smashed buildings in Shanghai, we knew it in our sitting rooms in Europe even before the injured were carried out. Incidents thousands of miles away overseas came vividly before our eyes. There was no shelter, no safety from constant awareness and involvement. There was no country to which you could escape, no way you could buy peace and quiet; all the time, everywhere, the hand of Fate took us and dragged us back into its insatiable game.

We have constantly had to subordinate ourselves to the demands of the state, a prey to the most stupid of policies, we have had to adjust to the most fantastic of vicissitudes, we have always been chained to a common fate, bitterly as we might resent it; it swept us irresistibly away. Those of us who passed through that time, or rather were hunted and hounded through it, have hardly had time to draw breath. We have experienced more history than any of our forefathers did. Even today we stand at another watershed, at an end and a new beginning. If I conclude this survey of my life at a certain particular date, I do so intentionally—that September day in 1939[1] drew the closing line under the epoch that had formed and reared those of us who are of the generation now reaching the age of sixty. But if we can salvage only a splinter of truth from the structure of its ruin, and pass it on to the next generation by bearing witness to it, we will not have lived entirely in vain.

I am well aware of the unfortunate circumstances, so characteristic of our times, in which I am trying to give some kind of form to these memoirs of mine. I write in the middle of the war, I write abroad and with nothing to jog my memory; I have no copies of my books, no notes, no letters from friends available here in my hotel room. There is nowhere I can go for information, because all over the world postal services between countries have been halted or are subject to censorship. We all live apart from each other, just as we did hundreds of years ago before the invention of steamships and railways, air travel and the postal system. I have nothing left of my past, then, but what I carry in my head. At this moment everything else is either lost or beyond my reach. But our generation has learnt the fine art of not mourning for what is lost, and perhaps the loss of documentation and detail will even be an advantage in this book of mine. For I regard memory not as a phenomenon preserving one thing and losing another merely by chance, but as a power that deliberately places events in order or wisely omits them. Everything we forget about our own lives was really condemned to oblivion by an inner instinct long ago. Only what I want to preserve for myself has any claim to be preserved for others. So I ask my memories to speak and choose for me, and give at least some faint reflection of my life before it sinks into the dark.

NOTE

1   3rd September 1939, the day when Britain (where Zweig was living in exile at the time) and France declared war on Germany.

THE WORLD OF
YESTERDAY

THE WORLD OF SECURITY

Reared as we are, in quiet and in peace,
Now all at once we're thrown upon the world.
Thousands of waves wash round us without cease,
Often delighted, sometimes pleased, we're whirled
From joy to grief, and so from hour to hour
Our restless feelings waver, change and sway.
Our senses know a strange, tumultuous power,
And in the turmoil find no place to stay.

Goethe

IF I TRY TO FIND some useful phrase to sum up the time of my childhood and youth before the First World War, I hope I can put it most succinctly by calling it the Golden Age of Security. Everything in our Austrian Monarchy, then almost a thousand years old, seemed built to last, and the state itself was the ultimate guarantor of durability. The rights it gave its citizens were affirmed by our parliament, a freely elected assembly representing the people, and every duty was precisely defined. Our currency, the Austrian crown, circulated in the form of shiny gold coins, thus vouching for its own immutability. Everyone knew how much he owned and what his income was, what was allowed and what was not. Everything had its norm, its correct measurement and weight. If you had wealth, you could work out precisely how much interest it would earn you every year, while civil servants and officers were reliably able to consult the calendar and see the year when they would be promoted and the year when they would retire. Every family had its own budget and knew how much could be spent on food and lodging, summer holidays and social functions, and of course you had to put a small sum aside for unforeseen contingencies such as illness and the doctor. If you owned a house you regarded it as a secure home for your children and grandchildren; property in town or country was passed on from generation to generation. While a baby was still in the cradle, you contributed the first small sums to its way through life, depositing them in a money box or savings account, a little reserve for the future. Everything in this wide domain was firmly established, immovably in its place, with the old Emperor at the top of the pyramid, and if he were to die the Austrians all knew (or thought they knew) that another emperor would take his place, and nothing in the well-calculated order of things would change. Anything radical or violent seemed impossible in such an age of reason.

This sense of security was an asset owned by millions, something desirable, an ideal of life held in common by all. Life was worth living only with such security, and wider and wider circles were eager to have their part in that valuable asset. At first only those who already owned property enjoyed advantages, but gradually the population at large came to aspire to them. The era of security was also the golden age of the insurance industry. You insured your house against fire and theft, your land against damage by storms and hail, your body against accidents and sickness; you bought annuities for your old age; you put insurance policies in your girl children's cradles to provide their future dowries. Finally even the working classes organised themselves to demand a certain level of wages as the norm, as well as health insurance schemes. Servants saved for their old age, and paid ahead of time into policies for their own funerals. Only those who could look forward with confidence to the future enjoyed the present with an easy mind.

But for all the solidity and sobriety of people's concept of life at the time, there was a dangerous and overweening pride in this touching belief that they could fence in their existence, leaving no gaps at all. In its liberal idealism, the nineteenth century was honestly convinced that it was on the direct and infallible road to the best of all possible worlds. The people of the time scornfully looked down on earlier epochs with their wars, famines and revolutions as periods when mankind had not yet come of age and was insufficiently enlightened. Now, however, it was a mere matter of decades before they finally saw an end to evil and violence, and in those days this faith in uninterrupted, inexorable 'progress' truly had the force of a religion. People believed in 'progress' more than in the Bible, and its gospel message seemed incontestably proven by the new miracles of science and technology that were revealed daily. In fact a general upward development became more and more evident, and at the end of that peaceful century it was swift and multifarious. Electric lights brightly lit the streets by night, replacing the dim lamps of the past; shops displayed their seductive new brilliance from the main streets of cities all the way to the suburbs; thanks to the telephone, people who were far apart could speak to each other; they were already racing along at new speeds in horseless carriages, and fulfilling the dream of Icarus by rising in the air. The comfort of upper-class dwellings now reached the homes of the middle classes; water no longer had to be drawn from wells or waterways; fires no longer had to be laboriously kindled in the hearth; hygiene was widespread, dirt was disappearing. People were becoming more attractive, stronger, healthier, and now that there were sporting activities to help them keep physically fit, cripples, goitres and mutilations were seen in the streets less and less frequently. Science, the archangel of progress, had worked all these miracles. Social welfare was also proceeding apace; from year to year more rights were granted to the individual, the judiciary laid down the law in a milder and more humane manner, even that ultimate problem, the poverty of the masses, no longer seemed insuperable. The right to vote was granted to circles flung wider and wider, and with it the opportunity for voters to defend their own interests legally. Sociologists and professors competed to make the lives of the proletariat healthier and even happier—no wonder that century basked in its own sense of achievement and regarded every decade, as it drew to a close, as the prelude to an even better one. People no more believed in the possibility of barbaric relapses, such as wars between the nations of Europe, than they believed in ghosts and witches; our fathers were doggedly convinced of the infallibly binding power of tolerance and conciliation. They honestly thought that divergences between nations and religious faiths would gradually flow into a sense of common humanity, so that peace and security, the greatest of goods, would come to all mankind.

Today, now that the word 'security' has long been struck out of our vocabulary as a phantom, it is easy for us to smile at the optimistic delusion of that idealistically dazzled generation, which thought that the technical progress of mankind must inevitably result in an equally rapid moral rise. We who, in the new century, have learnt not to be surprised by any new outbreak of collective bestiality, and expect every new day to prove even worse than the day just past, are considerably more sceptical about prospects for the moral education of humanity. We have found that we have to agree with Freud, who saw our culture and civilization as a thin veneer through which the destructive forces of the underworld could break at any moment. We have had to accustom ourselves slowly to living without firm ground beneath our feet, without laws, freedom or security. We long ago ceased believing in the religion of our fathers, their faith in the swift and enduring ascent of humanity. Having learnt our cruel lesson, we see their overhasty optimism as banal in the face of a catastrophe that, with a single blow, cancelled out a thousand years of human effort. But if it was only a delusion, it was a noble and wonderful delusion that our fathers served, more humane and fruitful than today's slogans.

26

And something in me, mysteriously and in spite of all I know and all my disappointments, cannot quite shake it off. What a man has taken into his bloodstream in childhood from the air of that time stays with him. And despite all that is dinned into my ears daily, all the humiliation and trials that I myself and countless of my companions in misfortune have experienced, I cannot quite deny the belief of my youth that in spite of everything, events will take a turn for the better. Even from the abyss of horror in which we try to feel our way today, half-blind, our hearts distraught and shattered, I look up again and again to the ancient constellations that shone on my childhood, comforting myself with the inherited confidence that, some day, this relapse will appear only an interval in the eternal rhythm of progress onward and upward.

Now that a great storm has long since destroyed it, we know at last that our world of security was a castle in the air. Yet my parents lived in it as if it were a solid stone house. Not once did a storm or a cold draught invade their warm, comfortable existence. Of course they had special protection from cold winds; they were prosperous people who grew rich, then even very rich, and wealth comfortably draught-proofed your windows and walls in those times. Their way of life seems to me typical of the Jewish middle classes that had made significant contributions to Viennese culture, only to be exterminated root and branch by way of thanks, and I can say impersonally of their comfortable and quiet existence that, in that era of security, ten or twenty thousand Viennese families lived just as my parents did.

My father's family came from Moravia. The Jewish communities there lived in small country towns and villages, on excellent terms with the peasants and the lower middle classes. They felt none of the sense of oppression suffered by the Jews of Galicia further to the east, nor did they share their impatience to forge ahead. Made strong and healthy by life in the country, they walked the fields in peace and security, just as the peasants of their native land did. Emancipated at an early date from orthodox religious observance, they were passionate supporters of the contemporary cult of 'progress', and in the political era of liberalism they provided parliament with its most respected deputies. When they moved from their places of origin to Vienna, they adapted with remarkable speed to a higher cultural sphere, and their personal rise was closely linked to the general economic upswing of the times. Here again, my family was entirely typical in its development. My paternal grandfather had sold manufactured goods. Then, in the second half of the century, came the industrial boom in Austria. Mechanical looms and spinning machines imported from Britain rationalised manufacturing, bringing a great reduction in costs by comparison with traditional handloom weaving, and Jewish businessmen, with their gift for commercial acumen and their international perspective, were the first in Austria to recognise the necessity of switching to industrial production and the rewards it would bring. Usually beginning with only a small capital sum, they founded swiftly erected factories, initially driven by water power, which gradually expanded to become the mighty Bohemian textiles industry that dominated all Austria and the Balkans. So while my grandfather, a middleman dealing in ready-made products, was a typical representative of the previous generation, my father moved firmly into the modern era at the age of thirty-three by founding a small weaving mill in northern Bohemia. Over the years, he slowly and carefully built it up into a business of considerable size.

Such caution in expanding the business, even when the economic situation looked enticingly favourable, was very much in the spirit of the times. It also exactly suited my father's reserved and far from avaricious nature. He had taken the 'safety first' creed of his epoch as his own watchword; it was more important to him to own a sound business (the ideal of

28

something sound and solid was also characteristic of the period), with the force of his own capital behind it, than to extend it to huge dimensions by taking out bank loans and mortgages. The one thing of which he was truly proud was that no one had ever in his life seen his name on a promissory note, and he had never failed to be in credit with his bank—which of course was the soundest bank of all, the Kreditanstalt founded by the Rothschilds. Any kind of transaction carrying the faintest suggestion of risk was anathema to him, and he never in all his years took part in any foreign business dealings. The fact that he still gradually became rich, and then even richer, was not the result of bold speculation or particularly farsighted operations, but of adapting to the general method of that cautious period, expending only a modest part of his income and consequently, from year to year, making an increasingly large contribution to the capital of the business. Like most of his generation, my father would have considered anyone who cheerfully spent half his annual income without thought for the future a dubious wastrel at the very least. Providing for the future was another recurrent idea in that age of security. Steadily setting profits aside meant rising prosperity. In addition, the state had no plans to take more than a few per cent of even the largest incomes in taxes, while state and industrial securities brought in good rates of interest, so that making money was quite a passive process for the well-to-do. And it was worth it; the savings of the thrifty were not stolen, as they are during times of inflation; no pressure was put on sound businesses, and even those who were particularly patient and refrained from any kind of speculation made good profits. Thanks to adapting to the general system of his time, in his fifties my father could be regarded as a very prosperous man by international standards. But the lifestyle of our family lagged well behind the increasingly rapid rise of its property. We did gradually acquire small comforts. We moved from a small apartment to a larger one, we hired a car for outings on spring afternoons, we travelled second class by train and booked a sleeper, but it was not until he was fifty that my father first allowed himself the luxury of taking my mother to Nice for a month in the winter. All things considered, he stuck to his basic attitude of enjoying wealth by knowing that he had it, rather than by making a great display of it. Even as a millionaire, my father never smoked any imported product but—like Emperor Franz Joseph with his cheap Virginia tobacco—the ordinary Trabuco cigars of the time, and when he played cards it was only for small stakes. He inflexibly maintained his restraint and his comfortable but discreet way of life. Although he was very much better educated than most of his colleagues, and culturally superior to them—he played the piano extremely well, wrote a good, clear hand, spoke French and English— he firmly declined any distinctions or honorary positions, and never in his life either aspired to or accepted any honour or dignity of the kind frequently offered to him in his position as a leading industrialist. His secret pride in never having asked anyone for anything, never having been obliged to say 'please' or 'thank you', meant more to him than any outward show.

There inevitably comes a moment in every man's life when he sees his father reflected in himself. That preference for privacy, for an anonymous way of life, is beginning to develop in me more and more strongly as the years go by, though in fact it runs contrary to my profession, which is bound to make my name and person to some extent public. But out of the same secret pride as his, I have always declined any form of outward honour, never accepted any decoration or title, or the presidency of any association. I have never been a member of an academy, nor have I sat on the board of any company or on any jury panel. Attending a festive occasion is something of an ordeal for me, and the mere thought of asking someone a favour is enough—even if my request were to be made through a third party—to make my mouth dry up before uttering the first word. I know that such inhibitions are out of tune with the times, in a world where we can remain free only through cunning and evasion, and where, as Goethe wisely said, "in the general throng, many a fool receives decorations and titles." But my father in me, with his secret pride, makes me hold back, and I cannot resist him. After all, it is my father I have to thank for what I feel is, perhaps, my one secure possession: my sense of inner freedom.

My mother, whose maiden name was Brettauer, was not of the same origin. Hers was an international family. She was born in Ancona in Italy, and Italian and German had both been the languages of her childhood. When she was discussing something with her mother, my grandmother or her sister, and they did not want the servants to know what they were saying, they would switch to Italian. From my earliest youth I was familiar with risotto, artichokes (still a rarity in Vienna at the time) and the other specialities of Mediterranean cookery, and whenever I visited Italy later I immediately felt at home. But my mother's family was not by any means Italian, and saw itself as more cosmopolitan than anything else. The Brettauers, who had originally owned a bank, came from Hohenems, a small town on the Swiss border, and spread all over the world at an early date on the model of the great Jewish banking families, although of course on a much smaller scale. Some went to St Gallen, others to Vienna and Paris. My grandfather went to Italy, an uncle to New York, and these international contacts gave the family more sophistication, a wider outlook, and a certain arrogance. There were no small tradesmen in the family, no brokers, they were all bankers, company directors, professors, lawyers and medical doctors; everyone spoke several languages, and I remember how naturally the conversation around my aunt's table in Paris moved from one language to

31

another. It was a family that thought well of itself, and when a
girl from one of its poorer branches reached marriageable age,
everyone contributed to providing her with a good dowry so that
she need not marry 'beneath herself'. As a leading industrialist,
my father was respected, but my mother, although theirs was the
happiest of marriages, would never have allowed his relations
to consider themselves the equals of hers. It was impossible to
root out the pride of their descent from a 'good family' from the
Brettauers, and in later years, if one of them wanted to show me
particular goodwill, he would condescend to say, "You're more
of a Brettauer really", as if stating approvingly that I took after
the right side of my family.

This kind of distinction, claimed for themselves by many Jewish
families, sometimes amused and sometimes annoyed my brother
and me, even as children. We were always hearing that certain
persons were 'refined', while others were less so. Enquiries were
made about any new friends of ours—were they from a 'good
family'?—and every ramification of their origins in respect
of both family and fortune was investigated. This constant
classification, which was in fact the main subject of all family
and social conversations, seemed to us at the time ridiculous and
snobbish, since after all, the only difference between one Jewish
family and another was whether it had left the ghetto fifty or a
hundred years ago. Only much later did I realise that this idea
of the 'good family', which seemed to us boys the farcical parody
of an artificial pseudo-aristocracy, expresses one of the most
mysterious but deeply felt tendencies in the Jewish nature. It is
generally assumed that getting rich is a Jew's true and typical aim
in life. Nothing could be further from the truth. Getting rich, to a
Jew, is only an interim stage, a means to his real end, by no means
his aim in itself. The true desire of a Jew, his inbuilt ideal, is to rise
to a higher social plane by becoming an intellectual. Even among
Orthodox Eastern Jews, in whom the failings as well as the virtues
of the Jewish people as a whole are more strongly marked, this

supreme desire to be an intellectual finds graphic expression going beyond merely material considerations—the devout Biblical scholar has far higher status within the community than a rich man. Even the most prosperous Jew would rather marry his daughter to an indigent intellectual than a merchant. This high regard for intellectuals runs through all classes of Jewish society, and the poorest pedlar who carries his pack through wind and weather will try to give at least one son the chance of studying at university, however great the sacrifices he must make, and will consider it an honour to the entire family that one of them is clearly regarded as an intellectual: a professor, a scholar, a musician. It is as if such a man's achievements ennobled them all. Unconsciously, something in a Jew seeks to escape the morally dubious, mean, petty and pernicious associations of trade clinging to all that is merely business, and rise to the purer sphere of the intellect where money is not a consideration, as if, like a Wagnerian character, he were trying to break the curse of gold laid on himself and his entire race. Among Jews, then, the urge to make a fortune is nearly always exhausted within two or at most three generations of a family, and even the mightiest dynasts find that their sons are unwilling to take over the family banks and factories, the prosperous businesses built up and expanded by the previous generation. It is no coincidence that Lord Rothschild became an ornithologist, one of the Warburgs an art historian, one of the Cassirer family was a philosopher, one of the Sassoons a poet; they were all obeying the same unconscious urge to liberate themselves from the mere cold earning of money that has restricted Jewish life, and perhaps this flight to the intellectual sphere even expresses a secret longing to exchange their Jewish identity for one that is universally human. So a 'good' family means more than a mere claim to social status; it also denotes a Jewish way of life that, by adjusting to another and perhaps more universal culture, has freed itself or is freeing itself from all the drawbacks and constraints and

THE WORLD OF YESTERDAY

pettiness forced upon it by the ghetto. Admittedly, it is one of the eternal paradoxes of the Jewish destiny that this flight into intellectual realms has now, because of the disproportionately large number of Jews in the intellectual professions, become as fatal as their earlier restriction to the material sphere.[1]

In hardly any other European city was the urge towards culture as passionate as in Vienna. For the very reason that for centuries Austria and its monarchy had been neither politically ambitious nor particularly successful in its military ventures, native pride had focused most strongly on distinction in artistic achievement. The most important and valuable provinces of the old Habsburg empire that once ruled Europe—German and Italian, Flemish and Walloon—had seceded long ago, but the capital city was still intact in its old glory as the sanctuary of the court, the guardian of a millennial tradition. The Romans had laid the foundation stones of that city as a *castrum*, a far-flung outpost to protect Latin civilization from the barbarians, and over a thousand years later the Ottoman attack on the West was repelled outside the walls of Vienna. The Nibelungs had come here, the immortal Pleiades of music shone down on the world from this city, Gluck, Haydn and Mozart, Beethoven, Schubert, Brahms and Johann Strauss, all the currents of European culture had merged in this place. At court and among the nobility and the common people alike, German elements were linked with Slavonic, Hungarian, Spanish, Italian, French and Flemish. It was the peculiar genius of Vienna, the city of music, to resolve all these contrasts harmoniously in something new and unique, specifically Austrian and Viennese. Open-minded and particularly receptive, the city attracted the most disparate of forces, relaxed their tensions, eased and placated them. It was pleasant to live here, in this atmosphere of intellectual tolerance, and unconsciously every citizen of Vienna also became a supranational, cosmopolitan citizen of the world.

This art of adaptation, of gentle and musical transitions, was

34

evident even in the outward appearance of the city. Growing slowly over the centuries, developing organically from its centre, with its two million inhabitants Vienna had a large enough population to offer all the luxury and diversity of a metropolis, and yet it was not so vast that it was cut off from nature, like London or New York. The buildings on the edge of the city were reflected in the mighty waters of the Danube and looked out over the wide plain, merged with gardens and fields or climbed the last gently undulating green and wooded foothills of the Alps. You hardly noticed where nature ended and the city began, they made way for one another without resistance or contradiction. At the centre, in turn, you felt that the city had grown like a tree, forming ring after ring, and instead of the old ramparts of the fortifications, the Ringstrasse enclosed the innermost, precious core with its grand houses. In that core, the old palaces of the court and the nobility spoke the language of history in stone; here Beethoven had played for the Lichnowskys; there Haydn had stayed with the Esterházys; the premiere of his *Creation* was given in the old university; the Hofburg saw generations of emperors, Napoleon took up residence at Schönbrunn Palace; the united rulers of Christendom met in St Stephen's Cathedral to give thanks for their salvation from the Turks, the university saw countless luminaries of scholarship and science in its walls. Among these buildings the new architecture rose, proud and magnificent, with shining avenues and glittering emporiums. But old Vienna had as little to do with the new city as dressed stone has to do with nature. It was wonderful to live in this city, which hospitably welcomed strangers and gave of itself freely; it was natural to enjoy life in its light atmosphere, full of elation and merriment like the air of Paris. Vienna, as everyone knew, was an epicurean city—however, what does culture mean but taking the raw material of life and enticing from it its finest, most delicate and subtle aspects by means of art and love? The people of Vienna were gourmets who appreciated good

35

food and good wine, fresh and astringent beer, lavish desserts
and tortes, but they also demanded subtler pleasures. To make
music, dance, produce plays, converse well, behave pleasingly
and show good taste were arts much cultivated here. Neither
military, political nor commercial matters held first place in
the lives of individuals or society as a whole; when the average
Viennese citizen looked at his morning paper, his eye generally
went first not to parliamentary debates or foreign affairs but
to the theatrical repertory, which assumed an importance
in public life hardly comprehensible in other cities. For to
the Viennese and indeed the Austrians the imperial theatre,
the Burgtheater, was more than just a stage on which actors
performed dramatic works; it was a microcosm reflecting the
macrocosm, a bright mirror in which society could study itself,
the one true *cartigiano* of good taste. In an actor at the imperial
theatre, spectators saw an example of the way to dress, enter a
room, make conversation, were shown which words a man of
taste might use and which should be avoided. The stage was not
just a place of entertainment but a spoken, three-dimensional
manual of good conduct and correct pronunciation, and an
aura of esteem, rather like a saint's halo, surrounded all who
had even the faintest connection with the court theatre. The
Prime Minister, the richest magnate, could walk through the
streets of Vienna and no one would turn to stare, but every
salesgirl and every cab driver would recognise an actor at the
court theatre or an operatic diva. When we boys had seen one
of them pass by (we all collected their pictures and autographs)
we proudly told each other, and this almost religious personality
cult even extended to their entourages; Adolf von Sonnenthal's
barber, Josef Kainz's cab driver were regarded with awe and
secretly envied. Young dandies were proud to have their clothes
made by the tailors patronised by those actors. A notable
anniversary in a famous actor's career, or a great actor's funeral,
was an event overshadowing all the political news. It was every

Viennese dramatist's dream to be performed at the Burgtheater, a distinction that meant a kind of ennoblement for life and brought with it a series of benefits such as free theatre tickets for life and invitations to all official occasions, because you had been a guest in an imperial house. I still remember the solemn manner of my own reception. The director of the Burgtheater had asked me to visit his office in the morning, where he informed me—after first offering his congratulations—that the theatre had accepted my play. When I got home that evening, I found his visiting card in my apartment. Although I was only a young man of twenty-six, he had formally returned my call; my mere acceptance as an author writing for the imperial stage had made me a gentleman whom the director of that institution must treat as on a par with himself. And what went on at the theatre indirectly affected every individual, even someone who had no direct connection with it whatsoever. I remember, for instance, a day in my earliest youth when our cook burst into the sitting room with tears in her eyes: she had just heard that Charlotte Wolter, the star actress of the Burgtheater, had died. The grotesque aspect of her extravagant grief, of course, lay in the fact that our old, semi-literate cook had never once been to that distinguished theatre herself, and had never seen Charlotte Wolter either on stage or in real life, but in Vienna a great Austrian actress was so much part of the common property of the entire city that even those entirely unconnected with her felt her death was a catastrophe. Every loss, the death of a popular singer or artist, inevitably became an occasion for national mourning. When the old Burgtheater where the premiere of Mozart's *The Marriage of Figaro* had been given was to be demolished, Viennese high society gathered there in a mood of solemn emotion, and no sooner had the curtain fallen than everyone raced on stage to take home at least a splinter from the boards that had been trodden by their favourite artists as a relic. Even decades later, these plain wooden splinters were kept in precious caskets in many bourgeois households, just as splinters of the Holy Cross are preserved in churches.

In my own day, we acted no more rationally when the so-called Bösendorfer Saal was torn down. In itself that little concert hall, which was reserved exclusively for chamber music, was a modest building, not suggesting any great artistic distinction. It had been Prince Liechtenstein's riding school, and was adapted for musical purposes only by the addition of interior boarding, without any ostentation. But it had the resonance of an old violin, and it was a sacred place to music-lovers because Chopin and Brahms, Liszt and Rubinstein had given recitals there, and many of the famous quartets had first performed in this hall. And now it was to make way for a new purpose-built concert hall; such a thing was beyond the understanding of those of us who had spent many memorable hours there. When the last bars of Beethoven died away, played better than ever by the Rosé Quartet, none of the audience left their seats. We shouted and applauded, some of the women were sobbing with emotion, no one was willing to admit that this was goodbye. The lights in the hall were extinguished to clear us out of the place. Still none of the four or five hundred people present left their seats. We stayed for half-an-hour, an hour, as if our presence could save the sacred hall by force. And as students, how we campaigned, with petitions and demonstrations and articles, to keep the house where Beethoven died from demolition! Whenever one of these historic Viennese buildings went, it was as if a part of our souls were being torn from our bodies.

This fanatical love of art, in particular the art of the theatre, was common to all classes of society in Vienna. Its hundreds of years of tradition had made the city itself a place with a clearly ordered and also—as I once wrote myself—a wonderfully orchestrated structure. The imperial house still set the tone, while the imperial palace represented not only the spatial centre of the city but also the supranational nature of the monarchy. Around that palace lay the grand residences of the Austrian, Polish, Czech and Hungarian nobility, forming what might be called a second rampart. Then came the houses of the members of 'good society'—the minor nobility, higher civil servants, captains of industry and the 'old families'. Below them came the lower middle class and the proletariat. All these social classes lived in their own circles and even in their own districts of the city: at the centre the great noblemen in their palaces, the diplomats in District Three, businessmen and industrialists near the Ringstrasse, the lower middle class in the inner districts, Districts Two to Nine, the proletariat on the periphery. However, they all came into contact with each other at the theatre and for major festivities such as the Floral Parade, when three hundred thousand spectators enthusiastically greeted the 'upper ten thousand' in their beautifully decorated carriages. Everything in Vienna that expressed itself in colour or music became an occasion for festivities: religious spectacles like the Corpus Christi procession, the military parades, performances by the outdoor musicians of the Burgmusik, even funerals attracted enthusiastic audiences, and it was the ambition of every true Viennese to end up as 'a handsome corpse' with a fine funeral procession and many companions escorting him on his last journey. A genuine Viennese turned even his death into a fine show for others to enjoy. The entire city was united in this sensitivity to everything colourful, musical and festive, in this delight in theatrical spectacle as a playful reflection of life, whether on the stage or in real space and time.

It was not difficult to make fun of the theatrical mania of the Viennese, whose delight in tracking down the tiniest details of the lives of their favourites sometimes became grotesque, and our Austrian political indolence and economic backwardness, by comparison with the determined German Reich next door, may indeed be partly ascribed to our overrating of sensuous pleasure. But in cultural terms the very high value placed on the arts created something unique—a great veneration for all artistic achievement, leading over the centuries to unequalled expertise, and finally, thanks in its own turn to that expertise, to outstandingly high standards in all cultural fields. An artist always feels most at ease and at the same time most inspired in a place where he is valued, even overvalued. Art always reaches its zenith where it is important in the life of an entire nation. And just as Renaissance Florence and Rome attracted painters and trained them to achieve greatness, because every one of them felt bound to keep outdoing others and himself, competing in front of the citizens as a whole, so musicians and actors knew how important they were in Vienna. At the Opera House, in the Burgtheater, nothing was overlooked, every wrong note was instantly detected, every incorrect entry or abridged passage deplored, and this keen surveillance was exercised not only by professional critics at premieres, but day after day by the alert ear of the public at large, honed as it was by constant comparison. While the attitude in politics, the administration and morality was easygoing, and one made allowances for a slipshod piece of work and showed leniency for an offence, no quarter was given in artistic matters. Here the honour of the city was at stake. Every singer, every actor, every musician must constantly give of his best, or his career was finished. It was wonderful to be a darling of the public in Vienna, but it was not easy to maintain that position. No lowering of standards was forgiven. And this awareness of being under constant and pitiless observation forced every artist in Vienna to do his best, bringing the art of the city as a whole to a very high level. All of us who lived there in our youth have brought a stern and implacable standard of artistic performance into our lives from those years. Those who saw discipline exercised down to the smallest detail at the Opera House under Gustav Mahler, and vitality combined with meticulous accuracy taken as the norm in music played by the Philharmonic, are rarely entirely satisfied with theatrical or musical performances today. But we also learnt to criticise our own artistic performance; the example before us was, and still is, a high level of achievement inculcated into rising artists in few other cities in the world. This understanding of the right rhythm and momentum went deep into the people themselves, for even the most unassuming citizen sitting over his *Heurige*,[2] demanded good music from the wind band just as he expected good value from the landlord. Similarly, people knew exactly which military band played with most verve in the Prater, whether it was the German Masters or the Hungarians. Anyone who lived in Vienna absorbed a sense of rhythm as if it were in the air. And just as that musicality expressed itself in writers in the particular attention we paid to writing particularly well-turned prose, in others the sense of delicacy was expressed in social attitudes and daily life. In what was known as 'high society', a Viennese with no appreciation of art or pleasure in form was unimaginable, but even among the lower classes the lives of the poorest showed a certain feeling for beauty drawn from the surrounding landscape and genial human attitudes. You were not truly Viennese without a love for culture, a bent for both enjoying and assessing the prodigality of life as something sacred.

For Jews, adaptation to the human or national environment in which they lived was not only a measure taken for their own protection, but also a deeply felt private need. Their desire for a homeland, for peace, repose and security, a place where they would not be strangers, impelled them to form a passionate attachment to the culture around them. And nowhere else, except for Spain in the fifteenth century, were such bonds more happily and productively forged than in Austria. Here the Jews who had been settled in the imperial city for over two hundred years met people who took life lightly and were naturally easygoing, while under that apparently light-hearted surface they shared the deep Jewish instinct for intellectual and aesthetic values. And the two came together all the more easily in Vienna, where they found a personal task waiting for them, because over the last century Austrian art had lost its traditional guardians and protectors: the imperial house and the aristocracy. In the eighteenth century Maria Theresia had had her daughters taught the pleasures of music, Joseph II had discussed Mozart's operas with him as a connoisseur, Leopold II was a composer himself, but the later emperors Franz II and Ferdinand had no kind of interest in art, and Emperor Franz Joseph, who in his eighty years of life never read or even picked up a book other than the Army List, even felt a decided antipathy to music. Similarly, the great noblemen had abandoned their former position as patrons; gone were the glorious days when the Esterházys gave house-room to Haydn, when the Lobkowitzes and Kinskys and Waldsteins competed for the first performance of a work by Beethoven to be given in their palaces, when Countess Thun went on her knees to that great daemonic figure asking him not to withdraw *Fidelio* from the Opera. Even Wagner, Brahms, Johann Strauss and Hugo Wolf no longer received the slightest support from them; the citizens of Vienna had to step into the breach to keep up the old high standard of the Philharmonic concerts and enable painters and sculptors to make a living, and it was the particular pride and indeed the ambition of the Jewish bourgeoisie to maintain the reputation of Viennese culture in its old brilliance. They had always loved the city, taking it to their hearts when they settled there, but it was their love of Viennese art that had made them feel entirely at home, genuinely Viennese. In fact they exerted little influence otherwise in public life; the lustre of the imperial house left all private wealth in the shade, high positions in the leadership of the state were in hereditary hands, diplomacy was reserved for the aristocracy, the army and the higher reaches of the civil service for the old-established families, and the Jews did not even try to look so high as to force their way into those privileged circles. They tactfully respected such traditional privileges as something to be taken for granted. I remember, for instance, that my father never in his life ate at Sacher's, not for reasons of economy—the price difference between Sacher and the other great hotels was ridiculously small—but out of a natural instinct for preserving a distance. He would have felt it embarrassing or unseemly to sit at the table next to one occupied by, say, Prince Schwarzenberg or Prince Lobkowitz. It was only in art that all the Viennese felt they had equal rights, because art, like love, was regarded as a duty incumbent on everyone in the city, and the part played by the Jewish bourgeoisie in Viennese culture, through the aid and patronage it offered, was immeasurable. They were the real public, they filled seats at the theatre and in concert halls, they bought books and pictures, visited exhibitions, championed and encouraged new trends everywhere with minds that were more flexible, less weighed down by tradition. They had built up virtually all the great art collections of the nineteenth century, they had made almost all the artistic experiments of the time possible. Without the constant interest of the Jewish bourgeoisie as stimulation, at a time when the court was indolent and the aristocracy and the Christian millionaires preferred to spend money on racing stables and hunts rather than encouraging art, Vienna would have lagged as far behind Berlin artistically as Austria did behind the German Reich in politics. Anyone wishing to introduce a novelty to Vienna, anyone from outside seeking understanding and an audience there, had to rely on the Jewish bourgeoisie. When a single attempt was made in the anti-Semitic period[3] to found a so-called National Theatre, there were no playwrights or actors or audiences available; after a few months the 'National Theatre' failed miserably, and that example first made it clear that nine-tenths of what the world of the nineteenth century celebrated as Viennese culture was in fact culture promoted and nurtured or even created by the Jews of Vienna.

For in recent years the Viennese Jews—like those of Spain before their similarly tragic downfall—had been artistically creative, not in any specifically Jewish style but, with miraculous empathy, giving especially intense expression to all that was Austrian and Viennese. As composers, Goldmark, Gustav Mahler and Schönberg were figures of international stature; Oscar Straus, Leo Fall and Kálmán brought the traditional waltz and operetta to new heights; Hofmannsthal, Arthur Schnitzler, Beer-Hofmann and Peter Altenberg gave Viennese literature new status in Europe, a rank that it had never before reached even at the time of Grillparzer and Stifter. Sonnenthal and Max Reinhardt revived the international reputation of Vienna as a city of the theatre; Freud and the great scientific experts attracted attention to the famous and ancient university— everywhere, as scholars, virtuoso musicians, painters, directors, architects, journalists, they claimed high and sometimes the highest positions in the intellectual life of Vienna. Through their passionate love of the city and their adaptability they had become entirely assimilated, and were happy to serve the reputation of Austria; they felt that the assertion of their Austrian identity was their vocation. In fact, it must be said in all honesty that a good part, if not the greater part, of all that is admired today in Europe and America as the expression of a newly revived Austrian culture in music, literature, the theatre, the art trade, was the work of the Jews of Vienna, whose intellectual drive, dating back for thousands of years, brought them to a peak of achievement. Here intellectual energy that had lost its sense of direction through the centuries found a tradition that was already a little weary, nurtured it, revived and refined it, and with tireless activity injected new strength into it. Only the following decades would show what a crime it was when an attempt was made to force Vienna—a place combining the most heterogeneous elements in its atmosphere and culture, reaching out intellectually beyond national borders—into the new mould of a nationalist and thus a provincial city. For the genius of Vienna, a specifically musical genius, had always been that it harmonised all national and linguistic opposites in itself, its culture was a synthesis of all Western cultures. Anyone who lived and worked there felt free of narrow-minded prejudice. Nowhere was it easier to be a European, and I know that in part I have to thank Vienna, a city that was already defending universal and Roman values in the days of Marcus Aurelius, for the fact that I learnt early to love the idea of community as the highest ideal of my heart.

We lived well, we lived with light hearts and minds at ease in old Vienna, and the Germans to the north looked down with some annoyance and scorn at us, their neighbours on the Danube who, instead of being capable and efficient like them and observing strict principles of order, indulged themselves, ate well, enjoyed parties and the theatre, and made excellent music on those occasions. Instead of cultivating German efficiency, which finally embittered and destroyed the lives of all other peoples, instead of the greedy will of Germany to rise supreme and forge a way forward, we Viennese loved to chat at our ease; we liked pleasant social gatherings, and in a kindly and perhaps lax spirit of concord we let all have their share without grudging it. 'Live and let live' was famous as a Viennese principle, a principle that still seems to me more humane than any categorical imperative, and it reigned supreme in all social circles. Poor and rich, Czechs and Germans, Christians and Jews lived peacefully together in spite of the occasional needling remark, and even political and social movements did not have that terrible spitefulness that eventually made its way into the bloodstream of the time as a poisonous residue of the First World War. In the old Austria you fought chivalrously; you might complain in the newspapers and parliament, but then the deputies, after delivering their Ciceronian tirades, would sit happily together over coffee or a beer, talking on familiar terms. Even when Lueger, leader of the anti-Semitic party,[4] became mayor of the city, nothing changed in private social relationships, and I personally must confess that I never felt the slightest coldness or scorn for me as a Jew either in school, at the university, or in literature. Hatred between country and country, nation and nation, the occupants of one table and those of another, did not yet leap to the eye daily from the newspaper, it did not divide human beings from other human beings, nations from other nations. The herd instinct of the mob was not yet as offensively powerful in public life as it is today; freedom in what you did or did not do in private life was something taken for granted—which is hardly imaginable now—and toleration was not, as it is today, deplored as weakness and debility, but was praised as an ethical force.

For I was not born into a century of passion. It was a well-ordered world with a clear social structure and easy transitions between the parts of that structure, a world without haste. The rhythm of the new speed had not yet transferred itself from machinery, the motor car, the telephone and the aeroplane to humanity. Time and age were judged by different criteria. People lived a more leisurely life, and when I try to picture the figures of the adults who played a large part in my childhood it strikes me how many of them grew stout before their time. My father, my uncle, my teacher, the salesmen in shops, the musicians in the Philharmonic at their music desks were all portly, 'dignified' men at the age of forty. They walked slowly, they spoke in measured tones, and in conversation they stroked their well-groomed beards, which were often already grey. But grey hair was only another mark of dignity, and a 'man of mature years' deliberately avoided the gestures and high sprits of youth as something unseemly. Even in my earliest childhood, when my father was not yet forty, I cannot remember ever seeing him run up or down a staircase, or indeed do anything in visible haste. Haste was not only regarded as bad form, it was in fact superfluous, since in that stable bourgeois world with its countless little safeguards nothing sudden ever happened. Those disasters that did take place on the periphery of our world did not penetrate the well-lined walls of our secure life. The Boer War, the Russo-Japanese War, even the Balkan Wars did not make any deep impression on my parents' lives. They skimmed all the war reporting in the paper as indifferently as they looked at the sports headlines. And what, indeed, did anything that happened outside Austria have to do with them, what change did it bring to their lives? In the serene epoch of their Austria, there was no upheaval in the state, no abrupt destruction of their values. Once, when securities fell by four or five points on the stock exchange, it was called a 'crash' and discussed with furrowed brow as a catastrophe. People complained of high taxes more out of habit that from any real conviction, and by comparison with those of the post-war period the taxes then were only a kind of little tip you gave the state. The most precise stipulations were laid down in wills for ways to protect grandsons and great-grandsons from any loss of property, as if some kind of invisible IOU guaranteed safety from the eternal powers, and meanwhile people lived comfortably and tended their small worries like obedient domestic pets who were not really to be feared. When an old newspaper from those days happens to fall into my hands, and I read the excitable reports of some small local council election, when I try to remember the plays at the Burgtheater with their tiny problems, or think of the disproportionate agitation of our youthful debates on fundamentally unimportant matters, I cannot help smiling. How Lilliputian all those anxieties were, how serene that time! The

47

generation of my parents and grandparents was better off, they lived their lives from one end to the other quietly in a straight, clear line. All the same, I do not know whether I envy them. For they drowsed their lives away remote from all true bitterness, from the malice and force of destiny; they knew nothing about all those crises and problems that oppress the heart but at the same time greatly enlarge it. How little they knew, stumbling along in security and prosperity and comfort, that life can also mean excess and tension, constant surprise, can be turned upside down; how little they guessed in their touching liberal optimism that every new day dawning outside the window could shatter human lives. Even in their darkest nights they never dreamt how dangerous human beings can be, or then again how much power they can have to survive dangers and surmount trials. We who have been hunted through the rapids of life, torn from our former roots, always driven to the end and obliged to begin again, victims and yet also the willing servants of unknown mysterious powers, we for whom comfort has become an old legend and security, a childish dream, have felt tension from pole to pole of our being, the terror of something always new in every fibre. Every hour of our years was linked to the fate of the world. In sorrow and in joy we have lived through time and history far beyond our own small lives, while they knew nothing beyond themselves. Every one of us, therefore, even the least of the human race, knows a thousand times more about reality today than the wisest of our forebears. But nothing was given to us freely; we paid the price in full.

NOTES

1   Zweig is referring to the ban imposed by Hitler's anti-Semitic regime on Jews in 'the intellectual professions'. They were no longer, for instance, allowed to practise as lawyers and doctors.

2   The wine of the new season's vintage.

3   The National Socialist regime, dating from Hitler's accession to power as Chancellor in 1933.

4   Karl Lueger, 1844-1910, leader of the Austrian Christian Socialist party. Although he did hold anti-Semitic opinions, he was generally regarded as a good mayor of Vienna. Zweig returns to him later in this chapter.

AT SCHOOL IN THE LAST CENTURY

I T WAS TAKEN FOR GRANTED that I would go on from elementary school to grammar school. If only for the sake of social standing, every well-to-do family was anxious to have 'educated' sons, who were taught English and French and familiarised with music. First governesses and then tutors were engaged to teach them good manners. But in those days of 'enlightened' liberalism, only an education regarded as academic and leading to university really counted, and as a result it was the ambition of every 'good' family for at least one son to have some kind of doctoral degree. The path to university was rather a long one, and by no means a bed of roses. You had to spend five to six hours a day sitting on the wooden school bench for five years of elementary school and eight of grammar school. In your free time you did homework, and in addition you had to master the subjects required for 'general culture' outside school: the living languages of French, English and Italian, classical Greek and Latin—that is to say, five languages in all as well as geometry, physics, and the other school subjects. It was more than too much, leaving almost no time for physical exercise, sporting activities, walking, and above all none for light-hearted amusements. I vaguely remember that at the age of seven we had to learn by heart some ditty about "happy, blissful childhood days" and sing it in chorus. I can still hear the tune of this simple, naive little song, but even at the time I could hardly bring myself to utter the words, and still less was my heart convinced of their message. For if I am to be honest, my entire school career was nothing but a constant surfeit of tedium, increased yearly by my impatience to escape this treadmill. I don't recollect ever having felt either 'happy' or 'blissful' during that monotonous, heartless, dismal schooling, which thoroughly spoilt the happiest days of our lives, and I will confess that even today I cannot resist a certain envy when I see how much happier, freer, and more independent childhood can be in the present century. It still strikes me as incredible that children today will talk to their teachers naturally, almost on a par with them, and that they hurry to school free of fear, instead of with our old constant sense of inadequacy. At school and at home today's children are often allowed to express the preferences and wishes of their young, inquisitive hearts openly—they are free, independent, natural creatures, while as soon as we entered the hated school building we had to keep our heads down, so to speak, to avoid coming up against the invisible yoke of servitude. School, to us, meant compulsion, dreary boredom, a place where you had to absorb knowledge of subjects that did not seem worth knowing, sliced into neat portions. This was scholastic material, or material made to seem scholastic, which we felt could have no connection with any real interests of our own. The old style of teaching meant a dull, dreary kind of learning for the mere sake of learning, not for the sake of life. And the one real moment of elation for which I have to thank my school was the day when I closed its doors behind me for ever.

Not that our Austrian schools need necessarily have been bad in themselves. Far from it; the curriculum had been carefully devised on the basis of a hundred years of experience, and if inspiringly taught could have laid the foundations of a fruitful all-round cultural education. But the very fact that it was taught according to a dry-as-dust plan made the lessons themselves dry and lifeless, a cold apparatus of learning that was never adjusted to the individual and, like an automaton programmed to recite the terms 'good, satisfactory, unsatisfactory', showed only how far we met the demands of the curriculum. It was this lack of human feeling, this sober impersonality and the barracks-like atmosphere about the whole process that subconsciously embittered us. We had our allotted quota of work to learn, and we were tested on what we had learnt; through the whole eight years of our secondary education no teacher ever asked what we personally wanted to learn, and the encouraging stimulation that is just what every young person secretly longs for was entirely lacking.

This sobriety was expressed even outwardly in the school building, a typically functional place erected hastily, thoughtlessly and on the cheap fifty years earlier. With its cold, poorly whitewashed walls, its low-ceilinged classrooms without pictures or any other kind of ornament to please the eye, and the smell of the lavatories that pervaded the whole building, this educational barracks was rather like an old piece of hotel furniture that had been used by countless people before us, and would be used by countless others with equal indifference or reluctance. To this day I have not forgotten the musty, mouldy odour clinging to that building, as it does to all Austrian official institutions. We described it as the 'treasury smell', a reek of overheated, overcrowded rooms. It settled first on your clothes and then on your soul. We sat in pairs, like convicts in their galley, on low wooden benches that made us bend our backs, and we sat there until our bones ached. In winter the bluish light of open gas flames flickered over our books, while in summer the windows were covered, in case we were to enjoy gazing wistfully at a small square of blue sky. The century of our youth had not yet discovered that young, still-developing bodies need fresh air and exercise. Ten minutes' break in the cold, narrow corridor were considered sufficient in the space of four or five hours of sitting still. Twice a week we were taken to the gym, where all the windows were carefully closed, to run around pointlessly on the wooden floorboards, from which dust rose high in the air at every step. That was enough to ensure hygiene, and meant that the state had done its duty to us in the cause of promoting *mens sana in corpore sano*. Passing the gloomy, dismal building even years later, I felt relieved to know that I no longer had to set foot in the dungeon of our youth, and when the fiftieth anniversary of that illustrious institution was celebrated, and as a former star pupil I was asked to deliver a speech on the occasion before the Minister of Education and the Mayor, I politely declined. I had no reason to be grateful to the school, and anything I said to that effect would have been a lie.

Our teachers were not to blame for the dreariness of school life. They were neither good nor bad, they were not tyrants, but on the other hand nor were they helpful companions— they were merely poor devils who, bound like slaves to the set pattern of the officially ordained curriculum, had to do their quota of work just as we had to do ours, and—as we clearly perceived—were as glad as we were when the school bell rang at midday, setting both them and us free. They didn't like us, they didn't hate us, and why should they? They knew nothing about us; after a couple of years they still knew very few of us by name, and in the spirit of the teaching methods of the time they had nothing to bother about apart from establishing how many mistakes a pupil had made in his last piece of homework. They sat raised above us at the schoolmaster's lectern, we sat down below; they asked questions and we had to answer. There was no other connection between us. For between teachers and students, the schoolmaster's lectern and the students' bench, visibly representing Above and Below respectively, stood the invisible barrier of authority preventing any contact. At the time it would have been beyond both a teacher's competence and his ability to consider a pupil as an individual whose particular qualities called for special attention, nor did he have to write reports on his work, which is taken for granted today, while on the other hand a private conversation would have diminished the teacher's standing, because it would have put us as pupils too much on the same level as a man set in authority over us. Nothing, to my mind, is more characteristic of the total lack of mental and intellectual connection between us and our teachers than the fact that I have forgotten all their names and faces. My memory retains, with photographic clarity, images of the schoolmaster's lectern and the class register, which we always tried to squint at because it contained our marks; I see the little red notebook in which categories were marked out, and the short black pencil entering our results; I see my own exercise books sprinkled with the teacher's corrections in red ink, but I can no longer conjure up the face of a single one of our mentors—perhaps because we always stood in front of them with our heads down or our eyes wandering elsewhere.

This dislike of school was not just my personal attitude; I can't remember one of my school friends who did not hate the way in which our best interests and intentions were inhibited, bored and suppressed on the scholastic treadmill. Only much later did I realise that negligence on the part of the state authorities was not to blame for this loveless, soulless method of educating the young, but that it expressed a definite if carefully concealed intention: the world ahead of us, or set in authority over us, with its mind entirely bent on its fetish of security, did not like young people, or rather it habitually distrusted them. Proud of its systematic 'progress' and good order, bourgeois society extolled leisurely moderation in all aspects of life as the sole effective human virtue; any haste in leading us forward was to be avoided. Austria was an old state ruled by an old emperor, governed by old ministers, a state that, having no ambition, hoped only to preserve itself intact by rejecting all radical changes in Europe. Young people, who instinctively always want such swift and radical changes, were therefore regarded as a suspect element that had to be neutralised or kept down as long as possible. So there was no reason to make our schooldays

55

pleasant for us; we could earn any rise in the world only by waiting patiently. When everything was constantly being put off in this way, the meaning of age was quite different from what it is today. A grammar-school boy of eighteen was treated like a child, punished if he was caught smoking a cigarette, had to put up a docile hand if he wanted to leave his place in class to answer the call of nature. Even a man of thirty was still considered immature, and a forty-year-old was not yet regarded as ready for a position of responsibility. When there was once an astonishing exception, and Gustav Mahler was appointed director of the Court Opera at the age of thirty-eight, horrified murmurs of astonishment ran through the whole of Vienna at the notion of entrusting the highest artistic institution in the country to 'such a young man' (no one stopped to think that Mozart had completed all his works at the age of thirty-six, and Schubert his at thirty-one). At the time this distrust of any young person as 'not quite reliable' was rife in all circles of society. My father would never have taken a young man into his business, and anyone unfortunate enough to look particularly young had to overcome suspicion wherever he went. Almost incredible as it may seem today, youth was an obstacle in every profession, only age was an advantage. While in today's entirely different atmosphere men of forty will try hard to look as if they were thirty, and sixty-year-olds to look forty, while these days youth, energy, drive and self-confidence are a recommendation, in that age of security anyone who wanted to get ahead in life had to try all conceivable methods of looking older than his age. Newspapers advertised methods of encouraging your beard to grow, young doctors of twenty-four or twenty-five who had only just qualified as physicians sported heavy beards and wore gold-rimmed glasses even if they had perfect eyesight, just to impress their patients by looking experienced. They wore long, black frock coats and cultivated a measured tread and, if possible, a slight embonpoint in order to achieve that desirably staid appearance, and if they were ambitious they took a good deal of trouble to dissociate themselves from the suspect immaturity of youth, at least in their outward appearance. In our sixth and seventh years at school we ourselves refused to carry the school satchels that branded us schoolboys, and carried briefcases instead. All that now appears enviable—the freshness of youth, its self-confidence, daring, curiosity and lust for life—was suspect at that time, which set store solely on all that was well established.

Only that odd attitude can explain the way the state exploited its schools as an instrument for maintaining its authority. Above all, we were to be brought up to respect the status quo — as perfect, our teachers' opinions as infallible, a father's word as final, brooking no contradiction, and state institutions as absolute and valid for all eternity. A second cardinal principle of educational theory, one that was also adopted in the family, was that young people should not have too easy a time. Before they were allowed rights of any kind they were supposed to learn that they had duties, above all the duty of total obedience. From the first it was to be impressed upon us that we had not yet done anything in life, we had no experience, we must be grateful for anything we were allowed, and we had no right to ask questions or make demands. In my day, this stupid method of intimidation was applied from early childhood on. Maidservants and silly mothers would terrify children of three or four by threatening to fetch 'the policeman' if they didn't stop being naughty at once. Even as grammar-school boys, if we brought home a bad mark in some unimportant subject we were threatened with being taken away from school and sent to learn a trade—returning to the proletariat being the worst threat imaginable in bourgeois society—and if young people, in an honest desire for education, sought enlightenment from adults on the serious problems of the day, they were fobbed off with a lofty, "You wouldn't understand that yet". This technique was used everywhere—at home, at school, by the state. It was always being impressed on a boy that he was not grown up yet, didn't understand anything, had no option but to listen, believing all he was told, although he must never join in a discussion himself, let alone contradict anyone. For the same reason the poor devil of a teacher at his high lectern at school was to remain unapproachable and aloof, restricting all our thoughts and endeavours to the curriculum. It made no difference whether we were happy at school or not. The sole purpose of school in the spirit of those times was not so much to bring us on as to hold us back, not to help us to shape our minds but to fit us into the established mould with as little resistance as possible, not to enhance our energies but to discipline them and level them out.

Such psychological or rather unpsychological pressure on the young can take effect in only one of two ways—it will either paralyse or stimulate them. The case histories in psychoanalysts' files show us how many inferiority complexes are the result of this absurd method of education; it may be no coincidence that the inferiority complex was revealed by men who had been through our old Austrian schools themselves. Myself, I owe to that pressure a passion for freedom that manifested itself early, one that the youth of today can hardly feel to the same extent, and with it a hatred for all that is authoritarian, all dictums issued from on high, and it has accompanied me all my life. Over the years my aversion to everything dogmatically established has become purely instinctive, and I had almost forgotten where it came from. But one day, when I was on a lecture tour and found out that I was to speak in the great auditorium of a university, standing at a raised lectern while the audience occupied benches below just as we schoolboys used to, I was suddenly overcome by uneasiness. I remembered how I had suffered all through my schooldays from being addressed from on high in that unfriendly, authoritarian, doctrinaire manner, and I was overwhelmed by a fear that speaking from a raised lectern might make me seem just as impersonal as our teachers did in the past. My sense of inhibition made that lecture the worst I ever gave.

Up to the age of fourteen or fifteen we coped with school reasonably well. We joked about the teachers, we learnt our lessons with cold curiosity. But then came the time when school bored and disturbed us more and more. A strange phenomenon had quietly taken place—after entering grammar school at the age of ten, we boys had intellectually overtaken the curriculum after the first four of our eight years of secondary education. We instinctively felt that there wasn't much of importance left for us to learn from it, and in many of the subjects that really interested us we even knew more than our poor teachers, who had never opened a book for their own interest since finishing their university studies. And another difference became more and more obvious daily—on the school benches where, in reality, only the seats of our trousers sat, we heard nothing new, or nothing that we felt was worth knowing, while outside there was a city full of thousands of things to stimulate our minds—a city of theatres, museums, bookshops, a university, music, a place where every day brought new surprises. So our pent-up thirst for knowledge, our intellectual, artistic and sensuous curiosity, finding no nourishment at school, ardently concentrated on all that was going on outside it. At first only two or three of us discovered that we had these artistic, literary and musical interests, then a dozen, and finally it was almost everyone.

For enthusiasm is infectious among young people. It passes from one to another in a school class like measles or scarlet fever, and by trying to outdo one another as fast as possible novices, in their childish vanity and ambition, will spur one another on. It is more or less a matter of chance what direction that enthusiasm takes; if there is a stamp-collector in the class he will soon infect a dozen with the same mania; if three boys wax lyrical about ballerinas then their classmates will be standing at the stage door of the Opera daily. Three years after ours, another whole class at our school was obsessed with football, and before us a class had been enthusiastic fans of socialism and Tolstoy. The fact that I happened to be in a year with other boys whose imagination turned to the arts may have decided my entire career.

In itself this enthusiasm for the theatre, literature and art was perfectly natural in Vienna; the Viennese daily paper devoted a particularly large amount of space to cultural events, and wherever you went you heard adults discussing the Opera or the Burgtheater; you saw the pictures of famous actors on display in all the stationery shops; sport was still considered a rather violent occupation and a grammar-school boy felt he ought to be ashamed of indulging in it; and the cinematograph, with its mass-market ideals, had not yet been invented. There was no opposition to be feared at home either: the theatre and literature were among the 'innocent' passions by comparison with playing cards or chasing girls. After all, my father, like all Viennese fathers, had been an enthusiastic theatre-goer himself in his youth, and had attended a performance of *Lohengrin* conducted by Richard Wagner with as much delight as we went to the premieres of works by Richard Strauss and Gerhart Hauptmann. It was only natural for us, as grammar-school boys, to throng to any premiere. How ashamed we would have been, meeting our luckier colleagues, if we couldn't have described every detail of a first night at school next morning! If our teachers had not been entirely indifferent to us they would surely have noticed that on the afternoon before the premiere of a major work—for which we had to begin queuing at three to get the only available places, standing room only—two-thirds of their pupils were mysteriously away sick. And if they had paid close attention, they would also have realised that the covers of our Latin grammars in fact concealed the poems of Rilke, and we were using our mathematics exercise books to copy out the best poems from books that we had borrowed. Every day we invented new means of exploiting the tedium of lessons for our own reading. While a master was giving his tired old account of Schiller's *Naive and Sentimental Poetry*, we read other things under the table, works by Nietzsche and Strindberg, whose names the good old man had never heard. It had come over us all like a fever; we had to know everything, acquire knowledge of all that was going on in every area of the arts and sciences. We crowded in with the university students in the afternoons to hear lectures, we went to all the art exhibitions, we went to the lecture theatres of the Department of Anatomy to watch dissections. Our curious nostrils sniffed at everything and anything. We stole into the rehearsals of the Philharmonic Orchestra, we rummaged around the second-hand bookshops, we looked at the booksellers' display windows every day for instant information on what had just been published. And most of all, we read; we read everything we could lay hands on. We borrowed books from all the public libraries, and lent anything we could find to one another. But our best cultural source for all novelty was the coffee house.

To understand this, you have to know that the Viennese coffee house is an institution of a peculiar kind, not comparable to any other in the world. It is really a sort of democratic club, and anyone can join it for the price of a cheap cup of coffee. Every guest, in return for that small expenditure, can sit there for hours on end, talking, writing, playing cards, receiving post, and above all reading an unlimited number of newspapers and journals. A Viennese coffee house of the better sort took all the Viennese newspapers available, and not only those but the newspapers of the entire German Reich, as well as the French, British, Italian and American papers, and all the major literary and artistic international magazines, the *Mercure de France* as well as the *Neue Rundschau*, the *Studio*, and the *Burlington Magazine*. So

61

we knew everything that was going on in the world at first hand, we heard about every book that came out, every theatrical performance wherever it took place, and we compared the reviews in all the newspapers. Perhaps nothing contributed so much to the intellectual mobility and international orientation of Austrians as the fact that they could inform themselves so extensively at the coffee house of all that was going on in the world, and at the same time could discuss it with a circle of friends. We sat there for hours every day, and nothing escaped us, for thanks to our collective interests we pursued the *orbis pictus*[1] of artistic events not with just with one pair of eyes but with twenty or so; if one of us missed something, another would point it out to him, since, with a childish wish to show off, we were always vying with each other, showing an almost sporting ambition to know the newest, very latest thing. We were engaged in constant competition for new sensations. For instance, if we were discussing the works of Nietzsche, who was still frowned upon at the time, one of us might suddenly remark, assuming a superior air: "But Kierkegaard is better on the subject of egotism," and at once we would all be jittery. "X knows about Kierkegaard and we don't, who is he?" Next day we would all be racing off to the library to find the works of the dead Danish philosopher, for we felt it was a slur on us not to know something new when another boy did. Discovering and being right up to date with the very latest, most recent, most extravagant and unusual subject, one that had not yet been flogged to death—in particular not by the official literary critics of our worthy daily papers—was our passion, and I myself have indulged it for very many years. We were particularly keen to know all about what was not yet generally acknowledged, was difficult to get hold of, extravagant, new and radical; nothing was so abstruse and remote that our collective and avidly competitive curiosity did not want to entice it out of hiding. During our schooldays Stefan George and Rilke, for instance, had been published in editions of only two or three hundred copies in all, and at most three or four of those copies had found their way to Vienna; no bookseller stocked them, no official critic had ever mentioned the name of Rilke. But through a miracle of the will, our little band knew every verse and every line of those poets. We beardless boys, not yet fully grown, who had to spend our days on the school bench, were the ideal readers for a young poet: curious, with enquiring and critical minds, and enthusiastic about enthusiasm itself. In fact we had a boundless capacity for enthusiasm. For years, we adolescents did nothing during our lessons, on the way to and from school, in the coffee house, at the theatre and on walks but discuss books, pictures, music, philosophy. Anyone who performed in public as an actor or conductor, anyone who had published a book or wrote in a newspaper, was a star in our firmament. I was almost alarmed when, years later, I found in Balzac's account of his youth the sentence: "*Les gens célèbres étaient pour moi comme des dieux qui ne parlaient pas, ne marchaient pas, ne mangeaient pas comme les autres hommes.*"[2] That was exactly what we used to feel—to have seen Gustav Mahler in the street was an event to be reported to your friends next morning like a personal triumph, and when once, as a boy, I was introduced to Johannes Brahms and he gave me a kindly pat on the shoulder, I was in a state of total confusion for days over this extraordinary event. It is true that, aged twelve, I had only a very vague idea of exactly what Brahms had done, but the mere fact of his fame and his aura of creativity exerted astonishing power over me. A premiere of a work by Gerhart Hauptmann intrigued our entire class for weeks before rehearsals began; we approached actors and the players of bit parts to find out—ahead of anyone else!—the course of the plot and the exact cast; we had our hair cut by the theatre barber (I do not shrink even from describing our absurdities), just to glean some secret piece of information about Wolter or Sonnenthal, and we particularly cultivated the company of a boy in a lower class, showing him all kinds of attentions, just because he was the nephew of a lighting inspector at the Opera and sometimes smuggled us in during rehearsals, and to tread that stage exceeded the awe felt by Dante when he climbed to the sacred circle of Paradise. So strongly did we feel the radiance of fame that even if it came at seventh hand, it still awed us; a poor old lady who was a great-niece of Franz Schubert appeared to us a supernatural being, and we looked respectfully at even Joseph Kainz's valet in the street because he was lucky enough to be personally close to that most popular and brilliant of actors.

Of course I am well aware now of all the absurdity in our undiscriminating enthusiasm, of how much of it was merely mutual mimicry, how much no more than a sportsman's instinct to come first, how much childish vanity there was in feeling arrogantly superior to the philistine environment of our families and our teachers in our high regard for the arts. But it still surprises me to think how much this close attention to our literary passions taught us boys at the time, how early our constant discussion and unravelling of the details of texts brought us the critical ability to discriminate. At seventeen, I had not only read all the poems of Baudelaire and Walt Whitman, I knew most of them by heart, and I think that in my entire later life I never read as intensively as I did in those years at school and university. It was taken for granted that names not honoured by the general public until a decade later were current among us, even the most ephemeral stayed in our minds because we fixed upon them so eagerly. Once I was telling my revered friend Paul Valéry how old my literary acquaintance with him really was. Thirty years ago, I said, I had already been reading his poems and loved them. The good-humoured Valéry merely smiled. "No pretence, please, my friend! My poems weren't published until 1916." He was astonished when I described in detail the colour and format of the small literary journal where, in 1898, we had found his first verses in Vienna. "But hardly anyone knew them even in Paris," he said in amazement. "How can you have got hold of them in Vienna?" I replied: "In just the same way as when you were a schoolboy yourself, in your provincial town, you got hold of the poems of Mallarmé, who was no better known at the time, nor part of the accepted literary canon." And he agreed with me: "Young people discover poets for themselves because they want to discover them." And it is a fact that we could scent what was in the wind even before it crossed the border, because we lived with our nostrils always distended to catch it. We found what was new because that was what we wanted, because we were hungry for something that belonged to us alone—not to the world of our fathers, not our environment. Young people, like certain animals, have an excellent instinct for changes in the weather, and so our generation felt, before our teachers and the universities knew it, that with the old century some of the old artistic ideas were also coming to an end, that a revolution or at least a change of values was in preparation. The good, solid masters of our fathers' time—in literature Gottfried Keller, in drama Ibsen, in music Johannes Brahms, in painting Leibl, in philosophy Eduard von Hartmann—had in them, as we saw it, all the measured deliberation of the world of security. In spite of their technical and intellectual mastery, they no longer interested us. Instinctively, we felt that their cold, temperate rhythm was not that of our own restless blood, was no longer in tune with the accelerating tempo of modernity. The most vigilant mind of the later German generation, Hermann Bahr, lived in Vienna. He struck out furiously, an intellectual marauder championing all that was on its way, all that was new, and with his aid the Secession movement's building was opened in Vienna, exhibiting, to the horror of the old school in Paris,

65

the Impressionists and Pointillists, Munch from Norway, Rops from Belgium, all manner of extreme artists pointing to their predecessors Grünewald, Greco and Goya, who were out of favour at the time. We suddenly learnt to see with new eyes, and at the same time we learnt new rhythms and tonal colours in music through the works of Mussorgsky, Debussy, Strauss and Schönberg. In literature, realism dawned with Zola, Strindberg and Hauptmann, the daemonic Slav spirit with Dostoevsky, and a previously unknown sublimation and refinement of lyrical art in the works of Verlaine, Rimbaud and Mallarmé. Nietzsche revolutionised philosophy; in architecture plain, functional buildings were introduced instead of the overloaded style of neoclassicism. Suddenly the old, comfortable order had been disrupted, its norms of the "aesthetically beautiful" (as Hanslick[3] would have put it) were questioned, and while the official critics of our solid bourgeois age often expressed horror at the experiments now being made, which were often bold, and sought to hold back the inexorable current by condemning such trends as 'decadent' or 'anarchic', we young people flung ourselves with gusto into the turbulent waves wherever they broke and foamed most wildly, We had a feeling that a time for us, our own time, was beginning, a time when youth would at last come into its own. So all at once our restlessly questing, enquiring passion had a point; we young people, still at school, could join the fray in these wild and often ferocious battles for the new art. Where an experiment was tried, perhaps a performance of a Wedekind play or a reading of modern poetry, we were sure to be there, lending our aid with the full force not only of our minds but also of our hands. I was a witness when, at the first performance of one of the atonal works of Arnold Schönberg's youth, one gentleman began hissing and whistling vigorously, whereupon my friend Buschbeck dealt him an equally vigorous blow. We were the vanguard, the shock troops promoting every kind of new art just because it *was* new, just because it would change the world for us, and it was our turn to live our own lives in the world now. *Nostra res agitur*[4], we felt.

However, something else about this new art interested and fascinated us inordinately: it was almost exclusively the work of young people. In our fathers' generation a poet or musician was esteemed only when he had 'proved himself', adjusting to the worthy tastes of bourgeois society. All the men whom we had been taught to respect bore themselves and behaved like people truly worthy of that respect. They had fine beards, sprinkled with grey, above poetical velvet jackets—Wilbrandt, Ebers, Felix Dahn, Paul Heyse, Lenbach, those now long-forgotten darlings of their time. They had themselves photographed with a pensive gaze, always in 'dignified' and 'poetic' attitudes, they behaved like the bearers of official titles, excellencies and councillors, and like them were awarded honours. Young poets or painters or musicians, however, were regarded at the most as promising; outright recognition was kept on ice for the time being. The age of caution did not like to bestow its favours ahead of time, before an artist had shown his merit through long years of solid achievement. The new poets, musicians, and painters, however, were all young: Gerhart Hauptmann, suddenly emerging from complete anonymity, dominated the German stage at the age of thirty; Stefan George and Rainer Maria Rilke had won literary fame and a fanatical following at twenty-three—before by Austrian law they had reached the age of adult responsibility. In our own city, the 'Young Vienna' group emerged overnight, with members like Arthur Schnitzler, Hermann Bahr, Richard Beer-Hofmann, Peter Altenberg—men in whom specifically Austrian culture found European expression for the first time by the refinement of all artistic means. But *one* figure above all fascinated us, seduced, intoxicated and inspired us—that wonderful and unique phenomenon Hugo von Hofmannsthal, in whom our youth saw not only its highest ambitions, but also absolute literary perfection, and in the shape of a man who was almost our contemporary.

67

The appearance of young Hofmannsthal is and will remain remarkable as one of the great miracles of early perfection. I know no other example in world literature, except in Keats and Rimbaud, of similar infallibility in the mastery of language at such a young age, of such a breadth of inspired ideas, such a mind, full of poetic substance even in the least of his lines, as in that great genius, who had written his way into the eternal annals of the German language in his sixteenth and seventeenth year with imperishable verse and prose that is still unrivalled today. His sudden emergence and instant achievement of perfection were a phenomenon of a kind unlikely to recur in the same generation. The outcome was that all who first heard of it were astonished by the improbability of what he represented. Hermann Bahr often told me about his amazement when he was sent an article for his magazine from Vienna written by one 'Loris', a pseudonym unknown to him—the educational authorities would not allow a schoolboy to publish under his own name. Never, among contributions coming in to him from all over the world, had he received an article like this, setting out such a wealth of ideas as if with the greatest ease, and in such lively, elevated language. "Who is 'Loris'?" he asked himself. "Who is this unknown? An old man, surely, who has distilled his discoveries in silence over the years, and in mysterious seclusion has cultivated the sublime essence of language to create an almost sensuous magic." To think that such a wise man, such a gifted writer lived in the same city, and he had never heard of him! Bahr wrote at once to the anonymous Loris and arranged to meet him for discussion at a coffee house—the famous Café Griensteidl, the haunt of the young literary lions. Suddenly a slender, still-beardless grammar-school boy, still in a boy's short trousers, entered, walking fast and lightly, went up to his table, bowed and said merely, in a high voice, still not completely broken, but with a firm note in it: "Hofmannsthal! I'm Loris." Years later, when Bahr spoke of his astonishment, excitement still overcame him. At first he couldn't believe it. A schoolboy who had acquired such artistry, such breadth and depth of vision, such a stupendous knowledge of life even *before* his life had really begun! Arthur Schnitzler told me almost the same. Schnitzler was still practising as a doctor at the time, since his first successful literary works seemed far from guaranteeing security, although he was already regarded as the leader of the Young Vienna group, and those who were even younger liked to turn to him for advice and his opinion. Visiting casual acquaintances, he had met the tall young schoolboy, whose quick intelligence impressed him, and when the schoolboy asked as a favour whether he could read him a short theatrical piece in verse, Schnitzler gladly invited him to his bachelor apartment, although without any great expectations—well, he thought, a schoolboy effort, it will be either sentimental or pseudo-classical. He invited some friends: Hofmannsthal turned up in his short trousers, rather nervous and awkward, and began to read. "After a few minutes," Schnitzler told me, "we suddenly pricked up our ears and exchanged surprised, almost alarmed glances. We had never before heard from any living soul verse of such perfection, so flawlessly graphic and with such musical feeling. In fact, we had thought it hardly possible since Goethe. But even more wonderful than this unique mastery of form (which has not been achieved by anyone writing in German since Hofmannsthal), was the knowledge of the world that could come only from some magical intuition in a boy who spent his days at school." When Hofmannsthal came to the end of his piece, they were all silent. "I had a feeling," Schnitzler told me, "that for the first time in my life I had met a born genius, and in all my life I have never again felt that with such force." A man who began like that at the age of sixteen—or rather did not begin but was already perfect when he began— must become a brother of Goethe and Shakespeare. And indeed, perfection seemed to become even more perfected:

after that first piece in verse, *Yesterday*, came the grand fragment *The Death of Titian*, in which the German language rose to the melodious sound of Italian, and the poems, every one of which was an event to us, and which I still know by heart years later. Then came the short dramas, and those essays that combined a wealth of knowledge, a perfect understanding of art and a width of vision, all crowding into the wonderfully small space of a few dozen pages. Everything that he wrote as a schoolboy and then a university student was like a crystal illuminated from within, dark and glittering at the same time. The verse and prose were like fragrant beeswax from Hymettus in his hands; by some unique miracle every work he wrote had its right measure, there was never too little and never too much of anything, one always felt that something unconscious and impossible to grasp must be guiding him along these paths to places hitherto untrodden.

I can hardly say how such a phenomenon fascinated those of us who had taught ourselves to take note of artistic values. What can be more intoxicating for a young generation than to know that there is a pure, sublime writer near them, among them in the flesh, just as they previously imagined him in the legendary figures of Hölderlin, Keats and Leopardi, but out of reach, half a dream and a vision? That is why I also remember so clearly the day when I first saw Hofmannsthal in person. I was sixteen years old, and as we were all avidly following what this ideal mentor of ours did, a small note hidden away in the newspaper excited me immensely. It announced a lecture on Goethe that he was to deliver at the Scientific Club (we could hardly imagine such a genius speaking in so modest a setting; in our schoolboy devotion, we would have expected the largest hall available to be crammed when a figure like Hofmannsthal stated publicly that he would be there). But on this occasion I found out how far in advance of the general public and the established critics we insignificant schoolboys were in our instinct for what would endure (an instinct which proved sound). An audience of about ten to twelve dozen had assembled in the small room, so I need not have set out half-an-hour too early, just to be sure of a seat. We waited for some time, and then a slender young man, inconspicuous in himself, walked past our ranks to the lectern and began speaking so suddenly that I hardly had time to study him properly. With his soft moustache, not yet fully mature, and his supple figure, Hofmannsthal looked even younger than I had expected. His face, with its keen profile and dark, rather Italianate complexion, seemed to show nervous tension, and the restlessness of his very dark, velvety, but extremely short-sighted eyes added to that impression. As if with a sudden single movement, he plunged into his lecture like a swimmer diving into a familiar torrent, and the longer he went on speaking, the more freely he gestured and the more confident was his manner. Once his initial awkwardness was over and he was in his intellectual element he was swept away—as I often noticed later in private conversation—by the wonderful ease and vitality of a man inspired. Only in the first few sentences did I notice that his voice was unattractive, sometimes very close to a falsetto and with a slight tendency to fall over itself, but soon his lecture was carrying us up to such heights of freedom that we no longer noticed his voice, hardly even his face. He spoke without a manuscript text, without notes, perhaps even without careful preparation, but his natural and magical sense of form left every sentence perfectly rounded. The most daring antitheses unfolded, dazzling us and resolving themselves in clear yet unexpected formulations. We had an irresistible feeling that what we were hearing was merely scattered before us out of much greater wealth, and that elated as he was, rising to higher spheres, he could go on for hours and hours without running short of ideas or sinking to a lower level. I still felt the magical force of "this creator's rolling song and sparkling, confident

71

dialogue", as Stefan George said in praise of him, in later years and in private conversation. He was restless, agitated, sensitive, reacting to every change in the atmosphere, often morose and nervous in private, and it was not easy to get close to him. But once a problem interested him he caught fire like a rocket, and in a single glittering, glowing flight he carried every discussion up into the sphere peculiar to *him*, truly accessible only to him. I have never known conversations on such an intellectual level with anyone else apart, sometimes, from Valéry, whose thinking was more measured and more crystalline, and from the impetuous Keyserling. At these truly inspired moments, everything vividly came back to his daemonically keen memory, every book he had read, every picture he had seen, every landscape; metaphor was linked to metaphor as naturally as hand to hand, perspectives rose like sudden backdrops beyond the horizon that had seemed to be finite. In that lecture, for the first time, and later in personal encounters, I truly felt the *flatus* comprehended by reason alone.

In a certain sense, Hofmannsthal never again surpassed the unique marvel that he represented from his sixteenth to about his twenty-fourth year. I admire many of his later works no less, his wonderful essays, the fragment *Andreas*, that torso of what might have been the finest novel in the German language, and certain parts of his dramatic output, but with his increasing links to the theatre of the day and the interests of his time, once he became clearly conscious of his ambitious plans some of the instinctive, apt certainty, the pure inspiration of those first youthful works was gone, and with it something of the intoxication and ecstasy of our own youth. With the magical knowledge that is peculiar to those not yet of age, we were aware in advance that this miracle of our youth was unique, and would not return to our own lives.

Balzac, in his own incomparable way, described how the example of Napoleon electrified an entire generation in France. To him, the dazzling rise of little Lieutenant Bonaparte to become emperor of the world meant not just the triumph of a man, but the victory of the idea of youth. The fact that you need not be born a prince to achieve power at an early age, that you could come from any insignificant, even poor family, yet still be a general before you were twenty-four, master of France at the age of thirty, and soon of the whole world—that unprecedented success drove hundreds to abandon their little careers and their provincial towns. Lieutenant Bonaparte went to the heads of a whole generation of young people. He urged them on to higher ambitions; he created the generals of the *Grande Armée* and the heroes and *arrivistes* of the *Comédie Humaine*. A single young man who reached hitherto unattainable heights at the first bold attempt always, merely by dint of his success, encourages all the young people around him and following him. In this sense we younger boys, whose energies were still developing, were spurred on to an enormous degree by Hofmannsthal and Rilke. Without hoping that any of us could ever emulate the miracle of Hofmannsthal, we were invigorated merely by his physical existence. It was visible evidence that there could still be a writer of distinction in our own time, our own environment. After all, his father, a bank manager, came from the same Jewish middle class as the rest of us; the genius had grown up in a home like ours, with the same furnishings and the same moral principles as other people of our social class. He had attended an equally tedious grammar school; he had learnt from the same textbooks and spent eight years wearing the seat of his trousers out on the same wooden benches; he was as impatient as we were, as passionately devoted to all intellectual values. And lo and behold, even when he was still sitting on those benches and having to trot around the gymnasium, he had succeeded surmounting the constraints of school, family and the city by virtue of that rise to the boundless heights. Hofmannsthal could be said to have demonstrated before our eyes that even at our age, even in the dungeon atmosphere of an Austrian grammar school, it was possible in principle to create a work of literature, indeed a perfect work of literature. It was even possible—what a tempting inducement to a boy's mind—to be published, discussed and famous, although at home and at school you might still be regarded as an insignificant adolescent.

As for Rilke, he represented a different kind of encouragement to us, and he reassuringly complemented Hofmannsthal. The idea of competing with Hofmannsthal would have appeared blasphemy to even the boldest among us. We knew he was an incomparable, inimitable miracle of early perfection, and if we, at sixteen, compared our verses with those famous specimens that he had written at the same age we felt frightened and ashamed, just as we felt humbled by the eagle flight with which he had soared through intellectual space while still at grammar school. Rilke too had begun writing and publishing poetry young, at seventeen or eighteen, but compared to Hofmannsthal's and even in the absolute sense, those early works of his were immature, childish and naive verses. There were a few golden traces of talent to be found, but you had to make made allowances. Only gradually, at twenty-two and twenty-three, did that wonderful poet, whom we loved beyond measure, begin to form his personal style, and that was a great consolation to us. So it was not essential to be perfect while still at grammar school, like Hofmannsthal; you could feel your way like Rilke, make attempts, create a structure for your work and enhance it. There was no need to give up at once because for the time being your work was inadequate, immature, irresponsible. Despite the Hofmannsthal miracle, you could emulate the quieter, more normal rise of Rilke.

For naturally we had all, long ago, begun writing prose or poetry, making music, giving readings; after all, it is unnatural for young people to be passively enthusiastic; it is in their nature not just to absorb impressions but to respond to them productively. For young people, a love of the theatre means at least wishing and dreaming of working in or for the theatre in some way themselves; ecstatic admiration for talent in all its forms leads them irresistibly to look at themselves, wondering whether they can perhaps detect a trace of that sublime essence in their own unexplored bodies or still partly unenlightened minds. In line with the Viennese atmosphere and the circumstances of that time, the drive to artistic production in our class at school was a positive epidemic. We all looked for some talent in ourselves and tried to develop it. Four or five of us wanted to be actors. They imitated the diction of the Burghof actors, they were always reciting and declaiming, they secretly took drama lessons and, during break at school, improvised whole scenes from the classics, dividing out the parts between them, while the rest of us formed an interested but severely critical audience. Two or three were very well trained musicians, but had not yet decided whether they wanted to be composers, virtuoso performers or conductors. It is to them that I owe my first acquaintance with modern music, which was still strictly excluded from the concerts given by the Philharmonic. The musicians, in turn, asked us to write texts for their lieder and choruses. Another boy, the son of a society painter who was famous at the time, drew in our exercise books during lessons, portraying all the future geniuses of the class. But far the strongest trend was towards literary endeavour. In spurring each other on to ever swifter achievement, and by dint of mutual criticism of every single poem, the level we reached at the age of seventeen was well above that of mere amateurs, and some of us approached genuine achievement, as was witness the fact that our work was published not merely in obscure provincial papers but by leading journals of the modern generation, and was even paid for, the most convincing of all proofs of merit. One of my

75

friends, Ph A, whom I idolised as a genius, shone in *Pan*, the de luxe literary journal, in the company of Dehmel and Rilke; another, A M, writing under the pseudonym of August Oehler, had made his way into the pages of the most inaccessible and eclectic of all German reviews, the *Blätter für die Kunst*—Leaves for Art—in which Stefan George usually published only the work of his canonised circle of writers. A third, encouraged by Hofmannsthal, wrote a drama on the subject of Napoleon, a fourth came up with a new theory of aesthetics and some important sonnets. I myself had something published in *Gesellschaft*—Society—the leading journal of modern literature, and Maxmilian Harden's *Zukunft*—Future—a weekly journal prominent in the political and cultural history of modern Germany. When I look back today, I must say perfectly objectively that the sum of our knowledge, the refinement of our literary technique, and our artistic level was really astonishing for boys of seventeen, and can be explained only by the inspiring example of that fantastic early maturing of Hofmannsthal which, if we were to hold our heads high in each other's company, meant that we had to exert ourselves to the utmost. We mastered all the tricks and extravagances and audacities of language, we had tried the technique of every verse form, making countless attempts at all styles from the Pindaric ode to the simple diction of the folk song, we showed our writings to each other every day, discussing the most fugitive of discrepancies and every metrical detail. While our worthy teachers, unaware of any of this, were still marking our school essays in red ink, pointing out missing commas, we criticised one another with a severity, artistic expertise and attention to detail greater than any of the official literary pundits of our great daily papers applied to the classic masterpieces. In our final years at school, our fanatical enthusiasm meant that in our expert judgements and stylistic ability to express ourselves, we were far ahead of famous critics in established positions.

This account of our literary precocity, which is genuinely faithful to the facts, might tempt one to think that we were a particularly talented class. By no means. The same phenomenon of fanatical enthusiasm and the same precocious talent was to be found at a dozen neighbouring schools in Vienna at the time. It could not be chance. There was something especially favourable to it in the air, something nurtured by the fertile artistic soil of the city, by the apolitical period and all the interlinking new literary and intellectual directions around the turn of the century. By a kind of chemical reaction, all this created in us the kind of desire to create literary works that is almost a compulsion at that age. At puberty every young person writes or feels the urge to write, although admittedly in most cases it is just a fleeting impulse, and it is rare for such an inclination, being a symptom of youth, to survive youth itself. None of our five would-be actors at school became an actor on the real stage. After that amazing initial surge of creativity had petered out, the young contributors to *Pan* and the *Blätter für die Kunst*[6] became staid lawyers or civil servants, and perhaps smile over their former ambitions with melancholy or irony today. Of them all, I am the only one in whom the creative passion has lasted, has become the meaning and core of my whole life. But I think back very gratefully to our comradeship. It helped me so much. Those fiery discussions, that hectic competition, that mutual admiration and criticism exercised my hand and my nerves at an early date, giving me a view of the intellectual cosmos, and their inspiration raised us all above the bleak and dismal atmosphere of our school. *Du holde Kunst, in wieviel grauen Stunden*[6] ... whenever I hear that immortal Schubert song I have a kind of three-dimensional vision in which we are sitting on those unpleasant school benches, shoulders hunched, and then going home with radiant, excited faces, reciting, criticising poems, forgetting time and space in our passionate enthusiasm, truly transported to a better world.

Such a monomaniac obsession with art, setting store on aestheticism to the point of absurdity, was of course bound to take its toll on the normal interests of young people of our age. If I wonder today where we found the time to read all those books, crammed as our days already were with lessons at school and private coaching, it is clear to me that it must have been mainly at the expense of our sleep and so our physical health. Although I had to get up at seven, I never put down whatever I was reading until one or two in the morning. Incidentally it was then that I acquired the bad habit of always reading for an hour or two before going to sleep, however late it is. So I do not remember ever setting off to school feeling as if I were well rested, and I used to set off in haste, eating my breakfast of a buttered roll on the way, after a mere lick and promise of a wash. No wonder that for all our high-flying intellectuality we cut a poor figure, looking as green as unripe fruit, and we were rather carelessly dressed. Every penny of our pocket money went on the theatre, concerts or books, and we did not feel it was important to appeal to girls when our minds were bent on impressing higher authorities. In fact going out with girls seemed to us a waste of time, since in our intellectual arrogance we regarded the opposite sex as intellectually inferior by their very nature, and we didn't want to spend our valuable time in idle chatter. It would be quite hard to get a modern young person to understand the extent to which we ignored and even despised all sporting activities. In the last century the wave of enthusiasm for sport had not yet spread from Britain to the continent of Europe. As yet there were no stadiums where a hundred thousand spectators roared with enthusiasm at the sight of one boxer landing a mighty punch on another boxer's jaw; the newspapers were not yet sending reporters off to fill columns with Homeric accounts of a hockey game. Wrestling matches, athletics clubs, heavyweight records were regarded in our time as spectacles fit only for the outer suburbs of the city, with the spectators consisting of butchers and porters. The nobler and more aristocratic sport of horse-racing might at most tempt high society to the racecourse a couple of times a year, but not us, since all physical activity struck us as a sheer waste of time. At thirteen, when I first caught our literary and intellectual infection, I stopped going ice-skating and spent the money my parents gave me for dancing lessons to buy books; at eighteen I still couldn't swim, dance or play tennis; to this day I can neither ride a bicycle nor drive a car, and in my general knowledge of sport any ten-year-old puts me to shame. Even today the differences between baseball and football, hockey and polo are not at all clear to me, and the sports section of a newspaper, with its mysterious symbols, might as well be written in Chinese. As for sporting records of speed or skill, I am still in the position of the Shah of Persia who, when it was suggested that he might go to a horse race for amusement, asked with oriental wisdom, "What's the point? I know that one horse can run faster than another, but which horse does it is a matter of indifference to me." Wasting time playing games seemed to us just as contemptible as physical training; chess was the only game to find some favour with us because it required intellectual effort. And even more absurdly, although we considered ourselves budding or at least potential poets, we took very little notice of nature. Throughout my first twenty years of life I saw almost nothing of the wonderful surroundings of Vienna; indeed, the hottest and most beautiful summer days, when the city was deserted, were particularly attractive to us because we could get our hands more quickly on a wider choice of newspapers and journals in our coffee house. It took me years, even decades, to get my sense of a proper balance back, and make up to some extent for my inevitable physical awkwardness, the result of overstraining myself in this childishly greedy way. But on the whole I have never regretted the enthusiasms of my time at grammar school, when I lived only through my eyes and my nerves. It gave me a passion for the things of the mind that I would never wish to lose, and all that I have read and learnt since then stands on the solid foundation of those years. One can make up later for neglecting to exercise the muscles, but the mind can be trained only in those crucial years of development to rise to its full powers of comprehension, and only someone who has learnt to spread his intellectual wings early will be able to form an idea of the world as a whole later.

The truly great experience of our youthful years was the realisation that something new in art was on the way—something more impassioned, difficult and alluring than the art that had satisfied our parents and the world around us. But fascinated as we were by this one aspect of life, we did not notice that these aesthetic changes were only the forerunners of the much more far-reaching changes that were to shake and finally destroy the world of our fathers, the world of security. A remarkable process of restructuring was going on in sleepy old Austria. The quiet, obedient masses who for decades had left power to the liberal bourgeoisie were suddenly becoming restive, organising themselves and demanding their own rights. In the last ten years of the century, politics disturbed the serene calm of comfortable Austrian life with keen gusts of a changing wind. The new century called for a new order, a new time.

The first of these great mass movements in Austria was the Socialist movement. Until now, what was misleadingly called the 'universal' franchise had been confined to prosperous citizens who could show that they paid a certain amount of tax. However, the lawyers and landed gentlemen whom this class elected sincerely and genuinely believed that they spoke for the people and represented their interests in parliament. They were very proud of being cultivated and even, where possible, academically educated men; they set store by dignity, correct manners and good diction, and as a result parliamentary sessions resembled an evening debate at a good club. Thanks to their liberal belief in a world that had become infallibly progressive, through tolerance and reason, these middle-class democrats honestly thought that they served the good of all Austrian subjects best by making small concessions and gradual improvements. But they had entirely forgotten that they represented only the fifty thousand or a hundred thousand prosperous men of the big cities, not the hundreds of thousands, even millions of people in the entire country. By now machinery had done its work and the working classes, once widely scattered, had gathered around the industries. Under an eminent leader, Dr Victor Adler,[7] a Social Democratic Party formed in Austria to carry through the demands of the proletariat, which wanted truly universal suffrage for every man. As soon as that was granted—or rather, forcibly introduced—it became clear what a small if useful part of society had been represented by Liberalism, and with it conciliation too disappeared from public political life; interests now clashed harshly, and the battle began.

I remember, from my earliest childhood, the day that brought the decisive change in the rise of the Social Democratic Party in Austria. By way of a visible demonstration of their power and their numbers, the workers had declared the first of May a holiday for the working class, and were going to march in close formation to the Prater[8] and down the Hauptallee itself, where only the horses and carriages of the aristocracy and the rich middle class usually went that day for their own traditional parade down the wide, handsome avenue lined with chestnut trees. This announcement paralysed the liberal middle classes with horror. Socialists—at the time, in Germany and Austria, the word had something of a bloodstained, terrorist aura about it, like the terms Jacobin before and Bolshevik after it. At first no one thought it possible that the red horde from the city suburbs would march without setting fire to houses, looting shops, and committing every imaginable act of violence. A kind of panic spread. The police of the entire city and its surroundings were stationed on Praterstrasse, with the army in reserve ready to open fire. No carriage or cab ventured near the Prater, shopkeepers rolled down the iron shutters over their windows, and I remember my parents strictly forbidding us children to go out into the street on that terrible day when Vienna might go up in flames. The workers, with their wives and children, marched to the Prater with exemplary discipline in ranks four abreast, all of them wearing red carnations, the party symbol, in their buttonholes. As they marched along they sang *The Internationale*, but then, in the beautiful green of the handsome avenue where they had never set foot before, the children struck up their carefree school songs. No one was abused, no blows were exchanged, no fists were clenched; the police officers and soldiers smiled at the workers in a comradely manner. Thanks to this blameless behaviour on the part of the workers, it was no longer possible for the bourgeoisie to brand them red revolutionaries, concessions were made on both sides—as usual in the wise old country of Austria. No one had yet devised the present system of eradicating demonstrators by clubbing them to the ground, and though the humanitarian ideal was already fading, it was still alive even among the party leaders.

No sooner did the red carnation emerge as a party symbol than another flower suddenly appeared in buttonholes, the white carnation, denoting membership of the Christian Socialist Party (how touching to think that, at that time, political symbols were flowers rather than jackboots, daggers and death's heads). The Christian Socialist party, drawn from the lower middle class, was really just the organic counter-movement to the proletarian workers, and basically was just as much a product of the victory of machinery over craftsmanship as they were. For while machinery, by bringing together large numbers in the factories, gave the workers power and social advancement, at the same time it threatened small crafts. Huge department stores and mass production were the ruin of the lower middle class and the small master craftsmen who were still plying their old trades. A clever and popular leader, Dr Karl Lueger, · exploited this discontent and anxiety and, with the slogan, 'We must help the little man', united the discontented lower middle class, whose envy of those more prosperous than themselves was considerably lesser than their fear of sinking from bourgeois status into the proletariat. This was exactly the same kind of social group living in a state of anxiety that Adolf Hitler later gathered around him to provide his first large body of followers. Karl Lueger was also his model in another sense by teaching him the usefulness of anti-Semitic slogans, thus showing the ⁓ disgruntled lower middle classes a visible enemy and at the same time imperceptibly diverting their hatred from the great landowners and feudal wealth. But the far greater vulgarisation ‑ and brutality of today's politics, the terrible relapse we have seen in our own century, is obvious if we compare the two men. Karl Lueger, an imposing figure with his soft, blond beard—he was known in Vienna as 'Handsome Karl'—had an academic education, and not for nothing had he been to school in an age that set the highest value on intellectual culture. He could speak in a way that appealed to the common man, he was vehement and witty, but even when speaking with his utmost ferocity— or what was taken as ferocity at the time—he never stepped beyond the bounds of decency, and while he had his equivalent of Julius Streicher,[9] he kept him carefully under control. This equivalent was a certain mechanic called Schneider whose anti-Semitic propaganda consisted of such vulgar nonsense as fairy tales about ritual murders. Lueger, whose private life was beyond reproach, always maintained a certain dignity towards his opponents, and his official anti-Semitism never kept him from helping his former Jewish friends and showing them goodwill. When his movement finally took control of the Viennese city

83

council, and he was appointed Mayor—an appointment that Emperor Franz Joseph, who loathed the anti-Semitic trend, had twice refused to sanction—his administration of the city was blamelessly just and in fact a model of democracy, and the Jews, who had been terrified by the triumph of the anti-Semitic party, continued to enjoy respect and equal rights. Venomous hatred and an urge towards mutual annihilation had not yet entered the bloodstream of that time.

But now a third symbolic flower appeared—the blue cornflower, Bismarck's favourite and the symbol of the German National party, which—not that anyone realised it at the time—was deliberately revolutionary, and worked with brute force for the destruction of the Austrian Monarchy, anticipating Hitler's dreams by aiming to set up a Greater Germany under Prussian and Protestant leadership. While the Christian Socialist party had its roots in Vienna and the country, and the Socialists in the industrial centres, the German Nationalists had their adherents almost solely in the Bohemian and Alpenland border areas; they were weak in numbers, but made up for their insignificance by ferocious aggression and mass brutality. Their few deputies became the terror and—in the old sense of the word—the shame of the Austrian parliament; Hitler, himself an Austrian from the border of the country, adopted their ideas and methods as his point of departure. He took on board the clarion cry, "Away from Rome!" thought up by Georg von Schönerer,[10] whom thousands of nationalist Germans had followed obediently in his time, infuriating the Emperor and the clergy by converting from Catholicism to Protestantism. Hitler also adopted his anti-Semitic theory of race—*In der Rass' liegt die Schweinerei*,[11] said a famous example—and above all, he took over Schönerer's use of ruthless storm troopers to strike out at random, and with it the principle where by a small group intimidates a numerically superior but humane and passive majority through terrorism. What the SA men did for National

Socialism, breaking up gatherings with rubber truncheons, attacking opponents by night and striking them down, was done for the German Nationalists in Austria at this time by the student groups which established a unparalleled, violently terrorist regime, under cover of academic immunity, and were ready to march with military organisation in any political action when they were called upon to do so. Grouped in so-called fraternities, their faces battered, drunk and brutal, they dominated the university hall because they did not just wear bands and caps like the other students, but were also armed with hard, heavy sticks. Ever provocative, they struck out now at Slavonic students, now at Jews, now at Catholics and now at Italians, driving the defenceless out of the university. During every 'casual stroll', as the student parades on Saturdays were called, blood was shed. The police, who thanks to the old privilege of the university could not enter its hall, watched helplessly from the sidelines as these cowardly thugs went on the rampage. Police officers had to confine themselves to carrying away the injured and bleeding who were flung down the steps and into the street by the violent nationalists. Whenever the tiny but loud-mouthed party of German Nationalists wanted to do something by force, it sent in this student storm troop; when Count Badeni,[12] with the consent of the Emperor and parliament had decided on the Language Ordinance that was intended to make peace between the nations of Austria, and would probably have extended the life of the monarchy itself by decades, this handful of young thugs moved in to occupy the Ringstrasse. The cavalry were sent in, swords were drawn, guns were fired. But in that tragically weak if touchingly humane and liberal era, so great was the horror of any violent tumult and bloodshed that the government gave way in the face of the German Nationalist terrorists. The Prime Minister resigned, and the Language Ordinance, a measure which had been backed by true loyalists, was annulled. The advent of brutality into politics chalked up its first success. When the underlying rifts between races and classes, mended so laboriously during the age of conciliation, broke open they widened into ravines and clefts. In fact, in that last decade before the new century, war waged by everyone against everyone else in Austria had already begun.

We young men, however, wholly absorbed in our literary ambitions, noticed little of these dangerous changes in our native land; our eyes were bent entirely on books and pictures. We took not the slightest interest in political and social problems; what did all this shrill squabbling mean in our lives? The city was in a state of agitation at election time; we went to the libraries. The masses rose up; we wrote and discussed poetry. We failed to see the writing on the wall in letters of fire. Like King Belshazzar before us, we dined on the delicious dishes of the arts and never looked apprehensively ahead. Only decades later, when the roof and walls of the building fell in on us, did we realise that the foundations had been undermined long before, and the downfall of individual freedom in Europe had begun with the new century.

NOTES

1   *The World in Pictures*—this was the title of a seventeenth-century educational work with illustrations by the Czech John Commenius, and came to be used for educational picture books in general.

2   *To me, famous people were like gods who did not talk, walk or eat like other human beings.*

3   Eduard Hanslick, an influential nineteenth-century Austrian writer on music. Zweig is alluding to, but slightly misquoting, the title of his best-known work, *Vom Musikalich-Schönen*—On the Musically Beautiful.

4   Latin tag meaning, roughly speaking—*Our business is involved.* Or as Zweig paraphrases—*It's our turn now.*

5   A note to the original German of Zweig's text reads: "Where August Oehler, who died young, is concerned, Stefan Zweig's memory is at fault."

6   *Thou sacred art, in many a dismal hour:* the opening of the words of Schubert's famous song *An die Musik*—To Music. The text was by Schubert's friend Franz von Schober.

7   Victor Adler, 1852-1918, founded the Austrian Social Democratic Party in 1889.

8   The Prater: the large and famous public park in Vienna; the Hauptallee is the main avenue through it.

9   Julius Streicher, 1885-1945, was editor and founder of the notoriously anti-Semitic Nazi newspaper *Der Stürmer.*

10   Georg von Schönerer, 1842-1921, founder of the Austrian Pan-German Party. It lasted little more than two decades, but Hitler and German National Socialism were influenced by its anti-Semitic and anti-Catholic stance.

11   *In the race lies the disgrace.* The general sense here is that the Jew's racial origin makes him a swine, a disgrace.

12   Count Kasimir Badeni, 1846-1909, Austrian politician and Prime Minister in 1895-1897, tried to bring in a 'Language Ordinance' giving equal status to German and Czech as languages in the affairs of Bohemia, part of the Austro-Hungarian empire at the time. German was generally the preferred language of the educated, and his proposed measure encountered violent opposition.

EROS MATUTINUS

D URING THOSE EIGHT YEARS at grammar school, one very
personal fact affected us all—starting as children of ten,
we gradually became sexually mature young people of sixteen,
seventeen, eighteen. Nature began to assert its rights. These
days, the awakening of puberty seems to be an entirely private
matter, to be dealt with for themselves by all young people as
they grow up, and it does not at first glance appear at all suitable
for public discussion. For our generation, however, the crisis of
puberty reached beyond its own real sphere. At the same time,
it brought an awakening in another sense—it taught us to look
more critically, for the first time, at the world of the society in
which we had grown up and its conventions. Children and even
adolescents are generally inclined to conform respectfully to the
laws of their environment at first. But they submit to the conventions enjoined upon them only as long as they see everyone else
genuinely observing them. A single instance of mendacity in
teachers or parents will inevitably make the young turn a distrustful and thus a sharper eye on their surroundings as a whole.
And it did not take us long to discover that all those authorities
whom we had so far trusted—school, the family, public morality—were remarkably insincere on one point—the subject of
sexuality. Worse than that, they wanted us, too, to dissimulate
and cover up anything we did in that respect.

The fact is that thirty or forty years ago, thinking on such
subjects was not what it is in the world of today. Perhaps
there has never been such a total transformation in any area

of public life within a single human generation as here, in the relationship between the sexes, and it was brought about by a whole series of factors—the emancipation of women, Freudian psychoanalysis, cultivation of physical fitness through sport, the way in which the young have claimed independence. If we try to pin down the difference between the bourgeois morality of the nineteenth century, which was essentially Victorian, and the more liberal uninhibited attitudes of the present, we come closest, perhaps, to the heart of the matter by saying that in the nineteenth century the question of sexuality was anxiously avoided because of a sense of inner insecurity. Previous eras which were still openly religious, in particular the strict puritanical period, had an easier time of it. Imbued by a genuine conviction that the demands of the flesh were the Devil's work, and physical desire was sinful and licentious, the authorities of the Middle Ages tackled the problem with a stern ban on most sexual activity, and enforced their harsh morality, especially in Calvinist Geneva, by exacting cruel punishments. Our own century, however, a tolerant epoch that long ago stopped believing in the Devil and hardly believed in God any more, could not quite summon up the courage for such outright condemnation, but viewed sexuality as an anarchic and therefore disruptive force, something that could not be fitted into its ethical system and must not move into the light of day, because any form of extramarital free love offended bourgeois 'decency'. A curious compromise was found to resolve this dilemma. While not actually forbidding a young man to engage in sexual activity, morality confined itself to insisting that he must deal with that embarrassing business by hushing it up. Perhaps sexuality could not be eradicated from the polite world, but at least it should not be visible. By tacit agreement, therefore, the whole difficult complex of problems was not to be mentioned in public, at school, or at home, and everything that could remind anyone of its existence was to be suppressed.

90

We, who have known since Freud that those who try to suppress natural instincts from the conscious mind are not eradicating them but only, and dangerously, shifting them into the unconscious, find it easy to smile at the ignorance of that naive policy of keeping mum. But the entire nineteenth century suffered from the delusion that all conflicts could be resolved by reason, and the more you hid your natural instincts the more you tempered your anarchic forces, so that if young people were not enlightened about the existence of their own sexuality they would forget it. In this deluded belief that you could moderate something by ignoring it, all the authorities agreed on a joint boycott imposed by means of hermetic silence. The churches offering pastoral care, schools, salons and the law courts, books and newspapers, fashion and custom all on principle avoided any mention of the matter, and to its discredit even science, which should have taken on the task of confronting all problems directly, also agreed to consider that what was natural was dirty, *naturalia sunt turpia*.[1] Science capitulated on the pretext that it was beneath its dignity to study such indecent subjects. Wherever you look in the books of the period—philosophical, legal, even medical—you find that by common consent every mention of the subject is anxiously avoided. When experts on criminal law met at conferences to discuss the introduction of humane practices to prisons and the moral damage done to inmates by life in jail, they scurried timidly past the real central problem. Although in many cases neurologists were perfectly well acquainted with the causes of a number of hysterical disorders, they were equally unwilling to tackle the subject, and we read in Freud how even his revered teacher Charcot admitted to him privately that he knew the real cause of these cases but could never say so publicly. Least of all might any writer of belles-lettres venture to give an honest account of such subjects, because that branch of literature was concerned only with the aesthetically beautiful. While in earlier centuries authors did not shrink from presenting an honest and all-inclusive picture of the culture of their time, so that in Defoe, the Abbé Prévost, Fielding and Rétif de la Bretonne we can still read unvarnished descriptions of the true state of affairs, the nineteenth century saw fit only to show the 'sensitive' and sublime, nothing embarrassing but true. Consequently you will find scarcely a fleeting mention in the literature of that era of all the perils and dark confusions of young city-dwellers of the time. Even when a writer boldly mentioned prostitution, he felt he should refine the subject, presenting a perfumed heroine as the Lady of the Camellias.[2] So we are faced with the strange fact that if young people today, wanting to know how their counterparts of the last couple of generations made their way through life, open the novels of even the great writers of that time, the works of Dickens and Thackeray, Gottfried Keller and Bjørnson,[3] they will find—except in Tolstoy and Dostoevsky, who as Russians stood outside the pseudo-idealism of Europe—accounts of nothing but sublimated, toned-down love affairs because the pressures of the time inhibited that whole generation in its freedom of expression. And nothing more clearly illustrates the almost hysterical over-sensitivity of our forebears' moral sense and the atmosphere in which they lived, unimaginable today, than the fact that even this literary restraint was not enough. Can anyone now understand how such a down-to-earth novel as *Madame Bovary* could be banned by a French court on the grounds of indecency? Or how Zola's novels, in my own youth, could be considered pornographic, or so well-balanced a writer of neoclassical epic works as Thomas Hardy could arouse indignation in England and America? Reserved as they were on the subject, these books had given away too much of the truth.

But we grew up in this unhealthily musty air, drenched with sultry perfumes. The dishonest and psychologically unrealistic morality of covering up sexuality and keeping it quiet weighed down on us in our youth, and as, thanks to the solidarity

92

maintained in this policy of hushing things up, there were no proper accounts available in literature and cultural history, it may not be easy for my readers to reconstruct what had actually happened, incredible as it might seem. However, there is one good point of reference; we need only look at fashion, because the fashions of a period, visibly expressing its tastes, betray its morality. It can be no coincidence that as I write now, in 1940, the entire audience in every town and village all over Europe or America bursts into wholehearted merriment when society men and women of 1900 appear on the cinema screen in the costumes of the time. The most naive of us today will smile at those strange figures of the past, seeing them as caricatures, idiots decked out in unnatural, uncomfortable, unhygienic and impractical clothing. Even we, who saw our mothers, aunts and girlfriends wearing those absurd gowns and thought them equally ridiculous when we were boys, feel it is like a strange dream for a whole generation to have submitted to such stupid costumes without protest. The men's fashions of the time— high, stiff collars, one of them known as the 'patricide', so stiff that they ruled out any ease of movement, the black frock coats with their flowing tails, top hats resembling chimney pipes, also provoke laughter. But most ridiculous of all is a lady of the past in her dress, difficult to put on and hard to wear, every detail of it doing violence to nature. Her body is cut in two at a wasp-waist obtained by a whalebone corset, her skirts billow out in an enormous bell, her throat is enclosed right up to the chin, her feet covered to the toes, her hair piled up into countless little curls and rolls and braids, worn under a majestically swaying monster of a hat, her hands carefully gloved even in the hottest summer—this creature, long ago consigned to history, gives the impression of pitiable helplessness, despite the perfume wafting around her, the jewellery weighing her down and all the costly lace, frills and trimmings. You see at first glance that once inside such garments and invulnerable as a knight in his armour, a

93

woman was no longer free, could not move fast and gracefully, but every movement, every gesture and indeed her whole bearing in such a costume was bound to be artificial and literally unnatural. Merely dressing to look like a lady—never mind all the etiquette of high society—just putting on such gowns and taking them off was a complicated procedure, and impossible without someone else's help. First there were countless little hooks and eyes to be done up behind a lady's back from waist to neck, a maid had to exert all her strength to tight-lace her mistress's corset, her long hair—and let me remind the young that thirty years ago all European women, with the exception of a handful of Russian women students, had hair that fell to their waists when they unpinned it—had to be curled, set, brushed and combed and piled up by a hairdresser called in daily and using a large quantity of hairpins, combs and slides, curling tongs and hair curlers, all this before she could put on her petticoats, camisoles, little bodices and jackets like a set of onion skins, turning and adjusting until the last remnant of her own female form had entirely disappeared. But there was a secret sense in this nonsense. A woman's real figure was to be so entirely concealed by all this manipulation that even at the wedding breakfast her bridegroom had not the faintest idea whether his future companion for life was straight or crooked, plump or thin, had short legs or long legs. That 'moral' age thought it perfectly permissible to add artificial reinforcements to the hair, the bosom and other parts of the body, for the purposes of deception and to conform to the general ideal of female beauty. The more a woman was expected to look like a lady, the less of her natural shape might be shown; in reality the guiding principle behind this fashion was only to obey the general moral tendency of the time, which was chiefly concerned with concealment and covering up.

But that wise morality quite forgot that when you bar the door to the Devil, he usually forces his way in down the chimney or through a back entrance. What strikes our uninhibited gaze today about those costumes, garments so desperately trying to cover every inch of bare skin and hide the natural figure, is not their moral propriety but its opposite, the way that those fashions, provocative to the point of embarrassment, emphasised the polarity of the sexes. While the modern young man and young woman, both of them tall and slim, both beardless and short-haired, conform to each other in easy comradeship even in their outward appearance, in that earlier epoch the sexes distanced themselves from each other as far as possible. The men sported long beards, or at least twirled the ends of a mighty moustache, a clearly recognisable sign of their masculinity, while a woman's breasts, essentially feminine sexual attributes, were made ostentatiously visible by her corset. The extreme emphasis on difference between the so-called stronger sex and the weaker sex was also evident in the attitudes expected of them—a man was supposed to be forthright, chivalrous and aggressive, a woman shy, timid and defensive. They were not equals but hunters and prey. This unnatural tension separating them in their outward behaviour was bound to heighten the inner tension between the two poles, the factor of eroticism, and so thanks to its technique—which knew nothing of psychology, of concealing sexuality and hushing it up—the society of the time achieved exactly the opposite. In its constant prudish anxiety, it was always sniffing out immorality in all aspects of life—literature, art and fashion—with a view to preventing any stimulation, with the result that it was in fact forced to keep dwelling on the immoral. As it was always studying what might be unsuitable, it found itself constantly on the alert; to the world of that time, 'decency' always appeared to be in deadly danger from every gesture, every word. Perhaps we can understand how it still seemed criminal, at that time, for a woman to wear any form of trousers for games or sports. But how can we explain the hysterical prudery that made it improper for a lady even to utter the word 'trousers'? If she mentioned such a sensually dangerous object as a man's trousers at all, she had to resort to the coy euphemism of 'his unmentionables'. It would have been absolutely out of the question for a couple of young people, from the same social class but of different sexes, to go out together by themselves—or rather, everyone's first thought at the mere idea would have been that 'something might happen'. Such an encounter was permissible only if some supervising person, a mother or a governess, accompanied every step that the young people took. Even in the hottest summer, it would have been considered scandalous for young girls to play tennis in ankle-length skirts or even with bare arms, and it was terribly improper for a well-brought-up woman to cross one foot over the other in public, because she might reveal a glimpse of her ankles under the hem of her dress. The natural elements of sunlight, water and air were not permitted to touch a woman's bare skin. At the seaside, women made their laborious way through the water in heavy bathing costumes, covered from neck to ankles. Young girls in boarding schools and convents even had to take baths in long white garments, forgetting that they had bodies at all. It is no legend or exaggeration to say that when women died in old age, their bodies had sometimes never been seen, not even their shoulders or their knees, by anyone except the midwife, their husbands, and the woman who came to lay out the corpse. Today, forty years on, all that seems like a fairy tale or humorous exaggeration. But this fear of the physical and natural really did permeate society, from the upper classes down, with the force of a true neurosis. It is hard to imagine today that at the turn of the century, when the first women rode bicycles or actually ventured to sit astride a horse instead of riding side-saddle, people would throw stones at those bold hussies. Or that, when I was still at school, the Viennese newspapers filled columns with discussions of the shocking innovation proposed at the Opera for the ballerinas to dance without wearing tights. Or that it was an unparalleled sensation when Isadora Duncan, although her style of dancing was extremely classical, was the first to dance barefoot instead of wearing the usual silk shoes under her tunic—which fortunately was long and full. And now think of young people growing up in such an age of watchfulness, and imagine how ridiculous these fears of the constant threat to decency must have appeared to them as soon as they realised that the cloak of morality mysteriously draped over these things was in fact very threadbare, torn and full of holes. After all, there was no getting around the fact that out of fifty grammar school boys, one would come upon his teacher lurking in a dark alley some day, or you heard in the family circle of someone who appeared particularly respectable in front of us, but had various little falls from grace to his account. The fact was that nothing increased and heightened our curiosity so much as this clumsy technique of concealment, and as it was undesirable for natural inclinations to run their course freely and openly, curiosity in a big city created its underground and usually not very salubrious outlets. In all classes of society, this suppression of sexuality led to the stealthy overstimulation of young people, and it was expressed in a childish, inexpert way. There was hardly a fence or a remote shed that was not scrawled with indecent words and graffiti, hardly a swimming pool where the wooden partition marking off the ladies' pool was not full of so-called knotholes through which a peeping Tom might look. Whole industries flourished in secret—industries that have now disappeared because morals and manners are more natural—in particular the trade in nude photographs offered for sale under the counter in bars to adolescent boys. Or the pornographic literature *sous le manteau*—since serious literature was bound to be idealistic and cautious—which consisted of books of the very worst sort, printed on poor-quality paper, badly written, and yet sure to sell well, like the 'titillating' magazines of a kind no longer available today, or not in such a repulsive and lecherous form.

As well as the court theatre, which paid homage to the ideals of the time with its noble sentiments and snow-white purity, there were theatres and cabarets with programmes entirely comprising the smuttiest of dirty jokes. What was suppressed found outlets everywhere, found ways around obstacles, ways out of difficulties. So ultimately the generation that was prudishly denied any sexual enlightenment, any form of easy social encounter with the opposite sex, was a thousand times more erotically obsessed than young people today, who have so much more freedom in love. Forbidden fruit excites a craving, only what is forbidden stimulates desire, and the less the eyes saw and the ears heard the more minds dreamt. The less air, light and sun was allowed to fall on the body, the more heated did the senses become. To sum up, the social pressure put on us as young people, instead of improving our morals, merely made us embittered and distrustful of those in authority. From the first day of our sexual awakening we instinctively felt that this dishonest morality, with its silence and concealment, wanted to take from us something that was rightfully ours in our youth, and was sacrificing our desire for honesty to a convention that had long ago ceased to have any real meaning.

However, the morality of this society, which on the one hand tacitly assumed the existence of sexuality running its natural course, but on the other would not publicly acknowledge it at any price, was in fact doubly mendacious. For while it turned a blind eye to young men and even, winking the other eye, encouraged them to 'sow their wild oats', as the jargon of the time jocularly put it, society closed both eyes in alarm and pretended to be blind when faced with women. Even convention had to admit tacitly that a man felt and must be allowed to feel certain urges. But to admit honestly that a woman was also subject to them, that for its eternal purposes creation required the feminine as well as the masculine principle, would have offended against the whole concept of women as sacred beings. Before Freud, it was an accepted axiom that a woman had no physical desires until they were aroused in her by a man, although of course that was officially permitted only in marriage. However, as the air of Vienna in particular was full of dangerously infectious eroticism even in that age of morality, a girl of good family had to live in an entirely sterilised atmosphere from her birth to the day when she went to the bridal altar. Young girls were not left alone for a moment, for their own protection. Girls had governesses whose duty it was to make sure that they did not—God forbid!—take a step outside the front door of their homes unescorted; they were taken to school, to their dancing classes and music lessons, and then collected again. Every book they read was checked, and above all young girls were kept constantly occupied in case they indulged in any dangerous ideas. They had to practise the piano, do some singing and drawing; they had to learn foreign languages and the history of art and literature; they were educated, indeed over-educated. But while the idea was to make them as educated and socially well brought up as possible, at the same time great care was taken to leave them ignorant of all natural things, in a way unimaginable to us today. A young girl of good family was not allowed to have any idea of how the male body was formed, she must not know how children came into the world, for since she was an angel she was not just to remain physically untouched, she must also enter marriage entirely 'pure' in mind. For a girl to be well brought up at the time was equivalent to leaving her ignorant of life, and that ignorance sometimes remained with women of those days all their lives. I am still amused by the grotesque story of an aunt of mine, who on her wedding night suddenly appeared back in her parents' apartment at one in the morning frantically ringing the bell and protesting that she never wanted to set eyes on the horrible man whom she had married again, he was a madman and a monster! In all seriousness, he had tried to take her clothes off. It was only with difficulty, she said, that she had been able to save herself from his obviously deranged demands.

I cannot deny that, on the other hand, this ignorance lent young girls of the time a mysterious charm. Unfledged as they were, they guessed that besides and beyond their own world there was another of which they knew nothing, were not allowed to know anything, and that made them curious, full of longing, effusive, attractively confused. If you greeted them in the street they would blush—do any young girls still blush? Alone with each other they would giggle and whisper and laugh all the time, as if they were slightly tipsy. Full of expectation of the unknown that was never disclosed to them, they entertained romantic dreams of life, but at the same time were ashamed to think of anyone finding out how much their bodies physically craved a kind of affection of which they had no very clear notion. A sort of slight confusion always animated their conduct. They walked differently from the girls of today, whose bodies are made fit through sport, who mingle with young men easily and without embarrassment, as their equals. Even a thousand paces away in our time, you could tell the difference between a young girl and a woman who had had a physical relationship with a man simply by the way she walked and held herself. Young girls were more girlish than the girls of today, less like women, resembling the exotically tender hothouse plants that are raised in the artificially overheated atmosphere of a glasshouse, away from any breath of inclement wind; the artificially bred product of a certain kind of rearing and culture.

But that was how the society of the time liked its young girls— innocent and ignorant, well brought up and knowing nothing, curious and bashful, uncertain and impractical, destined by an education remote from real life to be formed and guided in marriage by a husband, without any will of their own. Custom and decency seemed to protect them as the emblem of its most secret ideal, the epitome of demure feminine conduct, virginal and unworldly. But what a tragedy if one of these young girls had wasted her time, and at twenty-five or thirty was still unmarried! Convention mercilessly decreed that an unmarried woman of thirty must remain in a state of inexperience and naivety, feeling no desires—it was a state not at all suitable for her at her present age—preserving herself intact for the sake of the family and 'decency'. The tender image of girlhood then usually turned into a sharp and cruel caricature. An unmarried woman of her age had been 'left on the shelf', and a woman left on the shelf became an old maid. The humorous journals, with their shallow mockery, made fun of old maids all the time. If you open old issues of the *Fliegende Blätter* or another specimen of the humorous press of the time, it is horrifying to see, in every edition, the most unfeeling jokes cracked at the expense of aging unmarried women whose nervous systems were so badly disturbed that they could not hide what, after all, was their natural longing for love. Instead of acknowledging the tragedy of these sacrificial lives which, for the sake of the family and its good name, had to deny the demands of nature and their longing for love and motherhood, people mocked them with a lack of understanding that repels us today. But society is always most cruel to those who betray its secrets, showing where its dishonesty commits a crime against nature.

If bourgeois convention of the time desperately tried to maintain the fiction that a woman of the 'best circles' had no sexuality and must not have any until she was married—for anything else would make her an immoral creature, an outcast from her family—then it was still obliged to admit that such instincts really were present in a young man. And as experience had shown that young men who had reached sexual maturity could not be prevented from putting their sexuality into practice, society limited itself to the modest hope that they could take their unworthy pleasures extramurally, outside the sanctified precincts of good manners. Just as cities conceal an underground

101

sewage system into which all the filth of the cesspits is diverted under their neatly swept streets, full of beautiful shops selling luxury goods, beneath their elegant promenades, the entire sexual life of young men was supposed to be conducted out of sight, below the moral surface of society. The dangers to which a young man would expose himself did not matter, or the spheres into which he ventured, and his mentors at school and at home sedulously refrained from explaining anything about that to him. Now and then, in the last years of that moral society's existence, an occasional father with 'enlightened ideas', as it was put at the time, put some thought to the matter and, as soon as the boy began to show signs of growing a beard, tried to help him in a responsible way. He would summon the family doctor; who sometimes asked the young man into a private room, ceremoniously cleaning his glasses before embarking on a lecture about the dangers of sexually transmitted diseases, and urging the young man, who by this time had usually informed himself about them already, to indulge in moderation and remember to take certain precautions. Other fathers employed a still stranger method; they hired a pretty maidservant for their domestic staff, and it was this girl's job to give the young man practical instruction. Such fathers thought it better for a son to get this troublesome business over and done with under their own roof. This method also, to all appearances, preserved decorum and in addition excluded the danger that the young man might fall into the hands of some 'artful and designing person'. *One* method of enlightenment, however, remained firmly banned in all forms and by all those in authority—the open and honest one.

What opportunities were open to a young man of the bourgeois world? In all other classes of society, including the so-called lower classes, the problem was not a problem at all. In the country, a farm labourer of seventeen would be sleeping with a maidservant, and if there were consequences of the relationship it was not so very important. In most of our Alpine villages the numbers of illegitimate children far exceeded those born in wedlock. In the urban proletariat, again, a young working man would 'live in sin' with a woman of his class when he could not afford to get married yet. Among the Orthodox Jews of Galicia, a young man of seventeen who had only just reached sexual maturity was given a bride, and he could be a grandfather by the time he was forty. Only in our bourgeois society was the real solution to the problem, early marriage, frowned upon, because no paterfamilias would have entrusted his daughter to a young man of twenty-two or twenty. Someone so young was not thought mature enough. Here again we can detect dishonesty, for the bourgeois calendar was by no means synchronised with the rhythms of nature. While nature brings a young man to sexual maturity at sixteen or seventeen, in the society of that time he was of marriageable status only when he had a 'position in society', and that was unlikely to be before he was twenty-five or twenty-six. So there was an artificial interval of six, eight or ten years between real sexual maturity and society's idea of it, and in that interval the young man had to fend for himself in his private affairs or 'adventures'.

Not that he was given too many opportunities for them at that time. Only a very few and especially rich young men could afford the luxury of keeping a mistress, meaning renting an apartment for her and providing for her keep. Similarly, a few particularly lucky young men matched a literary ideal of the time in the matter of extramarital love—for extramarital love was the only kind that could be described in novels—and entered into a relationship with a married woman. The rest managed as best they could with shop girls and waitresses, affairs that provided little real satisfaction. Before the emancipation of women, only girls from the very poorest proletarian background had few

103

enough scruples and sufficient liberty to engage in such fleeting relationships when there was no serious prospect of marriage. Poorly dressed, tired out after working at a poorly paid job for twelve hours a day, neglectful of personal hygiene (a bathroom was the privilege of rich families in those days), and reared in a very narrow social class, these poor girls were so far below the intellectual level of their lovers that the young men themselves usually shrank from being seen with them in public. It was true that convention had found a way of dealing with this awkward fact in the institution of *chambres séparées*, as they were known, where you could eat supper with a girl in the evening unobserved, and everything else was done in the small hotels in dark side streets that had been set up exclusively for this trade. But all these encounters were bound to be fleeting and without any real attraction; they were purely sexual rather than erotic, because they were always conducted hastily and surreptitiously, like something forbidden. At best, there was the possibility of a relationship with one of those hybrid beings who were half inside society, half outside it—actresses, dancers, women artists, the only 'emancipated' women of the day. In general, however, the basis of eroticism outside marriage at that time was prostitution, which in a way represented the dark vaulted cellar above which rose the magnificent structure of bourgeois society, with its immaculately dazzling façade.

The present generation has little idea of the vast extent of prostitution in Europe before the world wars. While today prostitutes are seen in big cities as seldom as horses in the streets, at the time the pavements were so crowded with women of easy virtue that it was harder to avoid them than to find them. In addition there were all the 'closed houses' or brothels, the night-spots, cabarets and dance halls with their female dancers and singers, the bars with their hostesses. Feminine wares were openly offered for sale at such places, in every price range and at every time of day, and it really cost a man as little time and trouble to hire a woman for quarter-of-an-hour, an hour, or a night as to buy a packet of cigarettes or a newspaper. Nothing seems to me better evidence of the greater and more natural honesty of life and love today than the fact that these days it is possible, and almost taken for granted, for young men to do without this once indispensable institution, and prostitution has been partly eliminated, but not by the efforts of the police or the law. Decreasing demand for this tragic product of pseudo-morality has reduced it to a small remnant.

The official attitude of the state and its morality to these murky affairs was never really comfortable. From the moral standpoint, no one dared to acknowledge a woman's right to sell herself openly; but when hygiene entered the equation it was impossible to do without prostitution, since it provided a channel for the problem of extramarital sexuality. So the authorities resorted to ambiguity by drawing a distinction between unofficial prostitution, which the state opposed as immoral and dangerous, and licensed prostitution, for which a woman needed a kind of certificate and which was taxed by the state. A girl who had made up her mind to become a prostitute got a special licence from the police, and a booklet of her own certifying her profession. By placing herself under police control and dutifully turning up for a medical examination twice a week, she had gained business rights to hire out her body at whatever price she thought appropriate. Her calling was recognised as a profession along with other professions, but all the same—and here came the snag of morality—it was not *fully* recognised. If a prostitute had, for instance, sold her wares, meaning her body, to a man who then refused to pay the agreed price, she could not bring charges against him. At that point her demand had suddenly become an immoral one, and the authorities provided no protection—*ob turpem causam* was the reason given by the law, because it was a dirty trade.

105

Such details showed up the contradictions in a system that on the one hand gave these women a place in a trade permitted by the state, but on the other considered them personally outcasts beyond the common law. However, the real dishonesty lay in the fact that these restrictions applied only to the poorer classes. A Viennese ballerina who could be bought by any man at any time of day for two hundred crowns, just as a street girl could be bought for two crowns, did not, of course, need a licence; the great *demi-mondaines* even featured in newspaper reports of the prominent spectators present at horse-racing events— trotting races, or the Derby—because they themselves belonged to 'society'. In the same way, some of the most distinguished procuresses, women who supplied the court, the aristocracy and the rich bourgeoisie with luxury goods, were outside the law, which otherwise imposed severe prison sentences for procuring. Strict discipline, merciless supervision and social ostracism applied only to the army of thousands upon thousands of prostitutes whose bodies and humiliated souls were recruited to defend an ancient and long-since-eroded concept of morality against free, natural forms of love.

This monstrous army of prostitutes was divided into different kinds, just as the real army was divided into cavalry, artillery, infantry and siege artillery. In prostitution, the closest equivalent to the siege artillery was the group that adopted certain streets of the city as their own quarter. These were usually areas where, during the Middle Ages, the gallows, a leper house or a graveyard used to stand, places frequented by outlaws, hangmen and other social outcasts. The better class of citizens had preferred to avoid such parts of the city for centuries, and the authorities allowed a few alleys there to be used as a market for love. Two hundred or five hundred women would sit next door to one another, side by side, on display at the windows of their single-storey apartments, as twentieth-century prostitutes still do in Yoshiwara in Japan or the Cairo fish market. They were cheap goods working in shifts, a day shift and a night shift.

Itinerant prostitutes corresponded to the cavalry or infantry; these were the countless girls for sale trying to pick up customers in the street. Street-walkers of this kind were said in Vienna to be *auf den Strich*,[4] because the police had divided up the street with invisible lines, leaving the girls their own patches in which to advertise. Dressed in a tawdry elegance which they had gone to great pains to purchase, they paraded around the streets day and night, until well into the hours of dawn, even in freezing and wet weather, constantly forcing their weary and badly painted faces into an enticing smile for every passer-by. All the big cities today look to me more beautiful and humane places now that these crowds of hungry, unhappy women no longer populate the streets, offering pleasure for sale without any expectation of pleasure themselves, and in their endless wanderings from place to place, all finally going the same inevitable way—to the hospital.

But even these throngs of women were not enough to satisfy the constant demand. Some men preferred to indulge themselves more discreetly and in greater comfort than by picking up these sad, fluttering nocturnal birds of paradise in the street. They wanted a more agreeable kind of lovemaking in the light and warmth, with music and dancing and a pretence of luxury. For these clients there were the 'closed houses', the brothels. The girls gathered there in a so-called salon furnished with fake luxury, some of them in ladylike outfits, some already unequivocally clad in negligees. A pianist provided musical entertainment, there was drinking and dancing and light conversation before the couples discreetly withdrew to bedrooms. In many of the more elegant houses, brothels that had a certain international fame (to be found particularly in Paris and Milan), a naive mind could imagine that he had been invited to a private house with some rather high-spirited society ladies. In addition, the girls in these houses were better off than the street-walkers. They did not have to walk through the dirt of alleyways in wind and rain; they sat in a warm room, had good clothes, plenty to eat and in particular plenty to drink. In reality, however, they were prisoners of their madams, who forced them to buy the clothes they wore at extortionate prices, and played such arithmetical tricks with the expense of their board and lodging that even a girl who worked with great industry and stamina was always in debt to the madam in some way, and could never leave the house of her own free will.

It would be intriguing, and good documentary evidence of the culture of that time, to write the secret history of many of these houses, for they held the most remarkable secrets, which of course were well known to the otherwise stern authorities. There were secret doors, and special staircases up which members of the very highest society—even, it was rumoured, gentlemen from the court—could visit these places, unseen by other mortals. There were rooms lined with mirrors, and others offering secret views of the rooms next door, where couples engaged in sex unaware that they were being watched. There were all kinds of strange costumes for the girls to wear, from nuns' habits to ballerinas' tutus, kept in drawers and chests ready for men with special fetishes. And this was the same city, the same society, the same morality that expressed horror if young girls rode bicycles, and called it a violation of the dignity of science for Freud, in his clear, calm and cogent manner, to state certain truths that they did not like to acknowledge. The same world that so emotionally defended the purity of woman tolerated this horrifying trade in female bodies, organised it and even profited by it.

So we must not be misled by the sentimental novels and novellas of that period; it was not a good time for the young when girls were placed in airtight compartments under the control of their families, sealed off from life, their physical and intellectual development stunted, and when young men in turn were forced into secrecy and underhand behaviour, all in support of a morality that at heart no one believed in or obeyed. Straightforward, honest relationships, exactly what ought to have been bringing happiness and delight to these young people by the laws of nature, were granted to only very few. And any man of that generation trying to be honest in recollecting his very first encounters with women will find few episodes on which he can really look back with unclouded pleasure. For apart from the social constraints always urging young men to be cautious and preserve secrecy, there was another element at the time to cast a shadow on their minds, even at the most intimate moments—the fear of infection. Here again the young men of the time were at a particular disadvantage compared to those of today, for it must not be forgotten that forty years ago sexual diseases were a hundred times more prevalent than they are now, and above all a hundred times more dangerous and terrible in their effects, because clinical practice did not yet know how to deal with them. There was still no scientific possibility of curing them as quickly and radically as today, when they are little more than a passing episode. While thanks to the treatment developed by Paul Ehrlich,[5] weeks may now pass at the teaching hospitals of small and medium-sized universities without a professor's being able to show his students a new case of syphilis, statistics of that time showed that in the army, and in big cities, at least one or two in every ten young men had already contracted an infection. Young people at the time were constantly warned of the danger; walking through the streets of Vienna, you could read a plate on every sixth or seventh building proclaiming that a 'specialist in skin and venereal diseases' practised there, and to the fear of infection was added horror at the repellent, degrading nature of treatment at the time. Again, today's world knows nothing of that. The entire body of a man infected with syphilis was subjected to weeks and weeks of treatment by rubbing with quicksilver, which made the teeth fall out and caused other kinds of damage to the patient's health. The unfortunate victim of a bad attack felt not only mentally but also physically soiled, and even after such a terrible cure he could never for the rest of his life be sure that the malicious virus might not wake from its dormancy at any moment, paralysing him from the spinal marrow outwards and softening the brain inside his skull. No wonder that at the time many young men diagnosed with the disease immediately reached for a revolver, finding it intolerable to feel hopelessly suspect to themselves and their close family. Then there were the other anxieties resulting from a *vita sexualis* pursued only in secrecy. If I try to remember truthfully, I know hardly one of the comrades of my adolescent years who did not at some time look pale and distracted—one because he was sick or feared he would fall sick, another because he was being blackmailed over an abortion, a third because he lacked the money to take a course of treatment without his family's knowledge, a fourth because he didn't know how to pay the alimony for a child claimed by a waitress to be his, a fifth because his wallet had been stolen in a brothel and he dared not go to the police. So youth in that pseudo-moral age was much more dramatic and on the other hand unclean, much more exciting and at the same time oppressive, than the novels and plays of the court writers describe it. In the sphere of Eros, young people were almost never allowed the freedom and happiness proper to them at their time of life, any more than they were permitted it at school and at home.

All this has to be emphasised in an honest portrait of the time, because in talking to younger friends of the post-war generation, I often find it very hard to convince them that our young days were definitely not to be preferred to theirs.

110

Certainly, we had more freedom as citizens of the state than the present generation, who are obliged to do military service or labour service, or in many countries to embrace a mass ideology, and are indeed generally at the mercy of the arbitrary stupidity of international politics. We could devote ourselves undisturbed to our artistic and intellectual inclinations; we could pursue our private lives in a more individual and personal way. We were able to live in a more cosmopolitan manner; the whole world was open to us. We could travel anywhere we liked without passes and permits; no one interrogated us about our beliefs, our origins, our race or religion. We certainly did—I do not deny it—have immeasurably more individual freedom, and we did not just welcome that, we made use of it. But as Friedrich Hebbel once nicely put it, "Sometimes we have no wine, sometimes we have no goblet." Both are seldom granted to one and the same generation; if morality allows a man freedom, the state tries to remould him. If the state allows him freedom, morality will try to impose itself. We knew more of the world then, and knew it better, but the young today live their own youthful years more fully and are more aware of what they experience. Today, when I see young people coming out of their schools and colleges with heads held high, with bright, cheerful faces, when I see boys and girls together in free and easy companionship, competing with each other in studies, sport and games without false shame or bashfulness, racing over the snow on skis, rivalling each other in the swimming pool with the freedom known in the ancient world, driving over the countryside together in motor cars, engaging in all aspects of a healthy, untroubled life like brothers and sisters, without any internal or external pressure on them, I always feel as if not forty but a thousand years lay between them and those of us who had to look for any experience of giving and taking love in a hole-and-corner way in the shadows. I see genuinely happy expressions on their faces. What a great revolution in morality has taken place to the benefit of the young; how much freedom in life and love they have regained, and how much better they thrive both physically and mentally on this healthy new freedom! Women look more beautiful to me now that they are at liberty to display their figures; their gait is more upright, their eyes brighter, their conversation less stilted. What a different kind of confidence this new youth has acquired! They are not called upon by anyone else to account for what they do or do not do—they answer only to themselves and their own sense of responsibility, which has wrested control over them from mothers and fathers and aunts and teachers, and long ago threw off the inhibition, intimidation and tension that weighed down on their own development. They no longer know the devious secrecy we had to resort to to get the forbidden pleasures that they now correctly feel are their right. They happily enjoy their youth with the verve, freshness, lightness of heart and freedom from anxiety proper to their age. But the best of that happiness, it seems to me, is that they do not have to lie to others, while they can be honest with themselves and their natural feelings and desires. It is possible that the carefree way in which young people go through life today means they lack something of our own veneration for intellectual subjects when we were young. It may be that through the easy give and take that is accepted now, they lose an aspect of love that seemed to us particularly valuable and intriguing, they lose a certain reticence caused by shame and timidity, and certain especially tender moments. Perhaps they do not even have any idea how the awe of what is banned and forbidden mysteriously enhances one's enjoyment of it. But all this seems to me a minor drawback by comparison with the saving grace—the fact that young people today are free from fear and oppression, and enjoy in full what was forbidden us at their age, a sense of frank self-confidence.

NOTES

1 *What is natural is vile.*

2 *La Dame aux camélias,* novel by Alexandre Dumas *fils,* on which Verdi's famous opera *La Traviata* is based.

3 Bjørnstjerne Bjørnson, 1832-1910, Norwegian novelist who won the Nobel Prize for Literature in 1903.

4 *Strich*—line or break. To be *auf den Strich* has gone into the German language as an expression for street-walking or being on the game.

5 Paul Ehrlich, 1854-1915, distinguished German immunologist who won the Nobel Prize for Medicine in 1908.

UNIVERSITAS VITAE

A T LAST THE LONG-AWAITED MOMENT CAME, and with the last year of the old century we could also close the door of the hated grammar school behind us. After we had passed our final school examinations, not altogether easily—what did we know about mathematics, physics, and the rest of the scholastic curriculum?—the school principal honoured us with a valedictory speech, delivered with great feeling, an occasion for which we had to wear black frock coats. We were now grown up, he said, and our industry and efficiency must do credit to our native land. Eight years of companionship thus came to an end, and I have seen very few of my comrades in adversity since then. Most of us registered at the university, and those who had to reconcile themselves to other careers and occupations regarded us with envy.

For in those long-distant days in Austria there was still a special, romantic aura about university. The status of a student brought with it certain privileges that gave a young scholar a great advantage over all his contemporaries. I doubt whether much is known outside the German-speaking countries about the old-fashioned oddity of this phenomenon, so its anachronistic absurdity calls for explanation. Most of our universities had been founded in the Middle Ages, at a time when occupying your mind with academic knowledge appeared out of the ordinary, and young men were given certain privileges to induce them to study. Medieval scholars were not subject to the ordinary civil courts, they could not have writs served on them or be otherwise pestered by bailiffs in their colleges, they wore special clothing, had a right to fight duels with impunity, and were recognised as an exclusive guild with its own traditions—be they good or bad. In the course of time, with the gradual coming of democracy to public life and the dissolution of all other medieval guilds, academics in the rest of Europe lost this privileged position. Only in Germany and German-speaking Austria, where class consciousness still had the upper hand, did students cling tenaciously to privileges which had long ago lost any meaning. They even based their own student code of conduct on them. A German student set particular store by a specific kind of 'student honour', existing side by side with his honour as an ordinary citizen. Anyone who insulted him must give him satisfaction, meaning that if the man offering the insult was 'fit to give satisfaction' they must fight a duel. This smug student criterion of 'fitness to give satisfaction', in turn, could not be met by someone like a businessman or a banker, only a man with an academic education, a graduate, or a military officer—no one else, among millions, was good enough to have the honour of crossing swords with one of those stupid, beardless boys. Then again, to be considered a real student you had to have proved your courage, meaning you had fought as many duels as possible, and even showed the signs of those heroic deeds on your face in the form of duelling scars; unscarred cheeks and a nose without a nick in it were unworthy of an academic in the genuine German tradition. This meant that the students who wore fraternity colours, showing that they belonged to a particular student body, felt obliged to go in for mutual provocation, also insulting other perfectly peaceful students and officers so that they could fight more duels. In the fraternities, every new student had his aptitude for this worthy occupation tested on the fencing floor, and he was also initiated into other fraternity customs. Every 'fox', the term for a novice, was assigned to an older fraternity member whom he had to serve with slavish obedience, and who in turn instructed him in the noble arts required by the student code of conduct, which amounted to drinking until you threw up. The acid test was to empty a heavy tankard of beer in a single draught, proving in this glorious manner that you were no weakling, or to bawl student songs in chorus and defy the police by going on the rampage and goose-stepping through the streets by night. All this was considered manly, proper student behaviour, suitably German, and when the fraternities went out on a Saturday, waving their banners and wearing their colourful caps and ribbons, these simple-minded young men, with senseless arrogance fostered by their own activities, felt that they were the true representatives of intellectual youth. They looked down with contempt on the common herd who did not know enough to pay proper tribute to this academic culture of German manliness.

To a boy still wet behind the ears, coming to Vienna straight from a provincial grammar school, such dashing, merry student days may well have seemed the epitome of all that was romantic. For decades to come, indeed, when village notaries and physicians now getting on in years were in their cups, they would look up with much emotion at the crossed swords and colourful student ribbons hanging on the walls of their rooms, and proudly bore their duelling scars as the marks of their 'academic' status. To us, however, this stupid, brutish way of life was nothing short of abhorrent, and if we met a member of those beribboned hordes we sensibly kept out of his way. We saw individual freedom as the greatest good, and to us this urge for aggression, combined with a tendency towards servility en masse, was only too clearly evidence of the worst and most dangerous aspects of the German mind. We also knew that this artificially mummified romanticism hid some very cleverly calculated and practical aims, for membership of a duelling fraternity ensured a young man the patronage of its former members who now held high office, and would smooth the path for his subsequent career. Joining the Borussia fraternity

117

in Bonn was the one sure way into the German Diplomatic Service; membership of the Catholic fraternities in Austria led to well-endowed benefices in the gift of the ruling Catholic Socialist party, and most of these 'heroes' knew very well that in future their coloured student ribbons would have to make up for the serious studies they had neglected, and that a couple of duelling scars on their faces could be much more useful in a job application than anything they had inside their heads. The mere sight of those uncouth, militarised gangs, those scarred and boldly provocative faces, spoilt my visits to the university halls, and when other students who genuinely wanted to study went to the university library they, too, avoided going through the main hall, opting for an inconspicuous back door so as not to meet these pathetic heroes.

It had been decided long ago by my family, consulting together, that I was to study at the university. The only question was which faculty to choose. My parents left that entirely to me. My elder brother had already joined our father's business, so for me, as the second son, there was no great hurry. After all, it was just a case of making sure, for the sake of the family honour, that I gained a doctorate, never mind in what subject. Curiously enough, I didn't mind what subject either. I had long ago given my heart to literature, so none of the professionally taught academic branches of knowledge really interested me in themselves. I even had a secret distrust, which has not yet left me, of all academic pursuits. Emerson's axiom that good books are a substitute for the best university still seems to me accurate, and I am convinced to this day that one can become an excellent philosopher, historian, literary philologist, lawyer, or anything else without ever having gone to university or even a grammar school. In ordinary everyday life I have found confirmation, again and again, that in practice second-hand booksellers often know more about books than the professors who lecture on them; art dealers know more than academic art historians; and many of the most important ideas and discoveries in all fields come from outsiders. Practical, useful and salutary as academic life may be for those of average talent, it seems to me that creative individuals can dispense with it, and may even be inhibited by the academic approach, in particular at a university like ours in Vienna. It had six or seven thousand students, whose potentially fruitful personal contact with their teachers was restricted from the first by overcrowding, and it had fallen behind the times because of excessive loyalty to its traditions. I did not meet a single man there whose knowledge would have held me spellbound. So the real criterion of my choice was not what subject most appealed to me in itself, but which would burden me least and would allow me the maximum time and liberty for my real passion. I finally chose philosophy—or rather, 'exact philosophy', as the old curriculum called it in our time—but not out of any real sense of a vocation, since I do not have much aptitude for purely abstract thought. Without exception, my ideas come to me from objects, events and people, and everything purely theoretical and metaphysical remains beyond my grasp. But in exact philosophy the purely abstract material to be mastered was well within bounds, and it would be easy to avoid attending lectures and classes. I would only have to hand in a dissertation at the end of my eighth semester and take a few exams. So I drew up a plan for my time—for three years I would not bother with my university studies at all. Then, in my final year, I would put on a strenuous spurt, master the academic material and dash off some kind of dissertation. The university would thus have given me all I really wanted of it: a couple of years of freedom to lead my own life and concentrate on my artistic endeavours—*universitas vitae*, the university of life.

119

When I look back at my life I can remember few happier moments than those at the beginning of what might be called my non-university studies. I was young, and did not yet feel that I ought to be achieving perfection. I was reasonably independent, the day had twenty-four hours in it and they were all mine. I could read what I liked and work on what I liked, without having to account to anyone for it. The cloud of academic exams did not yet loom on the bright horizon. To a nineteen-year-old, three years are a long time, rich and ample in its possibilities, full of potential surprises and gifts!

The first thing I began to do was to make a collection—an unsparing selection, as I thought—of my own poems. I am not ashamed to confess that at nineteen, fresh from grammar school, printer's ink seemed to me the finest smell on earth, sweeter than attar of roses from Shiraz. Whenever I had a poem accepted for publication in a newspaper, my self-confidence, not naturally very strong, was boosted. Shouldn't I take the crucial step of trying to get a whole volume published? The encouragement of my friends, who believed in me more than I believed in myself, made up my mind for me. I was bold enough to submit the manuscript to the most outstanding publishing house of the time specialising in German poetry, Schuster & Löffler, the publishers of Liliencron, Dehmel, Bierbaum and Mombert,[1] in fact the whole generation of poets who, with Rilke and Hofmannsthal at the same period, had created the new German style. And then, marvellous to relate, along in quick succession came those unforgettably happy moments, never to be repeated in a writer's life even after his greatest successes. A letter arrived with the publisher's colophon on it. I held it uneasily in my hands, hardly daring to open it. Next came the moment, when, with bated breath, I read the news it contained—the firm had decided to publish my poems, and even wanted an option on my next one as a condition. After that came a package with the first proofs, which I undid with the greatest excitement to see the typeface, the design of the page, the embryonic form of the book, and then, a few weeks later, the book itself, the first copies. I never tired of looking at them, feeling them, comparing them with each other again and again and again. Then there was the childish impulse to visit bookshops and see if they had copies on display, and if so whether those copies were in the middle of the shop, or lurking inconspicuously in some corner. After that came the wait for letters, for the first reviews, for the first communication from unknown and unpredictable quarters—such suspense and excitement, such moments of enthusiasm! I secretly envy young people offering their first books to the world those moments. But this delight of mine was not self-satisfaction; it was only a case of love at first sight. Anyone can work out, from the mere fact that I have never allowed these *Silberne Saiten*—Silver Strings—the title of my now forgotten firstborn, to be reprinted, what I myself soon came to feel about those early verses, Nor did I not let a single one of them appear in my collected poetry. They were verses of vague premonition and unconscious empathy, arising not from my own experience but from a passion for language. They did show a certain musicality and enough sense of form to get them noticed in interested circles, and I could not complain of any lack of encouragement. Liliencron and Dehmel, the leading poets of the time, gave warm and even comradely recognition, to their nineteen-year-old author; Rilke, whom I idolised, sent me, in return for my "attractively produced book" a copy from a special edition of his latest poems inscribed to me "with thanks". I saved this work from the ruins of Austria as one of the finest mementos of my youth, and brought it to England. (I wonder ⸍ where it is today?) At the end, it seemed to me almost eerie that this kind present to me from Rilke—the first of many—was now forty years old, and his familiar handwriting greeted me from the domain of the dead. But the most unexpected surprise of all was that Max Reger, together with Richard Strauss the greatest living composer, asked my permission to set six poems from this volume to music. I have often heard one or another of them at concerts since then—my own verses, long forgotten and dismissed from my own mind, but brought back over the intervening time by the fraternal art of a master.

This unhoped-for approval, together with a friendly reception by the critics, encouraged me to take a step that, in my incurable self-distrust, I would never otherwise have taken, or not so early. Even when I was at school I had published short novellas and essays as well as poems in the modern literary journals, but I had never tried offering any of these works to a powerful newspaper with a wide circulation. There was really only one such quality newspaper in Vienna, the *Neue Freie Presse*, which with its high-minded stance, its concentration on culture and its political prestige occupied much the same position throughout the entire Austro-Hungarian Monarchy as *The Times* did in England and *Le Temps* in France. None of even the imperial German newspapers were so intent on maintaining a high cultural level. The editor, Moritz Benedikt, a man of inexhaustible industry and with a phenomenal talent for organisation, put all his positively daemonic energy into outshining all the German newspapers in the fields of literature and culture. When he wanted something from a famous author, no expense was spared; ten, twenty telegrams were sent off to him one after another, any kind of fee agreed in advance; the literary supplements of the holiday numbers at Christmas and New Year were whole volumes full of the greatest names of the time. Anatole France, Gerhart Hauptmann, Ibsen, Zola, Strindberg and Shaw found themselves keeping company in the paper on such occasions, and its influence on the literary orientation of the entire city and country was immeasurable. Progressive and liberal in its views as a matter of course, sound and circumspect in its opinions, this paper was a fine example of the high cultural standards of old Austria.

There was a special holy of holies in this temple of progress, the section known as the 'feuilleton' which, like the great daily papers of Paris, *Le Temps* and *Le Journal des Débats*, published the best and soundest essays on poetry, the theatre, music and art under a line at the bottom of the page, keeping it clearly distinct from the ephemera of politics and the news of the day. Only authorities who had proved their worth could write for this section. Nothing but sound judgement, wide experience over many years and perfect artistic form could get an author who had proved himself over the course of time into this sanctuary. Ludwig Speidel, a master essayist, and Eduard Hanslick had the same papal authority in the fields of the theatre and music as Sainte-Beuve in his columns known as *les Lundis* in Paris. The thumbs-up or thumbs-down of these critics determined the success in Vienna of a musical work, a play, a book, and often of its author or composer himself. At the time every one of these feuilleton essays was the talk of the town in educated circles; they were discussed and criticised, they aroused admiration or hostility, and when now and then a new writer's name appeared among the long-acknowledged feuilletonists, it created a sensation. Of the younger generation, only Hofmannsthal had sometimes found his way into the feuilleton with some of his best essays; other young authors had to be satisfied if they could contrive to get themselves into the separate literary supplement of the paper. As Vienna saw it, an author writing in the feuilleton on the front page had his name carved in marble.

How I found the courage to submit a small essay on poetry to the *Neue Freie Presse*, which my father regarded as an oracle and the abode of the Lord's anointed, is more than I can understand today. But after all, nothing worse than rejection could happen to me. The editor of the feuilleton interviewed would-be essayists only once a week, between two and three o'clock, since the regular cycle of famous and firmly established contributors very seldom left any room for an outsider's work.

With my heart racing, I climbed the little spiral staircase to his office and sent in my name. A few minutes later the servant came back—the editor of the feuilleton would see me, and I entered the small, cramped room.

The editor of the feuilleton of the *Neue Freie Presse* was Theodor Herzl, and he was the first man of international stature whom I had met in my life—not that I knew what great changes he would bring to the destiny of the Jewish people and the history of our times. His position at that point was rather contradictory and indeterminate. He had set out to become a writer, had shown dazzling journalistic talents at an early age, and became the darling of the Viennese public first as Paris correspondent of the *Neue Freie Presse*, then as a writer for its feuilleton. His essays are still captivating in their wealth of sharp and often wise observation, their felicity of style and their high-minded tone, which never lost its natural distinction even when he was in cheerful or critical mood. They were the most cultivated imaginable kind of journalism, and delighted a city that had trained itself to appreciate subtlety. He had also had a play successfully produced at the Burgtheater, and now he was a highly esteemed man, idolised by us young people and respected by our fathers, until one day the unexpected happened. Fate can always find a way to track down the man it needs for its secret purposes, even if he tries to hide from it.

Theodor Herzl had had an experience in Paris that shook him badly, one of those moments that change an entire life. As Paris correspondent, he had been present at the official degradation of Alfred Dreyfus. He had seen the epaulettes torn from the pale man's uniform as he cried out aloud, "I am innocent." And he had known in his heart at that moment that Dreyfus was indeed innocent, and only the fact that he was Jewish had brought the terrible suspicion of treason down on him. As a student,

Theodor Herzl had already suffered in his straightforward and manly pride from the fate of the Jews—or rather, thanks to his prophetic insight, he had anticipated all its tragic significance at a time when it hardly seemed a serious matter. At that time, with a sense of being a born leader, which was justified by both his extremely imposing physical appearance and the wide scope of his mind and his knowledge of the world, he had formed the fantastic plan of bringing the Jewish problem to an end once and for all by uniting Jews and Christians in voluntary mass-baptism. Always inclined to think in dramatic terms, he had imagined himself leading thousands upon thousands of Austrian Jews in a long procession to St Stephen's Cathedral, there to liberate his persecuted, homeless people for ever from the curse of segregation and hatred in an exemplary symbolic act. He had soon realised that this plan was impracticable, and years of his own work had distracted him from the problem at the heart of his life, although he saw solving it as his true vocation. However, at the moment when he saw Dreyfus degraded the idea of his own people's eternal ostracism went to his heart like a dagger. If segregation is inevitable, he said to himself, why not make it complete? If humiliation is always to be our fate, let us meet it with pride. If we suffer from the lack of a home, let us build ourselves one! So he published his pamphlet on *The Jewish State*, in which he pronounced all adaptation through assimilation and all hope of total tolerance impossible for the Jewish people. They would have to found a new home for themselves in their old homeland of Palestine.

When this pamphlet, which was short but had the power and forcefulness of a steel bolt, was published I was still at school, but I remember the general astonishment and annoyance it aroused in bourgeois Jewish circles in Vienna. What on earth, they said angrily, has that usually clever, witty and cultivated writer Herzl taken into his head? What stupid stuff is he saying and writing? Why would we want to go to Palestine? We speak German,

125

not Hebrew, our home is in beautiful Austria. Aren't we very well off under good Emperor Franz Joseph? Don't we make a respectable living and enjoy a secure position? Don't we have equal rights, aren't we loyal, established citizens of our beloved Vienna? And don't we live in a progressive time which will do away with all religious prejudice within a few decades? If he's a Jew who wants to help other Jews, why does he present our worst enemies with arguments, trying to segregate us from the German-speaking world when every day unites us more closely with it? Rabbis waxed indignant in their pulpits, the managing director of the *Neue Freie Presse* banned even the mention of the word Zionism in his allegedly progressive newspaper. Karl Kraus, the Thersites of Viennese literature and a past master of venomous mockery, wrote a pamphlet entitled *A Crown for Zion*, and when Theodor Herzl entered the theatre sarcastic murmurs ran through the rows of spectators: "Here comes His Majesty!"

At first Herzl could reasonably feel misunderstood—Vienna, where he thought himself most secure after enjoying years of popularity, was abandoning him, even laughing at him. But then the answer came thundering back with such a weight of approval that he was almost alarmed to see what a mighty movement, far greater than his own person, he had called into being with his few dozen pages. Admittedly the answer did not come from the well-situated, middle-class Western Jews with their comfortable lives, but from the great masses in the East, the Galician, Polish and Russian proletariat. Without knowing it, Herzl's pamphlet had fanned the heart of Judaism into flame. The Messianic dream, two thousand years old, of the return to the Promised Land as affirmed in the holy books, had been smouldering among the ashes of foreign domination. It was a hope and at the same time a religious certainty, the one thing that still gave meaning to life for those downtrodden and oppressed millions. Whenever someone, whether prophet or impostor, had plucked that string in the millennia of exile, the soul of the people had vibrated in sympathy, but never so powerfully as now, never echoing back with such a clamorous roar. One man, with a few dozen pages, had shaped a scattered and disunited throng into a single entity.

That first moment, when the idea was still taking dreamlike but uncertain shape, was to be the happiest in Herzl's short life. As soon as he began to define the aims of the movement in real terms, trying to combine its forces, he could not help seeing how different these people had become under various different nationalities, with their different histories, sometimes religious, sometimes free-thinking, some of them socialist and others capitalist Jews, stirring themselves up against each other in a wide variety of languages, and none of them willing to fall into line with a single unified authority. In the year 1901, when I first met him, he was in mid-struggle, and was perhaps at odds with himself as well; he did not yet believe in ultimate success enough to give up the post that earned him and his family a living. He had to divide himself between his lesser work of journalism and the mission that was his real life. It was as feuilleton editor that Theodor Herzl received me that day.

Theodor Herzl rose to greet me, and instinctively I felt there was a grain of truth in the ill-intentioned joke about the King of Zion—he really did look regal with his high forehead, his clear-cut features, his long and almost blue-black beard and his deep-blue, melancholy eyes. His sweeping, rather theatrical gestures did not seem affected, because they arose from a natural dignity, and it would not have taken this particular occasion to make him look imposing to me. Even standing in front of the shabby desk heaped high with papers in that miserably cramped editorial office with its single window, he was like a Bedouin desert sheikh; a billowing white burnous would have

127

looked as natural on him as his black morning coat, well-cut in an obviously Parisian style. After a brief and deliberately inserted pause—as I often noticed later, he liked such small effects, and had probably studied them at the Burgtheater—he deigned to give me his hand, though in a very friendly way. Indicating the chair beside him, he asked, "I think I've heard or read your name somewhere before. You write poetry, don't you?" I said that I did. "Well," he said leaning back, "so what have you brought me?"

I told him I would very much like to submit a little prose essay to him, and handed him my manuscript. He looked at the title page, turned to the end to assess its extent, and then leant back further in his chair. And to my surprise (I had not expected it) I saw that he had already begun to read the manuscript. He read slowly, turning the page without looking up. When he had finished the final page, he slowly folded the manuscript, then ceremoniously and still without looking at me put it into an envelope, and wrote something on the envelope in pencil. Only then, after keeping me in suspense for some time with these mysterious moves, did he raise his dark, weighty glance to me, saying with deliberate and slow solemnity, "I am glad to tell you that your fine piece is accepted for publication in the feuilleton of the *Neue Freie Presse*." It was like Napoleon presenting a young sergeant with the cross of the Légion d'Honneur on the battlefield.

This may seem a minor, unimportant episode in itself. But you would have to be Viennese, and Viennese of my generation, to understand what a meteoric rise this encouragement meant. In my nineteenth year, I had risen to a position of prominence overnight, and Theodor Herzl, who was kind to me from that first moment, used the occasion of our meeting to say, in one of his next essays, that no one should believe the arts were in decline in Vienna. On the contrary, he wrote, as well as Hofmannsthal there were now a number of gifted young writers around who might be expected to do great things, and he mentioned my name first. I have always felt it a particular distinction that a man of the towering importance of Theodor Herzl, in his highly visible and thus very responsible position, was the first to express support for me.

It was a difficult decision for me to make when I said later, with apparent ingratitude, that I felt I could not join his Zionist movement actively and even help him to lead it, as he had asked. However, I could never have made a real success of such a connection; I was alienated most of all by the lack of respect, hardly imaginable today, that his real comrades expressed towards Herzl himself. The Eastern Jews complained that he understood nothing about the Jewish way of life and wasn't even conversant with Jewish customs, while the economists among them regarded him as a mere journalist and feuilletonist. Everyone had his own objection, and did not always express it respectfully. I knew how much goodwill, particularly just then, those truly attuned to Herz's ideas, particularly the young, could and should owe him, and the quarrelsome, opinionated spirit of constant opposition, the lack of honest, heartfelt acceptance in the Zionist circle, estranged me from a movement that I would willingly have approached with curiosity, if only for Herzl's sake. Once, when we were discussing the subject, I openly confessed my dislike of the indiscipline in his ranks. He smiled rather bitterly and said, "Don't forget, we've been used to dealing with problems and arguing over ideas for centuries. After all, historically speaking, we Jews have gone two thousand years without any experience of bringing something real into the world. Unconditional commitment has to be learnt, and I still haven't learnt it myself. I still write for feuilletons now and then, I am still Feuilleton Editor of the *Neue Freie Presse*, when it should really be my duty to have only one thought in the world and never write a line about anything else. But I'm on my way to rectifying that; I'll have to learn unconditional commitment myself first, and then maybe the rest of them will learn with me." I still remember the deep impression these remarks made

129

on me, for none of us could understand why it took Herzl so long to give up his position with the *Neue Freie Presse*—we thought it was for his family's sake. But the world did not know until much later that such was not the case, and he had even sacrificed his own private fortune to the cause. This conversation showed me how much Herzl suffered personally in this dilemma, and many accounts in his diaries confirm it.

I met him many more times, but of all our encounters only one other seems to me really worth remembering, indeed unforgettable, because it was the last. I had been abroad, keeping in touch with Vienna only by letter, and met him one day in the city park. He was obviously coming away from the editorial offices, walking very slowly and not with his old, swinging step, but stooping slightly. I greeted him politely and was going to pass on, but he quickly came towards me, straightening his posture, and gave me his hand. "Now, why are you hiding away? There's no need for that." He approved of my frequent trips abroad. "It's our only way," he said. "All I know I learnt abroad. Only there do you get used to thinking on a wide scale. I'm sure that I would never have had the courage to form my first concept here, it would have been nipped in the bud. But thank God, when I came up with it, it was all ready, and they couldn't do anything but try tripping me up." He then spoke very bitterly about Vienna where, he said, he had found most opposition, and if new initiatives had not come from outside, particularly from the East and now from America too, he would have grown weary. "What's more," he said, "my mistake was to begin too late. Victor Adler was leader of the Social Democratic party at the age of thirty, the age when he was best fitted for the struggle, and I won't even speak of the great figures of history. If you knew how I suffer mentally, thinking of the lost years— regretting that I didn't find my vocation earlier. If my health were as strong as my will, then all would still be well, but you can't buy back the past." I went back to his house with him.

Arriving there, he stopped, shook hands with me, and said, "Why do you never come to see me? You've never visited me at home. Telephone first and I'll make sure I am free." I promised him, firmly determined not to keep that promise, for the more I love someone the more I respect his time.

But I did join him after all, only a few months later. The illness that was beginning to make him stoop at that last meeting of ours had suddenly felled him, and now I could accompany him only to the cemetery. It was a strange day, a day in July, and no one who was there will ever forget it. For suddenly people arrived at all the Viennese railway stations, coming with every train by day and night, from all lands and countres; Western, Eastern, Russian, Turkish Jews—from all the provinces and small towns they suddenly stormed in, the shock of the news of his death still showing on their faces. You never felt more clearly what their quarrels and talking had veiled over—the leader of a great movement was being carried to his grave. It was an endless procession. Suddenly Vienna realised that it was not only a writer, an author of moderate importance, who had died, but one of those original thinkers who rise victorious in a country and among its people only at rare intervals. There was uproar in the cemetery itself; too many mourners suddenly poured like a torrent up to his coffin, weeping, howling and screaming in a wild explosion of despair. There was an almost raging turmoil; all order failed in the face of a kind of elemental, ecstatic grief. I have never seen anything like it at a funeral before or since. And I could tell for the first time from all this pain, rising in sudden great outbursts from the hearts of a crowd a million strong, how much passion and hope this one lonely man had brought into the world by the force of his ideas.

The real significance to me of my ceremonial admission to the rank of feuilletonist on the *Neue Freie Presse* was in my private life. It gave me unexpected confidence within the family. My parents had little to do with literature, and did not presume to make literary judgements; to them, and to the entire Viennese bourgeoisie, important works were those that won praise in the *Neue Freie Presse*, and works ignored or condemned there didn't matter. They felt that anything published in the feuilleton was vouched for by the highest authority, and a writer who pronounced judgement there demanded respect merely by virtue of that fact. And now, imagine such a family glancing daily at the front page of their newspaper with reverent awe and one morning, incredibly, finding that the rather unkempt nineteen-year-old sitting at their table, who had been far from a high-flyer at school and whose writing they accepted with kindly tolerance as a harmless diversion (better than playing cards or flirting with disreputable girls, anyway), has been giving his opinions, not much valued previously at home, in that highly responsible journal among famous and experienced men. If I had written the finest poems of Keats, Hölderlin or Shelley, it would not have caused such a total change of attitude in my entire family circle. When I came into the theatre, they pointed this puzzling Benjamin of theirs out to each other, a lad who in some mysterious way had entered the sacred precincts of the old and dignified. And since I was published quite often in the feuilleton, almost on a regular basis, I soon risked winning high esteem and respect locally. But fortunately I avoided that danger in good time by telling my parents one morning, to their surprise, that I would like to spend the next semester studying in Berlin. My family respected me, or rather the *Neue Freie Presse* in whose golden aura I stood, too much not to grant my wish.

Of course I had no intention of 'studying' in Berlin. I called in at the university there, just as I had in Vienna, only twice in the course of a semester—once to register for lectures, the second time for certification of my alleged attendance at them. I was not looking for colleges or professors in Berlin, I wanted a greater and even more complete form of freedom. In Vienna, I still felt tied to my environment. The literary colleagues with whom I mingled almost all came from the same middle-class Jewish background as I did; in a small city where everyone knew everyone else, I was inevitably the son of a 'good' family, and I was tired of what was considered 'good' society'; I even liked the idea of decidedly bad society, an unconstrained way of life with no one checking up on me. I hadn't even looked in the university register to see who lectured on philosophy in Berlin. It was enough for me to know that modern literature was cultivated more actively and eagerly there than at home, that Dehmel and other writers of the younger generation could be met in Berlin, that new journals, cabarets and theatres were being opened, and in short, that the whole place was in a buzz.

In fact I arrived in Berlin at a very interesting moment in its history. Since 1870, when it had ceased to be the modest and by no means rich little capital of the Kingdom of Prussia and became the residence of the German Kaiser, this unassuming city on the river Spree had seen its fortunes soar to great heights. However, Berlin had not yet assumed leadership in culture and the arts. Munich, with its painters and writers, was still considered the real artistic centre; the Dresden Opera dominated music; the smaller capital cities of former princely states attracted notable artistic figures, but Vienna above all, with its centuries of tradition, concentrated cultural force, and wealth of natural talent had still, until this point, been considered greatly superior. In the last few years, however, with the rapid economic rise of Germany, all that had begun to change. Great industrial companies and prosperous families moved to Berlin, and new wealth accompanied by daring audacity opened up greater opportunities in architecture and the theatre there than in any other large German city. Under the patronage of Kaiser Wilhelm museums began to expand, the theatre found an excellent director in Otto Brahm, and the very fact that

133

there was no real cultural tradition going back for centuries encouraged young artists to try something new. For tradition also and always means inhibition. Vienna, bound to the old ways and idolising its own past, was cautious when faced with young people and bold experiments, waiting to see what came of them. In Berlin, on the other hand, a city seeking to mould itself quickly and in its own individual form, innovation was much in demand. It was only natural, then, for young people to come thronging to Berlin from all over the Reich and even from Austria, and the talented among them were proved right by the success they achieved. Max Reinhardt of Vienna, for instance, would have had to wait patiently for a couple of decades in his native city to reach the position that he was holding in Berlin within two years.

It was at exactly this point of its change from a mere capital city to an international metropolis that I arrived in Berlin. After the rich beauty of Vienna, a legacy of our great forebears, my first impression was rather disappointing; the crucial move towards the Westend district, where a new style of architecture was to replace that of the rather ostentatious buildings of the Tiergarten, had only just begun, and architecturally uninteresting Friedrichstrasse and Leipziger Strasse, with their ponderous splendours, still formed the centre of the city. Suburbs such as Wilmersdorf, Nikolassee and Steglitz could be reached only with some difficulty by tram, and in those days visiting the austerely beautiful lakes of the March of Brandenburg still meant quite an elaborate expedition. Apart from the old Unter den Linden, there was no real centre, no place for showy parades such as the Graben in Vienna, and old Prussian habits of thrift died hard—there was no sign of elegance in general. Women went to the theatre in unfashionable home-made dresses, and wherever you went you never found the light, skilful, prodigal touch that in Vienna and Paris could make something that cost very little looked enchantingly extravagant. Every detail showed the miserly economy of the period of Frederick the Great; the coffee was weak and bad because every bean was grudged, food was carelessly prepared and had no zest in it. Cleanliness and a strict, painstaking sense of order ruled here, not the musical verve of Vienna. Nothing seemed to me more typical than the contrast between my Viennese and my Berlin landladies. The woman from whom I rented rooms in Vienna was cheerful and talkative; she did not keep everything sparkling clean, and would carelessly forget things, but she was ready and willing to oblige her tenants. My landlady in Berlin was correct and kept the place immaculate, but on receiving her first monthly bill I found every small service she had done me charged in her neat, upright hand—three pfennigs for sewing on a trouser button, twenty pfennigs for removing a splash of ink from the table top, until finally, under a strong line ruled above, the total sum I owed for such labours, they amounted to sixty-seven pfennigs in all. At first this made me smile, but more telling was the fact that after a few days I myself was infected with this Prussian passion for meticulous order, and for the first and last time in my life found myself keeping precise accounts of my expenditure.

My friends in Vienna had given me a whole series of letters of introduction, but I did not use any of them. After all, the real point of my venture was to escape the secure, bourgeois atmosphere of home and instead live free of all ties, cast entirely on my own resources. The only people I wanted to meet were those to whom I found the way through my own literary endeavours—and I wanted them to be as interesting as possible. After all, not for nothing had I read Henri Murger's *Scènes de la vie de Bohème*,[2] and at the age of twenty I was bound to want to try the bohemian life for myself.

I did not have to search long for a lively and motley assortment of friends. Back in Vienna I had been contributing for some time to the leading journal of the Berlin modernists, which went by the almost ironic title of *Das Gesellschaft*—Society—and was edited by Ludwig Jacobowski. Shortly before his early death, this young writer had founded a society called 'Die Kommenden'—The Coming Generation—a name calculated to entice the young, which met once a week on the first floor of a coffee house on Nollendorfplatz. A truly heterogeneous company met in this society, which was created on the model of the Parisian 'Closerie des Lilas'—writers and architects, snobs and journalists, young women who liked to be regarded as artists or sculptors, Russian students and ash-blonde Scandinavian girls who had come to Berlin to perfect their German. From Germany itself came representatives of all its provinces—strong-boned Westphalians, unsophisticated Bavarians, Silesian Jews, all mingling freely in fervent discussion. Now and then poems or dramas were read aloud, but for all of us our main business was getting to know each other. Amidst these young people who deliberately called themselves bohemians sat one old, grey-bearded man, a figure like Father Christmas—Peter Hille, whom we all loved and respected because he was a real writer and a real bohemian. Hille, then aged seventy, gazed kindly and guilelessly at the curious crowd of children that we were to him. He always wore his grey raincoat, which hid a frayed suit and dirty linen, and would bring badly crumpled manuscripts out of one of his pockets and read his poems aloud. They were poems like no others, more like the improvisations of a poetic genius, but too loosely formed, with too much left to chance. He wrote them in pencil, on trams or in cafés, then forgot them, and had difficulty deciphering the words on the smudged, stained piece of paper when he read them aloud. He never had any money, but he didn't care about money, sleeping the night now at one friend's, now at another's, and there was something touchingly genuine about his total unworldliness and absolute lack of ambition. It was hard to work out when and how this kindly child of nature had made his way to the big city of Berlin, and what he wanted here. However, as in fact he

136

wanted nothing, not even to be famous or celebrated, thanks to his poetically dreamy nature he was more carefree and at ease with himself than anyone else I have ever met. Ambitious disputants shouted each other down in vociferous argument all around him; he listened quietly, did not argue with anyone, sometimes raised his glass to someone in friendly greeting, but he never joined in the conversation. You felt as if, even in the wildest tumult, words and verses were in search of each other in his shaggy and rather weary head, without ever quite touching and finding one another.

The aura of childlike truthfulness emanating from this naive poet, who is almost forgotten today even in Germany, may perhaps have distracted my attention from the chosen chairman of the Coming Generation, yet this was a man whose ideas and remarks were to have a crucial influence on the lives of countless people. Rudolf Steiner, the founder of anthroposophy, in whose honour his adherents built the most magnificent schools and academies to put his ideas into practice, was the first man I met after Theodor Herzl who was destined to show millions of human beings the way to go. In person he did not suggest a leader as strongly as Herzl, but his manner was more persuasive. There was hypnotic force in his dark eyes, and I could listen to him better and more critically if I did not look at him, for his ascetically lean face, marked by intellectual passion, was inclined to influence people by itself, men as well as women. At this time Rudolf Steiner had not yet worked out his own doctrines, but was still seeking and learning. He sometimes spoke to us about Goethe's theory of colour, and in Steiner's account of him the poet became more Faustian and Paracelsian. It was exciting to listen to him, for his learning was vast, and in particular it was magnificently wide and diverse by comparison with ours, which was confined to literature. After his lectures and many enjoyable private conversations I always went home both full of enthusiasm and slightly depressed. All the same—when I wonder

137

now whether, at the time, I could have foretold that this young man would have such strong philosophical and ethical influence on so many people, I have to confess, to my shame, that I would not. I expected his questing spirit to do great things in science, and it would not have surprised me at all to hear of some great biological discovery made by his intuitive mind, but when many years later I saw the great Goetheanum in Dornach, the 'school of wisdom' that his followers founded for him as the Platonic academy of anthroposophy, I was rather disappointed that his influence had declined so far into the ordinary and sometimes even banal. I will not presume to pronounce judgement on anthroposophy itself, for to this day it is not perfectly clear to me what it aims for and what it means; I am inclined to think that in essence its seductive force came not from an idea but from the fascinating person of Rudolf Steiner himself. But in any case, to meet a man of such magnetic power at that early stage, when he was still imparting his ideas to younger men in a friendly manner and without dogmatism, was an inestimable benefit to me. His astonishing and at the same time profound knowledge showed me that true universality, which with schoolboy arrogance the rest of us thought we had already mastered, cannot be achieved by superficial reading and discussion, but calls for many years of ardent effort.

However, at that receptive time of life when friendships are easily made, and social and political differences have not yet become entrenched, a young man really learns better from his contemporaries in the same line of business than from his superiors. Once again I felt—although now on a higher and more international level than at school—how fruitful collective enthusiasm is. While my Viennese friends almost all came from the bourgeoisie, and indeed nine-tenths of them from the Jewish bourgeoisie, so that we were merely duplicating and multiplying our own inclinations, the young people of this new world came from very different social classes both upper and lower. One might be a Prussian aristocrat, another the son of a Hamburg shipowner, a third from a Westphalian farming family. Suddenly I was living in a circle where there was also real poverty, people in ragged clothes and worn-out shoes; I had never been near anything like it in Vienna. I sat at the same table as heavy drinkers, homosexuals and morphine addicts, I shook hands—proudly—with a well-known con man who had served a jail sentence (and later published his memoirs, thus joining our company as a writer). What I had hardly credited in realist novels was present here, teeming with life, in the little bars and cafés that I frequented, and the worse someone's reputation was the more I wanted to know him personally. This particular liking for or curiosity about people living on the edge of danger has, incidentally, stayed with me all my life; even at times when more discrimination would have been seemly, my friends used to point out that I seemed to like mingling with amoral and unreliable people whose company might be compromising. Perhaps the very fact that I came from a solidly established background, and felt to some extent that this 'security' complex weighed me down, made me more likely to be fascinated by those who almost recklessly squandered their lives, their time, their money, their health and reputation—passionate monomaniacs obsessed by aimless existence for its own sake—and perhaps readers may notice this preference of mine for intense, intemperate characters in my novels and novellas. And then there was the charm of the exotic and outlandish; almost everyone presented my questing mind with a gift from a strange new world. For the first time I met a genuine Eastern Jew, the graphic artist E M Lilien, son of a poor Orthodox master turner from Drohobycz, and so I encountered an aspect of Jewishness previously unknown to me in its force and tough fanaticism. A young Russian translated for my benefit the finest passages from the *Brothers Karamazov*, unknown in Germany at the time; a young Swedish woman first introduced me to the pictures of Munch; I visited painters' studios to observe their technique (admittedly they were not very good painters), a believer in spiritualism took me to seances—I sensed the diversity of a thousand forms of life, and never tired of it. The intense interest which at school I had shown only in literary form, in rhymes, verses and words, was now bent on human beings. From morning to night, I was always with new and different acquaintances in Berlin, fascinated, disappointed, even sometimes cheated by them. I think that in ten years elsewhere I never have enjoyed such a variety of intellectual company as I did in that one short semester in Berlin, the first of my total freedom.

It would seem only logical for my creative impulse to have been enhanced to a high degree by all this stimulation. In fact exactly the opposite happened—much of my self-confidence, greatly boosted at first by the intellectual exhilaration of my schooldays, was now draining away. Four months after the appearance of that immature volume of poetry I couldn't understand how I had ever summoned up the courage to publish it. I still thought the verses good in themselves, skilful, some of them even remarkably craftsmanlike, the end result of my ambitious enjoyment of playing about with form, but there was a false ring to their sentimentality. In the same way, after this encounter with reality I felt there was a whiff of scented notepaper about my first novellas. Written in total ignorance of real life, they employed other people's techniques at second hand. A novel that I had brought to Berlin with me, finished except for the last chapter, was soon heating my stove, for my faith in my powers and those of my class at school in Vienna had suffered a severe setback after this first look at real life. I felt as if I were still a schoolboy and had been told to move two classes lower down. After that first volume of poems there was a gap of six years before I published a second, and only after three or four years did I publish my first prose work. Following the advice of Dehmel, to whom I am still grateful, I used my time translating from foreign languages, which I still regard as the best way for a young writer to gain a deeper, more creative understanding of the spirit of his own mother tongue. I translated Baudelaire, some poems by Verlaine, Keats, William Morris, a short play by Charles Van Lerberghe, and a novel by Camille Lemonnier[3] to get my hand in. The more personal turns of phrase in every foreign language initially present a translator with difficulties, and that in itself is a challenge to a young writer's powers of expression which will not come into play unsought, and this struggle to persist in wresting its essence from the foreign language and making your own equally expressive has always given me a special kind of artistic pleasure. Since this quiet and rather unappreciated work calls for patience and stamina, virtues that I had tended to ignore out of a sense of daring ease while I was at school, it became particularly dear to me, because in this modest activity of interpreting illustrious works of art I felt certain, for the first time, that I was doing something really meaningful which justified my existence.

I was now clear in my mind about the path I would tread for the next few years; I would see and learn a great deal, and only then would I really begin. I did not plan to present myself to the world with rashly premature publications—first I wanted to know what the world was all about! The astringency of Berlin had only increased my thirst for such knowledge. And I wondered what country to visit that summer. I opted for Belgium, which had seen a great artistic upturn around the turn of the century, in some ways even outshining France.

Khnopff and Rops in painting, Constantin Meunier and Minne in sculpture, van der Velde in arts and crafts, Maeterlinck, Eekhoud and Lemonnier in literature set high standards for modern Europe. But above all I was fascinated by Emile Verhaeren, because he showed an entirely new way ahead in poetry. He was still unknown in Germany—where for a long time the established critics confused him with Verlaine, just as they got Rolland mixed up with Rostand—and it could be said that I discovered him for myself. And to come to love someone in that way always redoubles one's affection.

Perhaps I should add a little parenthesis here. Today we get too much experience, and get it too fast, to remember it well, and I do not know if the name of Emile Verhaeren still means anything. Verhaeren was the first Francophone poet to try doing for Europe what Walt Whitman did for America—declare his belief in the present and the future. He had begun to love the modern world and wanted to conquer it for literature. While other writers regarded machines as evil, cities as ugly, the present as unpoetic, he felt enthusiasm for every new discovery and technical achievement, and his own enthusiasm spurred him on; he took a close interest in science so that he could feel that passion more strongly. The minor poems of his early work led on to great, flowing hymns. "*Admirez-vous les uns les autres*", marvel at one another, was his message to the nations of Europe. All the optimism of our generation, incomprehensible today at the time of our terrible relapse, found its first poetic expression in him, and some of his best poems will long bear witness to the Europe of the time and the kind of humanity that we dreamt of then.

I had really gone to Brussels on purpose to meet Verhaeren, but Camille Lemonnier, the fine and now unjustly forgotten author of *Un Mâle*, one of whose novels I had myself translated into German, told me regretfully that Verhaeren seldom left the little village where he lived to come to Brussels, and was not in that city now. To make up for my disappointment, he gave me valuable introductions to other Belgian artists. So I saw the old master Constantin Meunier, the greatest sculptor of the time to depict labour and a heroic labourer in his own field, and after him van der Stappen,[4] whose name is now almost forgotten in the history of art. But what a friendly man that small, chubby-cheeked Fleming was, and how warmly he and his tall, broad, cheerful Dutch wife welcomed their young visitor. He showed me his work, and we talked about art and literature for a long time that bright morning. The couple's kindness soon banished any awkwardness on my part. I told them frankly how disappointed I had been in Brussels to miss seeing the very man for whose sake I had really come to Belgium, Emile Verhaeren.

Had I said too much? Had I said something silly? I noticed both van der Stappen and his wife smiling slightly and glancing surreptitiously at each other. I felt that my words had set off some secret understanding between them. Feeling embarrassed, I said I must be going, but they wouldn't hear of it, and insisted on my staying to lunch. Once again that odd smile passed between their eyes. I felt that if there was some kind of secret here, then it was a friendly one, and was happy to abandon my original plan of going on to Waterloo.

It was soon lunchtime, we were already in the dining room—on the ground floor, as in all Belgian houses—where you looked out on the street through stained-glass panes, when suddenly a shadowy figure stopped, sharply outlined, on the other side of the window. Knuckles tapped on the stained glass, and the doorbell rang a loud peal. "*Le voilà*," said Mme van der Stappen, getting to her feet, and in he came with a strong, heavy tread. It was Verhaeren himself. I recognised the face that had long been familiar to me from his pictures at first glance. Verhaeren was their guest to lunch today, as he very often was, and when they heard that I had been looking for him in vain they had agreed, in that quick exchange of glances, not to tell me but to let his arrival take me by surprise. And now there he was before me, smiling at the success of their trick when he heard about it. For the first time I felt the firm grip of his sinewy hand, for the first time I saw his clear and kindly gaze. He came—as always—into the house as if full of vigour and enthusiasm. Even as he ate heartily, he kept talking. He had been to see friends, he told us, they had gone to a gallery, he still felt inspired by that visit. This was his usual manner of arrival, his state of mind intensified by chance experiences anywhere and everywhere, and this enthusiasm was his established habit. Like a flame, it leapt again and again from his lips, and he was master of the art of emphasising his words with graphic gestures. With the first thing he said, he reached into you because he was perfectly open, accessible to every newcomer, rejecting nothing, ready for everyone. He sent his whole being, you might say, out to meet you again and again, and I saw him make that overwhelming, stormy impression on many other people after experiencing it for myself on that first meeting. He knew nothing about me, but he already trusted me just because he had heard that I appreciated his works.

After lunch and that first delightful surprise came a second. Van der Stappen, who had long been meaning to fulfil an old wish of his own and Verhaeren's, had been working for days on a bust of the poet, and today was to be the last sitting. My presence, said van der Stappen, was a very lucky chance, because he positively needed someone to talk to Verhaeren—who was only too inclined to fidget—while he sat for the sculptor so that his face would be animated as he talked and listened. And so I looked deeply into his face for two hours, that unforgettable face with its high forehead, ploughed deeply by the wrinkled furrows of his bad years, his brown, rust-coloured hair falling over it, the hard, stern structure of his features surrounded by brownish weather-beaten skin, his chin jutting like a rock and above the narrow lips, large and lavish, his drooping moustache in the Vercingetorix style. All his nervousness was in his hands—those lean, firm, fine and yet strong hands where the veins throbbed strongly under the thin skin. The whole weight of his will was expressed in his broad, rustic shoulders; the intelligent, bony

144

head almost seemed too small for them. Only when he was moving did you see his strength. If I look at the bust of him now—and van der Stappen never did anything better than the work of that day—I know how true to life it is, and how fully it catches the essence of the man. It is documentary evidence of literary stature, a monument to unchanging power.

In those three hours I learnt to love the man as I have loved him all the rest of my life. There was a confidence in him that did not for a moment seem self-satisfied. He did not mind about money; he would rather live in the country than write a line meant only for the day and the hour. He did not mind about success either, did not try to increase it by granting concessions or doing favours or showing cameraderie—his friends of the same cast of mind were enough for him. He was even independent of the temptation so dangerous to a famous man when fame at last came to him at the zenith of his life. He remained open in every sense, hampered by no inhibitions, confused by no vanity, a free and happy man, easily giving vent to every enthusiasm. When you were with him, you felt inspired in your own will to live.

So there he was in the flesh before me, young as I then was—a poet such as I had hoped to find him, exactly as I had dreamt of him. And even in that first hour of our personal acquaintance my decision was taken; I would put myself at the service of this man and his work. It was a bold decision, for this hymnodist of Europe was little known at the time in Europe itself, and I knew in advance that translating his monumental body of poetry and his three-verse dramas would keep me from writing my own work for two or three years. But as I determined to devote all my power, time and passion to someone else's work, I was giving myself the best thing imaginable—a moral mission. My vague seeking, my own attempts, now had a point. And if I am asked today to advise a young writer who has not yet made up his mind what way to go, I would try to persuade him to devote himself first to the work of someone greater, interpreting or translating him. If you are a beginner there is more security in such self-sacrifice than in your own creativity, and nothing that you ever do with all your heart is done in vain.

In the two years that I spent almost exclusively in translating the poetry of Verhaeren and preparing to write a biography of him, I travelled a good deal at various times, sometimes to give public lectures. And I had already received unexpected thanks for my apparently thankless devotion to Verhaeren's work; his friends abroad noticed me, and soon became my friends too. One day, for instance, the delightful Swede Ellen Key came to see me—a woman who, with extraordinary courage in those still blind and backward times, was fighting for the emancipation of women, and in her book *The Century of the Child* pointed a warning finger, long before Freud, at the mental vulnerability of young people. Through her, I was introduced to the poetic circle in Italy of Giovanni Cena, and made an important friend in the Norwegian Johan Bojer. Georg Brandes, international master of the history of literature, took an interest in me, and thanks to my promotion of it the name of Verhaeren began to be better known in Germany than in his native land. Kainz, that great actor, and Moissi gave public recitations of his poems in my translation. Max Reinhardt produced Verhaeren's *Les Moines*—The Monks—on the German stage. I had good reason to feel pleased.

But now it was time to think of myself and remember that I had taken on other duties as well as those to Verhaeren. I had to bring my university career to a successful conclusion and take my doctorate in philosophy home. Now it was a matter of catching up within a few months with the entire scholastic material on which more conscientious students had been labouring for almost four years. With Erwin Guido Kolbenheyer, a literary friend of my youth who may not be too happily remembered today because he was one of the acknowledged public writers and academics of Hitler's Germany, I crammed by night. But the examination was not made difficult for me. In a private preliminary conversation the kindly professor, who knew too much about me from my public literary activities to trouble me with details, said with a smile, "I expect you'd rather not be tested in the field of exact logic," and then gently led me into spheres where he knew I was sure of myself. It was the first time that I had to take an examination, and I hope the last, and I passed with distinction. Now I was outwardly free, and all the years from then until the present day have been given to my struggle to remain equally free in my mind—a struggle that, in our times, is becoming ever harder.

NOTES

1   Detlev von Liliencron, pseudonym of Friedrich, Baron von Liliencron, poet, 1844-1909. Richard Dehmel, 1863-1920, poet. A close friend of Liliencron, and much influenced by Nietzsche. Otto Julius Bierbaum, 1865-1910, poet, novelist and dramatist. Alfred Mombert, 1872-1942, poet.

2   *Scenes from Bohemian Life*, the novel on which Puccini's opera *La Bohème* is based.

3   Charles Van Lerberghe, 1861-1907, Belgian Symbolist poet. Camille Lemonnier, 1844-1913, Belgian poet and novelist.

4   Charles Van der Stappen, 1843-1910, Belgian sculptor.

PARIS, THE CITY OF ETERNAL YOUTH

I HAD PROMISED MYSELF a present for the first year of my newly gained freedom—I would go to Paris. Two earlier visits had given me only a superficial knowledge of that city of inexhaustible delights, but I could tell that any young man who had spent a year there would be left with incomparably happy memories for the rest of his life. Nowhere but in Paris did you feel so strongly, with all your senses aroused, that your own youth was as one with the atmosphere around you. The city offers itself to everyone, although no one can fathom it entirely.

Of course I know that the wonderfully lively and invigorating Paris of my youth no longer exists; perhaps the city will never entirely recover that wonderful natural ease, now that it has felt the iron brand forcibly imprinted on it by the hardest hand on earth. Just as I began writing these lines, German armies and German tanks were rolling in, like a swarm of grey termites, to destroy utterly the divinely colourful, blessedly light-hearted lustre and unfading flowering of its harmonious structure. And now they are there—the swastika is hoisted on the Eiffel Tower, black-clad storm troopers march challengingly down Napoleon's Champs-Elysées, and even from far away I feel how hearts must be sinking in the buildings of Paris, how its downtrodden citizens, once so good-humoured, must be watching the conquerors tramp through its pleasant bistros and cafés in their jackboots. Few of my own misfortunes have dismayed me and filled me with despair as much as the humiliation of Paris, a city that was blessed like no other with the ability to make anyone who came there happy. Will it ever again be able to set future generations the wonderful example it set us—wise instruction in how to be both free and creative, open to everyone and made ever richer by such delightful extravagance?

I know, I know, Paris is not alone in its suffering today. It will be decades before that other Europe can return to what it was before the First World War. A certain gloom has never entirely lifted from the once-bright horizon of the continent since then, and from country to country, from one person to another, bitterness and distrust have lurked in the mutilated body of Europe corroding it like poison. However much progress in society and technology has been made during the quarter of a century between the two world wars, look closely and there is not a single nation in our small Western world that is not immeasurably worse off by comparison with its old natural *joie de vivre*. You could spend days describing the trustful, childlike cheerfulness of the Italians in the old days, even when they were in the direst poverty—how they laughed and sang in their trattorias, joking about their terrible *governo*, while now they have to march in sombre ranks, chins jutting, hearts heavy. Can anyone imagine an Austrian today as free and easy, as good-natured as he would once have been, devoutly trusting in his imperial ruler and in God, who used to make his life so pleasant? The Russians, the Germans, the Spanish, none of them know how much freedom and joy that heartless, voracious ogre the State has sucked from the marrow of their souls. The people of all nations feel only that an alien shadow, broad and heavy, looms over their lives. But we who knew the world of individual liberties in our time can bear witness that a carefree Europe once rejoiced in a kaleidoscopic play of variegated colours. We tremble to see how clouded, darkened, enslaved and imprisoned the world has now become in its suicidal rage.

And nowhere could you ever have experienced the artless yet wonderfully wise lightness of life more happily than in Paris, where it was gloriously affirmed in the city's beauty of form, mild climate, wealth and traditions. All of us young people absorbed a part of that lightness, and added our own mite to it. Chinese and Scandinavians, Spaniards and Greeks, Brazilians and Canadians, we all felt at home on the banks of the Seine. We were under no compulsion, we could speak, think, laugh and criticise as we liked, we lived as we pleased, with others or by ourselves, extravagantly or thriftily, luxuriously or in the bohemian style— there was room for every preference and all tastes were catered for. There were sublime restaurants where culinary magic was worked, wines at two hundred or three hundred francs, wickedly expensive cognacs from the days of Marengo and Waterloo; but you could eat and drink almost as well at any *marchand de vin* around the corner. In the crowded student restaurants of the Latin Quarter, a few sous would buy you the most delicious little *amuse-gueules* before and after your juicy steak, with red or white wine and a long stick of delicious white bread. You could dress as you liked; students promenaded along the boulevard Saint-Michel in their chic berets, while the *rapins*, the painters, sported broad-brimmed hats like giant mushrooms and romantic, black-velvet jackets. Meanwhile workers cheerfully went about on the smartest of boulevards in their blue blouses or their shirtsleeves, along with nursemaids in elaborately pleated Breton caps and vintners in blue aprons. A young couple might start dancing in the street any time, not just on the fourteenth of July, with a policeman smiling at them—the street was common property! No one felt shy with anyone; the prettiest girls didn't shrink from going into the nearest *petit hôtel* with a black man—who in Paris minded about such ridiculous bugbears as race, class and origin became later? You walked, talked, and slept with whoever you liked, regardless of what anyone else thought. To love Paris properly, you ought really to have known Berlin first, experiencing the natural servility of Germany with its rigid class differences, painfully clearly delineated, in which the

151

officer's wife did not talk to the teacher's wife, who in turn did not speak to the merchant's lady, who herself did not mix with the labourer's wife. In Paris, however, the inheritance of the Revolution was still alive and coursing through the people's veins; the proletarian worker felt himself as much of a free citizen as his employer, a man with equal rights; the café waiter shook hands in a comradely manner with the general in his gold-laced uniform; the industrious, respectable, neat and clean wives of the lower middle classes did not look down their noses at prostitutes who happened to live on the same floor in their building, but passed the time of day with them on the stairs, and their children gave the girls flowers. Once I saw a party of prosperous Norman farmers coming into a smart restaurant—Larue, near the Madeleine—after a christening service; they wore the traditional costume of their village, their heavy shoes tramped over the paving stones like horses' hooves; their hair was so thickly pomaded that you could have smelt it in the kitchen. They were talking at the top of their voices, which grew louder and louder the more they drank, uninhibitedly nudging their stout wives in the ribs. As working farmers they were not at all diffident about sitting among the well-groomed gentry in frock coats and grand dresses, and even the smooth-shaven waiter did not look down his nose at such rustic guests, as he would have done in Germany or Britain, but served them as politely and punctiliously as he waited on the ministers and excellencies, and the *maître d'hôtel* even seemed to take particular pleasure in giving a warm welcome to his rather boisterous customers. Paris accommodated everyone side by side; there was no above and below, no visible dividing line between de luxe streets and grubby alleys; life and cheerfulness reigned everywhere. Street musicians played in suburban yards, from the windows you heard midinettes singing at their work; there was always laughter in the air somewhere, or the sound of someone calling out in friendly tones. If a couple of cabbies got into an argument, they would shake hands afterwards, and drink a glass of wine together to wash down a few of the oysters that you could get really cheap. Nothing was stiffly formal. It was easy to meet women and easy to part with them again; there was someone for everyone; every young man had a cheerful girlfriend with no prudishness about her. What a carefree life that was! You could live well in Paris, especially when you were young! Even strolling about the city was a pleasure, and also instructive, because everything was open to everyone—you could go into a bookshop and spend a quarter-of-an-hour leafing through the volumes there without any morose muttering from the bookseller. You could visit the little galleries and enjoy looking around the bric-a-brac shops at your leisure, you could go to auction sales at the Hôtel Drouot just to watch, and talk to governesses out in the parks. Once you had really begun to stroll it wasn't easy to stop, for the street irresistibly led you on with it, always showing you something new, like the patterns of a kaleidoscope. If you felt tired, you could sit outside one of the ten thousand cafés and write letters on the free notepaper provided, while you listened to the street traders talking up the useless junk they had for sale. The only difficulty was in staying at home or going home, particularly when spring came, silvery light shone softly over the Seine, the trees in the boulevards began to put out green leaves, and every young girl wore a bunch of violets that had cost a mere sou. However, it didn't have to be spring in Paris for you to feel cheerful there.

At the time when I first knew the city it had not merged so completely into a single entity as it has today, thanks to the underground railway and motor cars. Most of the traffic in the streets still consisted of omnibuses drawn by heavy horses with steam rising from them. And there was no more comfortable way of discovering Paris than from the *impériale*, the top deck of those wide omnibuses, or from one of the open cabs which also ambled along at a leisurely pace. At that time it was still quite a journey to go from Montmartre to Montparnasse, and considering the thrifty habits of the *petit bourgeoisie* of Paris I thought it quite credible that, as legend had it, there were still Parisians on the Right Bank who had never set foot on the Left Bank, and children who played only in the Jardin du Luxembourg and had never been to the Tuileries or Parc Monceau. The Parisian resident or concierge preferred to stay at home in his own part of the city, making his own little Paris inside the great metropolis, and every arrondissement had its own distinct and even provincial character. So it was quite an important decision for a stranger to choose a place to stay. The Latin Quarter no longer enticed me. On an earlier brief visit, when I was twenty, I had gone straight there from the railway station, and on my very first evening I had sat in the Café Vachette, getting them to show me, with all due reverence, the place where Verlaine used to sit and the marble-topped table on which, when he was tipsy, he used to bang angrily with his heavy stick to get a respectful hearing. I was a novice drinker, unused to alcohol, but I ordered a glass of absinthe in his honour, not because I liked the taste of the greenish brew at all, but out of a sense that, as a young admirer of the great lyric poet of France, I ought to observe his own ritual in the Latin Quarter. At that time my idea of the right thing to do made me want to live in a fifth-floor attic near the Sorbonne, to give me a more faithful idea of the 'real' atmosphere of the Latin Quarter, which I knew from books. At twenty-five, however, I was no longer so naively romantic. The student quarter seemed to me too international, too un-Parisian. Above all, I no longer wanted to choose my permanent place of residence for reasons of literary reminiscence, but in order to work there as well as possible myself. I started looking around at once. The elegant Paris of the Champs-Elysées was not at all suitable, still less the quarter around the Café de la Paix, where all the rich visitors from the Balkans congregated and no one spoke French but the waiters. I was more attracted by the quiet district of Saint Sulpice, surrounded by churches and monasteries, where Rilke and Suarès also liked to stay. Most of all I would have liked to take lodgings on the Île St-Louis, so that I could feel I was linked to both sides of Paris, the Right Bank and the Left Bank. But in my exploration of the city I managed to find something even better in my very first week. Wandering around the Galeries du Palais-Royal, I discovered that among the eighteenth-century buildings constructed on the same pattern in that huge square by the duc d'Orléans, nicknamed Philippe Égalité, a single once grand *palais* had come down in the world, and was now a small and rather primitive hotel. I asked to be shown one of the rooms, and was charmed to find that its window had a view of the garden of the Palais-Royal, which was closed to the public after dark. All you could hear then was the faint roar of the city, an indistinct and rhythmic sound like waves breaking on a distant shore, you saw statues gleaming in the moonlight, and sometimes in the early hours of the morning the wind carried an aromatic scent of vegetables that way from the nearby food market of Les Halles. The writers and statesmen of the eighteenth and nineteenth centuries used to live in this historic quarter of the Palais-Royal. Opposite stood the building where Balzac and Victor Hugo had so often climbed the hundred steps up to the attic storey where the poet I loved so much, Marceline Desbordes-Valmore,[1] had lived. There stood the marble memorial at the place where Camille Desmoulins had called on the people to storm the Bastille, there was the covered walkway where the indigent young Lieutenant Bonaparte had looked for a patroness among the not very virtuous ladies promenading along. The history of France spoke from every stone here, and what was more, the Bibliothèque Nationale, where I spent my mornings, was only a street away. Also close were the Musée du Louvre with its pictures and the boulevards with crowds pouring along them. At last I was where I had wanted to be, in a place where the warm heart of France had been beating steadily for centuries, right in the centre of the city. I remember how André Gide once visited me and, amazed by such silence here in the heart of Paris, commented, "We have to ask foreigners to show us the most beautiful places in our own city." And sure enough, I couldn't have found anything more Parisian and at the same time more secluded than my romantic studio room in the very middle of the magic circle of the liveliest city in the world.

I wandered through the streets, seeing so much, looking for so much else in my impatience! For the Paris of 1904 was not the only one I wanted to know; my senses and my heart were also in search of the Paris of Henri IV and Louis XIV, of Napoleon and the Revolution, of Rétif de la Bretonne and Balzac, Zola and Charles-Louis Philippe, Paris with all its streets, its characters, its incidents. Here, as always in France, I felt how much strength a great literary tradition, with veracity as its ideal, can give back to its people, endowing them with immortality. In fact even before I saw it with my own eyes, I had become intellectually familiar in advance with everything in Paris through the art of the poets, novelists, and political and social historians who described it. It merely came to life when I arrived there. Actually seeing the city was really a case of recognition, the Greek *anagnosis* that Aristotle praises as the greatest and most mysterious of all artistic pleasures. All the same, you can never know a nation or a city in all its most secret details through books, or even by walking indefatigably around it, only through the best of those who live there. It is intellectual friendship with its people that gives you insight into the real connections between them and their land; outside observations convey a misleading and over-hasty image.

Such friendships were granted to me, and the best was with Léon Bazalgette. Thanks to my close connection with Verhaeren, whom I visited twice a week at St Cloud, I had been safeguarded in advance from being caught up, like most foreigners, in the dubious circle of international painters and men of letters who frequented the Café du Dôme and were really much the same wherever they went, in Munich, Rome or Berlin. With Verhaeren, however, I came to know those artists and writers who, in the midst of this lively and opulent city, lived in creative quiet as if on a desert island with their work; I saw Renoir's studio, and met his best pupils. To all outward appearance, the life of these Impressionists whose work now fetches tens of thousands of dollars was just like the life of a *petit bourgeois* living on a small income—a little house with a studio built on to it, none of the showy splendours of the grand villas imitating the Pompeian style favoured by Lenbach[2] and other celebrities in Munich. The writers whom I soon came to know personally lived as simply as the artists. Most of them held minor public office in a job which did not call for much strenuous work. The great respect for intellectual achievement felt in France, from the lowest to the highest ranks of society, meant that this ingenious method of finding discreet sinecures for poets and writers who did not earn large sums from their work had been devised years ago. For instance, they might be appointed to posts as librarians in the Naval Ministry or the Senate. Such employment gave them a small salary and not much work to do, since the Senators did not often want a book, and the fortunate occupant of the benefice could sit in comfort in the elegant old Senate Palace, with the Jardin du Luxembourg outside the windows, spending his working hours writing verse at his leisure without having to worry about getting paid for it. Modest security of this kind was enough for such writers. Others were doctors, like Duhamel and Durtain later; or ran a little picture gallery, like Charles Vildrac; or like Romains and Jean-Richard Bloch taught in grammar schools; they might keep office hours in a news agency, as Paul Valéry did in the Agence Havas, or be assistant editors in publishing houses. But none of them were pretentious enough to base their lives on the independent pursuit of their artistic inclinations, like those who came after them and had inflated ideas of themselves as a result of films and large print runs of their works. What these writers wanted from their modest posts, sought without professional ambition, was only a modicum of security in everyday life that would guarantee them independence in their true work. Thanks to that security, they could ignore the huge, corrupt daily newspapers of Paris, and write without any fee for the little reviews that were kept going at personal sacrifice, resigning themselves quietly to the fact that their plays would be performed only in small art theatres, and at first their names would not be known outside their own circle. For decades, only a tiny elite knew anything about Claudel, Péguy, Rolland, Suarès and Valéry. Alone among the people of this busy, fast-moving city, they seemed to be in no hurry. Living and working quietly, for a quiet life without raucous publicity mattered more to them than thrusting themselves forward; they were not ashamed to live in a modest way so that they could think freely and boldly in their artistic work. Their wives cooked and kept house; it was a simple life and so their friendly evening gatherings were all the warmer. They sat on cheap wicker chairs around a table laid with a plain check cloth— nothing grander than you would have found in the home of the workman on the same floor of their building, but they felt free and at ease. They had no telephones, no typewriters, no secretaries, they avoided all technical equipment just as they avoided the intellectual apparatus of propaganda; they wrote their books by hand as writers did a thousand years ago, and even in the big publishing houses such as the Mercure de France there was no dictation and no complicated machinery. No money was wasted on prestige and outward show. All these young French writers lived, like the people of France as a whole, for the joys of life, though to be sure in their most sublime form, joy found in creative work. These new friends of mine, with

158

their straightforward humanity, revised my ideas of French writers; their way of life was so different from that depicted by Bourget and other novelists of the time, to whom the salon meant all the world! And their wives taught me a great deal about the shockingly false picture we had gained at home, from our reading, of the Frenchwoman as a *mondaine* bent only on adventures, extravagance and the sight of her own reflection in the mirror. I never saw better, quieter housewives than in that fraternal circle—thrifty, modest, and cheerful even in the most straitened circumstances, conjuring up wonderful little dishes on a tiny stove, looking after their children, and at the same time in sympathy with their husbands' intellectual interests. Only someone who has lived in such circles as a friend and comrade knows what the real France is like.

What distinguished Léon Bazalgette—my greatest friend among them, a man whose name is unjustly forgotten in most accounts of modern French literature—as an extraordinary figure in that literary generation was his readiness to lavish his creative powers exclusively on works in foreign languages, thus saving all his wonderful intensity for those people he loved. In him, a good comrade by nature, I met the embodiment of a self-sacrificing human being, truly devoted and seeing his vocation entirely in helping the important figures of his time to be properly appreciated, not even indulging in well-justified pride in discovering and promoting them. His active enthusiasm was merely a natural function of his moral consciousness. Although fervently anti-militarist, he was rather military in appearance, and he showed the cordiality of a true friend in everything he did. Always ready to offer help and advice, staunchly honourable, punctual as clockwork, he cared about everything that happened to others but never sought any personal advantage. Where a friend's welfare was concerned, time and money meant nothing to him—and he had friends all over the world, a small but select circle of them. He had spent ten years bringing Walt Whitman to the French by translating his poems and writing a monumental biography of him. With Whitman before him as the model of a free man who loved the world, it became his aim in life to direct the intellectual gaze of his nation beyond its own borders, making his countrymen more straightforward and friendly, He was the best of Frenchmen, and at the same time passionately opposed to nationalism.

We soon became friends as close to each other as brothers; we neither of us felt solely devoted to our fatherlands, we enjoyed serving the works of others devotedly and without any outward advantage, and we saw intellectual independence as the great aim in life. I first came to know the 'underground' of France through him; when I read later, in Romain Rolland,[3] how Olivier met the German Jean-Christophe I felt almost as if it were an account of our personal experience. But the best and to me the most unforgettable part of our friendship was that it held good in spite of a delicate and persistent problem which, in normal circumstances, would have been sure to stand in the way of honest and genuine intimacy between two writers. The delicate problem was that Bazalgette, a wonderfully honest man, disliked everything I was writing at the time very much. He liked me personally, and felt respect and gratitude for my devotion to the work of Verhaeren. Whenever I came to Paris, he was sure to be there at the station to welcome me; he helped me wherever he could; we agreed better than brothers on all important matters. But he did not like my own works at all. He had read poetry and prose of mine in the translations by Henri Guilbeaux—who went on to play an important part in the First World War as a friend of Lenin—and he frankly said he did not like them. They had nothing to do with reality, he unsparingly told me; this was esoteric literature—which he hated—and he was annoyed to find me, of all people, writing it. Absolutely honest with himself, he would make no concessions on this point, even for the sake of civility. When he was editing a journal, for instance, he asked for my help—but in finding him German contributors of substance, meaning people who would write him contributions better than mine. He stuck to his guns in neither asking for nor publishing a line by me, his closest friend, although at the same time he self-sacrificingly and without asking any fee, purely out of true friendship, revised the translation into French of one of my books for a publisher. The fact that this curious circumstance never once in ten years made any difference to our fraternal friendship made it particularly dear to me. And no approval ever pleased me more than Bazalgette's when, during the Great War, I had finally reached a new kind of personal expression in my work, and I destroyed all that had gone before. I knew that his approval of my new approach was as honest as his firm rejection of it had been for the last ten years.

If I write the great name of Rainer Maria Rilke here in the pages devoted to my days in Paris, even though he was a German poet, it is because I spent most time with him there, and in the best way, and in my mind's eye I always see his face against the background of the city that he loved more than any other. When I think of him today, and of other masters of words that might have been written in finely wrought gold, when I think of those revered names that shone down on my youth, like constellations far beyond my reach, a sad question irresistibly comes into my mind: can there ever again be such pure poets, devoted only to lyrical form, in our present time of turbulence and general destruction? Am I lovingly mourning a lost generation, one without any immediate descendants in our own days as the hurricanes of fate storm through them? These writers wanted no kind of outward show, not the interest of the public at large, no honours and dignities and profit, all they wanted was to link verse to verse perfectly in quiet yet passionate endeavour, every line singing with music, shining with colour, glowing with images. A guild formed, an almost monastic order in the midst of our noisy lives; they deliberately turned away from everyday life, and thought nothing in the universe more important than the delicate sound—I say delicate, although it will outlast the thunder of our days—when rhyme fitting to rhyme set in motion an indescribable rhythm that, more softly than the sound of a leaf falling in the wind, yet vibrated in the most distant souls. Think how inspiring it was for us young people to be in the presence of such stern servants and guardians of language, admirably true to themselves, loving only the resonant word, a word meant not for today and the newspapers but for what would last and endure. You felt almost ashamed to look at them, for they led such quiet lives, as if inconspicuous or invisible—one in rustic style in the country, another in a small career, a third as a 'passionate pilgrim' travelling the world, all of them known only to a few but loved all the more deeply by those few for it. One lived in Germany, another in France, yet another in Italy, but they all inhabited the same homeland, for they really lived only in their poetry. In sternly renouncing everything ephemeral while they created works of art, each also made a work of art out of his own life. It always seems to me amazing that we had such flawless poets among us in our youth. But for that very reason I also keep wondering, with a kind of secret anxiety: can such artists sworn entirely to the art of poetry exist in our own times, in our new way of life, which chases people out of their own peace of mind like animals running from a forest fire? I know that poets do miraculously appear again and again over time, and Goethe's moving and consoling words in his dirge for Lord Byron are eternally true: "For the earth will bring them forth as it brought them forth before." Again and again such poets miraculously appear, and at intervals immortality always gives this precious pledge even to the most unworthy of times. But is it not true that ours, of all times, is one that allows no quiet moments even to the purest and most private minds, none

162

of the stillness to help them wait, mature, meditate and collect their thoughts that they were granted in the kindlier, calmer time of the European pre-war world? I do not know how highly all these poets, Valéry, Verhaeren, Rilke, Pascoli, Francis Jammes are still regarded today, how much they mean to a generation that has been deafened for years by the clattering millwheel of propaganda, and twice by the thunder of the guns, instead of hearing this soft music. All I know, and I feel it my duty to say so gratefully, is what a lesson and a delight the presence of such poets was to us, artists sworn to the sacred cause of perfection in a world already becoming mechanised. Looking back at my life, I am aware of no more important part of it than the privilege of being personally close to many of them, often able to turn my early admiration into an enduring friendship.

Of all these poets, perhaps none lived a quieter, more mysterious and inconspicuous life than Rilke. But his was not a deliberately assumed solitude, or one draped in priestly and mystical airs such as those adopted, for instance, by Stefan George[4] in Germany. Stillness, so to speak, formed around him wherever he went and wherever he was. Because he avoided any kind of fuss and even his own fame—that "sum of all the misunderstandings gathering around his name", as he once aptly put it himself—the wave of curiosity surging around him in vain reached only his name, never the man himself. It was difficult to get in touch with Rilke. He had no house, no address where he could be visited, no home, he did not live anywhere permanently, he held no official position. He was always travelling through the world, and no one, not even Rilke himself, knew ahead of time where he would go next. To his extremely sensitive and impressionable mind, any firm decision, any plan or advance announcement was too much of a burden, so you never met him except by chance. You might be standing in an Italian art gallery when you sensed, without being really aware how or from where, a quiet, friendly smile coming your way.

163

Only then did you recognise blue eyes that, when they looked at you, brought an inner light to animate Rilke's features, not in themselves striking. In fact his unobtrusive appearance was the deepest mystery of his nature. Thousands of people may have passed the young man whose fair moustache drooped in a slightly melancholy way, and whose rather Slavonic face was not notable for any one feature, without guessing that this was a poet, one of the greatest of our century. The distinctive quality of his restraint became obvious only when you knew him more closely. He had an indescribably quiet way of approaching and speaking to you. When he entered a room full of company, he did it so quietly that hardly anyone noticed him. Then he would sit listening in silence, sometimes instinctively looking up when an idea seemed to enter his mind, and when he himself began to speak it was never with any affectation or vigorous emphasis. He spoke naturally and simply, like a mother telling her child a fairy tale, and just as lovingly; it was wonderful to listen to him and hear how graphically and cogently he discussed even the most unimportant subject. However, as soon as he felt that he was the centre of attention in a company of any size, he would break off and go back to listening in attentive silence. Every movement and every gesture of his was gentle, and even when he laughed, it was a sound that merely hinted at laughter. A muted tone was a necessity to him, so nothing disturbed him more than noise and any kind of emotional vehemence. "People who spout their emotions like blood exhaust me," he once told me, "and so I can take Russians only in very small doses, like a liqueur." Order, cleanliness and silence were real physical necessities to him, and so was moderate behaviour. Having to travel in an overcrowded tram or sitting in a noisy bar could upset him for hours. He could not bear vulgarity of any kind, and although he lived in straitened circumstances, he always dressed with the utmost care, cleanliness and good taste. His clothing itself was a masterpiece of well thought-out and carefully composed discretion, and there was always some unobtrusive but very personal touch about it, some little thing that secretly gave him pleasure, such as a thin silver bracelet around his wrist, for his aesthetic sense of perfection and symmetry extended to the most intimate personal details. I once saw him in his rooms packing his case before leaving—he rightly declined my help as irrelevant—and it was like a mosaic, every single item lovingly lowered into the place carefully left free for it. It would have been sacrilege to destroy that almost floral arrangement by lending a helping hand. And he applied his fundamental sense of beauty to the most insignificant details. Not only did he write his manuscripts carefully on the finest paper in his rounded calligraphic hand, so that line matched line as if drawn with a ruler, he chose good paper for even the most unimportant letter, and that calligraphic handwriting, pure and round, covered it regularly right up to the margin. He never, even in the most hastily written note, allowed himself to cross out a word. Once he felt that some sentence or expression was not quite right, he would rewrite the whole letter with the utmost patience. Rilke never let anything that was less than perfect leave his hands.

This muted and at the same time concentrated quality of his had a compelling effect on everyone who knew him well. It was unimaginable for Rilke himself to do anything violent, and nor could anyone else in his company; the powerful resonance of his silence dispelled any inclination to make a loud, assertive noise. His restraint was expressed as an educational and moral force, mysteriously exerting continuous influence. After a conversation of any length with him you were incapable of any kind of vulgarity for hours, even days. On the other hand, it is true that this constant moderation of his nature, his unwillingness ever to give himself fully, set limits at an early stage to any particular warmth of expression. I think that few could boast of having been 'friends' with Rilke. Almost no one is ever addressed as a friend in the six published volumes of his correspondence, and he seems to have used the familiar *du* pronoun to hardly anyone after his schooldays. With his extraordinary sensitivity, he could not bear to let anyone or anything come too close to him, and in particular anything strongly masculine made him physically uncomfortable. He found it easier to converse with women. He wrote to them a great deal, and liked writing to them, and was much less constrained in their presence. Perhaps it was the absence of grating, guttural sounds from a woman's voice that he liked; harsh voices positively made him suffer. I still see Rilke before me in conversation with an aristocratic grandee, his back hunched and his shoulders tense, even keeping his eyes cast down so that they would not show how unwell the man's unpleasant falsetto made him feel. But it was good to be with him when he was well-disposed to someone; then you felt his inner kindness—although he rarely expressed it in words and gestures—like a warming, healing charisma that reached your heart.

One reason why the shy, reserved Rilke appeared far more expansive in the warm-hearted city of Paris may have been that his work and his name were still unknown there, and anonymity always made him feel happier and more liberated. I visited him in two different rented rooms in Paris. They were both plain and tasteless in themselves, yet the sense of beauty that ruled him immediately lent them its quiet stylishness. He could never take a room in a large boarding house with neighbours making a lot of noise; he preferred an old if less comfortable building where he could make himself at home, and wherever he was his sense of order immediately imposed harmony on his surroundings, in line with his own nature. He never had many things around him, but there were always flowers in a vase or a bowl, perhaps a woman's gift, perhaps lovingly brought home by himself. And there were always books in shelves on the wall, beautifully bound or carefully covered in paper, for he loved books like pet animals. His pencils and pens lay perfectly aligned on his desk, new sheets of paper were stacked in a rectangular pile, and a

Russian icon and a Catholic crucifix which, I think, went with him on all his travels gave a slightly religious touch to the place where he worked, not that his sense of religion was linked to any particular dogma. You felt that every detail had been carefully chosen and was tenderly cared for. If you lent him a book that he had not yet read, it would be returned to you wrapped in smooth tissue paper and tied with a coloured ribbon, like a present; I still remember how he brought the manuscript of his *Die Weise von Liebe und Tod*—The Song of Love and Death—to my room, a precious gift, and to this day I have the ribbon that was tied around it. But best of all was to go walking in Paris with Rilke, for that meant seeing the importance of the most insignificant things, as if with new eyes; he noticed every little thing, and if the names on the brass plates of businesses seemed to him rhythmical he would recite them out loud. Knowing every nook and cranny of the city of Paris was his passion. Once, when we were visiting mutual friends, I told him that the previous day I had happened to come upon the old *barrière* where the last victims of the guillotine had been buried in the Cimetière de Picpus, among them André Chénier. I described the touching little expanse of grass with its scattered graves, a place that strangers seldom visited, and how on the way back I saw, through the open gate of a convent, some *béguines*[5] telling their rosaries without a word, and walking in a circle as if in a devout reverie. It was one of the few times I saw that quiet, self-controlled man almost impatient; he had to see it all for himself, he said, both André Chénier's grave and the convent. Would I take him there? We went the very next day. He stood looking at that lonely cemetery in a kind of enchanted silence, and called it "the most poetic burial place in Paris". But on the way back the convent gate turned out to be closed. I was able to observe the silent patience that he had mastered both in life and in his works. "Let's wait for our chance," he said, and placed himself, head slightly bent, where he could see through the gate if it opened.

167

We waited like that for perhaps twenty minutes. Then a nun came along the street and rang the bell. "Now," he breathed in quiet excitement. But the nun had noticed him standing there in silence, listening—as I said earlier, you noticed everything about him in the air, from a distance—and went up to him asking if he was waiting for something. He gave her that soft smile of his that immediately made anyone trust him, and said frankly that he would so much have liked to see the cloisters. She was very sorry, said the nun, returning his smile, but she couldn't let him in. However, she said, if he went to the gardener's cottage next door, he could get a good view from the window on the upper floor. And so his wish was granted in this as in so much else.

Our paths crossed several times later, but whenever I think of Rilke, I see him in Paris. He was spared the sight of the city's saddest hour.

Meeting people of his rare kind was a great advantage to a novice, but I had yet to receive the crucial lesson, one that was to influence my entire life. It came to me by chance. At Verhaeren's, we had entered into a discussion with an art historian who lamented the fact that, as he said, the days of the great sculptors and painters were over. I strongly disagreed. Wasn't Rodin still alive, no less of a creative artist than the great names of the past? I began enumerating his works, and as always when you are opposing a contrary opinion, I soon got quite heated on the subject. Verhaeren smiled to himself. "A man who loves Rodin so much ought to meet him in person," he said when I had finished. "I'm visiting his studio tomorrow. If you don't mind, I'll take you with me."

If I didn't mind? I couldn't sleep for my delight. But when I met Rodin my voice dried up. I couldn't say a word to him, and stood among the statues like one of them myself. Strangely enough, he seemed pleased with this awkwardness of mine, for when we left the old man asked if I would like to see his real studio in Meudon, and even asked me to lunch there. That was the first lesson—great men are always the kindliest.

The second lesson was that they nearly always lead the simplest lives. At the home of this man whose fame filled the world, whose works lineament by lineament, were as vividly present to our generation as our closest friends, you ate as simply as at the table of a moderately prosperous farmer—good nourishing meat, a few olives, plenty of fruit, all washed down by strong country wine. That gave me more courage, and in the end I was speaking freely again, as if I had known this old man and his wife well for years.

After lunch we went over to the studio. It was a huge room full of replicas of the most important of his works, but among them stood or lay hundreds of delightful little individual studies—of a hand, an arm, a horse's mane, a woman's ear, usually just in plaster. To this day I still remember in detail many of these sketches, which he did just to keep his hand in, and I could talk for hours on end about that one hour I spent in Rodin's studio. Finally the master led me over to a plinth on which his latest work, the portrait of a woman, was still hidden under damp cloths. He removed them with his heavy, furrowed peasant hands, and stepped back. Instinctively, I cried with bated breath, "*Admirable!*" and was then ashamed of saying something so banal. But with calm objectivity in which there was not a grain of vanity, he only murmured in agreement, as he viewed his own work, "*N'est-ce pas?*" Then he hesitated. "Ah, except there, by the shoulder … just a moment!" He took off his indoor jacket, put on his white coat, picked up a spatula, and with a master's touch smoothed the shoulder of the soft feminine skin that breathed as if it were alive. Once again he stepped back. "Here, too," he murmured. Yet again a tiny detail enhanced the effect. Then he said no more. He stepped forwards, stepped back, looked at the figure reflected in a mirror, growled and uttered indistinct sounds, made changes and corrections. His eyes, which had been full of friendly abstraction at the lunch table, now flashed with strange light; he seemed to have grown taller and younger. He was working, working and working with all the passion and power of his mighty, heavy body. Whenever he took a vigorous step forwards or back, the floorboards creaked. But he didn't hear them. He did not notice that a young man was standing behind him, never making a sound, his heart in his mouth, happy to be able to watch such a unique master at work. He had entirely forgotten me. To him, I simply wasn't there. Only his creation and his work existed for him, and beyond them, unseen, the vision of absolute perfection.

This went on for quarter-of-an-hour, half-an-hour, I don't now remember just how long. Great moments are always outside time. Rodin was so deeply absorbed in his work that a clap of thunder wouldn't have aroused him. His movements became more and more decisive, almost irate; a kind of wildness or intoxication had come over him, he was working faster and faster. Then his hands slowed down. They seemed to have understood that there was no more for them to do. Once, twice, three times he stepped back to look, without making any more changes. Then he murmured something quietly into his beard, and replaced the cloths around the figure as affectionately as you might place a shawl around the shoulders of the woman you love. He took a deep breath, released from tension. His figure seemed to grow heavier again. The fire had gone out. Then came the great lesson for me, something I could hardly grasp. He took off his white coat, put his jacket on again, and turned to go. He had entirely forgotten me during that hour of extreme concentration. He no longer knew that a young man whom he had taken to the studio himself, to show him the place where he worked, had been standing behind him holding his breath, fascinated, as motionless as his own statues.

He made for the door. As he was about to open it, he saw me and looked at me almost angrily. Who was this young stranger who had stolen into his studio? But next moment he remembered, and came towards me, as if ashamed of himself. "*Pardon, monsieur*," he began. However, I would let him say no more, I just gratefully took his hand. I could happily have kissed him. In that hour I had seen opened up to me the eternal secret of all great art, indeed of every earthly achievement, every artist's concentration, the unification of all a man's powers and senses, a state of being outside himself, outside the world. I had learnt a lesson to last me all my life.

I had meant to leave Paris for London at the end of May. However, I had to bring my departure forward by two weeks because unforeseen circumstances made my delightful lodgings uncomfortable for me. This was a curious episode that amused me greatly, and at the same time gave me useful insight into the thinking of different parts of French society.

I had been out of Paris for the two days of the Whitsun holiday, going away with friends to look round beautiful Chartres Cathedral, which I had not seen before. When I came back to my room on the Tuesday morning, intending to change my clothes, I could not find my trunk, which had been standing in the corner all these months. I went downstairs to see the proprietor of the little hotel, who spent the day taking turns with his wife in the tiny porter's lodge. He was a small, sturdy, red-cheeked man, a native of Marseilles. I had often joked with him, and sometimes we had gone to the café just opposite to play his favourite game of backgammon. He instantly became very upset and, as he thumped the table with his fist, bitterly uttered the mysterious words, "So that's it!" Quickly putting on his coat—he had been sitting in his shirtsleeves, as usual—and changing his comfortable slippers for a pair of shoes, he explained what had happened, and if my readers are to understand it perhaps I should point to a peculiarity of Parisian buildings. In Paris, the smaller hotels and most of the private houses do not have front-door keys, and instead the concierge, that is to say the caretaker, operates the automatic door-opener from the porter's lodge as soon as someone out in the street rings the bell. In the smaller hotels and houses the owner or concierge does not spend all night in the porter's lodge, but can open the door from his conjugal bed by pressing a button—usually while he is still half-asleep. Anyone wanting to leave the building has to call, *"Le cordon, s'il vous plaît,"* and anyone wishing to enter from outside must call his name so that, in theory, no stranger can steal into the house by night. So at two in the morning in my hotel the bell was rung outside; on coming in the new arrival gave a name which sounded like that of one of the hotel guests, and he took a key that was still hanging in the porter's lodge. It should really have been the duty of this Cerberus to check the late-night visitor's identity through the glass pane of the lodge, but obviously he had felt too sleepy. However, when the call of, *"Le cordon, s'il vous plaît,"* came again an hour later, this time from inside, it struck the proprietor, who had opened the front door once already, that now someone wanted to go out after two in the morning. He had got up, looked down the street, and seeing that someone had just left the hotel with a trunk set off at once in his dressing-gown and slippers to follow the suspicious figure. However, as soon as he saw the man disappear into a small hotel in the rue des Petits Champs, he naturally enough concluded that he was not a thief or burglar, and went peacefully back to bed.

Upset as he was now by his mistake, he hurried off with me to the nearest police station. The police immediately made inquiries at the hotel in the rue des Petits Champs, and found that my trunk was indeed still there, but not the thief, who had obviously gone out to drink his morning coffee in some nearby bar. Two detectives waited for the villain in the porter's lodge of the hotel in the rue des Petits Champs, and half-an-hour later, when the thief returned, suspecting nothing, he was arrested at once.

Now the two of us, my landlord and I, had to go back to the police station to be present at the official proceedings. We were taken into the office of the *sous-préfet*, an extremely stout, moustached gentleman of comfortable appearance, who was sitting with his coat unbuttoned at a very untidy desk covered with documents. The entire office smelt of tobacco, and a large bottle of wine on the table showed that the man was by no means one of the more cruelly austere members of the holy brotherhood of peacekeepers. First the trunk was brought in, at his request, and I was asked to look and see if anything important was missing. The only apparent object of value was a letter of credit for two thousand francs, much of which had already been spent after the months of my stay in Paris, but of course it was of no use at all to anyone else, and sure enough lay untouched at the bottom of the trunk. After a report had been drawn up, to the effect that I recognised the case as my property, and nothing had been removed from it, the official ordered the thief to be brought in. I looked at him with no little curiosity.

And he was worth a look. Between two powerful sergeants, who made his thin, weedy figure look even more grotesque, stood a poor devil, rather shabby and wearing no collar. He had a small, drooping moustache and a sad, visibly half-starved, mouse-like face. Evidently he was not much of a thief, as witness his error of judgement in failing to make off with the trunk early in the morning. He stood there with his eyes cast down, trembling slightly as if he were freezing in front of the power of the law, and to my shame be it said that not only did he arouse my pity, I even felt a kind of sympathy for him. And my sympathetic interest increased when a police officer solemnly laid out on a large board all the items that had been found on him when he was searched. A stranger collection can hardly be

173

imagined—a very dirty, torn handkerchief; a dozen duplicate and skeleton keys of all shapes and sizes, jingling musically against each other on a keying; a shabby wallet, but fortunately no weapon, which at least showed that this thief went about his job in a fairly knowledgeable but non-violent way.

First the wallet was investigated before our eyes. The result was surprising. It did not contain thousand-franc or hundred-franc notes, or indeed a single banknote of any denomination—no, it held no less than twenty-seven photographs of dancers and actresses in low-cut dresses, as well as three or four nude photographs, evidence of nothing criminal, only of the fact that this thin, melancholy character was a passionate devotee of feminine beauty. Far beyond his reach as these stars of the Parisian theatre were, he wanted at least their pictures resting against his heart. Although the *sous-préfet* examined the nudes and the risqué photographs with a severe expression, I realised that this strange collector's passion in a delinquent like our thief amused him as much as it amused me. My own sympathy for this poor wrongdoer had been considerably increased by his love of the aesthetically beautiful, and when the official, solemnly picking up his pen, asked me if I wished to *porter plainte*, meaning to lay a complaint against the thief, I replied with a quick "No", as if that reply were to be taken for granted.

A little parenthesis may be useful here for an understanding of the situation. While in Austria and many other countries a complaint follows *ex officio* when a crime has been committed, that is to say the state imperiously takes justice into its own hands, in France the injured party can choose whether or not to bring charges. Personally I see this concept of justice as more even-handed than the severity of inflexible justice, since it offers you a chance of forgiving the person who has wronged you, while in Germany, for instance, if a woman fires a revolver at her lover in a fit of jealousy and wounds him, no begging and pleading from the injured party can protect her from the rigours of the law. The state steps in to tear the woman forcibly away from the man she has wounded in a moment of agitation, and who perhaps loves her all the more for her passion, and throws her into prison, while in France, once the man has forgiven her, the couple can go home arm-in-arm and consider the case settled between themselves.

As soon as I had said my decided 'no' three things happened. The thin man between the two policemen suddenly straightened up and gave me an extraordinary glance of gratitude, one I shall never forget. The *sous-préfet*, satisfied, laid his pen down again, and he too was visibly pleased that my decision not to prosecute the thief further saved him any more paperwork. My landlord, however, did not take it in the same way at all. He went scarlet in the face and began shouting angrily at me, saying I couldn't do that, such scum—*cette vermine*—had to be exterminated. I had no idea, he told me, of the harm characters of that kind did. A decent man must be on his guard day and night against such rogues, and if you let one of them go it would only encourage a hundred others. His was an explosion of all the upright principles and honesty of a *petit bourgeois* disturbed while minding his own business, and at the same time showed his pettiness; in view of all the trouble the matter had given him, he said, roughly and even menacingly, he insisted on my withdrawing my decision not to prosecute. But I stuck to my guns. I had my trunk back, I told him firmly, so I could not complain of suffering any damage, and that settled the matter so far as I was concerned. I had never in my life, I added, brought legal proceedings against another human being, and I would enjoy a good beefsteak at lunch today with a far easier mind if I knew that no one else was obliged to subsist on a prison diet on my account. My landlord answered back, more agitated than ever, and when the officer of the law explained that the decision had been not his but mine, and that once I refrained from laying charges the case was closed, he suddenly turned on his heel, left the room in a rage, and slammed the door after him with a loud bang. The *sous-préfet* got to his feet, smiled as he watched the infuriated man storming out, and shook hands with me in silent concord. With that the official business was over, and I reached for my trunk to carry it back. But then an odd thing happened; the thief approached with an air of humility. "*Ah non, monsieur,*" he said. "I'll carry it back for you." And so I marched along the four streets back to my hotel, with the grateful thief carrying my trunk behind me.

So an affair that had begun badly seemed to have concluded in the best and happiest way. But two epilogues followed in rapid succession—incidents which made some illuminating contributions to my understanding of the French mind. When I went to see Verhaeren next day, he welcomed me with a mischievous smile. "You certainly have some strange adventures here in Paris," he said jovially. "I never knew that you were such a rich man!" At first I had no idea what he was talking about. Then he handed me the newspaper, and lo and behold, there was a long account of yesterday's events, except that I hardly recognised the real facts in this romanticised version. The reporter, with great journalistic skill, described the theft from a distinguished foreigner—I had been made 'distinguished' so as to sound more interesting—who was staying at a hotel in the city centre, of a case containing a number of objects of great value, including a letter of credit for twenty thousand francs— the two thousand had multiplied by ten overnight—as well as other irreplaceable items (in fact consisting exclusively of shirts and ties). At first, said the report, it had seemed impossible to find any clues, since the thief had committed his crime with the utmost dexterity and was apparently closely acquainted with the neighbourhood. But the *sous-préfet* of the arrondissement, Monsieur So-and-so, with his "well-known energy" and "*grande perspicacité*", had immediately taken all the proper steps. On his instructions, conveyed by telephone, all the hotels and boarding houses in Paris had been thoroughly searched within the hour, and these inquiries, carried out with the usual meticulous precision of the police, had very quickly led to the arrest of the miscreant. The head of the police force had immediately expressed his particular appreciation of the outstanding achievement of the excellent *sous-préfet*, whose vigorous and far-sighted actions had, yet again, provided a shining example of the model organisation of the Parisian police.

Of course none of this story was true; the excellent *sous-préfet* had not had to make the effort of leaving his desk for so much as a minute, and we had delivered the thief and the trunk to him ourselves. However, he had taken this good opportunity to make capital for himself in the press.

The whole episode might have turned out well for both the thief and the high-ranking police, but not for me. From then on my once-jovial landlord did all he could to spoil my pleasure in staying at his hotel any longer. I would walk downstairs and give his wife a civil greeting as she sat in the porter's lodge; she did not answer, but with an injured expression turned away her face—the face of a good citizen. The servant no longer cleaned and tidied my room properly; letters mysteriously disappeared. Even in the nearby shops and the tobacconist's, where I was usually welcomed as a true *copain* because of my large consumption of tobacco, I suddenly encountered frosty faces. The injured *petit bourgeois* morale not only of the household but of the whole street and even the arrondissement closed ranks against me because I had 'helped' the thief. In the end there was nothing for it but for me to move out, with the trunk I had retrieved, and leave the comfortable hotel under as much of a cloud as if I had been the criminal myself.

After Paris, the effect of London on me was like stepping suddenly into shade on a day that is rather too hot—at first you instinctively shiver, but your eyes and senses soon get used to the change. I had planned to spend two or three months in England as a kind of duty—for how was I to understand and evaluate our world without knowing the country that had kept the wheels of that world on the rails for centuries? I also hoped to improve my rusty English—which has never become really fluent—by working hard at conversation and keeping lively company. My plan did not work; like all of us Continentals, I had few literary contacts on that side of the Channel, and I felt miserably inadequate in all the breakfast conversations and small talk at my little boarding house about the court and racing and parties. When people discussed politics I couldn't follow them; they talked about 'Joe' and I didn't know that they meant Joseph Chamberlain. Similarly I was unaware that a knight is called only by his first name after the honorific 'Sir', and for a long time my ears, closed as if by wax, could make no sense of the cabbies' cockney accent. So I did not improve my English as quickly as I had hoped. I did try to study good diction by listening to preachers in the churches, two or three times I watched proceedings in the law courts; I went to the theatre to hear English well spoken—but I always had difficulty in finding company, camaraderie and cheerfulness, all of which came flowing towards a visitor to Paris. I found no one with whom to discuss the things that mattered most to me, and to those of the English who were well disposed to me I, in turn, probably seemed rather uncouth, tedious company with my boundless indifference to sport, gambling, politics and the other subjects that interested them. I did not manage to forge close links with any group or circle, so I spent nine-tenths of my time in London working in my room or in the British Museum.

At first I did try walking. In my first week I walked all over London until I was footsore. With a student sense of duty, I saw all the sights listed in Baedeker, from Madame Tussaud's to the Houses of Parliament. I learnt to drink ale, I smoked a pipe in the manner of the country instead of the cigarettes of Paris; I tried to adapt in a hundred little details, but I never made any real contacts in society or literature, and those who know England only from the outside miss the essential part of it—they miss, for instance, the wealthy City companies which show you nothing on the outside but the usual well-polished brass plate. When I was introduced to a club I didn't know what to do there; the mere sight of the deep leather armchairs, like the atmosphere in general, induced a kind of intellectual drowsiness in me because I had not earnt such relaxation, like the others there, by concentrated activity or sport. An idler, a mere observer, unless he was worth millions and knew how to raise idling to the level of a high convivial art, was rejected by this city as a foreign body, while Paris happily accepted him into its congenial activities. My mistake, as I realised too late, had been not to spend my two months in London in some kind of occupation, as a volunteer in a business or a secretary on a newspaper, and then at least I would have dipped my finger a little way into English life. As just an outside observer I learnt little, and only many years later, during the war, did I come to know something about the real Britain.

Of poets writing in English, I visited only Arthur Symons. He in turn got me an invitation to visit W B Yeats, whose poetry I loved, and whose exquisite verse drama *The Shadowy Waters* I had translated purely for the pleasure of it. I didn't know that it was to be an evening of reading; a small and select party had been invited; we sat crowded together in a rather small room, some of us even on stools or on the floor. At last Yeats began, having first lit two thick, huge altar candles standing beside a black or black-covered lectern. All the other lights in the room were put out, so his energetic head with its black locks emerged from the candlelight like a sculpture. Yeats read slowly, in a deep and melodious voice, without ever lapsing into a declamatory tone, but giving every line its full, metallic weight. It was beautiful, and truly solemn. The only thing that disturbed my

179

pleasure was the stagy setting, the black cassock-like garment that gave Yeats a rather priestly look, the burning of the fat wax candles that, I think, had a slightly aromatic perfume. All this lent the literary event—which itself gave me a new kind of pleasure—more of the flavour of a celebration of poetry than a spontaneous reading. I couldn't help comparing this occasion with my memory of Verhaeren reading his own poems in his shirtsleeves, so that his sinewy arms could keep time with the rhythm better, and without any pompous stage-setting—or with Rilke now and then reciting a couple of verses from a book, speaking simply and clearly in the quiet service of language. This was the first 'staged' reading I ever attended, and if despite my love for the work of Yeats I thought there was something rather suspect about the cult-like presentation, he had a grateful guest on that occasion all the same.

However, the real poetic discovery I made in London was not of a living artist but of one almost forgotten at the time—William Blake, that lonely and difficult genius, who fascinates me to this day with his mixture of awkwardness and sublime perfection. A friend had advised me to go to the print room of the British Museum, which was in the care of Lawrence Binyon at this time, and get them to show me Blake's colourfully illustrated books *Europe, America* and *The Book of Job*. Today they are great rarities in second-hand bookshops, and I was captivated. Here, for the first time, I saw one of those magical natures that, without any very clear idea of their path, are borne up by visions as if on the wings of angels as they pass through every wilderness of the imagination. I spent days and weeks trying to make my way deeper into the labyrinth of Blake's naive yet daemonic mind, and translated some of his poems into German. I became almost avidly ambitious to own a sheet of paper from his own hand, but that at first seemed impossible except in my dreams. Then one day my friend Archibald G B Russell, even then the leading expert on Blake, told me that one of the 'visionary portraits', included in the Blake exhibition he was about to arrange, was for sale, in his—and my—opinion the finest of the master's pencil drawings, his *King John*. "You'll never get tired of it," he assured me, and he was right. Of all my books and pictures, that single sheet of paper was my companion for thirty years, and the magically inspired face of the mad king has looked at me again and again from my wall. It is this drawing that, in my wanderings, I miss more than any other of my possessions now lost and far away. I had tried in vain to recognise the genius of England in its streets and cities; suddenly it was revealed to me in the truly astral figure of Blake. And to the many things I ' loved in the world, I had added another.

NOTES

1   Marceline Desbordes-Valmore, 1786-1859, French poet of the Romantic period, was also a singer and actress.

2   Franz von Lenbach, 1836-1904, German Painter.

3   Romain Rolland, 1865-1944, French novelist whose best-known work was probably his cycle of ten novels unified by the character Jean-Christophe, alluded to here. He was also a musicologist, and prominent as a pacifist. He and Zweig, as will be seen, became close friends.

4   Stefan George, 1868-1933, prominent German poet who did indeed promote mystic and messianic ideas. He was also an influence on Schönberg and Webern in music. Zweig has already mentioned the *Blätter für die Kunst*, the journal of the *Georgekreis* (George Circle). Interesting as George was, few would doubt that Zweig is right in considering Rilke the greater poet.

5   *Béguines*—women who form a lay community living in a convent, as distinct from nuns who have taken vows.

DETOURS ON THE WAY TO MYSELF

P ARIS, ENGLAND, ITALY, SPAIN, Belgium, Holland—this wandering gypsy life to satisfy my curiosity had been enjoyable in
itself, and rewarding in many ways. But ultimately one needs a
fixed point, a place to set out from and return to again and again.
No one knows that better than I do today, when I no longer wander from country to country of my own free will. In the years
since I left school I had acquired a small library as well as pictures and other mementoes; thick packages of my manuscripts
were beginning to stack up, and after all, though I was attached
to these things, I couldn't keep dragging them around the world
with me in trunks and suitcases. So I took a small apartment in
Vienna, not meant to be a permanent residence but only a *pied-
à-terre*, as the French so graphically put it. Until the Great War,
in fact, my life was still governed in some odd way by the idea
that everything was only temporary. Nothing that I did, I told
myself, was the real thing—not in my work, which I regarded
as just experimenting to discover my true bent, not the women
with whom I was on friendly terms. Like this, my young self
could feel that it was not yet fully committed to anything, while
I still had the carefree pleasure of tasting, trying and enjoying
whatever was offered. At an age when other men had been married for some years, had children, held responsible positions, and
must strain every nerve to the limit, I still thought of myself as
a young man, a novice, a beginner with endless time ahead of
me, and I hesitated to commit myself to anything definite. Just
as I regarded my writing as a prelude to the real work I would do

183

some day, a kind of visiting card, I meant my apartment to be little more than a temporary address. I deliberately chose a small place in the suburbs so that the expense would not curtail my freedom. I did not buy particularly good furniture, in case I felt I had to 'spare' it, as I had seen my parents do in their own apartment, where every single chair had a cover that was removed only when visitors came. On purpose, I set out to avoid feeling permanently settled in Vienna, and thus forming sentimental links with a particular place. For many years I thought that my deliberate training of myself to feel that everything was temporary was a flaw in me, but later on, when I was forced time and again to leave every home I made for myself and saw everything around me fall apart, that mysterious lifelong sensation of not being tied down was helpful. It was a lesson I learnt early, and it has made loss and farewells easier for me.

Not that I had many treasures to keep in that first apartment. But the drawing by Blake that I had bought in London hung on my wall, and so did the manuscript of one of Goethe's most beautiful poems in his bold, free handwriting—at the time it was the jewel in my collection of autographs, which I had begun while I was still at school and, with the same herd instinct that had our whole literary group writing, we pursued writers, actors and singers for their signatures. Most of us gave up both writing and autograph-hunting on leaving school, but in me the passion for these earthly shades of men of genius only increased and grew deeper. I was indifferent to mere signatures, and I was not interested in the extent of a man's international fame or what his work would fetch; I wanted the original manuscripts or drafts of written works or musical compositions because, more than anything else, I was interested in the biographical and psychological aspects of the creation of a work of art. Where else can we locate that mysterious moment of transition when

the vision and intuition of a genius brings a verse or a melody
out of invisibility into the earthly realm, giving it graphic form,
where can we observe it if not in the first drafts of creative
artists, whether achieved with great effort or set down as if in
a trance? I do not know enough about an artist if I have only
his finished work before me, and I agree with Goethe who said
that, to understand great works fully, we should not just look at
them in their final form but trace the course of their creation.
Even visually, a preliminary sketch by Beethoven with its wild,
impatient strokes, its turbulent confusion of motifs begun and
then rejected, the creative fury of his daemonic energy con-
densed into a few pencil markings, has a physically stimulating
effect on me because the sight of it excites my mind so much.
I can stare at a sheet full of such hieroglyphics enchanted and
beguiled, as others might gaze at a perfect picture. A page of a
proof corrected by Balzac, where almost every sentence is torn
apart, every line ploughed up, the white margins invaded by
black lines, markings and words, symbolises to me the eruption
of a human Vesuvius, and when I first see a poem that I have
loved for decades in its original draft, its first earthly form, I am
moved by a religious sense of awe; I hardly dare to touch it. My
pride in owning several such first drafts went hand in hand with
the almost sporting pleasure of acquiring them, hunting them
down at auctions or in catalogues. I owe to that pursuit many
hours of excitement and many fortuitous events. I might be just
a day too late to buy something, or then again an item I wanted
badly might turn out to be a fake, but another time a miracle
might happen—I found myself the owner of a small Mozart
manuscript, but my joy was not unconfined because a line of
the music had been cut away. And then the piece of paper
containing that line of music, cut off fifty or a hundred years
ago by some vandal enamoured of it, suddenly turned up at a
Stockholm auction, and the whole aria could be fitted together
again just as Mozart left it a hundred and fifty years before. My

literary earnings were certainly not enough for me to buy on a large scale at that time, but every collector knows how much the pleasure of owning something is increased if you have to deny yourself another pleasure in order to acquire it. I also asked for contributions to my collection from all my writer friends. Rolland gave me a volume from his *Jean-Christophe* series, Rilke his most popular work, *Die Weise von Liebe und Tod*, Claudel the *Annonce faite à Marie*, Gorky a sketch of some length, Freud a treatise; they all knew that no museum would take more loving care of their manuscripts. So many of them are now scattered to the four winds, along with other, lesser pleasures!

I discovered only later, quite by chance, that the strangest and most valuable museum piece of all, although not in my own collection, was hidden away in the same house in the suburbs of Vienna. An elderly, grey-haired spinster lady lived in the apartment above mine, both of them modest places. She was a piano teacher by profession, and one day addressed me in a friendly way on the stairs, saying that she didn't like to think of my being the involuntary audience to the lessons she gave while I was working, and she hoped the imperfect skills of her girl pupils did not disturb me too much. As we talked, it emerged that her mother, who was half-blind and hardly left her room any more, lived with her, and that this eighty-year-old lady was no less than the daughter of Goethe's physician Dr Vogel, and at her christening in 1830 had been held in the arms of her godmother Ottilie von Goethe, while Goethe himself had been present at the ceremony. I felt a little dizzy—to think that in 1910 there was still someone alive on whom Goethe's sacred glance had rested! I had always felt particular reverence for every earthly manifestation of genius, and besides those manuscript pages I was making a collection of any relics I could lay hands on. Later, in what I called my second life, a whole room in my house was given up to the objects of my devotion. It contained Beethoven's desk, and the little money box from which he would hand small sums to his maidservant as he lay in bed, his shaking hand already touched by Death. I also had a page from his household accounts and a lock of his prematurely grey hair. I kept a quill pen that had belonged to Goethe in a glass case for years, to avoid the temptation of taking it in my own unworthy hand. But these things, after all, were lifeless, not to be compared with a living, breathing human being at whom Goethe's dark, round eyes had looked with affection—this fragile earthly creature was a last thin thread, one that could break at any moment, linking the Olympian world of Weimar with Number Eight Kochgasse, the suburban house in Vienna where we both happened to live. I asked permission to visit Frau Demelius; the old lady was happy to meet me, spoke very kindly, and in her room I found several items from the immortal poet's household goods that she had been given by Goethe's granddaughter, her childhood friend—the pair of candlesticks that used to stand on Goethe's table and other items from his house on the Frauenplan in Weimar. But the real marvel was surely the mere fact of this old lady's existence as she sat with a neat little cap on her now thin white hair, her wrinkled mouth happily telling me about the first fifteen years of her youth, spent in the house on the Frauenplan. At that time it was not the museum that it has become today, but its contents were still preserved, untouched, after the greatest of German poets left his home and this world for ever. Like all old people, she remembered her young days vividly. I was touched by her indignation on hearing of the indiscretion committed by the Goethe Society in publishing her childhood friend Ottilie von Goethe's love letters "so soon"—she forgot that Ottilie had been dead for half-a-century! To her, Goethe's darling was still present and still young, and what to us had long been legends of the past were still real to her. I always felt a sense of something ghostly in her presence. I lived in this stone building, I talked on the telephone, used electric light, dictated letters to be written on a typewriter—but twenty-two steps upstairs and I was back in another century, standing in the sacred shadow of the world where Goethe lived.

On several later occasions I met women whose heads, now white, rose into the heights of the heroic Olympian world—Cosima Wagner, Liszt's daughter, hard and stern, yet magnificent in her emotional gestures; Elisabeth Förster, Nietzsche's sister, small, delicate, flirtatious; Olga Monod, Alexander Herzen's daughter, who often used to sit on Tolstoy's knee as a child. And I have heard Georg Brandes talk, in his old age, about his meetings with Walt Whitman, Flaubert and Dickens, and Richard Strauss describing the first time he saw Richard Wagner. But nothing moved me as much as the face of that old lady, the last living soul to have been seen by Goethe with his own eyes. And perhaps, in my turn, I am the last who can say today: "I knew someone on whose head Goethe's hand rested affectionately for a moment."

So for the time being I had found myself a place where I could live between my travels. More important, however, was another home that I found at the same time—the publishing house that has fostered and promoted my work for thirty years. The choice of a publisher is an important decision in a writer's life, and mine could not have turned out better. Some years before, a highly cultivated literary dilettante had decided to spend his personal fortune not on a riding stable but on some intellectual project. Alfred Walter Heymel, not himself a significant writer, decided to found a firm of his own in Germany, where, as elsewhere, publishing was run mainly on a commercial basis. His publishing house, however, even although it anticipated long-term losses, would not set its sights on material profit, instead taking the true merit of a work, rather than sales figures, as the chief criterion for the selection of works to be published. Light literature, however lucrative it might be, would not appear under its imprint; instead, the firm offered a home to subtle

188

and experimental books. The motto of this exclusive publishing house which, proudly proclaiming its isolation, called itself 'Die Insel'—The Island—and later became Insel Verlag, depended entirely at first on the small public of those who genuinely appreciated literature, and set out to publish only works written in the purest form and with the purest artistic intentions. Nothing was to be printed in a standard format; every book was to have a design of its own reflecting its nature. So the frontispiece, the type area, the typeface and paper of every single book always presented choices to be made; passionate interest and care were lavished even on the catalogue and letterheads of this ambitious firm. In thirty years, for instance, I do not remember ever finding a single typographical error in one of my books, or even a corrected line in a letter from the firm; everything, down to the smallest detail, aspired to perfection.

Poetry by both Hofmannsthal and Rilke was published under the Insel Verlag imprint, and their presence on the list made the highest of standards all-important from the outset. Imagine my pride and delight in being dignified with the status of an established Insel author at the age of twenty-six! In terms of the outside world, publication by Insel meant a rise in literary rank, and for the writer himself it reinforced his own commitment. Anyone who entered this select circle must exercise self-discipline and restraint, could never allow himself any literary carelessness or indulge in journalistic haste—for thousands and later hundreds of thousands of readers, the Insel Verlag colophon on a title guaranteed both high literary quality and perfect book-production.

There could be no better luck for a rising young author than to come upon a young publishing house and grow in stature with it; there is nothing like such parallel development for creating a vital, organic link between him, his work, and the world. I was soon a close friend of the director of Insel Verlag, Professor Kippenberg, and our friendship was reinforced by our mutual understanding of our own private passion for collecting. In the thirty years of our association, Kippenberg's Goethe collection developed at the same time as I was adding to my own collection of autograph manuscripts, which eventually grew to the most monumental proportions ever achieved by a private collector. He gave me valuable advice and equally valuable warnings, while with my special knowledge of foreign literature I was able to offer him some useful ideas in return. And so, as a result of one of my suggestions, the Insel Bücherei series was founded. It sold millions of copies, and the imprint grew into a mighty metropolis built around the original 'ivory tower', making Insel the most highly regarded of German publishing houses. Thirty years made a great difference to us—at the end of them the small venture was one of the most powerful of publishing houses, while the writer whose works had initially appealed only to a small circle was now one of the most widely read authors in German-speaking countries. In fact it took a global catastrophe and the most brutal of laws to break a connection that had been natural and happy for both of us. I must admit it was easier to leave my home and my native land that not to see the familiar colophon on my books any more.

Now my path lay open before me. I had begun to publish my work at an almost indecently early age, but privately I was convinced that at the age of twenty-six I had not yet written any real works of literature. Mingling with the best creative artists of the time as a friend had been the great achievement of my youth, but curiously enough that stood in the way of my own creativity. I had learnt to understand genuine values too well; it made me hesitant. Thanks to this timidity, all I had published so far, apart from translations, was confined, with cautious economy, to small-scale works such as novellas and poems. It was a long time before I found the courage to begin a novel (another thirty years, in fact). My initial venture into a genre on a larger scale was with drama, and after my very first attempt many good omens tempted me to pursue it. I had written a play in the summer of 1905 or 1906—in the style of the time it was, of course, a verse drama in the classical manner. It was called *Thersites*, and the fact that—as with almost everything I wrote before I was thirty-three—I have never had it reprinted renders it superfluous for me to give my present opinion of this play. Only its form was any good. All the same, the play did indicate a certain personal tendency of mine never to take the side of the supposed 'heroes' of my works, seeing the tragedy of the losers instead. I am always most attracted to the character who is struck down by fate in my novellas, and in my biographies it is those who are morally right but never achieve success who appeal to me—Erasmus and not Luther, Mary Stuart and not Elizabeth, Castellio[1] and not Calvin. Even in that early place I took not Achilles as my heroic character but the most insignificant of his opponents, Thersites—the man who suffers, not the man whose strength and sure aim inflict suffering. I did not show the play to any actors when I had finished it, not even those who were friends of mine; I knew the world well enough to be aware that dramas in blank verse and performed in ancient Greek costume, even if written by Sophocles or Shakespeare, are not calculated to be a big box-office success. For form's sake I sent a few copies to the large theatres, and then forgot the whole thing entirely.

Imagine my surprise, then, when a letter arrived for me some three months later, in an envelope bearing the imprint 'Royal Berlin Theatre'. Why on earth, I thought, was the Prussian state theatre writing to me? Again to my surprise, the director Ludwig Barnay, formerly one of our greatest actors, wrote to say that my play had made a great impression on him, and it was particularly welcome because in Achilles he had found the right part for Adalbert Matkowsky, something he had long been searching for. He would be glad, he said, if I would let the Royal Theatre in Berlin put on the first production.

I was delighted, but almost frightened. The German-speaking countries had two great actors at the time, Adalbert Matkowsky and Josef Kainz. The former, a North German, was unsurpassed in the elemental force of his nature, projecting passion that enraptured audiences—the latter, our own Josef Kainz in Vienna, delighted them with his fine intellect, his perfect diction, his mastery of both soaring eloquence and a harsher, more metallic tone. And now Matkowsky was going to bring my character to life, speak my verse, the most highly regarded theatre in the capital of the German Reich was to stand sponsor to my play—a wonderful career as a dramatist seemed to open up before me, although I had never thought of such a thing before.

Since then, however, I have learnt never to look forward expectantly to a performance until the curtain actually rises. The rehearsals did indeed begin, one following another, and friends assured me that Matkowsky had never been better or more virile than when he spoke my verse at these rehearsals. I had already booked a train ticket in a sleeping car to Berlin when, at the last moment, a telegram arrived—the premiere was postponed because Matkowsky had fallen ill. I thought it was just an excuse, which is usually the case in the theatre when an engagement or a promise cannot be met. But a week later the papers published the news of Matkowsky's death. My verses had been the last to pass his wonderfully eloquent lips.

So that's that, I said to myself. All over. It was true that now two other court theatres of distinction, in Dresden and Kassel, wanted the play, but my own interest had waned. I couldn't imagine anyone but Matkowsky playing Achilles. Then, however, an even more astonishing piece of news arrived; a friend woke me one morning saying that he was there on behalf of Josef Kainz, who happened to have come upon the play and saw a part for himself in it—not Achilles, the role that Matkowsky had been going to take, but the tragic role of his adversary Thersites.

192

Kainz was going to get in touch with the Burgtheater at once, he said. Schlenther, the director of the theatre, had come there from Berlin as a pioneer of contemporary realism, and to the considerable annoyance of the Viennese was managing the theatre on those lines. He wrote to me at once, saying that he could see the interest of my drama, but unfortunately there was no likelihood of lasting success after the premiere.

That's that, I said to myself again, doubtful as I had always been of myself and my literary work. Kainz, however, felt bitter about it. He invited me to visit him at once, and for the first time I saw before me the idol of my youth. We schoolboys would happily have kissed his hands and feet. His figure was lithe, his intellectual face still animated by fine dark eyes in his fiftieth year. It was a pleasure to hear him speak. Even in private conversation, he articulated every word clearly, every consonant was sharply pronounced, every vowel full and clear; there are many poems that, if I ever heard him recite them, I cannot read now without recalling the incantatory power of his voice, its perfect rhythm, its heroic and sweeping range. I have never again taken such pleasure in the sound of the German language. And lo and behold, this man, whom I revered like a god, was actually apologising to me, young as I was, because he had not managed to persuade the theatre to put on my play. However, he assured me, we would not lose sight of each other now. In fact he had a favour to ask me—I almost smiled to think of Kainz asking me a favour!—and this was it: he was giving a great many guest performances these days, he said, and had two one-act plays for the purpose. He could do with a third, and what he had in mind was a small piece, preferably in verse, and if possible with one of those lyrical cascades of words that he—alone in the world of the German theatre—thanks to his magnificent elocution and breath control, could deliver like a crystalline waterfall of sound falling on a large audience that held its own breath as it listened. Could I write him a one-acter like that, he asked.

I promised to try. And as Goethe said, poetry sometimes lets the will command it—I sketched out a one-act play entitled *Der verwandelte Komödiant*—The Actor Transformed—a light, rococo piece with two big lyrical and dramatic monologues built into it. Instinctively, I had gone along with precisely what Kainz wanted by feeling my way into his mind and even his manner of speech with all the passion of which I was capable, and this occasional piece was one of those lucky chances that only enthusiasm can create, not mere dexterity. After three weeks I was able to show Kainz the half-finished sketch with one of the aria-like monologues already incorporated. Kainz was genuinely enthusiastic. He immediately recited that cascading monologue from the manuscript twice, the second time with unforgettable perfection. Visibly impatient, he asked how much longer I would need. A month, I said. Excellent! That would suit him very well! He was going away now for several weeks on tour in Germany, and when he came back the rehearsals for this play, to be staged at the Burgtheater, must begin at once. And then, he promised me, wherever he travelled he would take it with him in his repertory; it fitted him like a glove. "Like a glove!" He kept repeating the phrase, shaking hands with me warmly three times.

Obviously he had imposed his will on the Burgtheater before he went away, because the director in person telephoned me asking to see the one-act play, even though it was still in draft form, and he accepted it at once in advance. The supporting parts had already been sent to the theatre's actors for reading. Once again I seemed to have won the highest prize without staking anything much on it—a work of mine was to be produced at the Burgtheater, the pride of our city, and what was more, the man who shared with Eleonora Duse the reputation of being the greatest actor of the time was to appear in it at that same theatre. It was almost too much for a beginner. There was only one danger left—suppose Kainz changed his mind

about the play when it was finished? But that was very unlikely!
The impatience was all on my side now. At last I read in the
newspaper that Josef Kainz had come back from touring. Out
of civility, I waited two days so as not pester him the moment he
had arrived. But on the third day I summoned up my courage,
went to the Hotel Sacher, where Kainz was staying, and handed
my card to the old clerk at the reception desk, whom I knew well.
"For Herr Kainz, the actor at the court theatre!" I said. The old
man looked at me over the top of his pince-nez in surprise. "Oh,
don't you know, Doctor?" No, I knew nothing. "They took him
away to the sanatorium this morning." This was the first I had
heard of it—Kainz had come back severely ill from his tour in
Germany, where he had performed his great roles for the last
time, heroically overcoming terrible pain in front of audiences
that had no idea of it. Next day he had an operation for cancer.
Reading the bulletins in the newspaper, we still dared to hope he
would recover, and I visited him. He lay there looking exhausted
and emaciated, the dark eyes in his gaunt face looking even larger
than usual, and I was horrified. For the first time, a moustache
as grey as ice showed above the eternally young lips that spoke
so eloquently. I was looking at an old man on his deathbed. He
gave me a melancholy smile. "Will the good Lord allow me to
act our play? That might yet cure me." But a few weeks later we
were standing beside his coffin.

My uneasiness about persisting in the dramatic vein will be
easily understood, and so will the anxiety I now felt as soon as
I had delivered a new play to a theatre. I am not ashamed to
say that the deaths of the two greatest actors in the German-
speaking countries, when the last parts they had been rehearsing
were written by me, made me superstitious. It was not until a
few years later that I could bring myself to try writing another
dramatic work, and when the new artistic director of the

Burgtheater, Alfred Baron Berger, an eminent man of the theatre and a master of eloquent oratory himself, immediately accepted my play I looked almost anxiously at the list of actors he had selected. Paradoxically, I breathed a sigh of relief: "Thank God, no famous name among them!" There was no one to be the victim of disaster. Yet the improbable happened all the same; close one door to misfortune and it will come in by another. I had been thinking only of the actors, not the director of the play. Berger was planning to direct my tragedy *Das Haus am Meer*— The House by the Sea—himself, and had already been working on the prompt copy. Sure enough, fourteen days before the first rehearsals were to begin he died. So it seemed that the curse on my dramatic works was still in force. Even when my *Jeremiah* and *Volpone* were staged in many different languages after the Great War, more than a decade later, I did not feel secure. And in 1931 I deliberately acted against my own interests when I had finished a new play, *Das Lamm des Armen*—The Poor Man's Ewe Lamb. I had sent it to my friend Alexander Moissi, and I received a telegram from him asking me to reserve the lead part in the first production for him. Moissi, who had brought with him from his native Italy a feeling for sensuous, melodious language previously unknown on the German stage, was the sole successor to Josef Kainz's crown at this time. A man of captivating appearance, clever, lively, and in addition kindly and inspiring, he imbued every play with some of his personal magic; I could not have wished for a better actor in the part. All the same, when he put the proposition to me, I remembered Matkowsky and Kainz, and made an excuse for declining Moissi's request without telling him the real reason. I knew that he had inherited the ring known as the Iffland[2] ring from Kainz; it was always passed on by the greatest German actor of his time to his greatest successor. Was he to inherit Kainz's fate as well? I for one did not want to bring disaster down on the greatest German actor of the day for the third time. So out of superstition and friendship, I sacrificed what would almost certainly have been an ideal performance of my play. Yet although I would not let him take the part, and although I wrote no more plays after that, even this sacrifice of mine could not protect him. I was still, through no fault of my own, to be involved in bringing misfortune on others.

I realise that at this point I shall be suspected of telling a ghost story. Matkowsky and Kainz can be explained away as mere coincidence. But what about Moissi after them, when I had not let him take the part he wanted and I had not written any more plays? It happened like this: years later—I am anticipating events here—in the summer of 1935, I was in Zurich, with no idea of any looming threat, when I suddenly had a telegram from Alexander Moissi in Milan. He said he was coming to Zurich that evening on purpose to see me, and he asked me to be sure to meet him at the railway station. Strange, I thought, what could be so urgent? I had no new play, and had felt no great interest in the theatre for years. But of course I happily went to meet him; I loved that warm-hearted man like a brother. He got out of his carriage and rushed towards me; we embraced in the Italian way, and even in the car driving away from the station he was pouring out, with his usual wonderful verve, the gist of what I could do for him. He had a favour to ask me, a great favour, he said. Pirandello had honoured him by giving him rights for the first production of his new play, *Non si sa mai*[3]. This was to be not just the Italian premiere but the world premiere—and it was to be in Vienna and performed in German. This was the first time, said Moissi, that such an Italian master had given precedence to a foreign country for the premiere of one of his works. He had never even brought himself to allow a world premiere in Paris. And Pirandello, fearing that the musicality and nuances of his prose might be lost in translation, had one wish very much at heart; he did not want just any translator to produce the German version of his play, he had long admired my linguistic skill and would very much like me to do it. Pirandello had of course had scruples about wasting my time on translations, and so, said Moissi, he had taken it upon himself to deliver the playwright's request. In fact at this time I had done no translation for years. But I revered Pirandello, whom I had met on several pleasant occasions, too much to disappoint him, and most of all I·was delighted to be able to give such a close friend as Moissi proof of my comradely feeling. I dropped my own work for one or two weeks, and a few weeks after that Pirandello's play had its international premiere in Vienna, in my translation. The political background of the time meant that it was to be staged on a particularly grand scale. Pirandello had said that he would come in person, and since Mussolini was still regarded as the friend of Austria that he declared himself to be, members of many official circles, headed by the Chancellor, had said they would attend. The evening was to be a political demonstration of Austro-Italian friendship (in reality, it marked Austria's new status as an Italian protectorate).

I happened to be in Vienna myself when the first rehearsals were to begin. I looked forward to seeing Pirandello again, and I was curious to hear the words of my translation spoken with Moissi's musicality. But by eerie coincidence, the events of a quarter-of-a-century earlier were repeated. When I opened the newspaper first thing in the morning, I heard that Moissi had arrived from Switzerland with a bad attack of flu. Flu, I thought, that can't be too serious. But my heart was thudding as I approached his hotel—thank God, I said to myself, not the Hotel Sacher, the Grand Hotel—to visit my sick friend. The memory of that futile visit to Kainz came back to me like a shudder running down my spine. And the events of over twenty-five years ago were repeated, once again affecting the greatest actor of his time. I was not allowed in to see Moissi; he had fallen into a fevered delirium. Two days later I was not at a rehearsal but standing by his coffin, just as I had stood beside the coffin of Kainz.

I have looked ahead in time by mentioning that final instance of the mysterious curse on my ventures into the theatre. Of course I see nothing but coincidence in that succession of events. But undoubtedly the deaths of Matkowsky and Kainz, so soon after one another, affected the direction my life took at the time. If my first plays, written when I was twenty-six, had been performed by Matkowsky in Berlin and Kainz in Vienna, then thanks to their art, which could make a success even of the weakest play, I would quickly have come to wide public notice, perhaps more quickly than would have been good for me, and would thus have missed my years of slow learning and getting to know the world. At the time, understandably enough, I felt like a victim of Fate, since at the very beginning of my career the theatre offered me opportunities I would never have dared to dream of, temptingly holding them out and then cruelly taking them away again at the last minute. But only in youth does coincidence seem the same as fate. Later, we know that the real course of our lives is decided within us; our paths may seem to diverge from our wishes in a confused and pointless way, but in the end the way always leads us to our invisible destination.

NOTES

1   Sebastian Castellio, 1515-63, French Protestant theologian, who was in conflict with Calvin over the latter's savage persecution of heretics.

2   August Wilhelm Iffland (1759-1814) was a famous German actor of his time; this ring bore a picture of him.

3   Zweig means Pirandello's 1934 play, *Non si sa come—No One Knows How.*

BEYOND EUROPE

D ID TIME MOVE FASTER THEN than it does today, when it is crammed with incidents that will change our world utterly for centuries? Or do the last years of my youth, before the first European war, seem blurred to me now only because they were spent steadily working? I was writing, my work was published, my name was known in Germany and Austria and to some extent further afield. There were some who liked my work and—which really says more for its originality—some who did not. I could write for any of the major newspapers of the Reich; I no longer had to submit articles but was asked for them. Inwardly, however, I do not deceive myself into thinking that anything I did and wrote in those years matters today. Our ambitions, anxieties, setbacks and reasons for embitterment of that time now seem to me positively lilliputian. Inevitably, the dimensions of the present day have changed our point of view. If I had begun this book several years ago, I would have mentioned conversations with Gerhart Hauptmann, Arthur Schnitzler, Beer-Hofmann, Dehmel, Pirandello, Wassermann, Shalom Asch and Anatole France. (The last of those would have made an amusing story, for the old gentleman dished us up risqué anecdotes all afternoon, but with distinguished gravity and indescribable grace.) I could have written about great premieres—of Gustav Mahler's *Tenth Symphony*[1] in Munich, of *Der Rosenkavalier* in Dresden, of Karsavina and Nijinsky dancing. As a man easily able to travel and full of curiosity, I was present at many artistic events now considered historic. But anything unconnected with the prob-

201

lems of today pales in importance when judged by our sterner criteria. Today, the men who directed my attention to literature in my youth seem to me not nearly as important as those who diverted it to reality.

First and foremost among them was a man involved with the fate of the German Reich at one of he most tragic epochs of its history, and who suffered the first murderous onslaught of the National Socialists eleven years before Hitler took power. This was Walther Rathenau. Our friendship was warm and of long standing; it had begun in a strange way. One of the first to give me encouragement at the age of nineteen was Maximilian Harden, whose journal *Die Zukunft*—The Future—played an important part in the last decades of the Imperial Reich of Kaiser Wilhelm II. Harden, personally introduced into politics by Bismarck, who liked to use him as a mouthpiece or lightning conductor, was behind the fall of ministers, brought the Eulenburg affair[2] to the point of explosion, and had the Imperial Palace trembling every week for fear of more attacks and revelations. In spite of all that, Harden's private love was for the theatre and literature. One day *Die Zukunft* published a series of aphorisms signed by a pseudonymous name that I no longer remember, and I was greatly impressed by the author's clever mind and powers of linguistic concentration. As a regular contributor, I wrote to Harden asking: "Who is this new writer? I haven't seen such polished aphorisms for years."

The answer came not from Harden but from a man signing himself Walther Rathenau who, as I learnt from his letters as well as other sources, was none other than the son of the all-powerful director of the Berlin Electricity Company, a big businessman and industrialist himself, the director of many companies—one of the new breed of German businessmen who, in a phrase of Jean Paul's, knew what was what in the world. He wrote to me warmly, thanking me and saying that my letter had been the first positive mention he had received for his literary venture. Although at least ten years older than me, he frankly admitted that he was not sure whether he should really try to publish a whole book of his reflections and aphorisms. After all, he said, he was an outsider, and so far he had been active only in the field of economics. I gave him my honest encouragement, and we stayed in touch by correspondence. When I next visited Berlin I called him on the telephone. A hesitant voice answered: "Ah, it's you. What a pity, I have to set out at six tomorrow morning for South Africa ... " I interrupted him: "Then let's meet some other time." But the voice went on, slowly thinking aloud: "No, wait a moment ... this afternoon is full of meetings ... this evening I have to go to the Ministry, and then there's a dinner at the club ... but could you call on me at eleven-fifteen?" I agreed, and we talked until two in the morning. At six he did indeed leave for South West Africa—on a mission from the Kaiser of Germany, as I later discovered.

I mention this detail because it is so characteristic of Rathenau. Busy as he was, he always had time for a friend. I saw him in the most desperate days of the war, and just before the Conference of Genoa, and a few days before his assassination I drove with him in the very car in which he would be shot taking the same route as he did that day. He always had his day divided up to the minute, yet he could switch from subject to subject without any difficulty because his mind was always alert, an instrument of such precision and speed as I have never known in any other human being. He spoke as fluently as if he were reading aloud from an invisible sheet of paper, yet forming every sentence so clearly and graphically that if anyone had taken down his conversation in shorthand the text could have gone straight into print. He spoke French, English and Italian as well as his native German—his memory never let him down, he never needed special preparation for any subject. When you talked to him you felt simultaneously stupid, inadequately educated, uncertain and confused in the face of his calm objectivity as he assessed and clearly surveyed the subject of conversation. But there was something in the dazzling brilliance and crystal clarity of his mind that had an uncomfortable effect, just as the finest of furniture and pictures felt not quite right in his apartment. His mind was like a brilliantly constructed mechanism, his apartment like a museum, and you could never really feel at ease in his feudal castle of the time of Queen Luise[3] in the March of Brandenburg, it was so neat and tidy and well-ordered. There was something as transparent as glass and thus insubstantial in his thinking; I seldom felt the tragedy of the Jewish identity more strongly than I did in him. In spite of his obvious distinction, he was full of profound uneasiness and uncertainty. My other friends, for instance Verhaeren, Ellen Key and Bazalgette, were not one-tenth as clever nor one-hundredth as knowledgeable and experienced as he was, but they were sure of themselves. With Rathenau, I always felt that for all his extraordinarily clever mind he had no solid ground beneath his feet. His whole life was a conflict of contradictions. He had inherited great power from his father, yet he did not want to be his heir. He was a businessman, and wanted to feel that he was an artist; he owned millions and toyed with socialist ideas; he felt that he was Jewish but flirted with Christianity. His thinking was international, but he idolised the Prussian spirit; he dreamt of a people's democracy, yet always felt highly honoured to be received and questioned by Kaiser Wilhelm, whose weaknesses and vanities he clearly saw without being able to overcome some vanity of his own. So his constant busy activity may have been just an opiate to dull private nervousness and dispel the solitude of his real nature. Only at his hour of responsibility when in 1919, after the collapse of the German armies, he was given the hardest task in history—the reconstruction of the shattered state from chaos to a point where it was capable of life again—did the great potential forces in him suddenly unite, and he rose to the greatness natural to his genius by devoting his life to the single idea of saving Europe.

Along with many stimulating conversations, perhaps comparable only to my conversations with Hofmannsthal, Valéry and Count Keyserling, along with the way he broadened my horizons from being purely literary to include the history of my time, I owe Rathenau his suggestion that I should look beyond Europe. "You can't understand Great Britain when all you know is the island itself," he told me. "And you can't understand our continent until you have gone beyond it at least once. You're a free agent, use your freedom! Literature is a wonderful profession, because haste is no part of it. Whether a really good book is finished a year earlier or a year later makes no difference. Why don't you go to India and America?" This casual remark made an impression on me, and I decided to take his advice at once.

India had a stranger and more oppressive effect on me than I had expected. I was shocked by the poverty of the emaciated figures I saw there, the joyless gravity of their dark glances, the often cruel monotony of the landscape, and most of all the rigid distinction between classes and races. I had already seen a sample of that on the voyage. Two charming girls, black-eyed and slender, well-educated and well-mannered, modest and elegant, were travelling on our ship. On the very first day I noticed that they kept away from the rest of us, or perhaps were kept away by some invisible barrier. They did not come to the shipboard dances, they did not join in conversation, but instead sat on their own reading books in French and English. Only on the second or third day did I discover that they were not avoiding the English passengers of their own accord, the English passengers kept aloof from them because they were 'half-castes', although these delightful girls were the daughters of a Parsee businessman and a Frenchwoman. They had been on absolutely equal terms with

205

everyone else for the last two or three years at their boarding school in Lausanne and then their finishing school in England, but a cool, invisible and yet cruel form of social ostracism set in as soon as they began their voyage home to India. This was the first time I had experience of the menace of delusions of racial purity, a plague that has affected our world more disastrously than the real plague ever did in earlier centuries.

This first encounter with it alerted my eye from the start. Feeling rather ashamed of it, I enjoyed the respectful awe—no longer felt, and it is our own fault—shown to a European as a kind of white god when he went on a tourist expedition ashore, like the one I made to Adam's Mount in Ceylon, inevitably accompanied by twelve to fourteen servants. Anything less would have been beneath a European's dignity. I couldn't shake off the uncomfortable feeling that future decades and centuries were bound to bring change and reversal to this absurd state of affairs, but in our comfortable and apparently secure Europe, we dared not begin to imagine that. Because of these observations I did not see India in a rosy, romantic light, as did Pierre Loti and his like; I saw it as a warning, and during my travels I did not gain most from the wonderful temples, the weather-worn old palaces, the Himalayan landscapes, but from the people I met, people of another kind and from another world than those whom a writer used to meet in the interior of Europe. Anyone who travelled beyond Europe at that time, when we were more cautious about money and Cook's Tours were not yet so well organised, was almost always a man whose position gave him a certain standing—a merchant who travelled was not a small shopkeeper with modest horizons but a big businessman; a doctor was a true research scientist; an entrepreneur was like the conquistadors of the past, adventurous, generous, reckless— even a writer was likely to have a high degree of intellectual curiosity. In the long days and nights of my journey, which were not yet filled by the chatter of the radio, I learnt more about the forces and tensions that move our world from these people than from a hundred books. A change in distance from my native land brought about a change in my standards. On my return I began to see many small things that used to occupy my mind unduly as petty, and Europe no longer seemed to me the eternal axis of the universe.

One of the men whom I met on my travels in India has had an incalculable if not openly visible influence on the history of our time. Travelling on a river boat along the Irrawaddy from Calcutta to Indochina, I spent hours every day with Karl Haushofer, on his way to Japan with his wife to take up the post of German military attaché. An upright, thin man with a bony face and sharply aquiline nose, he gave me my first insight into the extraordinary qualities and disciplined mind of a German officer of the general staff. In Vienna, of course, I had already mingled at times with military men—pleasant and even amusing young fellows whose families were usually not very prosperous, and had joined the army to get the best they could out of military service. However, you sensed at once that Haushofer came from a cultivated upper-middle-class family—his father had published quite a number of poems, and I think had been a university professor—and his education was wide even outside military life. Commissioned to study the battlefields of the Russo-Japanese war on the spot, both he and his wife had familiarised themselves with the language and even the literature of Japan. I saw him as another example of the way in which if any branch of knowledge, including the military, is understood in a broad sense it must inevitably reach beyond its narrow specialist area and touch all other branches. On board the river boat he worked all day, following every detail of the voyage with his field glasses, writing diaries or reports, studying encyclopedias; I seldom saw him without a book in his hands. He was very observant and good at describing what he had seen. In conversation with him, I learnt a great deal about the mysteries of the East, and once home I stayed in friendly touch with the Haushofer family. We corresponded, and visited each other in Salzburg and Munich. Serious lung trouble kept him in Davos and Arosa for a year, and while he was not serving in the army he was able to devote himself to science, but during the First World War he took over a military command. After the defeat of Germany I often thought of him with great sympathy; I could only imagine how he must have suffered, after spending years building up a German position of power and perhaps, in his discreet manner, the war machine itself, when he saw Japan, where he had made many friends, side with the victorious enemy.

He soon turned out to be one of the first to think systematically and on a large scale of a reconstruction of German power. He was editing a geopolitical journal and, as so often happens, I did not understand the true meaning of this new movement at first. I genuinely believed it merely studied the interplay of international forces, and even the word *Lebensraum*,[4] as a term for "living-space" for the nations (I think he coined the term), was something that I understood only in Spengler's[5] sense, as the relative energy released by every nation at some point in the cycle of time, and changing from epoch to epoch. And there seemed to me nothing wrong about Haushofer's demand for closer study of the individual qualities of nations, and the construction of a permanent educational apparatus of a scientific nature. I thought that these investigations were solely meant to bring different nations together. Perhaps—I cannot say—Haushofer's original intentions had not been political. At least, I read his books with great interest (he once, incidentally, quoted me) and with no suspicion of anything amiss; I heard his lectures praised as uncommonly instructive by all impartial people, and no one accused him of putting his ideas to the service of a new policy of power and aggression, designed solely to give a new form of ideological justification to the old demands for a Greater Germany. One day, however, when I happened to mention his name, someone said, "Ah, Hitler's friend!" in a tone suggesting that everyone knew it. I couldn't have been more surprised. For one thing, Haushofer's wife was certainly not 'racially pure', and his very talented and agreeable sons could never have satisfied the Nuremberg Laws affecting Jews; in addition, I could not see any direct intellectual link between a highly cultivated scholar whose mind ranged widely, and a ferocious agitator obsessed with German nationalism in its most narrow and brutal sense. But one of Haushofer's pupils had been Rudolf Hess, and he had forged the link. From the first, Hitler, who in himself was far from open to other people's ideas, had an instinct for appropriating everything that could be useful to his personal aims. So for him, the be-all and end-all of geopolitics was to further National Socialist policies, and he drew on as much of that branch of science as could serve his purpose. The National Socialist method was always to shore up its obviously selfish instinct for power with ideological and pseudo-moral justifications, and with this concept 'living-space' at last found a philosophical cover for its naked will to aggression. The catchphrase was so vaguely defined as to be apparently innocuous, but it meant that any successful annexation, even the most autocratic, could be justified as an ethical and ethnological necessity. So my old travelling companion—whether knowingly and willingly I do not know—was to blame for the fundamental change for the worse in Hitler's idea of his aims, which had previously been confined to national and racial purity—a change that was to affect the rest of the world. The theory of 'living-space' degenerated into the slogan, "Germany is ours today, tomorrow the whole world"—as obvious an example of the way a single, succinct phrase can turn the immanent power of words into action and disaster as the demand of the *encyclopédistes* to let reason reign supreme, which led to terror and mass emotionalism, the very opposite of reason. Haushofer

himself, so far as I know, never held a prominent position in
the Party and may not even have been a Party member. I do
not by any means see him, like today's ingenious journalists,
as a demonic 'grey eminence' behind the scenes, hatching
dangerous plans and whispering them in the Führer's ear. But
there is no doubt that the theories of Haushofer, rather than
anything thought up by Hitler's most deranged advisers, were
responsible for the aggressive policy of National Socialism,
whether deliberately or not giving it universal instead of strictly
national proportions. Only posterity, with better documentation
than is available to us today, will be able to see him in the correct
historical light.

After this first overseas journey my second, to America, followed
a little later. It too was for no other purpose than to see the
world and, if possible, a little of the future that lay ahead of us.
I believe I really was one of the few writers at the time to have
travelled there not to make financial or journalistic capital out
of the United States, but just to compare my rather vague idea
of the New World with the reality.

That vague idea, I am not ashamed to say, was extremely
romantic. To me, America meant Walt Whitman, the land
of new rhythm, the coming brotherhood of the whole world.
Before making the crossing I reread the wild, long lines of
the great *Camerado*,[6] a flowing torrent like a cataract, and so I
entered Manhattan with an open-minded sense of fraternity
instead of the European's usual arrogance. I remember how
the first thing I did was to ask the hotel receptionist where Walt
Whitman's grave was, so that I could visit it. My question had
the poor man, an Italian, in great difficulty; he had never even
heard the poet's name.

My first impression was very striking, although New York
did not yet have its present captivating nocturnal beauty. The

foaming cascades of light in Times Square were still to come, and so was the city's dream-like starry firmament shining up at the real sky by night with billions of artificial stars. The general layout of the city and its traffic were not as bold and generous as today; the new architecture was still uncertainly trying its hand at a few high-rise buildings, and only a tentative beginning was being made on the astonishingly lavish and tasteful displays in store windows. But to look down from Brooklyn Bridge, always swaying slightly, at the harbour, and wander through the stony ravines of the avenues was discovery and excitement enough, although admittedly after two or three days it gave way to another and stronger feeling, a sense of great loneliness. I had nothing to do in New York, and at the time a man with no occupation was more out of place there than anywhere. The city did not yet have cinemas where you could amuse yourself for an hour, or comfortable little cafeterias; there were not as many art galleries, libraries and museums as today, and culturally everything was still far behind Europe. After I had spent two or three days dutifully seeing the museums and the main sights, I drifted like a rudderless boat along the icy, windy streets. Finally the sense that I was pointlessly wandering the streets became so strong that I could overcome it only by tricking myself into seeing it as more attractive. I invented a game to play. I told myself that I was wandering around here all alone, one of the countless emigrants who didn't know what to do with themselves and had only seven dollars in their pockets. You are voluntarily doing, I said to myself, what they do from necessity. Imagine that you are obliged to earn your bread after three days at the latest. Look around and see how you could start out in life here as a stranger, with no connections or friends, so you must look for a job at once. I began going from employment bureau to employment bureau, studying the notes tacked to their doors. A baker was wanted here, an assistant clerk with a knowledge of French and Italian there, a bookshop assistant somewhere

211

else. This last was a chance for my imaginary self. So I climbed an iron spiral staircase three floors up, asked about the pay, and compared it with the newspaper ads quoting prices for a room in the Bronx. After two days of job-hunting I had, in theory, found five posts with which I could have earnt my living, so I had convinced myself better than by merely strolling around of how much space and how many possibilities this young country held for everyone willing to work. That impressed me. In my wanderings from agency to agency, imagining myself working in the various businesses, I had also gained an insight into the country's wonderful freedom. No one asked about my nationality, my religion, my origin, and what was more—an amazing thing to imagine in our modern world of fingerprints, visas and police permits—I had travelled without a passport. But there was work waiting for people to do it, and that was all that counted. Fabulous as it now seems, a contract could be instantly agreed without today's inhibiting intervention of state formalities and trade unions. Thanks to my job-hunting, I learnt more about America in those first few days than in later weeks, when travelling in comfort as a tourist I saw Philadelphia, Boston, Baltimore and Chicago, spending a few companionable hours in Boston with Charles Loeffler, who had composed music for some of my poems, but otherwise always alone. Only once did a surprise interrupt the total anonymity of my existence. I remember that moment clearly. I was strolling down a broad avenue in Philadelphia; I stopped outside a large bookshop to get a sense of something familiar to me from the names of the authors at least. Suddenly I gave a start. There were six or seven German books on display to the left of the bookshop window, and my own name jumped out at me from one of them. I gazed as if I were under a spell, and began thinking. So something of my Self, the Self now drifting unknown and apparently aimlessly through strange streets, had been here before me, known to no one, noticed by no one. The bookseller must have written my name on an order form to get that book travelling over the ocean for ten days. For a moment my sense of isolation was dispelled, and when I visited Philadelphia again two years ago, I kept looking for that bookshop without meaning to.

I did not have the courage to reach San Francisco—Hollywood had not yet been invented. But there was at least one other place where I could have the view of the Pacific Ocean that I longed for, a view that had fascinated me since, as a child, I had read accounts of the first circumnavigation of the world. It was a place now gone, a place that no mortal eye will ever see again—the last mounds of earth from the Panama Canal, which was then being built. I had travelled in a small ship past Bermuda and Haiti. Our literary generation had been educated by Verhaeren to admire the technical marvels of our time with the same enthusiasm as our forefathers admired the buildings of Roman antiquity. Panama itself was an unforgettable sight, a river bed excavated by diggers, glaring ochre-yellow burning the eye even through dark glasses, air like the fires of hell teeming with millions upon millions of mosquitoes. You could see their victims in endless rows in the cemetery. How many had fallen victim to this project, begun by Europe and to be completed by America? Only now, after thirty years of disasters and disappointments, was it really taking shape. A few months before the final work on the sluices was done, then a finger pressing an electric button, and after thousands of years the two oceans would flow into each other again for ever. I was one of the last of my time to have seen them before they joined, in the full and conscious awareness that this was a historic moment. That view of its greatest creative act was a good way to say goodbye to America.

NOTES

1   Zweig means Mahler's *Eighth Symphony*, the 'Symphony of a Thousand', premiered in Munich in 1910. The composer left a tenth symphony unfinished when he died.

2   A scandal concerning accusations of homosexuality in high places.

3   Queen Luise of Prussia, 1776-1810, wife of King Friedrich Wilhelm III.

4   *Lebensraum* was of course a notorious Nazi term for territory that Hitler planned to annex to Germany.

5   Oswald Spengler, 1880-1936, whose most famous book was *The Decline of the West*. In it, he proposed the theory that nations and whole continents follow a natural cycle of growth, maturity and decline.

6   *As I Lay With My Head in Your Lap Camerado*, Walt Whitman, 1867.

BRIGHTNESS AND SHADOWS OVER EUROPE

I HAD NOW LIVED THROUGH TEN YEARS of the new century; I had seen India, part of America, and I began thinking of Europe with a new and better-informed sense of pleasure. I never loved our old world *more* than in those last years before the First World War; I never hoped more for a united Europe; I never believed more in its future than at that time, when we thought there was a new dawn in sight. But its red hue was really the firelight of the approaching international conflagration.

Today's generation has grown up amidst disasters, crises, and the failure of systems. The young see war as a constant possibility to be expected almost daily, and it may be difficult to describe to them the optimism and confidence in the world that we felt when we ourselves were young at the turn of the century. Forty years of peace had strengthened national economies, technology had speeded up the pace of life, scientific discoveries had been a source of pride to the spirit of our own generation.. The upswing now beginning could be felt to almost the same extent in all European countries. Cities were more attractive and densely populated year by year; the Berlin of 1905 was not like the city I had known in 1901. From being the capital of a princely state it had become an international metropolis, which in turn paled beside the Berlin of 1910. Vienna, Milan, Paris, London, Amsterdam—whenever you came back to them you were surprised and delighted. The streets were broader and finer, the public buildings more imposing, the shops more elegant. Everything conveyed a sense of the growth and wider

215

distribution of wealth. Even we writers noticed it from the editions of our books printed; in the space of ten years the number of copies printed per edition tripled, then multiplied by fivefold and by tenfold. There were new theatres, libraries and museums everywhere. Domestic facilities such as bathrooms and telephones that used to be the prerogative of a few select circles became available to the lower middle class, and now that hours of work were shorter than before, the proletariat had its own share in at least the minor pleasures and comforts of life. There was progress everywhere. Who dared, won. If you bought a house, a rare book, a picture you saw its value rise; the bolder and more ambitious the ideas behind an enterprise, the more certain it was to succeed. There was a wonderfully carefree atmosphere abroad in the world—for what was going to interrupt this growth, what could stand in the way of the vigour constantly drawing new strength from its own momentum? Europe had never been stronger, richer or more beautiful, had never believed more fervently in an even better future, and no one except a few shrivelled old folk still bewailed the passing of the 'good old days'.

And not only were the cities more beautiful, their inhabitants too were more attractive and healthier, thanks to sporting activities, better nutrition, shorter working hours and a closer link with nature. People had discovered that up in the mountains winter, once a dismal season to be spent gloomily playing cards in taverns or feeling bored as you sat around in overheated rooms, was a source of filtered sunlight, nectar for the lungs that sent blood coursing deliciously just beneath the skin. The mountains, the lakes and the sea no longer seemed so far away. Bicycles, motor cars, electric railways had shrunk distance and given the world a new sense of space. On Sundays thousands and tens of thousands, clad in brightly coloured sportswear, raced down the snowy slopes on skis and toboggans; sports centres and swimming baths were built everywhere. You could see the change clearly

216

in those swimming baths—while in my own youth a really fine figure of a man stood out among all the bull-necked, paunchy or pigeon-chested specimens, nowadays athletically agile young men, tanned by the sun and fit from all their sporting activities, competed cheerfully with each other as they did in classical antiquity. Only the most poverty-stricken stayed at home now on a Sunday; all the young people went walking, climbing or competing in all kinds of sports. When they went on holiday they did not, as in my parents' time, find somewhere to stay near the city, or at the most no further away than the Salzkammergut. Their curiosity about the world had been aroused; they wanted to see if it was as beautiful everywhere, or maybe beautiful in a different way in other places, and while once only the privileged few travelled abroad, now bank clerks and small tradesmen went away to Italy or France. Foreign travel had become cheaper and more comfortable, but above all a new bold, adventurous attitude made travellers willing to venture further afield, less thrifty, less anxious—indeed, anxiety was something to be ashamed of. That whole generation was determined to be more youthful; unlike young people in the world of my parents, everyone was proud of youth. Suddenly beards disappeared, first in the younger men, then shaved off by their elders, imitating them so as not to be thought of as old. Youthful freshness was more desirable than dignity. Women threw away the corsets that had constricted their breasts, stopped fearing fresh air and sunlight and gave up sunshades and veils; they shortened their skirts so that they could move more freely when they played tennis, and they were not shy about showing a well-turned pair of legs. Fashions became more and more natural, men wore breeches, women dared to ride astride, and the sexes stopped concealing themselves from each other. There was more freedom as well as more beauty in the world.

It was the health and self-confidence of the generation after ours that also laid claim to freedom for itself in manners and morals. For the first time, you saw young girls enjoying excursions and sporting activities in open and confident friendship with young men, and without a governess going along as chaperone. They were no longer timid and prudish; they knew what they wanted and what they did not. Escaping the anxious authority of their parents, earning their own living as secretaries or clerks, they took control of their own lives. This new, healthier freedom led to a clear decrease in prostitution, the sole permitted erotic institution of the old world, and prudery of every kind now seemed old-fashioned. Increasingly, the wooden partitions in swimming baths that used to divide the gentlemen's and ladies' pools from each other were taken down. Women and men were not ashamed to show their figures any more. In those ten years there was more freedom, informality and lack of inhibition than there had been in the entire preceding century.

For the world was moving to a different rhythm. A year—so much could happen in a year now! Inventions and discoveries followed hard on each other's heels, and each in turn swiftly became a general good. For the first time the nations all felt in common what was for the benefit of all. On the day when the Zeppelin[1] rose in the air for its first flight, I was on my way to Belgium and happened to be in Strasburg where, to shouts of jubilation from the crowd, it circled the Münster as if bowing to the thousand-year-old cathedral while it hovered in the air. That evening, at the Verhaerens', news came that the airship had crashed in Echterdingen. Verhaeren had tears in his eyes, and was badly upset. Belgian though he was, this German catastrophe did not leave him unmoved; it was as a European, a man of our time, that he felt for our common victory over the elements as well as this common setback. When Blériot made the first cross-Channel flight in an aeroplane, we rejoiced in Vienna as if he were a hero of our own nation; pride in the triumphs of our technology and science, which succeeded one another by the hour, had led for the first time to a European sense of community, the development of a European identity. How pointless, we said to ourselves, frontiers were if it was child's play for any aircraft to cross them, how provincial and artificial were customs barriers and border guards, how contrary to the spirit of our times that clearly wished for closer links and international fraternity! This upward surge of feeling was no less remarkable than the upward rise of aircraft; I feel sorry for all who did not live through these last years of European confidence while they were still young themselves. For the air around us is not a dead and empty void, it has in it the rhythm and vibration of the time. We absorb them unconsciously into our bloodstream as the air carries them deep into our hearts and minds. Perhaps, ungrateful as human beings are, we did not realise at the time how strongly and securely the wave bore us up. But only those who knew that time of confidence in the world know that everything since has been regression and gloom.

That world was a wonderful tonic, its strength reaching our hearts from all the coasts of Europe. At the same time, however, although we did not guess it, what delighted us was dangerous. The stormy wind of pride and confidence sweeping over Europe brought clouds with it. Perhaps the upward movement had come too fast, states and cities had made themselves powerful too swiftly—and an awareness of having power always leads states, like men, to use or misuse it. France was extremely wealthy, yet it wanted still more, it wanted another colony although it did not have enough people for the old ones, and it almost went to war over Morocco. Italy had its eye on Cyrenaica[2]; Austria annexed Bosnia; Serbia and Bulgaria advanced on Turkey; and Germany, although inactive for the moment, was flexing its claws to strike in anger. All the states were suffering a rush of blood to the head. Everywhere, and at the same time, the productive wish for consolidation at home began to develop, like an infectious illness, into a greedy desire for expansion. High-earning French industrialists agitated against their German counterparts, who were also rolling in riches, because both Krupp and Schneider-Creusot wanted to be able to supply more artillery. The Hamburg shipping industry, which earned huge dividends, was vying with shipping based in Southampton, Hungarian and Bulgarian agriculture were in competition, one group of companies was set against all the rest—the economic situation had maddened them all in their frantic wish to get their hands on more and more. If today, thinking it over calmly, we wonder why Europe went to war in 1914, there is not one sensible reason to be found, nor even any real occasion for the war. There were no ideas involved, it was not really about drawing minor borderlines; I can explain it only, thinking of that excess of power, by seeing it as a tragic consequence of the internal dynamism that had built up during those forty years of peace, and now demanded release. Every state suddenly felt that it was strong, and forgot that other states felt exactly the same; all states wanted even more, and wanted some of what the others already had. The worst of it was that the very thing we loved most, our common optimism, betrayed us, for everyone thought that everyone else would back down at the last minute, and so the diplomats began their game of mutual bluff. In four or five instances, for instance in Agadir and in the Balkan Wars, it was still only a game, but the great coalitions drew closer and closer together and became increasingly militant. Germany introduced a war tax in the middle of peacetime, France extended its term of military service. Finally the accumulated head of steam had to be released. And the weather over the Balkans showed the way the wind was blowing as the clouds approached Europe.

There was no panic yet, but there was a constant sense of smouldering uneasiness; we still felt only slightly uncomfortable when shots rang out from the Balkans. Was war really going to descend on us, when we had no idea why? Slowly—but too slowly, too hesitantly, as we now know—the forces rejecting

220

war came together. There was the Socialist Party, millions of people on all sides, with a programme opposing war; there were powerful Catholic groups under the leadership of the Pope and several international groups of companies; there were a few reasonable politicians who spoke out against any undercover dealings. We writers also ranged ourselves against war, although as usual we spoke in isolation, expressing ourselves as individuals rather than closing ranks to speak firmly as an organisation. Most intellectuals, unfortunately, adopted an indifferent and passive stance, for our optimism meant that the problem of war, with all its moral consequences, had not yet entered our personal field of vision—you will not find a single discussion of the principles involved, or a single passionate warning, in the major works of the prominent writers of that time. We thought we were doing enough if we thought in European terms and forged fraternal links internationally, stating in our own sphere—which had only indirect influence on current events—that we were in favour of the ideal of peaceful understanding and intellectual brotherhood crossing linguistic and national borders. And the younger generation was more strongly attached than anyone to this European ideal. In Paris, I found my friend Bazalgette surrounded by a group of young people who, in contrast to the older generation, had abjured all kinds of narrow-minded nationalism and imperialist aggression. Jules Romains, who was to write a great work on Europe at war, Georges Duhamel, Charles Vildrac, Durtain, René Arcos,[3] Jean-Richard Bloch, meeting first in the Abbaye and then in the Effort Libre groups, were passionate in their pioneering work for the future unity of Europe, and when put to the crucial test of war, were implacable in their abhorrence of every kind of militarism. These were young people of such courage, talent and moral determination as France has not often produced. In Germany, it was Franz Werfel with his collection of poems entitled *Der Weltfreund*—Friend of the World—who promoted

221

international fraternity most strongly. René Schickele, an Alsatian whose fate it therefore was to stand between the two opposing nations, worked passionately for understanding; G A Borgese sent us comradely greetings from Italy, and encouragement came from the Scandinavian and Slavonic countries. "Come and visit us!" one great Russian author wrote to me. "Show the pan-Slavists who urge us to go to war that you are against it in Austria!" How we all loved our time, a time that carried us forward on its wings; how we all loved Europe! But that overconfident faith in the future which, we were sure, would avert madness at the last minute, was also our own fault. We had certainly failed to look at the writing on the wall with enough distrust, but should not right-minded young people be trusting rather than suspicious? We trusted Jaurès and the Socialist International, we thought railway workers would blow up the tracks rather than let their comrades be loaded into trains to be sent to the front as cannon fodder; we relied on women to refuse to see their children and husbands sacrificed to the idol Moloch; we were convinced that the intellectual and moral power of Europe would assert itself triumphantly at the critical last moment. Our common idealism, the optimism that had come from progress, meant that we failed to see and speak out strongly enough against our common danger.

Moreover, what we lacked was an organiser who could bring the forces latent in us together effectively. We had only one prophet among us, a single man who looked ahead and saw what was to come, and the curious thing about it was that he lived among us, and it was a long time before we knew anything about him, although he had been sent by Fate as a leader. To me, finding him in the nick of time was a crucial stroke of luck, and it was hard to find him too, since he lived in the middle of Paris far from the hurly-burly of *la foire sur la place*.[4] Anyone who sets out to write an honest history of French literature in the twentieth century will be unable to ignore a remarkable phenomenon—the names of all kinds of writers were lauded to the skies in the Parisian newspapers of the time, except for the three most important of them, who were either disregarded or mentioned in the wrong context. From 1900 to 1914 I never saw the name of Paul Valéry mentioned as a poet in *Le Figaro* or *Le Matin*; Marcel Proust was considered a mere dandy who frequented the Paris salons, and Romain Rolland was thought of as a knowledgeable musicologist. They were almost fifty before the first faint light of fame touched their names, and their great work was hidden in darkness in the most enquiring city in the world.

It was pure chance that I discovered Romain Rolland at the right time. A Russian woman sculptor living in Florence had invited me to tea, to show me her work and try her hand at a sketch of me. I arrived punctually at four, forgetting that she was, after all, a Russian, so time and punctuality meant nothing to her. An old babushka who, I discovered, had been her mother's nurse, took me into the studio—the most picturesque thing about it was its disorder—and asked me to wait. In all there were four small sculptures standing around, and I had seen them all within two minutes. So as not to waste time, I picked up a book, or rather a couple of brown-covered journals lying about the studio. These were entitled *Cahiers de la Quinzaine*,[5] and I remembered having heard that title in Paris before. But who could keep track of the many little magazines that sprang up all over the country, short-lived idealistic flowers, and then disappeared again? I leafed through one of them, containing *L'Aube*, by Romain Rolland, and began to read, feeling more astonished and interested as I went on. Who was this Frenchman who knew Germany so well? Soon I was feeling grateful to my Russian friend for her unpunctuality. When she finally arrived, my first question was, "Who is this Romain Rolland?" She couldn't give me any very clear information, and only when I had acquired other issues of the magazine (the next was still in production) did I know that here at last was a work serving not just one European nation, but all of them and the fraternal connection between them. Here was the man, here was the writer who brought all the moral forces into play—affectionate understanding and an honest desire to find out more. He showed a sense of justice based on experience, and an inspiring faith in the unifying power of art. While the rest of us were squandering our efforts on small declarations of faith, he had set to work quietly and patiently to show the nations to one another through their most appealing individual qualities. This was the first consciously European novel being written at the time, the first vital call for fraternity, and it would be more effective in reaching a wider readership than Verhaeren's hymns, and in being more cogent than all the pamphlets and protests. What we had all unconsciously been hoping and longing for was being quietly written here.

The first thing I did in Paris was to ask about him, bearing in mind what Goethe had said: "He has learnt, he can teach us." I asked my friends about him. Verhaeren thought he remembered a play called *The Wolves* that had been staged at the socialist Théâtre du Peuple. Bazalgette had heard that Rolland was a musicologist and had written a short book on Beethoven. In the catalogue of the Bibliothèque Nationale I found a dozen works of his about old and modern music, and seven or eight plays, all of which had appeared under the imprint of small publishing houses or in the *Cahiers de la Quinzaine*. Finally, by way of a first approach to him, I sent him a book of my own. A letter soon arrived inviting me to visit him, and thus began a friendship that, together with my relationships with Freud and Verhaeren, was one of the most fruitful and often crucial of my life.

Notable days in our lives have a brighter aura about them than the ordinary kind. So I now remember that first visit with great clarity. I climbed five narrow, winding flights of stairs in an unpretentious building in the boulevard Montparnasse, and even outside the door I felt a special kind of stillness; the noise in the street sounded hardly any louder than the wind blowing in the trees of an old monastery garden below the windows. Rolland opened the door and took me into his small room, which was crammed with books up to the ceiling. For the first time I saw his remarkably bright blue eyes, the clearest and at the same time kindest eyes I ever saw in any human being, eyes that drew colour and fire from his inmost feelings in conversation, darkly shadowed in sorrow, appearing to grow deeper when he was thinking, sparkling with excitement—those unique eyes, under lids that were a little overtired, easily became red-rimmed when he had been reading or staying up late, but could shine radiantly in a congenial and happy light. I observed his figure with a little anxiety. Tall and thin, he stooped slightly as he walked, as if the countless hours at his desk had weighed his head down; his very pale complexion and angular features made him look rather unwell. He spoke very quietly and was sparing of physical effort in general; he almost never went out walking, he ate little, did not drink or smoke, but later I realised, with admiration, what great stamina there was in that ascetic frame, what a capacity for intellectual work lay behind his apparent debility. He would write for hours at his small desk, which was piled high with papers; he would read in bed for hours, never allowing his exhausted body more than four or five hours of sleep, and the only relaxation in which he indulged was music. He played the piano very well, with a delicate touch that I shall never forget, caressing the keys as if to entice rather than force the notes out of them. No virtuoso—and I have heard Max Reger, Busoni and Bruno Walter playing in small gatherings—gave me such a sense of direct communication with the master composers he loved.

His knowledge was very wide, putting most of us to shame; although he really lived only through his reading eyes; he had a fine command of literature, philosophy, history, and the problems of all nations at all times. He knew every bar of classical music; he was familiar with even the least-known works of Galuppi and Telemann, and with the music of sixth-rate or seventh-rate composers as well, yet he took a passionate interest in all events of the present day. The world was reflected in this monastic cell of his as if in a camera obscura. He had been on familiar terms with the great men of his time, had been a pupil of Renan, a guest in Wagner's house, a friend of Jaurès. Tolstoy had written him a famous letter that would go on record as human appreciation of his literary works. Here—and this always rejoices my heart—I sensed a human and moral superiority, an inner freedom without pride, something to be taken for granted in a strong mind. At first sight, and time has proved me right, I recognised him as the man who would be the conscience of Europe in its time of crisis. We talked about his *Jean-Christophe* novels. Rolland told me that he had tried to make the work fulfil a triple purpose—conveying his gratitude to music, his commitment to the cause of European unity, and an appeal to the nations to stop and think. Now we must all do what we could in our own positions, our own countries, our own languages. It was time, he said, to be more and more on our guard. The forces working for hatred, in line with their baser nature, were more violent and aggressive than the forces of reconciliation, and there were material interests behind them which, of their very nature, were more unscrupulous than ours. I found such grief over the fragility of earthly structures doubly moving in a man whose entire work celebrated the immortality of art. "It can bring comfort to us as individuals," he replied to me, "but it can do nothing against stark reality."

This was in 1913. It was the first conversation that showed me it was our duty not to confront the possibility of a European war passively and unprepared. When the crucial moment came, nothing gave Rolland such great moral superiority over everyone else as the way he had already, and painfully, strengthened his mind to face it in advance. Perhaps the rest of our circle had done something too. I had translated many works, I had promoted the best writers in the countries that were our neighbours, I had accompanied Verhaeren on a lecture tour all over Germany in 1912, and the tour had turned out to be a symbolic demonstration of Franco-German fraternity. In Hamburg Verhaeren and Dehmel, respectively the greatest poets of their time writing in French and German, had embraced in public. I had interested Reinhardt in Verhaeren's new play; our collaboration on both sides had never been warmer, more intense or more unconstrained, and in many hours of enthusiasm we entertained the illusion that we had shown the world the way that would save it. The world, however, took little notice of such literary manifestations, but went its own way to ruin. There was a kind of electrical crackling in the structural woodwork as if of invisible friction. Now and then a spark would fly up—the Zabern Affair,[6] the crises in Albania, the occasional unfortunate interview. Never more than a spark, but each one could have caused the accumulation of explosive material to blow up. We in Austria were keenly aware that we were at the heart of the area of unrest. In 1910 Emperor Franz Joseph passed the age of eighty. The old man, an icon in his own lifetime, could not last much longer, and a mystical belief began to spread among the public at large that after his death there would be no way to prevent the dissolution of the thousand-year-old monarchy. At home, the pressure of opposing nationalities grew; abroad Italy, Serbia, Romania and to some extent even Germany were waiting to divide up the Austrian empire. The war in the Balkans, where Krupp and Schneider-Creusot competed in trying out their artillery on 'human material', just as later the Germans and Italians tried out their aeroplanes during the

Spanish Civil War, drew us further and further into the raging torrent. We kept waking with a start, but to breathe again and again, with a sigh of relief, "Not this time. Not yet, and let us hope never!"

As everyone knows, it is a thousand times easier to reconstruct the facts of what happened at a certain time than its intellectual atmosphere. That atmosphere is reflected not in official events but, most conspicuously, in small, personal episodes of the kind that I am going to recount here. To be honest, I did not believe that war was coming at the time. But I twice had what might be called a waking dream of it, and woke with my mind in great turmoil. The first time was over the 'Redl Affair', which like many of those episodes that form a backdrop to history is not widely known.

Personally I knew Colonel Redl, the central character in one of the most complex of espionage dramas, only slightly. He lived a street away from me in the same district of Vienna, and once, in the café where this comfortable-looking gentleman, who appreciated the pleasures of the senses, was smoking his cigar, I was introduced to him by my friend Public Prosecutor T. After that we greeted each other when we met. But it was only later that I discovered how much secrecy surrounds us in the midst of our daily lives, and how little we really know about those who are close to us. This colonel, who looked very much the usual capable Austrian officer, was in the confidence of the heir to the throne. It was his important responsibility to head the army's secret service and thwart the activities of their opposing counterparts. It came out that during the crisis of the war in the Balkans in 1912, when Russia and Austria were mobilising to move against each other, the most important secret item in the hands of the Austrian army, the 'marching plan', had been sold to Russia. If war had come, this would have been nothing short of disastrous, for the Russians now knew in advance, move by move, every tactical manoeuvre for attack planned by the Austrian army. The panic set off among the General Staff of the army by this act of treachery was terrible. It was up to Colonel Redl, as the man in charge, to apprehend the traitor, who must be somewhere in the very highest places. The Foreign Ministry, not entirely trusting the competence of the military authorities, also let it be known without first informing the General Staff—a typical example of the jealous rivalry of those organisations—that they were going to follow the matter up independently, and to this end gave the police the job of taking various measures, including the opening of letters from abroad sent poste restante, regardless of the principle that such correspondence was strictly private.

One day, then, a post office received a letter from the Russian border station at Podvolokzyska to a poste-restante address code-named 'Opera Ball'. On being opened, it proved to contain no letter, but six or eight new Austrian thousand-crown notes. This suspicious find was reported at once to the chief of police, who issued instructions for a detective to be stationed at the post-office counter to arrest the person who came to claim the suspect letter on the spot.

For a moment it looked as if the tragedy was about to turn into Viennese farce. A gentleman turned up at midday, asking for the letter addressed to 'Opera Ball'. The clerk at the counter instantly gave a concealed signal to alert the detective. But the detective had just gone out for a snack, and when he came back all that anyone could say for certain was that the unknown gentleman had taken a horse-drawn cab and driven off in no-one-knew-what direction. However, the second act of this Viennese comedy soon began. In the time of those fashionable, elegant cabs, each of them a carriage and pair, the driver of the cab considered himself far too good to clean his cab with his own hands. So at every cab rank there was a man whose job it was

229

to feed the horses and wash the carriage. This man, fortunately, had noticed the number of the cab that had just driven off. In quarter-of-an-hour all police offices had been alerted and the cab had been found. Its driver described the gentleman who had taken the vehicle to the Café Kaiserhof, where I often met Colonel Redl, and moreover, by pure good luck, the pocketknife that the cabby's unknown fare had used to open the envelope was found still in the cab. Detectives hurried straight off to the Café Kaiserhof. By then the gentleman described by the cabby had left, but the waiters explained, as if it were the most natural thing in the world, that he could only be their regular customer Colonel Redl, and he had just gone back to the Hotel Klomser.

The detective in charge of the case froze. The mystery was solved. Colonel Redl, the top espionage chief in the Austrian army, was also a spy in the pay of Russia. He had not only sold Austrian secrets and the army's marching plan, it also instantly became clear why, over the last year, the Austrian agents he sent to Russia had been regularly arrested, tried and found guilty. Frantic telephone conversations began, finally reaching Franz Conrad von Hötzendorf, Chief of General Staff of the Austrian army. An eyewitness of this scene told me that on hearing the first few words he turned white as a sheet. Phone calls to the Hofburg palace ensued, discussion following discussion. What should be done next? The police had now made sure that Colonel Redl could not get away. When he was leaving the Hotel Klomser, and was giving the hotel porter some instructions, a detective unobtrusively approached him, offered him the pocketknife and asked, in civil tones, "Did you happen to leave this pocketknife in your cab, Colonel?" At that moment Redl knew that the game was up. Wherever he turned, he saw the familiar faces of secret policemen keeping watch on him, and when he returned to the hotel, two officers followed him up to his room and put a revolver down in front of him, for by now a decision had been reached in the Hofburg—the end of an affair showing the Austrian army in such an ignominious light would be best hushed up. The two officers stayed on duty outside Redl's room in the Hotel Klomser until two in the morning. Only then did they hear the sound of the revolver being fired inside the room.

Next day a brief obituary of the highly regarded officer Colonel Redl, who had died suddenly, appeared in the evening papers. But too many people had been involved in tracking him down for the secret to be kept. Gradually, moreover, details that explained a great deal in psychological terms came to light. Unknown to any of his superiors or colleagues, Colonel Redl's proclivities had been homosexual, and for years he had been a victim of blackmailers who finally drove him to this desperate means of extricating himself from their toils. A shudder of horror passed through the entire army. Everyone knew that if war came, this one man could have cost the country the lives of hundreds of thousands, bringing the monarchy to the brink of the abyss. Only then did we Austrians realise how very close we had been to world war already during the past year.

That was the first time I felt terror take me by the throat. Next day I happened to meet Bertha von Suttner, the generous and magnificent Cassandra of our times. An aristocrat from one of the first families in the land, in her early youth she had seen the horrors of the Austro-Prussian War of 1866 come close to their hereditary castle in Bohemia. With the passion of a Florence Nightingale, she saw only one task in life for herself—preventing a second war, preventing war in general. She wrote a novel entitled *Die Waffen nieder*—Lay Down Your Arms—which was an international success; she organised countless pacifist meetings, and the great triumph of her life was that she aroused the conscience of Alfred Nobel, the inventor of dynamite. He was induced to make up for the damage his invention had done by setting up the Nobel Peace Prize to foster international understanding. She came towards me in a state of great agitation. "People don't realise what's going on," she cried out loud in the street, although she usually spoke in quiet, kindly and composed tones. War was so close, and they were hiding everything from us and keeping it secret as usual. "Why don't you young people do something? It's more your business than anyone's! Resist, close ranks! Don't keep leaving everything to a few old women like us. No one listens to us!"

I told her that I was going to Paris, and perhaps we could try to draw up a joint manifesto there.

"Why 'perhaps'?" she urged me. "Things look worse than ever, the wheels have begun turning." Uneasy as I was myself, I had difficulty in calming her down.

But it was in France that a second, personal episode was to remind me how prophetically the old lady, who was not taken very seriously in Vienna, had foreseen the future. It was a very small incident, but it made a powerful impression on me. In the spring of 1914 I had left Paris, with a woman friend, to spend a few days in Touraine, where we were going to see the grave of Leonardo da Vinci. We had walked along the banks of the Loire in mild, sunny weather, and were pleasantly weary by evening. So we decided to go to the cinema in the rather sleepy town of Tours, where I had already paid my respects to the house in which Balzac was born.

It was a small suburban cinema, not at all like our modern picture palaces made of chromium and shining glass. Only a hall perfunctorily adapted for the purpose, and full of labourers, soldiers, market women, a crowd of ordinary people enjoying a gossip and blowing clouds of Scaferlati and Caporal tobacco smoke into the air, in defiance of a No Smoking sign. First on the screen came a newsreel—'News From All Over the World'. A boat race in England; the people talked and laughed. Then a French military parade, and again the audience took little notice. But the third item was entitled: 'Kaiser Wilhelm Visits Emperor Franz Joseph in Vienna'. Suddenly I saw on the screen the familiar platform of the Westbahnhof in Vienna, an ugly railway station building, along with a few policemen waiting for the train to come in. Then a signal was given, and old Emperor Franz Joseph walked past the guard of honour to welcome his guest. As the old Emperor appeared on the screen, stooping slightly and not entirely steady on his feet as he passed the line of men, the audience in Tours smiled kindly at the old gentleman with his white side whiskers. Then there was a picture of the train coming in, the first, the second and the third carriages. The door of the saloon car was opened, and out stepped Wilhelm II, the ends of his moustache bristling, wearing the uniform of an Austrian general.

At the moment when Kaiser Wilhelm appeared in the picture a storm of whistling and stamping broke out entirely spontaneously in the dark hall. Everyone was shouting and whistling, men, women and children all jeering as if they had been personally insulted. For a second the kindly people of Tours, who knew nothing about the world beyond what was in their newspapers, were out of their minds. I was horrified, deeply horrified. For I felt how far the poisoning of minds must have gone, after years and years of hate propaganda, if even here in a small provincial city the guileless citizens and soldiers had been roused to fury against the Kaiser and Germany—such fury that even a brief glimpse on the screen could provoke such an outburst. It was only a second, a single second. All was forgotten once other pictures were shown. The audience laughed heartily at the comedy that now followed, slapping their knees loudly with delight. Only a second, yes, but it showed me how easy it could be to whip up bad feeling on both sides at a moment of serious crisis, in spite of all attempts to restore understanding, in spite of our own efforts.

The entire evening was spoilt for me. I couldn't sleep. If it had happened in Paris, it would have made me just as uneasy, but it would not have shaken me so much. However, seeing how far hatred had eaten into the kindly, simple people here in the depths of the provinces made me shudder. In the next few days I told the story of this episode to many friends. Most of them didn't take it seriously. "Remember how we French mocked stout old Queen Victoria, and two years later came the Entente Cordiale with Britain. You don't know the French; they don't feel deeply about politics." Only Rolland saw it in a different light. "The simpler the people, the easier it is to win them over. Things have looked bad since Poincaré was elected. His journey to Petersburg will not be a pleasure jaunt." We talked for a long time about the International Socialist Congress that had been fixed for that summer in Vienna, but here too Rolland was more sceptical than most. "Who knows how many will stand firm once the posters ordering mobilisation go up? We have entered a time of mass emotion, crowd hysteria, and we cannot see yet what power it will have if war comes."

But, as I said earlier, such moments of anxiety passed by like gossamer blowing in the wind. We did think of war now and then, but in much the same way as one sometimes thinks of death—a possibility but probably far away. And Paris was too beautiful at that time, and we ourselves too young and happy to think of it much. I still remember a delightfully farcical ceremony devised by Jules Romains in which the idea of a *prince des poètes* was to be superseded by the crowning of a *prince des penseurs*, a good if rather simple-minded man who let the students lead him to the statue of Rodin's *Thinker* outside the Panthéon. In the evening we made merry like schoolboys at a parody of a banquet. The trees were in blossom, the air was sweet and mild; who wanted to think of something as unimaginable as war in the face of so many pleasures?

My friends were more my friends than ever, and I was making new friends too in a foreign land—an 'enemy' land. The city was more carefree than ever before, and we loved its freedom from care along with our own. In those final days I went with Verhaeren to Rouen, where he was to give a reading. That night we stood outside the cathedral, its spires gleaming magically in the moonlight—did such mild miracles belong to only one fatherland, didn't they belong to us all? At Rouen station, where one of the railway engines he had celebrated in verse was to crush him two years later,[7] we said our goodbyes. Verhaeren embraced me. "I'll see you on the first of August at Caillou qui Bique!" I promised to be there. I visited him at his place in the country every year to translate his new poems, working in close collaboration with him, so why not this year too? I said goodbye to my other friends without a care, goodbye to Paris, an unsentimental goodbye such as you say to your own house when you are just going away for a few weeks. My plan for the next few months was clear. I was off to Austria, to somewhere secluded in the country to get on with my work on Dostoevsky (which as things turned out could not be published until five years later), and thus complete my book on *Three Masters of Their Destiny*, depicting three great nations through the work of their greatest novelists. Then I would visit Verhaeren, and perhaps make my long-planned journey to Russia in winter, to form a group there as part of our movement for intellectual understanding. All lay plain and clear before me in this, my thirty-second year; that radiant summer the world offered itself like a delicious fruit. And I loved it for the sake of what it was now, and what it would be in an even greater future.

Then, on 28th June 1914, a shot was fired in Sarajevo, the shot that in a single second was to shatter the world of security and creative reason in which we had been reared, where we had grown up and were at home, as if it were a hollow clay pot breaking into a thousand pieces.

NOTES

1   This Zeppelin was the fourth model of the rigid airships developed by Count Ferdinand von Zeppelin through the last years of the nineteenth century; the first took to the air in 1900. The one described by Zweig, LZ 4, landed at Echterdingen near Stuttgart in 1906 to satisfy the requirements of the German army, which was thinking of buying it. But it then tore away from its moorings in the air and was wrecked. Luckily there was no one inside it at the time.

2   Cyrenaica, a region of modern Libya occupied by Italy in 1911.

3   René Arcos, 1881-1959, French poet and novelist.

4   *The Market in the Square*, the subtitle of the first of Romain Rolland's ten novels in the *Jean-Christophe* series. It was published in 1908.

5   The magazine in which Rolland's *Jean-Christophe* novels were first published in serial form.

6   Also known as the Saverne Affair, from Saverne (in German Zabern) in Alsace, where incidents illustrating Prussian militarism foreshadowed the Great War.

7   Emile Verhaeren was run over by a train and died at Rouen station in 1916.

THE FIRST HOURS OF THE 1914 WAR

E VEN WITHOUT THE DISASTER it brought down on the whole
of Europe, that summer of 1914 would have been unforgettable. I have seldom known a summer more luscious, more
beautiful, I am tempted to say more *summery*. The sky was a silken
blue day after day, the air was soft and sultry, the meadows warm
and fragrant, the woods dark and lush with young green growth.
Even today, when I say the word 'summer', I instinctively think
of the glorious July days that I spent in Baden near Vienna that
year. I had gone to stay quietly there, in the romantic little spa
town that Beethoven liked to visit in summer. I was planning to
concentrate entirely on work for that month, and then spend
the rest of the summer with my revered friend Verhaeren at
his little house in the Belgian countryside. When you are staying in Baden, you do not have to go out of the town to enjoy
the landscape. Beautiful woods, covering the gently rolling hills
nearby, make their way imperceptibly in among the low-built,
Biedermeier houses, which still have the simplicity and charm of
Beethoven's time. You can sit out of doors when you visit a café
or restaurant, mingling as you please with the cheerful guests
relaxing at the spa resort, promenading in the park or losing their
way as they stroll along secluded woodland paths.

It was 29th June, celebrated by staunchly Catholic Austria
as the Feast of St Peter and St Paul, and the day before a great
many visitors had arrived from Vienna. In pale summer clothes,
happy and carefree, the crowd walked around the spa park to
the sound of music. The day was mild, there was not a cloud in

the sky above the spreading chestnut trees, it was a day to feel happy. Soon it would be the holiday season for these people and their children, and with this first festival of summer they were looking forward, so to speak, to the whole season with its delightful air, lush green leaves, and a chance to forget all their daily anxieties. At the time I was sitting a little way off from the crowd in the spa park, reading a book with interest and close attention. I still remember what book it was—Mereshkovski's *Tolstoy and Dostoevsky.* Yet the wind in the trees, the birdsong and the music wafting through the air from the park still made their way into my mind. I clearly heard the melody of the music without letting it distract me, for the ear is so adaptable that when there is a continuous noise, for instance the thunder of traffic in the street or the babbling of a brook, the conscious mind will have adjusted to it within a few minutes, and after that only an unexpected break in the rhythm will attract the hearer's attention.

So my mind was instinctively distracted from my reading when the music abruptly stopped. I did not know what musical piece the spa band had been playing, I only sensed that the music had suddenly broken off, and I automatically looked up from my book. A change also seemed to come over the crowd promenading among the trees like a single pale entity flowing along. It too stopped walking up and down. Something must have happened. I stood up and saw the musicians leaving the bandstand. That was strange as well, because the band usually performed for an hour or more. There must be some reason why it had stopped so abruptly. Coming closer, I saw that excited groups of people were crowding around a communiqué that had just been pinned up on the bandstand. A few minutes later I discovered that it was the text of the telegram announcing that His Imperial Highness Franz Ferdinand, the heir to the throne, and his wife, both of them in Bosnia to inspect military manoeuvres, had been the victims of a political assassination in Sarajevo.

More and more people came up, thronging around this notice. The unexpected news passed from mouth to mouth. But to be honest, there was no special shock or dismay to be seen on the faces of the crowd, for the heir to the throne had not by any means been popular. I still remember another day, in my earliest childhood, when Crown Prince Rudolf, the Emperor's only son, was found shot dead at Mayerling. Then, the whole city had been in emotional turmoil, and enormous crowds had gone to see him lying in state, expressing their overwhelming sympathy for the Emperor and their horror at the idea that his only son and heir, of whom the nation had cherished great expectations as a progressive member of the Habsburg dynasty who was personally unusually likeable, had died in the prime of life. Franz Ferdinand, however, lacked what mattered most for anyone to win true popularity in Austria—an attractive personality, natural charm and a friendly manner. I had often seen him at the theatre. He sat there in his box, a powerful, broad figure with cold, fixed eyes, never casting a single friendly glance at the audience, or encouraging the actors by applauding them warmly. You never saw him smile, no photograph showed him in a relaxed mood. He had no feeling for music and no sense of humour, and his wife looked just as unapproachable. There was a chilly aura around the couple. It was common knowledge that they had no friends, and that the old Emperor heartily disliked his heir, who was not tactful enough to conceal his impatience to come to the throne and begin his reign. And my almost eerie presentiment that this man with the bulldog neck and cold, staring eyes would bring some kind of misfortune on us was not peculiar to me, but widespread in the country, so that the news of his assassination did not arouse any deep sympathy. Two hours later there was no sign of real grief to be seen. People were talking and laughing, later that evening musicians performed in the cafés again. There were many in Austria who secretly breathed a sigh of relief that day, because now the old Emperor's former heir had been replaced by young Archduke Karl, a far more popular figure.

Over the next few days, of course, the newspapers published extensive obituaries expressing appropriate horror at the assassination. There was nothing, however, to indicate that the incident would be exploited in the cause of political action against Serbia. Initially, the death of the Emperor's heir to the throne left the Imperial House in a very different quandary, concerning the nature of the funeral. In view of his rank as next in line to the throne, and particularly the fact that he had died while doing his duty on behalf of the monarchy, Franz Ferdinand would of course normally have been laid to rest in the Capuchin vault, the historical burial place of the Habsburgs. However, after a long and bitter battle with the Imperial Family, he had married a Countess Chotek, who did indeed come from the upper ranks of the aristocracy but, according to the mysterious centuries-old tradition of the Habsburgs, was not his equal by birth, and the Archduchesses insisted that on great occasions they had the right of precedence over the wife of the heir to the throne, whose children also had no hereditary claim to the succession. In its arrogance, the Court disowned her even now that she was dead. Was a mere Countess Chotek to be buried in the Habsburg imperial vault? Heaven forbid! A tremendous intrigue began, with the Archduchesses up in arms against the old Emperor. While deep mourning for the whole nation was officially decreed, acrimony was rife at the Hofburg Palace, and as might have been expected the dead woman came off worst. The masters of ceremonies invented a story, to the effect that Franz Ferdinand's own wish had been to be buried in the small provincial Austrian town of Artstetten, and on this pseudo-respectful pretext they were able to suppress any idea of a public lying-in-state or funeral procession, with all the quarrels over rank and precedence that would entail.

The coffins of the two assassination victims were quietly taken to Artstetten and laid to rest there. Vienna, deprived of an occasion to satisfy its eternal love of a good spectacle, was already beginning to forget the whole incident. After all, the violent deaths of Empress Elisabeth and the Crown Prince,[1] and the scandalous defection from court of many members of the Imperial House, had long ago accustomed the Austrians to the idea that the old Emperor, alone and solid as a rock, would survive his entire family, doomed as they seemed to be like the descendants of the house of Atreus. Another few weeks, and the name and person of Franz Ferdinand would have disappeared from history for ever.

However, about a week later a good deal of verbal sniping suddenly began to appear in the papers, all of it reaching a crescendo too simultaneously to be entirely a matter of chance. The Serbian government was accused of collusion in the assassination, and it was insinuated that Austria could not let the murder of its allegedly beloved heir to the throne pass without any repercussions. It was impossible not to feel that the press was preparing the country for action of some kind, but no one thought of war. No banks, businesses or private citizens changed their plans. There was skirmishing with Serbia all the time anyway. Fundamentally, as everyone knew, it had started over some trade agreements concerning the export of Serbian pigs, but what did that dispute have to do with us? My bags were packed for my journey to Belgium to visit Verhaeren, my work was going well; how could the dead Archduke in his sarcophagus affect my life? It was a beautiful summer, and promised to get even better; we all felt carefree as we looked out at the world. I remember how a friend and I were walking through the vineyards on my last day in Baden, and an old workman there told us, "We've not had a summer like this many a long year. We'll have a great vintage if the weather holds. Ah, folks will remember this summer for a long while to come!"

The old man in his blue vintner's overall had no idea how dreadfully true his words were.

And in Le Coq, the little seaside resort near Ostend where I was planning to spend two weeks before going to stay at Verhaeren's little country house, as I did every year, the mood was equally carefree. Visitors enjoying their holiday lay on the beach in brightly coloured tents or bathed in the sea, the children flew kites, young people danced outside the cafés on the promenade laid out on the harbour wall. All imaginable nations were gathered companionably together there. In particular, a great deal of German was spoken, because as usual holidaymakers from the nearby Rhineland liked to come to the Belgian beaches. The mood was broken only by newspaper boys crying their wares by bawling out the menacing headlines of the Paris papers. 'Austria challenges Russia.' 'Germany prepares to mobilise.' You could see people's faces darken as they bought newspapers, but as yet only for a few minutes. After all, we had had these diplomatic conflicts for years, and they were always satisfactorily settled at the last moment before anything really serious happened. So why not this time too? Half-an-hour later, you could see the same people splashing about in the water again, spluttering happily; the kites rose in the air, seagulls flew overhead, and the sun shone down on the peaceful scene, bright and warm.

But bad news kept on coming, and it was more and more threatening. First there was Austria's ultimatum to Serbia, then the evasive answer to it, telegrams exchanged by the monarchs, and finally mobilisation, which could hardly be kept under wraps any longer. I could not linger in this small, remote place. I took the small electrified railway over to Ostend every day to find out the latest news, and it was getting worse and worse. The seaside visitors were still bathing, the hotels were still full, there was still a crowd of smiling, talking summer visitors on the promenade.

But for the first time a new note had been struck. Suddenly there were Belgian soldiers in uniform around the place, a sight never usually seen on the beach. By a strange caprice of the Belgian army, its machine guns were transported on little carts with dogs harnessed to them.

At the time I was sitting in a café with a couple of Belgian friends, a young painter and the writer Crommelynck. We had been spending the afternoon with James Ensor, the greatest modern Belgian painter, a very strange, reserved, hermit of a man, who was much prouder of the rather feeble little polkas and waltzes for military band that he composed than of his amazing paintings, executed in brilliant colours. He had shown us his works, if rather reluctantly—for the idea that someone might want to buy one made him comically anxious. His real dream, as his friends told me, was to sell them at a high price but at the same time be able to keep them all, because he was as fond of money as of every single one of his own works. Parting from one always cast him into deep despair for a couple of days. All the odd fancies of this Harpagon[2] of genius made us laugh, and when a troop of soldiers passed by with a dog pulling a machine gun along one of us got up and patted the dog, much to the annoyance of the officer escorting the party, who was afraid that a caress bestowed on an item of war *matériel* could detract from the dignity of a military institution. "Why all this stupid marching about?" one of us murmured. To which someone else replied quite heatedly, "Well, precautions have to be taken." "Nonsense!" I said with genuine conviction, for in that world of the past we still believed that treaties were sacred. "If something were to make France and Germany annihilate each other to the last man, you Belgians would still be sitting safely here in comfort!" But our friend the pessimist stuck to his point. There must be some reason, he said, why such measures were being ordered in Belgium. Years ago, word had gone round of a secret plan made by the German general staff—if there was ever an attack on France, the German army would advance through Belgium in defiance of all the treaties that had been signed. I was not giving way either. It seemed to me utterly absurd that, while thousands and tens of thousands of Germans were casually and happily enjoying the hospitality of this neutral little country, there could be a German army stationed on the frontier ready to invade. "Ridiculous!" I said. "If the Germans march in I'll hang myself from this lamppost!" I am still grateful that my friends didn't hold me to my word later.

But then came those last, critical days in July, and every hour brought contradictory news—news of Kaiser Wilhelm's telegrams to the Tsar, the Tsar's telegrams to Kaiser Wilhelm, Austria's declaration of war on Serbia, the assassination of Jaurès.[3] We sensed that matters were getting serious. All of a sudden a cold wind of fear was blowing over the beach, sweeping it clear. People left their hotels in thousands, there was a rush for the trains, even the most confident began to pack their bags in a hurry. As soon as news of the Austrian declaration of war on Serbia came I myself bought a railway ticket, and not before time, for the Ostend express on which I travelled was the last train to leave Belgium for Germany. We stood in the corridors, agitated and impatient, all talking to each other. No one could sit still or read; we rushed out at every station to get the latest news, imbued by the mysterious hope that some determined hand could still restrain the fateful forces now set loose. We still did not believe in war, and even less in an invasion of Belgium; we couldn't believe it because we didn't want to believe anything so crazy. Gradually the train approached the frontier, and we passed Verviers, the Belgian border station. German conductors boarded the train here. In ten minutes' time we would be on German territory.

But halfway to Herbesthal, the first German station, the train suddenly stopped in the middle of the countryside. We crowded to the corridor windows. What had happened? And then, in the darkness, I saw freight train after freight train coming the other way towards us, with open trucks covered by tarpaulins under which I thought I saw the menacing shapes of cannon. My heart missed a beat. This must be the vanguard of the German army. But perhaps, I consoled myself, it was just a safety precaution, merely the threat of mobilisation, not mobilisation itself. There is always a strong desire to go on hoping in an hour of danger. Finally the signal came, the line was clear, and the train moved on and came into Herbesthal station. I jumped down the steps from the carriage to find a newspaper and make enquiries. But the station was occupied by soldiers. When I tried to go into the waiting room a stern, white-bearded official was standing in front of the closed door keeping people out—no one was allowed in the station buildings, he said. However, I had already heard the faint clink and clatter of swords, and the hard sound of rifle butts grounded on the floor behind the carefully curtained glass panes in the door. There was no doubt about it, this monstrous thing was in progress—the Germans were invading Belgium in defiance of the statutes of international law. No, there was no more doubt of it; I was on my way into a country at war.

Next morning, in Austria, there were notices up in every station announcing general mobilisation. The trains were full of recruits who had just joined up, flags waved, music boomed out, and in Vienna I found the whole city in a fever. The first shock of the war that no one wanted, not the people or the government, the war that, contrary to the intentions of the diplomats who had been playing games of bluff, had slipped out of their clumsy hands, had now turned to sudden enthusiasm. Parades formed in the streets, suddenly there were banners, streamers, music everywhere. The young recruits marched along in triumph, their faces bright because they, ordinary people who passed entirely unnoticed in everyday life, were being cheered and applauded.

245

To be perfectly honest, I must confess that there was something fine, inspiring, even seductive in that first mass outburst of feeling. It was difficult to resist it. And in spite of my hatred and abhorrence of war, I would not like to be without the memory of those first days. Thousands and hundreds of thousands of people felt, as never before, what they would have been better advised to feel in peace—that they belonged together. A city of two million, a country of almost fifty million, felt at this moment that they were witnessing history being made, experiencing a moment that would never return, and that everyone was called upon to fling his tiny self into this ardent fire to be cleansed there of all egotism. Differences of social station, language, class and religion were submerged at this one moment in a torrential stream of fraternal feeling. Strangers spoke to one another in the street; people who had avoided each other for years shook hands. Every single individual felt his own ego enhanced; he was no longer the isolated human being he had been before, he was a part of the whole, one of the people, and his person, formerly ignored, had acquired significance. Every little post office worker who usually worked from morning to night, Monday to Saturday, sorting letters without a break, every clerk, every cobbler suddenly saw another possibility lying ahead—he could be a hero, the women were already making much of men in uniform, those who were not going to the front respectfully bestowed the romantic term of hero in advance on those who were. They acknowledged the unknown power that was raising them above their ordinary lives; even their grieving mothers and anxious wives were ashamed, in these first hours of elation, to show their only too natural feelings. But perhaps there was a deeper, more mysterious force at work in this intoxicating frenzy. The great wave broke over humanity so suddenly, with such violence, that as it foamed over the surface it brought up from the depths the dark, unconscious primeval urges and instincts of the human animal—what Freud perceptively described as a rejection of civilisation, a longing

246

to break out of the bourgeois world of laws and their precepts for once and indulge the ancient bloodlust of humanity. And perhaps these dark powers also played their part in the wild intoxication that mingled alcohol with the joy of self-sacrifice, a desire for adventure and sheer credulity, the old magic of the banners and patriotic speeches—an uncanny frenzy that eludes verbal description but is capable of affecting millions, the frenzy that for a moment gave wild and almost irresistible momentum to the worst crime of our time.

Today's generation, who have seen only the outbreak of the Second World War with their own eyes, may perhaps be wondering: Why didn't *we* feel the same? Why did the masses not burn with the same enthusiasm in 1939 as in 1914? Why did they simply obey the call to arms with grave determination, silently, fatalistically? Wasn't it the same as before, was there not even something higher and more sacred at stake in the war now being fought,[4] which began as a war of ideas and was not just about borders and colonies?

The answer is simple—they did not feel the same because the world in 1939 was not as childishly naive and gullible as in 1914. At that earlier time people still blindly trusted the authorities governing them; no one in Austria would have ventured to think that, in his eighty-fourth year, the venerated father of his country Emperor Franz Joseph would have called on his people to fight without extreme necessity, or would have asked men to sacrifice their own blood if evil, malicious and criminal adversaries were not threatening the peace of the realm. The Germans, in their turn, had read their Kaiser's telegrams to the Tsar, in which he strove to keep the peace. Ordinary men still felt a great respect for those in high places, government ministers and diplomats, and were sure of their insight and honesty. If war was upon them, then it could be only have happened against the will of their own statesmen, who could not themselves be to blame in any way; no one in the entire country was to be blamed at all.

247

Consequently the criminals and warmongers must all be on the other side; it was in self-defence that they were taking up arms, self-defence against a villainous and malicious enemy who had attacked the peaceful countries of Germany and Austria for no reason whatsoever. In 1939, on the other hand, this almost religious faith in the honesty or at least the ability of your own government had disappeared throughout the whole of Europe. Nothing but contempt was felt for diplomacy after the public had watched, bitterly, as it wrecked any chance of a lasting peace at Versailles. At heart, no one respected any of the statesmen in 1939, and no one entrusted his fate to them with an easy mind. The nations remembered clearly how shamelessly they had been betrayed with promises of disarmament and the abolition of secret diplomatic deals. The least of French road-workers mocked Daladier; in Britain any faith in Chamberlain's vision had gone after Munich, when he brought home "peace for our time" from negotiations, and in Italy and Germany the people looked apprehensively at Mussolini and Hitler. Where, they asked themselves, will they drive us now? Of course they could put up no resistance—the fatherland was at stake, so soldiers must bear arms and women must let their children go, although not now, as in the past, believing firmly that the sacrifice was unavoidable. They obeyed, but in no spirit of jubilation. Men went to the front, but not dreaming of becoming heroes; nations and individuals alike felt that they were merely the victims of either ordinary political folly or the power of an incomprehensible and malicious fate.

And what did the people as a whole know about war in 1914, after almost half-a-century of peace? They had no idea what it was like, they had hardly ever thought of it. War was a legend, and its distance in time from them made it seem heroic and romantic. They still saw it as it was shown in school textbooks and the picture galleries in museums—daring attacks by cavalrymen in immaculate uniforms, fatal shots always

248

obligingly fired straight through the heart, the whole campaign an exultant triumphal march. "We'll be home for Christmas!" cried the recruits in 1914, smiling at their mothers. Who in the whole country still remembered what war was really like? At the outside, a few old men who had fought in 1866 against Prussia, now our ally, and what a swift, bloodless, faraway war that had been, a campaign of three weeks ending before anyone had stopped to draw breath, and without too many casualties! A quick excursion into the realms of romance, a bold and virile adventure—that was how the ordinary man imagined war in 1914, and young people were genuinely afraid they might miss out on this wonderfully exciting event in their lives. That was why they impetuously flocked to join the army; that was why they sang cheerfully in trains taking them to the slaughter. A red wave of blood surged feverishly through the veins of the entire Reich. But the generation of 1939 knew about war. They no longer deceived themselves. They knew that war was barbaric, not romantic. They knew it would last for years and years, a part of their lifespan that they would never get back. They knew that you did not set out adorned with oak leaves and coloured ribbons to attack the enemy; instead, thirsty and infested with lice, you vegetated for weeks on end in trenches and military quarters waiting to be smashed to pieces or mutilated from a distance, without ever having set eyes on your adversary. You knew in advance from the newspapers and cinema newsreels about the new and terrible arts of technological destruction, you knew that huge tanks crushed the wounded in their path and aircraft blew women and children to pieces in their beds, you knew that a world war in 1939, thanks to its soulless mechanisation, would be a thousand times worse, more bestial ⁄ and inhuman than any earlier war mankind had seen. None of the generation of 1939 believed in a just war with God on their side any longer, and yet worse, they did not even believe in the just and lasting peace that it was supposed to usher in. They still remembered only too clearly all the disappointments the last war had brought—poverty instead of prosperity, bitterness instead of satisfaction, famine, hyperinflation, riots, the loss of civil liberties, enslavement to the state, nerve-racking insecurity and the mutual suspicion of all and sundry.

That was the difference. The war of 1939 had intellectual ideas behind it—it was about freedom and the preservation of moral values, and fighting for ideas makes men hard and determined. In contrast, the war of 1914 was ignorant of the realities; it was still serving a delusion, the dream of a better world, a world that would be just and peaceful. And only delusion, not knowledge, brings happiness. That was why the victims went to the slaughter drunk and rejoicing, crowned with flowers and wearing oak leaves on their helmets, while the streets echoed with cheering and blazed with light, as if it were a festival.

I cannot claim to have owed my immunity to this sudden patriotic intoxication to any particular sobriety or clarity of vision, only to the form my life had taken so far. Two days before the World War broke out, I had been on 'enemy' territory, and as a result I had been able to convince myself that the great majority of Belgians were as peaceable and unsuspecting as our own people. In addition, I had lived a politically cosmopolitan life too long to change all of a sudden, indeed overnight, to hating a world that was as much mine as my own native country. I had distrusted politics for years, and recently in particular I had discussed the absurdity of any possibility of belligerence countless times with my French and Italian friends. My distrust thus inoculated me, so to speak, against the infection of patriotic fervour, and prepared as I was to resist the feverish fit of the first few hours, I was determined not to let my conviction of the necessity for a unified Europe be shaken by an internecine war brought about by incompetent diplomats and the leaders of the brutal munitions industries.

As a result, I was sure in my heart from the first of my identity as a citizen of the world. However, it was difficult to decide how to behave as a citizen of my country. Although I was only thirty-two years old I had no military duties incumbent on me yet, because all the committees examining men for military service had declared me unfit for it, and I had been very glad of that at the time. For one thing, their rejection spared me a year wasted on stupid army service, and for another I thought it an anachronistic crime, in the twentieth century, to be trained in the use of murderous weapons. In any war the correct conduct for a man of my convictions would have been to declare himself a conscientious objector. But in Austria—unlike Britain—severe penalties lay in wait for conscientious objectors, and you needed a martyr's strong-minded determination to face those. My own nature, as I am not ashamed to confess frankly, is unheroic. My natural reaction to all dangerous situations has been to keep well out of their way, and I may indeed have been at fault—and not just on this occasion—for being indecisive, a charge frequently levelled against my revered master in another century, Erasmus of Rotterdam. On the other hand, at a time like this it was unthinkable for a relatively young man to wait until he was unearthed from his hiding place and sent to some place unsuited to him. So I looked around for something I could do without being involved in any violent activity, and the fact that one of my friends, a high-ranking military officer, worked in the War Archive, helped me to get a post there. My job was to act as a librarian, in which capacity my knowledge of languages came in useful, and to polish up the style of the bulletins intended for public consumption—not a very glorious way of spending my time, I readily admit, but one that seemed to me personally more appropriate than sticking a bayonet into some Russian peasant's guts. But what really made me decide to take the job was that after I had carried out my not very arduous duties, I still had time for what I saw as my most pressing obligation in this war, to work for future mutual understanding.

My position within my circle of friends proved more difficult than my position in the War Archive. Most of our Austrian writers, who had little European experience and saw life entirely from the German point of view, thought their best course was to reinforce the enthusiasm of the masses, promoting the alleged glories of war with literary calls to arms or scholarly ideologies. Almost all the German writers, headed by Hauptmann and Dehmel, thought it their duty to imitate the bards of ancient Germanic times and inspire the advancing warriors, by singing lays and casting runes, to go willingly to their death. Poems rhyming *Krieg*—war—with *Sieg*—victory—and *Not*—necessity—with *Tod*—death—came thick and fast. Writers swore to have nothing to do culturally with a Frenchman or an Englishman ever again. Indeed, overnight they took to denying that there had ever been any such thing as British or French culture. It was all slight and worthless, they said, by comparison with German art and the German nature. Scholars were even worse—all of a sudden philosophers could think of nothing better than to call the war an "immersion in steel", which would have a beneficial effect by keeping the strength of the nations from being sapped. They were joined by the medical doctors, who sang the praises of their new prosthetic limbs so eloquently that you almost felt like having a healthy leg amputated, so as to get it replaced by an artificial limb. The clerics of all religious faiths were not to be outdone and joined the chorus. Sometimes it was like listening to the rantings of a horde of men possessed, yet they were all figures whose reason, creative power and humane attitudes we had admired only a week or a month ago.

But the worst of this madness was that the majority of its proponents were honest men. Most of them were too old to do military service, or physically incapable of it, but felt it was their right and proper duty to make some kind of helpful contribution to the war. They owed what they had done in life to their language and their country, so now they wished to serve the country with its language. They would tell people what they wanted to hear—that right was entirely on one side in this conflict and wrong entirely on the other; Germany would triumph and the enemy be shamefully defeated—with no idea that they were betraying the writer's true mission of preserving and defending values in common to all humanity. It is true that, once the fumes of that first intoxicating enthusiasm had dispersed, many of them were soon nauseated by the bitter taste of their own words in their mouths. But during those first months, the more wildly you raved the more of a hearing you got, and so writers on both sides shouted and sang in a crazy chorus.

To me, the most typical and distressing case of such well-meant yet pointless ecstasy was embodied in Ernst Lissauer. I knew him well. He wrote succinct, cogent and harsh little poems, yet he was the kindest man imaginable. Even now I remember how I had to tighten my lips to hide a smile when he first visited me. Instinctively, I had pictured the author of those pithy verses, which aimed for the utmost concision, as a lean, bony young poet. But into my room waddled a stout little man, fat as a barrel, with a friendly face above two double chins, bubbling over with enthusiasm and a sense of his own importance as his words tumbled over themselves. He was possessed by poetry; it was impossible to stop him quoting and reciting his own verses over and over again. For all his absurdities, you couldn't help liking him because he was warm-hearted, honest and a good friend, and had an almost daemonic devotion to his art.

He came from a prosperous German family, had been educated at the Friedrich Wilhelm Grammar School in Berlin, and he was perhaps the most Prussian or Prussian-assimilated Jew I knew. He spoke no living language apart from German, and had never been outside Germany. Germany was the whole world to him, and the more German something was the more enthusiastic he felt about it. His heroes were Yorck, Luther and Stein;[5] the German War of Liberation of 1813-1815 was his favourite subject. Bach was his musical idol; he played him very well in spite of his short, stubby, thick and doughy fingers. No one knew more about German poetry; no one was more in love with the German language or more enchanted by it—like many Jews whose families came to German culture only quite late in the day, he believed more fervently in Germany than the most fervent of native Germans.

When the war broke out, therefore, the first thing he did was hurry to the barracks and volunteer. I can imagine the mirth of the recruiting sergeants and their men as his stout form, panting for breath, made its way up the steps. They sent him straight away again. Lissauer was in despair, but now, like other writers, he wanted at least to serve Germany with his pen. As he saw it, everything the German newspapers and military communiqués said was Gospel truth. His country had been attacked, and the worst offender—this was how they had staged the scenario in Wilhelmstrasse[6]—was Lord Grey, the perfidious British Foreign Minister. Lissauer vented his belief that Britain was chiefly to blame for opposition to Germany and for the war in a *Hymn of Hate For England*, a poem—I do not now have it before me—which in cutting, succinct verse raised the writer's abhorrence of that country to an eternal oath never to forgive England for its 'crime'. Disastrously, it was soon obvious how easy it is to set the forces of hatred working, for here the stout, deluded little Jew Lissauer was anticipating Hitler. His poem had all the effect of a bomb thrown into an ammunition depot. Perhaps no poem made the rounds of Germany as quickly as his notorious Hymn of Hate, not even *The Watch on the Rhine.*[7] The Kaiser was enthusiastic, and gave Lissauer the Order of the Red Eagle; the poem was printed in all the newspapers, schoolteachers read it to their pupils, army officers at the front recited it to their men until everyone knew the litany of hatred by heart. But even that was not enough. The little poem, set to music and arranged for a chorus, was performed in theatres; soon there was not a single one of the seventy million Germans populating the country at the time who did not know the *Hymn of Hate For England* from the first line to the last, and not long after that so did the whole world—if with rather less enthusiasm. Overnight, Ernst Lissauer had won the most fiery reputation that any poet ever did in that war. Later, it was to burn him like the shirt of Nessus. For no sooner was the war over, businessmen were beginning to trade again and politicians were genuinely making efforts to achieve a rapprochement, than they did all they could to disown a poem calling for eternal hostility to England. And to absolve themselves of any blame, they pilloried poor Lissauer, the 'England-hater', as the man solely responsible for the crazy hysteria of hatred that in point of fact was shared by everyone in 1914. All who had praised him then now turned ostentatiously away from him. The papers stopped printing his poems, and when he appeared among his literary colleagues a dismayed silence fell. Finally, deserted by one and all, he was exiled by Hitler from the Germany he loved with every fibre of his heart and died a forgotten man, a tragic victim of that one poem that had raised him so high, only to dash him down to the depths again.

But they were all like Lissauer. These poets and professors, the sudden patriots of that time, were honest about what they felt and thought they were acting honourably. I do not deny it. However, after a very short time it was obvious what terrible

255

harm their praise of the war and orgies of hatred had done. All the bellicose nations were in an overheated frame of mind anyway in 1914; the worst rumours were rapidly turned into the truth, the most ridiculous slanders were believed. Germans swore in dozens that just before the outbreak of war they had seen, with their own eyes, cars laden with gold driving from France to Russia. On the third or fourth day horror stories of eyes put out and hands cut off, anecdotes that promptly emerge in every war, filled the newspapers. How little the poor innocents who spread such lies knew that the technique of accusing enemy soldiers of every imaginable atrocity is as much a part of war as ammunition and aircraft, or that similar stories are regularly brought out of storage in the first few days of any conflict. War cannot be conducted with reason and proper feeling. It requires an exaggerated emotional state, enthusiasm for one side and hatred for the other.

It is not in human nature for strong emotion to be prolonged for ever, in either an individual or a nation, and the military organisations understand that. They therefore need artificial incitement, agitation administered like a constant drug, and it was supposed to be the intellectuals—the writers and authors, the journalists—who did their country the service of whipping up feeling in this way, with a good or a guilty conscience, either honestly or as a matter of professional routine. They had beaten the drum of hate and beaten it loud and long, until the ears of every impartial person rang with the sound and their hearts were afraid. Almost everyone in Germany, France, Italy, Russia and Belgium obediently served this war propaganda, and thereby served the mass delusion and mob hatred of war instead of resisting it.

The consequences were devastating. At this point, when propaganda had not yet become ineffective in times of peace, in spite of thousands of disappointments people of all nations still thought that everything they saw in print was true. And so the pure, fine, sacrificial enthusiasm of the first few days gradually turned into an orgy of the worst and most stupid emotionalism. Battles against France and Britain were fought in Berlin and Vienna, on the Ringstrasse and Friedrichstrasse, all of them considerably more agreeable battlefields than the real front. Any notices in French and English put up in shops had to be taken down, a 'Convent of the *Englischen Fräulein*' had to change its name because of public indignation, since it was not understood that in this context the adjective *englisch* meant 'angelic' rather than 'English'. Modest tradesmen stuck or stamped the slogan *Gott strafe England*—God punish England—on their envelopes, society ladies swore never to speak a word of French again, and wrote to the newspapers saying so. Shakespeare was exiled from German theatres, Mozart and Wagner from French and British concert halls, German professors explained that Dante had really been of Germanic birth, the French claimed Beethoven as a Belgian—in fact the cultural treasures of enemy countries were unscrupulously plundered as if they were supplies of grain or metal ore. As if it was not enough for thousands of the peaceful citizens of those countries to be killing each other at the front daily, behind the lines the famous dead of the hostile nations, who had rested quietly in their graves for hundreds of years, were abused and vilified. Mental confusion grew worse all the time. The cook at the stove, who had never left her town and hadn't opened an atlas since she was at school, was sure that Austria could not survive without the acquisition of Sandshak (a small border village somewhere in Bosnia). In the street, cabbies disputed the amount of war reparations to be demanded of France, fifty billion or a hundred billion, without knowing how much a billion was. There was no town, no social group that did not fall victim to the terrible hysteria of hatred. Priests preached from their pulpits, the Social Democrats who had branded militarism the greatest of all crimes only a month before made if anything more noise than anyone else to avoid incurring Kaiser Wilhelm's accusation of being men with no fatherland. It was the war of a naive generation, and the greatest danger of all in it was the still-intact belief of the nations in the justice of their own cause alone.

Gradually, in those first weeks of the war in 1914, it became impossible to have a reasonable conversation with anyone. The kindest and most friendly acquaintances seemed to be drunk on the smell of blood. Friends whom I had always known as inveterate individualists, even intellectual anarchists, became rabid patriots overnight, and from patriotism they moved on to an insatiable desire to annex land. Every conversation ended either in such stupid phrases as, "If you don't know how to hate then you don't know how to love properly either", or in outright suspicion. Friends with whom I had never quarrelled in years accused me to my face of being no true Austrian any more and said I should go over to France or Belgium. They even cautiously suggested that opinions such as my view that war was a crime ought to be brought to the notice of the authorities, for 'defeatists'—a word recently coined in France— were committing the worst of crimes against the fatherland.

All I could do was withdraw into myself and keep quiet while everyone else persisted in a feverish state of turmoil. It was not easy. For even life in exile—as I have come to know only too well—is not as bad as life *alone* in one's own country. In Vienna, my old friends were estranged from me, and this was no time to look for new ones. Only with Rainer Maria Rilke did I sometimes have conversations in which he showed profound understanding. We had managed to get Rilke to come and work for our out-of-the-way War Archive as well. With his over-sensitive nervous system, which meant that dirt, smells and noise caused him actual physical nausea, he would have been a useless soldier. I can never help smiling when I think of him in uniform. One day there was a knock on my door, and there stood a soldier, looking hesitant. Next moment I started up in

258

alarm. It was Rilke—Rainer Maria Rilke in military disguise! He looked pathetically clumsy, his collar constricting him, upset by the thought of having to salute any officer by clicking the heels of his boots. And as in his urge for perfectionism he wanted to carry out even this pointless formality precisely in accordance with the rules, he was in a state of constant dismay. "I've had this uniform since I was at cadet school," he told me in his quiet voice. "I thought I'd said goodbye to it for ever. And now I'm wearing it again forty years on!" Luckily there were helping hands to protect him, and thanks to a kindly medical examiner he was soon discharged. He came back to my room once, in civilian clothes again, to say goodbye to me. I might almost say that the wind blew him in, he always moved so very quietly. He wanted to thank me for trying, through Rolland, to save his library in Paris, where it had been confiscated. For the first time he no longer looked young; it was as if the idea of the horrors of war had exhausted him. "Ah, to go abroad!" he said. "If only one could go abroad! War is always a prison." Then he left, and I was all alone again.

A few weeks later, determined to get away from the dangerous crowd psychosis of the time, I moved to a countrified little suburb to begin waging my personal war against the betrayal of reason by the mass hysteria of the time.

NOTES

1   Empress Elisabeth was stabbed to death by an anarchist in 1898; Crown Prince Rudolf had already committed suicide with his mistress Mary Vetsera in 1889.

2   Harpagon—the name of the miser in Molière's play of the same name.

3   Jean Jaurès, a French socialist politician opposed to the war, was assassinated by a nationalist on 31st July 1914.

4   It should be remembered that Zweig wrote these comments, and died, before the end of the Second World War.

5   Field Marshal Count Yorck, 1759-1830, a famous Prussian military commander. Baron vom Stein, 1757-1831, a reforming Prussian statesman.

6   The street in Berlin where the Reich Chancellery stood.

7   *Die Wacht am Rhein*—The Watch (or Guard) on the Rhine—a German patriotic song dating from the mid-19th century, when Germany feared that France would try to seize the left bank of the Rhine. It was much sung in the Franco-Prussian war and again in the Great War.

THE FIGHT FOR INTERNATIONAL FRATERNITY

W ITHDRAWING INTO SECLUSION was no help in itself. The atmosphere remained oppressive. For that very reason, I was well aware that such merely passive conduct as refraining from joining in furious abuse of the enemy was not enough. After all, I was a writer, I had words at my disposal, and I therefore had a duty to express my convictions in so far as I could at a time of censorship. I tried to do that. I wrote an essay entitled *To Friends Abroad*, in which, rejecting outright the hatred for the enemy being trumpeted here at home; I addressed all my friends in other countries, saying that I would be loyal to them even if closer links were impossible at the moment, so that at the first opportunity I could go on working with them to encourage the construction of a common European culture. I sent it to the most widely read German newspaper. To my surprise, the *Berliner Tageblatt* did not hesitate to print it almost as I had written it, without savage cuts. Only one sentence—"if and when someone emerges victorious"—fell victim to the censor, because at the time no one was allowed to imply the faintest doubt that Germany would emerge from this World War as the natural victor. Even without that reservation of mine, the article brought me indignant letters from the ultra-patriotic, protesting that they did not understand how I could have anything to do with our villainous enemies at such a time as this. They did not hurt my feelings very much. I had never in my life wanted to convert anyone else to my own beliefs. It was enough for me to make them known and be able to do so in public.

Fourteen days later, when I had almost forgotten the article, I received a letter with a Swiss stamp and the censor's imprint on it, and the familiar handwriting told me that it was from Romain Rolland. He must have read the article, for he wrote: "I for one will never forsake my friends." I realised at once that his few lines were designed to find out whether it was possible to exchange letters with an Austrian friend during the war. I replied to him at once. From then on we wrote regularly, and our correspondence continued for more than twenty-five years, until the Second World War, which turned out to be even more brutal than the First, cut off all communication between the countries of Europe.

The moment when that letter arrived was one of the happiest in my life. It was like a white dove flying to me out of an ark full of roaring, trampling, raging animals. I felt that I was not alone any more; at last I was in touch with a like-minded friend. I was fortified by Rolland's great strength of mind, for I knew how wonderfully well he maintained a humanity transcending all borders. He had found the one appropriate path for a writer to tread at such a time, one that meant taking no part in destruction and killing but instead—following the great example of Walt Whitman, who had served as a nursing orderly in the American Civil War—actively bringing humane help to others. Living in Switzerland, and exempted from any kind of war service by his frail health, he had immediately made himself available to the Red Cross in Geneva, where he happened to be when war broke out, and he was employed day after day, in crowded rooms, in the fine work of that organisation. I did my best to pay public tribute to it in an article entitled *The Heart of Europe*. After the fierce fighting of the first few weeks, every kind of contact with the front had been lost. Soldiers' families in all the European countries involved did not know whether their sons, brothers and fathers had fallen, were merely missing, or had been taken prisoner, and they had no idea where to turn for information, because none was to be expected from the 'enemy'. In the midst of all the horror and cruelty, the Red Cross took on the task of relieving people at least of the agony of not knowing what had happened to their dear ones, which was the worst of their torments, by forwarding letters from prisoners now in enemy countries to their native lands. Of course the organisation, although set up decades before, had never expected to deal with a demand of such huge dimensions for its services, with the numbers of letters running into millions. More and more volunteer workers had to be taken on daily, even hourly, for every hour of waiting in torment was an eternity to the families at home. At the end of December 1914 the Red Cross had already handled thirty thousand letters, and more kept coming. In the end, twelve hundred people were crowded into the cramped premises of the Musée Rath, handling and answering the post that arrived every day. And working among them, instead of selfishly devoting himself to his own compositions, was the most humane of all writers, Romain Rolland.

But he had not forgotten his other duty, the artist's duty to express his convictions even in the face of opposition from his own country and the disapproval of the entire world now waging war. As early as autumn 1914, when most writers were competing to outdo each other in their diatribes of hatred, yapping and discharging their venom at one another, he had written that remarkable confession *Au-dessus de la mêlée*—Above the Turmoil—in which he opposed intellectual hostility between nations, and called for artists to be just and humane even in the middle of war. It was an essay that stirred up more controversial feeling than anything else written at the time, and gave rise to a whole series of articles supporting or attacking his propositions.

For this was something on the credit side that distinguished the First World War from the Second—words were still powerful then. They had not yet been devalued by the systematic lies of propaganda. People still took notice of the written word and looked forward to reading it. In 1939 no writer's expression of opinion had any effect at all, either for better or worse, nor has a single book, pamphlet, essay or poem touched the hearts of the public at large to this day, let alone influenced its thinking, but in 1914 a fourteen-line poem such as Lissauer's *Hymn of Hate* was an event in itself. The same was true of the foolish *Manifesto of Ninety-three German Intellectuals*, and on the other side of Romain Rolland's eight-page essay and Barbusse's novel *Le Feu*—Fire. The moral conscience of the world was not yet as exhausted and drained as it is today; it reacted vehemently, with all the force of centuries of conviction, to every obvious lie, every transgression against international law and common humanity. A breach of law such as Germany's invasion of neutral Belgium which today, now that Hitler has made lying perfectly natural and disregard for humanity a law, would be unlikely to be seriously condemned, had the world in uproar from end to end at that time. Thanks to an outburst of universal moral indignation, the execution by firing squad of Nurse Cavell and the torpedoing of the *Lusitania* did Germany more harm than losing a battle. It was therefore not a hopeless prospect for my French friend to speak out at a time when the ear and mind were not yet flooded by the constant chatter of radio waves. On the contrary, the spontaneous manifesto of a great writer had an effect a thousand times greater than all the statesmen's official speeches, which everyone knew were tactically and politically adapted to the expediency of the moment and at best contained only half the truth. The sense that a writer could be trusted as the best guarantor of independent opinion inspired far greater faith in the minds of that generation, even if they were to be severely disappointed. But as the military men also knew that writers were figures of authority, they themselves tried to recruit men of high moral and intellectual prestige for their own ends, to stir up feeling. Writers were expected to provide explanations of what was going on, evidence of it, affirmation, and eloquent appeals to the effect that all the wrong and evil was on the enemy side, and all the justice and truth on the side of their own nation. Rolland was not lending himself to such purposes. He did not see it as any task of his to heat the already sultry and overcharged atmosphere any further, but instead to cleanse it.

Anyone reading that famous essay *Au-dessus de la mêlée* now will probably be unable to understand its immense influence at the time, for if it is read with a clear, cool mind, it will seem that everything Rolland proposed in it is to be taken for granted as the most natural thing in the world. But those words of his were written at a time of mass intellectual insanity which we can hardly imagine today. When that article appeared, the French ultra-patriots set up such an outcry that you might have thought they had accidentally picked up a piece of red-hot iron. Overnight, Rolland's oldest friends boycotted him, booksellers dared not display the *Jean-Christophe* novels in their windows, the military authorities, who needed hate to motivate their forces, were already contemplating measures against him, pamphlet after pamphlet was published, arguing that: "What a man gives to humanity during war is stolen from his native land." But as usual the outcry proved that the full weight of the blow had gone home. There was no stopping discussion about the proper attitude for intellectuals to adopt in war now. Every one of them was unavoidably confronted by the question.

In writing these memoirs of mine, there is nothing I regret more than no longer having access to Rolland's letters to me in those years. The idea that they may be destroyed or lost in this new Deluge weighs on my mind, a heavy responsibility. For much as I love his published works, I think it is possible that later his letters will be considered the finest and most humane utterances of his great heart and passionate intellect. Written to a friend on the other side of the frontier—and thus officially an enemy—in the deep distress of a compassionate mind, and with the full, bitter force of impotence, they represent perhaps the most powerful moral documents of a time when it was a massive achievement to understand what was going on, and keeping faith with your own convictions called in itself for great courage. Soon our friendly correspondence led to a positive suggestion—Rolland thought we might try inviting the major intellectual figures of all nations to a joint conference in Switzerland, to agree on the adoption of a common and more dignified attitude, perhaps even, in a spirit of solidarity, to draw up an appeal to the world for mutual reconciliation. Based as he was in Switzerland, Rolland would invite French and other foreign intellectuals to take part, while I, living in Austria, was to sound out German and Austrian writers and scholars, or rather those of them who had not yet compromised themselves by publicly disseminating the propaganda of hate. I set to work at once. The most outstanding and highly regarded German writer of the time was Gerhart Hauptmann. With a view to making it easier for him to agree— or disagree—I did not want to write to him directly. So I wrote to our mutual friend Walther Rathenau asking him to approach Hauptmann in confidence. Rathenau declined, whether with or without Hauptmann's agreement I never found out, saying it was not yet time to talk about peace between intellectuals. That really put an end to the idea, for at the time Thomas Mann was in the opposite camp, and in an essay on Frederick the Great had just put forward the German legal standpoint. Rilke, who I knew was on our side, said that on principle he would not participate in any joint public action. Dehmel, once a socialist, was now signing his letters with childishly patriotic pride as 'Lieutenant Dehmel', and private conversations had shown me that I could not count on Hofmannsthal and Jakob Wassermann. So there was not much to hope for on the German side, and Rolland fared little better in France. In 1914 and 1915 it was still too soon, and for those not at the front the war still seemed too far away. We were alone.

But not entirely alone. We had gained something from our correspondence—an initial idea of the few dozen people who, in their hearts, could be counted on and thought along the same lines as we did, whether they lived in neutral countries or those at war. We could draw each other's attention to books, articles and pamphlets on both sides of the front, and we could be sure that where ideas had crystallised, new support might be attracted to them, hesitantly at first, but then more strongly as the pressure grew greater. This sense that we did not exist entirely in a void encouraged me to write more articles, so that the answers and reactions I received would bring those who felt as we did, in private or in hiding, out into the light of day. After all, I could write for any of the major newspapers of Germany and Austria, which meant reaching a wide circle of readers, and as I never wrote on the political subjects of the day I need not fear opposition on principle from the authorities. The influence of the liberal spirit of respect for literature was still very strong, and when I look now at the articles I managed to smuggle out to a wide public at the time, I have to say that I respect the magnanimity of the Austrian military powers. In the middle of the Great War, I was able to write enthusiastic praise of Bertha von Suttner, the founder of the pacifist movement, who denounced war as the worst of all crimes, and I also published an extensive study of Barbusse's *Le Feu* in an Austrian newspaper. Of course we had to invent a certain technique for conveying these unfashionable views of ours to a wide audience in wartime. If I, writing in Austria, wanted to describe the horrors of war, and the indifference to them of those not at the front, I did it by dwelling on the suffering of a 'French infantryman' in an article on *Le Feu*, but hundreds of letters from the Austrian front showed me how clearly the Austrians themselves recognised their own plight. Or we might choose the device of appearing to disagree with each other in order to express our convictions. For instance, one of my French friends, writing in the *Mercure de France*, attacked my essay *To Friends Abroad*, but in what was supposed to be a denunciation he had printed the whole of it in French translation, down to the very last word, so he had successfully smuggled it into France, where anyone could now read it, which had been our real intention all along. These signals of understanding flashed from one side of the border to the other. Later, a little incident showed how well those for whom they were meant understood them. In 1915, when Italy declared war on its former ally Austria, a wave of hatred swept through our country. No one had a good word to say for any Italian. As it happened, the memoirs of a young Italian called Carlo Poerio of the time of the Risorgimento had just been published, and in them he described a visit to Goethe. I deliberately wrote an article entitled *An Italian Calls on Goethe*, to make the point, in the midst of all this outcry, that the Italians had always been on the best of terms with our own culture, and as Poerio's memoirs had a foreword by Benedetto Croce I took my chance of writing a few words expressing my profound respect for Croce. At a time when, in Austria, no tribute was supposed to be paid to a writer or scholar from any enemy country, this was of course an obvious statement of intent, and it was understood as such well beyond the borders of the country. Croce, who was a minister in the Italian government at the time,[1] told me later that a man in his ministry who did not himself read German had told him, in some dismay, that there was an article attacking him in the Austrian enemy's major newspaper—it never entered his head that a mention of his minister could be anything but hostile. Croce got hold of the *Neue Freie Presse*, and was first surprised and then amused to find a tribute to him instead.

I do not mean to overestimate these small, isolated attempts of ours. Of course they had no influence at all on the course of events. But they helped us ourselves and many unknown readers. They alleviated the dreadful isolation and despair in which a man with genuinely humane feelings in the twentieth century found himself, and now, twenty-five years later, finds himself again—just as powerless, if not more so, against all-powerful opposition. I was well aware at the time that I could not rid myself of the real burden with these little protests and devious literary ruses. Gradually, the plan of a book began to take shape in my mind. It was to be a book in which I did not just make a few points, but set out in detail my attitude to the time and its people, to catastrophe and war.

But for a literary discussion of war as a whole, there was something I still lacked: I had never seen it at first-hand. I had now been anchored to the War Archive office for almost a year, and the reality, war in its true and terrible aspect, was in progress far away and out of sight. I had more than once been offered an opportunity to visit the front; major newspapers had asked me three times to go there as a war reporter for them. But any account I wrote in that capacity would have committed me to presenting the war in an exclusively positive, patriotic light, and I had sworn to myself—an oath that I kept after 1940 as well—never to write a word approving of the war or denigrating any other nation. Now, by chance, an opportunity did offer itself. The great Austrian-German offensive had broken through the Russian lines at Tarnów in the spring of 1915, conquering Galicia and Poland in a single determined advance. The War Archive wanted the originals of all the Russian proclamations and placards to be collected for its libraries from the Austrian-occupied area before they could be torn down or otherwise destroyed. The Colonel, who happened to know about my collecting methods, asked if I would handle the assignment. I naturally set out at once, and an all-purpose permit was made out enabling me to travel by any military train and move freely wherever I liked, without being dependent on any particular authority or directly subordinate to an office or a superior. Producing this document led to some odd incidents—I was not an officer, only an acting sergeant major, and I wore a uniform without any distinguishing marks on it. But when I showed my mysterious permit it aroused great respect, for the officers at the front and the local officials alike suspected that I must be some kind of general-staff officer travelling incognito or carrying out a secret mission. As I avoided the officers' messes and stayed only in hotels, I also had the advantage of being outside the huge army machine, and could see what I wanted to without needing 'guidance'.

My real task of collecting the proclamations was not difficult. Whenever I went to a Galician town, to Tarnów, Drohobych or Lemberg, there would be several Jews at the station, known as 'factors', whose professional business it was to supply anything a visitor might want. It was enough for me to tell one of these jacks-of-all-trades that I would like to get the proclamations and placards from the Russian occupation, and the factor would scurry off quick as a weasel, passing on the job in some mysterious way to dozens of sub-factors, and three hours later, without moving a step myself, I would have the material all collected and as complete as it could possibly be. Thanks to this excellent organisation I had time to see a great deal, and I did. Above all, I saw the wretched state of the civilian population, whose eyes were still darkened by the horror of what they had experienced. I saw the misery of the Jews in their ghettos, something of which I had entertained no idea, living eight or twelve to a room on the ground floor or in the basement of a building. And I saw the 'enemy' for the first time. In Tarnów, I came upon the first transport carrying Russian prisoners of war. They sat penned up in a large rectangular space on the ground, smoking and talking, guarded by two or

270

three dozen middle-aged Tyrolean reservists, most of them bearded, looking as ragged and unkempt as the prisoners, a far cry from the smart, clean-shaven soldiers in their neat uniforms pictured at home in the illustrated papers. There was nothing at all martial or draconian in their manner. The prisoners showed no inclination to escape, and the Austrian reservists obviously had no idea of strictly observing their guard duties. They sat with their prisoners in a comradely fashion, and the fact that they could not communicate in each other's languages amused both sides inordinately. They exchanged cigarettes and laughed. One Tyrolean reservist took photographs of his wife and children out of his dirty old wallet and showed them to the 'enemy', who all in turn admired them, asking questions with their fingers—was this particular child three or four years old? I had an irresistible feeling that these simple, even primitive men saw the war in a much clearer light than our university professors and writers; they regarded it as a misfortune that had befallen them, there was nothing they could do about it, and anyone else who was the victim of such bad luck was a kind of brother. This was a consoling realisation to accompany me on my entire journey, past towns that had been shot to pieces and shops that had obviously been looted, because bits of furniture lay about in the middle of the street like broken limbs and gutted entrails. And the well-cultivated fields among the war-torn areas made me hope that within a few years all traces of the destruction would have disappeared. Of course at the time I could not yet guess that, just as quickly as the traces of war would disappear from the face of the earth, so too the memory of its horrors could be blotted out of human memory.

And I had not yet seen the real horror of war in those first days; when I did, it was worse than my worst fears. Almost no regular passenger trains were running, so I travelled sometimes on open artillery carriages, sitting on the limber of a field gun, sometimes in one of those cattle trucks where exhausted men slept in the stench among and on top of each other, looking like cattle already butchered even as they were taken to the slaughter. But worst of all were the hospital trains, which I had to use two or three times. How different they were from those well-lit, white, clean hospital trains where the Archduchesses and high-born ladies of Viennese society had undergone training as nurses at the beginning of the war! What I now saw, shuddering, was ordinary freight carriages without real windows, only a narrow vent for air, and lit inside by oil lamps black with soot. Primitive stretchers stood side by side, all of them occupied by groaning, sweating men, pale as death, struggling for air in the dense stink of excrement and iodoform. The soldiers acting as medical orderlies were so exhausted that they swayed rather than walked; there was no sign of the immaculate white sheets of the official photographs. Men lay on straw or the hard stretchers, covered with bloodstained blankets, and in every carriage there were already two or three dead among their groaning, dying comrades. I spoke to the doctor who, as he admitted to me, had really been only a dentist in a small Hungarian town and had not done any surgery for years. He had already telegraphed ahead to seven stations for morphine, but it was all gone, and he had no cotton wool or clean bandages left to last the twenty hours before we reached the Budapest hospital. He asked me to assist him, because his staff were so tired that they couldn't go on. I did my best, clumsily enough, but I could at least make myself useful by getting out at every station and helping to carry back a few buckets of water—impure, dirty water, meant for the locomotive, but now it was a blessing to help us at least wash the men a little and scour the blood off the carriage floors. And the soldiers of all imaginable nationalities, cast up together in this moving coffin, were in additional personal difficulty because of the Babel of different languages. Neither the doctor nor the medical orderlies knew Ruthenian or Croatian. The only man who could do anything at all to help was a white-haired old

272

priest who, in the same way as the doctor feared running out of morphine, lamented his inability to perform his sacred duty because he had no oil for the sacrament of the Last Unction. He said he had never administered it to so many people in his life before as in this last, single month. And it was from him that I heard a comment I have never forgotten, uttered in his harsh, angry voice. "I am sixty-seven years old. I have seen a great deal. But I never thought humanity capable of such a crime."

The hospital train on which I travelled back came into Budapest early in the morning. I went straight to a hotel, first to get some sleep; the only place to sit in the train had been on my suitcase. I slept until about eleven, for I had been exhausted, and then quickly dressed to go and find some breakfast. But after taking only my first few steps I kept feeling that I ought to rub my eyes to see whether I was dreaming. It was one of those bright, sunny days that are still spring-like in the morning but are summer by midday, and Budapest was as beautiful and carefree as I had ever seen it. Women in white dresses promenaded arm-in-arm with officers, who suddenly looked to me as if they belonged to some army entirely different from the one I had seen only yesterday and the day before yesterday. With the smell of iodoform from the transport of wounded soldiers still clinging to my clothes, still in my mouth and my nostrils, I saw them buying little bunches of violets and presenting them gallantly to the ladies, I saw immaculate cars being driven down the streets by immaculately shaved, well-dressed gentlemen. And all this eight or nine hours by express train away from the front line! But did anyone have a right to blame these people? Wasn't it the most natural thing in the world for them to be alive and trying to enjoy their lives? Wasn't it natural for them to seize on everything that they still could, a few nice clothes, the last happy hours, perhaps out of the very feeling that all this was under threat? It was precisely when you had seen what frail, vulnerable creatures human beings are, lives capable of being shattered in a thousandth of a second, together with all their memories and discoveries and ecstasies, that you understood how the prospect of a morning spent promenading by the shining river brought thousands out to see the sun, perhaps more keenly aware than ever before of themselves, their own blood, their own lives. I was almost reconciled to what had shocked me at first. But then, unfortunately, an obliging waiter brought me a Viennese newspaper. I tried to read it, and now revulsion did overcome me in the shape of real anger. I saw all those phrases about an inflexible will to victory, the low casualties among our own troops and the huge losses suffered by the enemy—the lies of wartime leapt out at me naked, gigantic and shameless. The ladies and gentleman casually parading in that carefree way were not the guilty ones, the guilty were those using words to stir up bellicose feeling. But we too were guilty if we did not do our best to counter them.

Now I really did feel a powerful urge to do something against the war! I had the material ready to hand; to get me started I had needed only this last visible confirmation of what instinct told me. I had recognised the enemy whom I must fight—the false heroism that would rather send others to suffering and death, the cheap optimism of unscrupulous prophets promising political and military victory, keeping the slaughter going, and behind them the chorus they had hired, the "wordsmiths of war",[2] as Werfel called them in his fine poem. Anyone who expressed reservations was disturbing them in their patriotic business; anyone who uttered a warning was derided as a pessimist; anyone who opposed the war which inflicted no suffering on them personally was branded a traitor. It was always the same, the whole pack throughout history who

274

called cautious people cowards, humane people weak, only to be at a loss themselves in the hour of disaster that they had rashly conjured up. Because the pack were always the same. They had mocked Cassandra in Troy, Jeremiah in Jerusalem, and I had never before understood the tragedy of those great figures as I did now, in a time so like theirs. From the first I had not believed in 'victory', and I knew only one thing for certain—even if victory could in fact be gained at the expense of countless victims, it did not justify that sacrifice. But I was alone among my friends with these warnings, and the wild howl of triumph even before the first shot was fired, the division of the spoils even before the first battle, often made me doubt whether I myself was mad among all these clever heads, or perhaps was the only person to be shockingly sober amidst their intoxication. So it was only natural for me to describe my own situation—the tragic situation of the 'defeatist', a word that had been coined to impute a wish for defeat to those anxious for reconciliation—and I did it in the form of a play. As a symbol, I chose the character of Jeremiah, the prophet issuing warnings in vain. But I was not setting out to write a 'pacifist' drama, expressing truisms in verse to the effect that peace is better than war; I wanted to show that a man despised as weak and fearful in a time of enthusiastic feeling is generally the only one who, when defeat comes, not only endures but rises above it. From the time of my very first play, *Thersites*, I had constantly turned to the question of the mental superiority of the defeated. I was always attracted to showing how any form of power can harden a human being's heart, how victory can bring mental rigidity to whole nations, and to contrasting that with the emotional force of defeat painfully and terribly ploughing through the soul. In the middle of war, while others, celebrating triumph too soon, were proving to one another that victory was inevitable, I was plumbing the depths of the catastrophe and looking for a way to emerge from them.

Unconsciously, however, by choosing a Biblical subject I had touched on something that so far had lain in me unexploited— my common ground with the Jews and their story, founded in either blood or tradition. Were not they my people, who had been defeated again and again by all other nations, over and over again, and yet had endured thanks to a mysterious power? And was that power not the one that, through a strong effort of the will, could overcome defeat by always enduring it? Our prophets had known in advance about the constant persecution and exile that still keeps us apart today, like chaff thrown into the street, and had taken defeat as an affirmation and even a blessed way to God. Had a time of trial not always been a gain to society and to individuals? I felt that was so as I wrote my play, the first of my works that I myself thought was really worth something. I know today that without all that I went through then in the Great War, without that fellow feeling and anticipation of the future, I would still have been the writer I was before the war, *con moto*—with emotion—as the musical term puts it, but gently so, not intensely moved to my very heart. Now, for the first time, I had the feeling that I was really speaking for myself and for my times. In trying to help others, I helped myself to write what is my most personal and private work, together with *Erasmus*, in which I made my way out of a similar crisis in 1934, the period of Hitler. From the moment when I began trying to construct it, I did not suffer so deeply from the tragedy of the times.

I had not expected any visible success from this play. Tackling as it did so many questions posed by prophets, by pacifists, by Jews, and through the choral construction of the closing scenes, rising to a hymn by the defeated to their fate, the extent of the play had grown so far beyond the usual length of a drama that in performance it would have occupied two or even three evenings in the theatre. And then, how was anyone going to produce a play on the German stage that spoke of defeat, even praised it, while every day the newspapers were urging, 'Death

276

or victory!'? I could consider it a miracle if the text was ever printed, but even in the worst case, that is that it was not, it had at least helped me through the worst of those times. I had said in my dialogue everything I could not say in conversation with those around me. I had thrown off the burden weighing on my mind and recovered my true self. At the very moment when everything in me was saying, 'No', to what was going on, I had found a way of saying 'Yes' to myself.

NOTES

1   Benedetto Croce did not become a minister until 1920-21. [This note appears in the German original.]

2   *Die Wortemacher des Kriegs*, an anti-war poem by Franz Werfel written in August 1914.

277

IN THE HEART OF EUROPE

W HEN MY TRAGEDY *Jeremiah* was published in book form in
Easter, 1917, I had a surprise. I had written it in a spirit of
bitter personal protest against the times we were living through,
so I thought that I must expect it to arouse equally bitter hostility.
But exactly the opposite happened. Twenty thousand copies were
sold at once, a fantastic number for a play in book form. Not only
did friends like Romain Rolland publicly applaud it, so did some
who had previously been in the opposite camp, like Rathenau and
Richard Dehmel. Theatrical directors, to whom I had not even
offered the drama—any performance in Germany or Austria during the war was, after all, unthinkable—wrote asking me to reserve
rights to its premiere for them once peace came. Even my pro-war
opponents were civil and respectful. It was not at all what I had
expected.

What had happened? Nothing, except that the war had now
been going on for two-and-a-half years. Time had done its work,
bringing cruel sobriety. After the terrible bloodletting on the
battlefields, the fever began to die down. People looked war in
the face with cooler, harder eyes than in those first months of
enthusiasm, and their sense of solidarity began to weaken, since
no one could see any sign of the great 'moral cleansing' that
philosophers and writers had so grandiloquently proclaimed.
A deep rift ran right through the nation; the country could be
said to have fallen apart into two different worlds. First came
the world of the soldiers who fought and suffered the most cruel
deprivation, then the world of those who had stayed at home and

went on living their old lives, going to the theatre and still making money out of the misery of others. The world at the front and the world behind the lines presented a sharper contrast than ever. A frenzy of protectionism, wearing a hundred disguises, had made its way through the doors of the civil service offices; everyone knew that money or good connections could still bring profitable orders for some people, while farmers or labourers, already shot half to pieces, were driven back to the trenches. Everyone began ruthlessly looking after his own interests as best he could. Essential everyday items grew more expensive daily, thanks to shameless deals done by middlemen, food was getting scarcer and scarcer, and above the grey morass of general wretchedness there hovered, like a will-o'-the-wisp, the phosphorescent light of the provocative luxury in which war profiteers lived. Embittered distrust began to take hold of people's minds—distrust of the currency, which was rapidly losing value, distrust of the generals, the officers, the diplomats. distrust of every announcement made by the state or the general staff, distrust of the news and the newspapers, distrust of the war itself and its alleged necessity. So it was not the literary merit of my play that brought it this surprising success; I had only put what no one else dared say openly into words: they hated the war, they would distrust even victory.

However, to express such sentiments in words spoken live on stage was surely impossible. There would inevitably have been demonstrations, so I felt it likely that I could not hope to see this first anti-war play performed while the war was still going on. Then, suddenly, I had a letter from the director of the Zurich Playhouse, saying he would like to stage my *Jeremiah* immediately, and inviting me to go to Zurich myself for the production. I had forgotten that—as also in the Second World War—one small but precious German-speaking nation had been granted the grace to keep out of hostilities, a democratic country where you were still free to say what you thought and stand by your opinions. Of course I agreed at once.

At this point, clearly, I could agree to go to Zurich for the production only in principle, since I would have to get permission to stay away from Austria and my employment in the War Archive for some time. Luckily it turned out that all the countries at war had a department for 'cultural propaganda' (no such thing has been set up this time). I keep having to stress the difference between our situation now and in the countries of that time, when the leaders, the Kaiser, the Kings had been raised in a humanitarian tradition, and must have been subconsciously ashamed of the war. Nation after nation rejected the accusation of being or having been 'militaristic' as a wicked slander; instead, they vied with each other in declaring that they were 'cultural nations' and making a great display of it. In 1914, facing a world that valued culture more than violence, and would have shunned such slogans as *sacro egoismo*[1] and *Lebensraum* as immoral, they wanted nothing more badly than recognition of universally valid cultural achievement. All the neutral countries, therefore, were swamped with artistic performances. Germany sent orchestras with world-famous conductors to Switzerland, Holland and Sweden, Vienna sent its Philharmonic; even poets, writers and scholars were sent, not to praise military deeds or celebrate the annexation of territory, but simply to show, through their verses and other works, that the Germans were not 'barbarians', and produced not just flame-throwers and deadly poison gas but works of absolute value to the whole of Europe. In the years 1914 to 1918—I must emphasise yet again—the conscience of the world was still a force whose favour the authorities wanted to win; the artistically creative, moral side of a nation at war was a strength respected for its influence, the states were still competing for human sympathy and not—like Germany in 1939—simply hammering it into the ground with inhumane terror. In view of that, I had a fair chance of succeeding if I asked for leave so that I could go to Switzerland for the production of my play. At the worst there might be difficulties on the grounds that this was an anti-war play in which an Austrian writer anticipated defeat as a possibility, even if in symbolical form. I asked to see the head of my department at the Ministry and put my request to him. To my great astonishment he immediately said he would do all he could to get me permission, adding, remarkably enough: "Thank God, you've never been one of those loud-mouthed warmongering idiots. Well, off you go and do what you can to bring this business to an end." Four days later I had my leave and a passport to travel abroad.

I had been rather surprised to hear one of the most highly placed officials in an Austrian ministry speak so freely while the war was still going on. But since I was unacquainted with the secret corridors of political power, I had no idea that in 1917, under our new Emperor Karl, a quiet movement had already begun in the higher circles of government to break free of the dictatorship of the German army, which ruthlessly, and against the will of our country itself, was towing Austria along in the wake of its own frenzied expansionism. Our general staff hated Ludendorff's brutal arrogance, the Foreign Office was desperately resisting being drawn into support for extensive U-boat hostilities, which was bound to make America our enemy, even the people were grumbling about 'Prussian presumption'. So far all this was expressed only in cautious undertones and apparently casual remarks. But in the days that followed I was to discover more, and I came unexpectedly close to one of the great political secrets of that time sooner than most.

It was like this—on my way to Switzerland I stopped off in Salzburg, where I had bought a house. I intended to live there when the war was over. There was a small clique of ardent Catholics in Salzburg, two of whom were to play crucial parts in the history of post-war Austria—Heinrich Lammasch and

Ignaz Seipel. The former was one of the outstanding teachers of jurisprudence of his time, and had chaired peace conferences in The Hague; the latter, Ignaz Seipel, a Catholic priest of extraordinary intelligence, was destined to take over the leadership of our little country after the collapse of the Austrian Monarchy, and in that capacity to give outstanding evidence of his political genius. Both were convinced pacifists, devout Catholics, passionate believers in the old Austria, and thus firmly opposed to German, Prussian and Protestant militarism, which as they saw it could not be reconciled with the traditional ideas of Austria and its Catholic mission. My play *Jeremiah* had found favour in these religious and pacifist circles, and as Seipel had just gone away, Councillor Lammasch asked me to come and see him in Salzburg. The distinguished old scholar spoke to me warmly about my book, saying it upheld the Austrian ideal of working towards reconciliation, and he very much hoped, he added, that it would be influential beyond the purely literary sphere. Then, to my amazement, and with the frankness that was evidence of his courageous nature, he confided a secret to me, a man he had never seen before: here in Austria we were on the brink of a crucial turn of events. Since the military elimination of Russia from the war, he said, there was no longer any real reason for Austria not to make peace, or Germany either if it would relinquish its aggressive tendencies. This was the moment, and it should be grasped. And if the pan-Germanic clique in Germany continued to oppose negotiations, then it was up to Austria to take the lead and negotiate independently. He indicated that young Emperor Karl had promised to lend his support to this endeavour, and we might soon see what effect the Emperor's own policies had. Everything now, he said, depended on whether Austria could summon up the energy to go ahead with peace through reconciliation, instead of the principle of 'peace through victory' that the German military party demanded, disregarding any future victims of the war.

In an emergency, however, extreme measures must be taken: Austria must withdraw from the alliance before being dragged down into disaster by the German militarists. "No one can blame us for disloyalty," he said in firm, decided tones. "We have suffered over a million dead. We have done and sacrificed enough! Not one more human life, not a single one, should be thrown away in the cause of German world-domination!"

He took my breath away. We had often thought all these things in private, but no one had had the courage to say in broad daylight: "Let us break with the Germans and their policy of annexation in good time." It would have looked like disloyalty to our brother-in-arms. And here was a man who, as I already knew, enjoyed the confidence of the Emperor at home, and the highest esteem abroad because of his work in The Hague, saying these things to me, almost a stranger, calmly and firmly. I immediately guessed that a separatist Austrian action had been in preparation for some time, and was well advanced. It was a bold idea either to induce Germany to be more amenable to negotiations by threatening to make a separate peace, or if need be carry out the threat itself. As history showed, it was the one last chance that could have saved the Austro-Hungarian Empire, the monarchy, and thus Europe at that time. Unfortunately the plan was not implemented with the determination that had accompanied its conception. Emperor Karl did indeed send his brother-in-law the Prince of Parma to Clemenceau with a secret letter, to sound out the chances of peace without previously seeking agreement with the Court in Berlin, even perhaps to start negotiating. Just how this secret mission came to the knowledge of Germany has not, I think, ever been cleared up, but when it did, disastrously, Emperor Karl was not bold enough to stand publicly by his convictions, perhaps because—as is widely thought—Germany threatened to send an invading force into Austria, or perhaps, since he was a Habsburg, because he shrank from the odium

of ending an alliance concluded by Franz Joseph and sealed
with so much blood at this crucial moment. Anyway, he did
not appoint Lammasch and Seipel to the prime-ministerial
positions. This hesitation was fatal, for they were the only men
who, as Catholics with an international reputation, would have
had the strength of their moral convictions in shouldering the
odium of breaking with Germany. Both did get the prime-
ministerial post later, in the mutilated Austrian Republic rather
than under the old Habsburg Monarchy, yet no one would have
been more capable of defending an apparently unjust course of
action to the world than these important and highly esteemed
men. By openly threatening to secede from the German alliance,
or actually doing so, Lammasch would not only have saved
Austria, he would also have saved Germany from its insidious
internal danger, its boundless desire to annex more territory.
Europe today would be better off if the action confided to me
frankly then by Lammasch, that wise and devout man, had not
foundered on weakness and lack of diplomacy.

Next day I travelled on and crossed the Swiss border. It is
hard to convey an idea of what it meant then to move into the
neutral zone from a country cut off from others and already
half-starved. Changing from one railway station to another
took only a few seconds, but in the very first of those seconds
you felt as if you were suddenly stepping out of a stale, musty
atmosphere into bracing air full of the smell of snow. It was
a kind of dizzy sensation in the brain, running on through all
the nerves and senses. Even years later, when I was travelling
from Austria and passed this station—whose name I would
never otherwise have remembered—that abrupt breath of fresh
air instantly came back to me. You got off the train, and there
in the station buffet—the first surprise—were all the things
that had once been taken for granted at home but were now

285

forgotten—plump, golden oranges, bananas, chocolate and ham, which were to be had only furtively in Austria, under the counter. There was bread and meat for sale without ration cards—and the travellers, like famished animals, positively fell on the food, which was both delicious and cheap. There was a post and telegraph office from which you could write and wire uncensored letters and telegrams to all quarters of the compass. There were French, Italian and English newspapers for sale, and you could buy, open and read them without fear of repercussions. Forbidden fruit was allowed here, five minutes from the other side of the border where it was still out of reach. The absurdity of European wars was made physically evident to me by the close spatial proximity of conditions on the two sides—over there, on the Austrian side of this little border town, its placards and signs still clearly legible with the naked eye, men were being taken out of every little house and hovel, put on trains and sent to the Ukraine and Albania to murder and be murdered; here, five minutes away, men of the same age could sit at ease with their wives outside their ivy-clad doors, smoking their pipes. I could not help wondering whether the fish on the right bank of this little river at the border were also at war, while the fish here on the left bank were neutral. A second after I had crossed the border, I was already thinking differently, more freely, with more vigour and less subservience, and next day I discovered from experience how the physical organism as well as the mind suffers from being inside a war zone. I had been invited to visit relations of mine, and unthinkingly drank a cup of black coffee at the end of our meal and then smoked a Havana cigar—I suddenly felt dizzy and had palpitations of the heart. After many months of substitutes, my body and nerves were not strong enough for real coffee and real tobacco any more. Even the body had to readjust to its natural element of peace on coming out of the unnatural element of war.

That pleasant dizziness transferred to my mind as well. Every tree seemed to me more beautiful, every mountain had a greater air of freedom about it, every landscape was lovelier—for in a country at war the blessed sight of a meadow seems to the sad eyes of its people like impertinence on the part of indifferent Nature, every crimson sunset reminds them of all the blood that has been shed. But here, in a natural state of peace, Nature's indifference seemed noble, right and proper again, and I loved Switzerland more than I had ever loved it before. I had always liked visiting the country, a delightful place of inexhaustible variety within its small territory. But never before had I felt the force of its ideals so much—the Swiss idea of the co-existence of originally different nationalities in the same place without hostility, its ability to take that wisest of maxims and, by dint of mutual respect within an honest democratic system, raise linguistic and national differences to a sense of fraternity. What an example to the rest of our confused continent of Europe! A place of refuge from all kinds of persecution, the native land of peace and freedom for centuries, hospitable to all opinions while faithfully preserving its own unique qualities—how important the existence of this one supranational state was for the world as a whole! It seemed to me only right that Switzerland was blessed with beauty and wealth. No one need feel a stranger here; all free and independent human beings were more at home in Switzerland at this time of worldwide tragedy than in their own native lands. I went walking through the streets of Zurich and on the banks of the lake for hours by night. The lights shone peacefully, the citizens here still lived their lives at ease. I seemed to sense that there were no women lying awake behind the windows, unable to sleep for thinking of their sons; I saw no maimed or wounded men, no young soldiers who would be loaded into trains tomorrow or the day after tomorrow. You felt justified in being alive here, whereas in a country at war an unmutilated body seemed almost something to be ashamed of.

But my first, most pressing wish was not to discuss the performance of my play or meet my Swiss and other friends.

Most of all I wanted to see Rolland, the man who, I knew, could help me to be firmer and more active and clarify my mind. I also wanted to thank him for what his words and his friendship had meant to me in days of bitter mental isolation. He must be the first person I saw, and so I immediately went to Geneva. And now the two of us, supposed to be enemies, were in a rather complicated position. Naturally, the governments of the opposing countries did not like to see their citizens mingling on friendly terms, while on neutral ground, with the citizens of 'hostile' nations. On the other hand, there was no law against it. There was not a single clause forbidding meetings on pain of some penalty. Only business dealings, 'trafficking with the enemy', were banned and regarded as high treason, and so as not to incur suspicion of the faintest infringement of that law, we made a point of not offering one another a cigarette, because there was no doubt that we were being watched all the time by countless secret agents. So as the simplest way of avoiding any suspicion of having a guilty conscience or reason to feel afraid, we two friends of different nationalities were perfectly open about it. We did not write to each other under a cover address or poste restante, we did not steal away in secret to meet by night, but instead walked down the street and sat in cafés together in full view of everyone. As soon as I had arrived in Geneva and given my full name at the registration desk of my hotel, I said I would like to speak to Monsieur Romain Rolland, just because it would make things easier for the German and French intelligence services if they could report back saying who I was and whom I was visiting. To us, of course, it was perfectly natural for two old friends not to keep out of one another's way all of a sudden because they happened to be of different nationalities, and their nations were at war. We did not feel it our duty to act absurdly because of the absurd behaviour of the world.

So there I was in his room at last—and it looked almost the same as his room in Paris. I saw his chair and a table piled high with books, exactly as before. The desk was overflowing with journals, documents and papers. He was working in the usual plain, almost monastic cell that he created around him wherever he went—but a monastic cell connected with the whole world. For a moment I could not think of a word to say in greeting; we just shook hands. Rolland's was the first French hand that I had been able to take for three years, he was the first Frenchman I had spoken to for those three years, yet in that time we had come closer to each other than ever before. I could speak to him in French more freely and with more familiarity than I could talk to anyone in German at home in Austria. I was well aware that in my friend's presence I was looking at the most important man of our time, and the moral conscience of Europe was speaking to me. Only now could I appreciate all that he was really doing, and had done, in his fine work to promote international understanding. Working night and day, always alone, without any assistant or secretary, he kept track of everything that was going on in every country, he wrote to countless correspondents who turned to him for advice on matters of conscience, he wrote pages and pages of his diary every day. He had a greater sense than anyone else in those times of his responsibility to do what he could at a historical moment, and he felt a need to leave it on record for posterity. (I wonder what has happened to those many handwritten volumes of diaries that will one day provide a complete account of all the moral and intellectual conflicts of the First World War? Where are they now?) At the same time he was publishing articles, every one of which was an international sensation at the time, and working on his novel *Clerambault*—it all illustrated his commitment, the unceasing, constant, self-sacrificing commitment of his entire existence to the vast responsibility he had assumed of setting an example, always acting humanely and with justice in the fit of madness then afflicting humanity. He left no letter unanswered, no pamphlet on the problems of the day unread. It was this frail, delicate man, whose health was seriously threatened at this of all times, who could speak only softly and always had to struggle with a slight cough, who could never go out into the open air without a scarf and had to keep stopping to rest if he had been walking fast, who now showed improbable strength of character in dealing with the demands made on him. Nothing could shake him, no attack, no perfidy; he looked clearly and fearlessly at the turmoil of the world. I saw the heroism of his mind, intellectual and moral heroism like a memorial in the shape of a living man. Perhaps I have not described Rolland fully enough even in my book on him, because when a writer's subject is still alive he feels some reservations about praising him to the skies. Even days after seeing him in that tiny room, from which powerful influences invisibly radiated out to all parts of the world, I could still feel in my blood how shaken and, if I may say so, cleansed I had been by our meeting. And I know that the invigorating, bracing force exerted by Rolland in his fight alone, or almost alone, against the senseless hatred of millions is one of those imponderables that cannot be measured or calculated. Only we, the contemporaries who knew him, realise what his character and his exemplary steadfastness meant at the time. The moral conscience of a Europe run mad lived on in him.

In our conversations that afternoon and during the next few days, I felt the slight melancholy latent in all he said, something I had also felt when discussing the war with Rilke. He was full of bitterness against the politicians who could never get enough foreign sacrifices to satisfy their national vanity. At the same time, his sympathy always went out to those who were suffering and dying for something that they themselves did not understand and that was in fact sheer nonsense. He showed me a telegram from Lenin who, before leaving Switzerland in his famous sealed train, had urged him to go to Russia with him because he knew what a boost Rolland's moral authority would give his own cause. But Rolland had set his mind firmly against supporting any one group. He wanted to continue independently serving a single cause, the common cause of humanity. Just as he never demanded unthinking acceptance of his own ideas, he declined to be linked with anyone. Those who loved him should, he thought, also remain independent, and the only example he wished to set was to show how we can remain free and stand up for our own convictions, even against the opposition of the whole world.

On my first evening in Geneva I also met the little group of French and other foreigners working on two small independent newspapers, *La Feuille* and *Demain*—P J Jouve, René Arcos, and Frans Masereel.[2] We became close friends at once, taking an instant liking to each other in a way that usually happens only in youth. But we instinctively felt that we stood at the beginning of a whole new life. Most of our old connections were not so close any more; former comrades had been dazzled by the spirit of patriotism. We needed new friends, and as we were all fighting on the same front, in the same trenches of the mind and intellect and against the same enemy, a kind of passionate comradeship formed spontaneously between us. After twenty-four hours we were as familiar with each other as if we had known one another for years, and we were already using the familiar '*du*', as men usually do on every front line. We were all aware—*we few, we happy few, we band of brothers*[3]—of both our personal danger and the audacity of our meeting like this. We knew that five hours' journey away any German who saw a Frenchman and any Frenchman who saw a German would charge at him with a bayonet or throw a grenade at him, and get a decoration for it; we knew that millions on both sides dreamt only of annihilating their adversaries and wiping them off the face of the earth; we knew that newspaper columnists almost foamed at the mouth whenever they mentioned 'the enemy', while we, a tiny handful among those millions upon millions, were not only sitting peacefully around the same table but doing so in an honest, even a consciously impassioned spirit of fraternity. We knew how that set us against all that was official and within the rules, we knew that by declaring loyal friendship for each other we were placing ourselves in danger in our native lands, but the sense of our audacity in itself took what we were doing to almost ecstatic heights. We wanted to do something daring, and we enjoyed it, for only its daring gave our protest real weight. I even gave a public reading with P J Jouve in Zurich, a unique event for the First World War, he reading his poems in French, I reading extracts from my *Jeremiah* in German—and just by putting our cards on the table so openly we showed that we were playing our bold game honestly. We didn't mind what they thought of it in our consulates and embassies, even if it meant that, like Cortez,[4] we were burning the boats that would have taken us home. For our minds were deeply imbued by the idea that *we* were not the traitors, those were the writers who betrayed the artist's mission to humanity when it suited them. How heroic these young Frenchmen and Belgians were! Among them was Frans Masereel, carving an enduring graphic monument of protest against the horrors of war before our eyes in his woodcuts, haunting images in black and white that, in their forceful anger, are equal even to Goya's *Desastres de la guerra*. Day and night, he worked tirelessly cutting new scenes and figures out of the silent wood, his small room and his kitchen were both full of his woodcut blocks, and every morning *La Feuille* printed another of his graphic accusations. They accused not one particular nation, but our joint enemy, the war. We dreamt of being able to distribute them over cities and armies by dropping them from aircraft, like bombs, so that anyone, even without words or a knowledge of languages, could understand their grim, savage denunciations. I am sure they would have stopped the war in its tracks. But unfortunately they appeared only in that little paper *La Feuille*, which was hardly read at all outside Geneva. Everything we said and tried to do was confined to Switzerland, and took effect only when it was too late. Privately we did not delude ourselves—we were powerless against the mighty machinery of general staffs and political offices, and if they did not pursue us it may have been because we could not endanger them, since all we said was stifled and we had little freedom of action. But the very fact that we knew how few and alone we were brought us closer together, fighting side by side, heart to heart. Never again, in my more mature years, did I know such enthusiastic friendship as in those days in Geneva, and it stood the test of all later times.

From the psychological and historical—though not the artistic—point of view the most remarkable figure in this group was Henri Guilbeaux; in him, more than anyone else, I saw affirmation of the irrefutable law of history that in times of abrupt political upheaval, particularly during war or revolution, courage and daring will do more in the short term than steadiness of character. When time surges on at breakneck speed, those who can fling themselves into its torrential waves without hesitation have a head start. And at that time, the torrent raised many fundamentally lightweight figures such as Béla Kun and Kurt Eisner above their natural level to positions for which they were not really adequate. Guilbeaux, a slender, blond little man with keen, restless grey eyes and a liking for fiery harangues, was not himself greatly gifted. Although he had translated my poems into French almost a decade earlier, if I am to be honest I must describe his literary talent as slight. His command of language was no more than average, his education not profound; his one gift was for polemics. An unfortunate character trait made him one of those men who always have to be opposing something and do not really mind what. He was happy only if he could strike out like a street urchin, mounting an attack on some stronger opponent. In Paris before the war, although at heart he was a kind man, he had always been vigorous in attacking

293

various literary trends and figures. Then he moved into radical circles, where no one was radical enough for him. Now, as an anti-militarist in wartime, he had suddenly found himself a vast enemy—the Great War itself. The anxiety and timidity of the majority, while he threw himself into the struggle with bold audacity, made him important and even indispensable in world affairs for a brief moment. He was attracted to what deterred others—danger. The fact that those others would dare so little and he alone so much gave this fundamentally insignificant man of letters sudden stature, enhancing his journalistic and combative abilities—a phenomenon that could also be observed during the French Revolution among the little lawyers of the Gironde. While others kept silent, while we ourselves hesitated and carefully considered what to do or not do on every occasion, he took determined action, and it will be to the lasting credit of Guilbeaux that he founded and edited the one intellectually important anti-war journal of the First World War, *Demain*, a document that should be read by everyone who really wants to understand the intellectual currents of that era. He gave us what we needed—a forum for international and supranational discussion in the midst of war. The support of Rolland was crucial in the significance of the journal, since thanks to his moral authority and his connections he could get Guilbeaux contributors of the highest calibre from Europe, America and India. On the other side, the revolutionaries still exiled from Russia, Lenin, Trotsky and Lunacharsky, trusted Guilbeaux's radicalism, and they wrote for *Demain* regularly. For twelve or twenty months, as a result, there was no more interesting and independent journal anywhere in the world, and if it had survived the war it might perhaps have been crucial in influencing public opinion. Guilbeaux also undertook to speak up in Switzerland for those radical French groups whom Clemenceau's firm hand had gagged. He played a historic part at the Socialist Congresses of Kienthal and Zimmerwald, where those who still thought internationally split away from those who had now switched to the patriotic line. No Frenchman, not even Captain Sadoul who had gone over to the Bolsheviks in Russia, was so feared during the war in the political and military circles of Paris as little, fair-haired Guilbeaux. At last the French secret service managed to trip him up. Blotting paper and copies of documents were stolen from a German agent's hotel room in Berne. In fact all they proved was that German organisations had subscribed to a few copies of *Demain*—harmless enough in itself, since those copies had probably, in the painstaking German spirit, been ordered for various libraries and offices. But it was enough of a pretext in Paris for Guilbeaux to be described as an agitator in the pay of Germany, and a trial was held. He was condemned to death in his absence—entirely unjustly, as witness the fact that the death sentence was quashed ten years later. But soon after that his vehemence and intransigence, which were beginning to endanger Rolland and the rest of us, brought him into conflict with the Swiss authorities. He was arrested and imprisoned. However, Lenin, who liked him personally and owed him a debt of gratitude for his help at a very difficult time, rescued him by turning him into a Russian citizen with a stroke of his pen and sending him to Moscow on the second sealed train. Now he could have developed his creative powers, for in Moscow, where he was credited with all the merits of a real revolutionary, including imprisonment and a death sentence passed in his absence, he had a second chance to do good work. Thanks to Lenin's confidence in him, he might have done something positive to help the reconstruction of Russia, just as he might have done something positive in Geneva with Rolland's help. And because of his brave stance in the war, few others seemed such an obvious choice to play a leading post-war part in France in parliament and in the eyes of the public. All the radical groups considered him a truly active and courageous man, a born leader. However, it turned out that there was nothing of the real leader about Guilbeaux. He was only, like so many wartime writers and revolutionary politicians, the product of a brief hour, and after a sudden rise to prominence these unbalanced characters always fall again. In Russia, as in the past in Paris, Guilbeaux the incorrigible polemicist squandered his gifts on futile quarrels, falling out even with people who had respected his courage, first Lenin, then Barbusse and Rolland, and finally all the rest of us. He ended in a small way, as he had begun, writing pamphlets of no great significance and unimportant polemics. He dropped out of the public eye, and died in Paris soon after his death sentence had been quashed. The boldest and bravest to oppose war during wartime, a man who, if he could have assessed the chance that the times offered him and exploited it properly, might have been one of the great figures of our epoch, he is now entirely forgotten, and I may be one of the last who still think gratefully of what he did in the war by publishing *Demain*.

I went back to Zurich after a few days in Geneva to begin discussions of the rehearsals for my play. I had always loved that city for its beautiful position by the lake, overshadowed by the mountains, and no less for its fine if rather conservative cultural tradition. But because of the way peaceful Switzerland nestled among the states now at war, Zurich was no longer as tranquil as it had been. Overnight, it had become the most important city in Europe, a meeting place for all intellectual movements, although also of a wide variety of profiteers, speculators, spies and propagandists, who were regarded with justified distrust by the native population when they took a sudden fancy to the place. You heard any number of languages in the restaurants, cafés, trams and streets of Zurich; you met acquaintances whom you liked and others whom you disliked, and you found yourself willy-nilly in the midst of a torrent of discussions. For the lives of all these people, cast up here by Fate, depended on the outcome of the war. Some were here on government business, others had been persecuted and exiled, but they had all had been torn away from their real lives and were now at the mercy of chance. As none of them had any homes, they were always looking for friendly company, and because it was beyond their power to influence military and political events they discussed them day and night, in a kind of intellectual fever that was both stimulating and tiring. After keeping our mouths shut at home for months and years, it was really hard to avoid wanting to speak out; we felt an urge to write, to publish, now that we could think and write again uncensored for the first time. Everyone was strung up to a high pitch, and as I have shown in the case of Guilbeaux, even mediocrities became more interesting than they had ever been before or would ever be again. Writers and politicians of many different languages and shades of opinion met here. It was in Zurich that Alfred H Fried, winner of the Nobel Peace Prize, published his *Die Friedenswarte*—The Peace Watch; Fritz von Unruh, formerly a Prussian officer, read from his dramas; Leonhard Frank wrote his provocative *Der Mensch ist gut*—Mankind is Good; Andreas Latzko created a sensation with his *Menschen im Kriege*—Humanity at War; and Franz Werfel came to give a lecture. I met men of all nationalities in the old Hotel Schwerdt where I was staying, like Casanova and Goethe before me in their time. I saw Russians who went on to play a part in the Revolution and whose real names I never discovered, Italians, Catholic priests, intransigent socialists and equally intransigent members of the German war party. Among the Swiss, the excellent Pastor Leonhard Ragaz and the writer Robert Faesi ranged themselves beside us. I met my translator Paul Morisse in the French bookshop, I saw the conductor Oskar Fried in the concert hall—everyone was there, everyone passed by, you heard all kinds of opinions, from the wisest to the most absurd, people waxed angry and enthusiastic. Journals were founded, controversial opinions voiced, conflicts were resolved or intensified, groups formed or dispersed. I never met such a varied and impassioned mixture of people and opinions in so concentrated a form, as if it were under a head of steam, as in those days in Zurich—or rather nights, when our discourse went on until the lights were being switched off in the Café Bellevue or the Café Odeon, and then we quite often went on to wherever one or another of us was staying. No one in this enchanted world took any more notice of the landscape, the mountains, the lakes and their gentle calm. We lived for the newspapers, the latest news and rumours, opinions, discussions. And strangely enough, we experienced the war more intensely here than in our native lands which were actually *at* war, because it felt like an objective problem, separate from any national interest in victory or defeat. It was not seen from any political standpoint in Zurich, only from the European angle as a cruel, violent event that would change not just a few frontiers on the map, but the form and future of our world.

As if I already had some inkling of my own future fate, I was most moved by those of the people here who had no homeland, or even worse, had not just one but two or three, and privately still did not feel sure where they belonged. There was one young man with a small brown beard, whose keen, dark eyes were hidden behind glasses with noticeably thick lenses, and who usually sat alone in a corner of the Café Odeon. I was told that he was a very talented English writer. When I was introduced to James Joyce a few days later, he firmly denied any connection with England. He was Irish, he said. He did write in the English language, but his thinking was not English, nor did he want it to be. "I would like," he told me, "a language above other languages, a language serving them all. I can't express myself entirely in English without making myself part of a certain tradition." I didn't quite understand this. I did not know that he was already writing *Ulysses* at the time. He had lent me his

298

Portrait of the Artist as a Young Man, the only copy he possessed, and his little play *Exiles*. I thought at the time that I would like to help him by translating it. The better I came to know him, the more his fantastic knowledge of languages amazed me. All the words of every idiom seemed to be stored behind that curving, almost chiselled brow, which shone as smoothly as porcelain in electric light, and he played on those words brilliantly. One day, when he asked me how I would render a difficult sentence from the *Portrait of the Artist as a Young Man* in German, we tried to work it out together in both German and Italian. He had four or five alternatives in each language for every word, including some dialect words, and understood every nuance of their meaning and weight. There was always a certain bitterness about him, but I think this irritability was in fact what gave him the strength to be so vigorous and creative. His resentment of Dublin, England and certain people had taken the form of dynamic energy that was set free only in his writing. However, he appeared to be happy enough with his own dour disposition; I never saw him laugh, or look really cheerful. He always seemed like some dark, concentrated force, and when I met him in the street, with his narrow lips pressed firmly together, always walking fast and as if towards some particular destination, I sensed the defensive isolation of his nature even more strongly than in conversation. I was not at all surprised when, later, he wrote that extremely original book,[5] entirely of its own kind. It fell into our times like a meteor.

Another who lived like an amphibian between two worlds was Ferruccio Busoni, Italian by birth and education, German by choice. From my youth on I had loved his work more than that of any other virtuoso. When he gave a piano recital, a wonderfully dreamy light came into his eyes. His hands tirelessly made music of unique perfection, while above those hands his handsome head, tilted slightly back, listened intently to the music he himself was creating, his expression full of feeling. He always seemed to be transfigured at such moments. How often, spellbound, I had seen that luminous face as the musical notes entered into me, softly arousing feeling with silver clarity. Now I saw him again. His hair had gone grey, and his eyes were shadowed by grief. "Where do I belong?" he once asked me. "When I wake up in the middle of a dream at night, I know I was speaking Italian in my dream. And then, when I write, I think in German." His pupils were now scattered all over the world—perhaps shooting each other—and at this time he dared not go on with his real work, his opera *Doctor Faust*, because he felt too disturbed. He wrote a small, light, musical one-act work to free himself, but the cloud hovering above him did not lift all through the war. I seldom heard that wonderfully whole-hearted musical laughter of his that I had liked so much before. And once I met him late at night in the railway station restaurant, where he had been sitting alone drinking two bottles of wine. As I passed he called me over. "Anaesthetic!" he said, indicating the bottles. "Not getting drunk. But sometimes I need to anaesthetise myself or I couldn't bear it. Music can't always do it, and I can work only at good times."

The situation was hardest, however, for the Alsatians, who were torn both ways, and among the Alsatians it was hardest of all for those who, like René Schickele, were French at heart but wrote in German. The war was really about their territory, and the scythe sheared right through their hearts. They were being pulled in two directions at the same time as attempts were made to force them to acknowledge Germany or France, but they hated being confronted with an 'either ... or' dilemma, when it was impossible for them to decide. Like all of us, they wanted fraternity between France and Germany, they were in favour of reconciliation rather than alienation, and so they felt for both and suffered for both.

And all around was the throng of those whose loyalties were divided—mixed marriages, the English wives of German army officers; French mothers of Austrian diplomats; families where sons were fighting on opposing sides, and where parents on both sides were waiting for letters. Here, what little they had was confiscated; there, they lost their jobs. All these people between two camps had taken refuge in Switzerland to escape the suspicion they attracted in both their old and their new countries. Afraid of compromising those on both sides, they avoided speaking either French or German, and stole about like shadows, their lives distressed and disrupted. The more truly European someone's way of life was in Europe, the harder he was hit by the fist shattering the continent.

Meanwhile the time for the premiere of *Jeremiah* had come. It was a great success, and although the *Frankfurter Zeitung* sent a report back to Germany denouncing it, and saying that the American Ambassador and several prominent Allied figures had been in the audience, that did not trouble me much. We felt that the war, now in its third year, was losing impetus all the time, and opposition to persisting with it, on which only Ludendorff really insisted, was no longer as dangerous as in the first dreadful days when it had been glorified. The autumn of 1918 would have to bring a final decision. But I did not want to spend the time until then waiting about in Zurich, for my glance had become more observant and watchful. In my first enthusiasm on arriving in Switzerland, I had expected to find genuine like-minded comrades among all the pacifists and opponents of militarism there, people honestly determined to fight for a rapprochement in Europe. But I soon realised that among those who claimed to be refugees or martyrs to their heroic convictions, some dubious figures had smuggled themselves in. They were paid by German intelligence to question and observe others. Peaceful, stolid Switzerland, as we could all soon see from our own experience, was being undermined by secret agents from both

sides working busily away like moles. The chambermaid who
emptied your waste-paper basket, the telephonist, the waiter
who served you noticeably slowly and at very close quarters,
were all in the service of an enemy power. Indeed, one and
the same man was often working for both sides. Suitcases were
mysteriously opened, sheets of blotting paper photographed,
letters disappeared on the way to or from the post office; elegant
women smiled enticingly at you in hotel lobbies, strangely
outspoken pacifists of whom we had never heard before
suddenly turned up inviting us to sign proclamations, or asking
hypocritically for the addresses of 'reliable' friends. A self-styled
socialist offered me a suspiciously high fee to give a lecture to the
working men of La Chaux de Fonds, who knew nothing about
it. You always had to be on your guard. It was not long before I
realised how small the number of those who could be regarded
as absolutely reliable was, and as I did not want to get drawn
into politics I mixed with fewer and fewer friends. But even with
those who *were* reliable, I was getting bored by the uselessness of
their never-ending discussions and their insistence on dividing
people up into radical, liberal, anarchist, Bolshevik and apolitical
groups. For the first time I really came to understand the eternal
character of the professional revolutionary who feels that he is
raised from his personal insignificance merely by adopting a
stance of opposition, and clings to dogmatism because he has
no resources of his own to support him. Staying much longer in
this atmosphere of loquacious confusion would mean cultivating
equally confused and insecure company, and endangering the
moral certainty of my own convictions. So I withdrew. In fact
none of those coffee-house conspirators ever embarked on a
real conspiracy, and of all those who improvised identities for
themselves as international politicians, not one understood how
to come up with a policy when it was needed. When positive
action began in the process of reconstruction after the war, they
were still their old fault-finding, captious, negative selves, just

302

as very few of the anti-war writers of those days wrote anything that was much good after the war. It had been the fever of the times speaking out of them, discussing, scoring political points, and like every group that has only temporary existence and does not owe its community to anything in real life, that whole circle of gifted and interesting people fell apart as soon as what it had been working against, the war, was over.

I chose a small inn in Rüschlikon as the place for me. It was about half-an-hour's journey from Zurich. There was a view from the top of a hill over the whole lake, and the towers of the city were very small and far away. Here I need see only the guests I invited, my real friends, and they came—Rolland and Masereel. Here I could do my own work and use the time that was still inexorably passing. The entry into the war of America made the defeat of Germany seem inevitable to all whose eyes were not dazzled and ears deafened by patriotic propaganda. When the Kaiser suddenly announced that from now on he was going to rule the country 'democratically', we knew that the game was up. I will frankly admit that we Austrians and Germans, in spite of our linguistic and intellectual affinities, were all impatient for the swift advent of what was now inevitable, and in many ways it came as a relief when Kaiser Wilhelm, who had sworn to fight to the last breath of every man and every horse, escaped over the border and Ludendorff, who had sacrificed millions of men to his idea of a victorious peace, disguised himself with a pair of blue-tinted glasses and took refuge in Sweden. For we believed—and the whole world believed with us—that this had been the war to end all wars, that the beast which had been laying our world waste was tamed or even slaughtered. We believed in President Woodrow Wilson's grand programme, which was ours too; we saw the faint light of dawn in the east in those days, when the Russian Revolution was still in its honeymoon period of humane ideals. We were foolish, I know. But we were not alone. Anyone who lived through that time will remember how

303

the streets of all the great cities echoed to cries of jubilation, hailing President Wilson as the saviour of the world, and how enemy soldiers embraced and kissed each other. There was never such trusting credulity in Europe as in those first days of peace. For now at last there was space on earth for the long-promised rule of justice and fraternity, now or never the hour for the united Europe of which we dreamt had come. Hell lay behind us, what could make us fear now? Another world was beginning. And as we were young, we told ourselves—It will be our world, the world of our dreams, better and more humane.

NOTES

1   *Sacred egotism*, a phrase coined by the Prime Minister of Italy in late 1914.

2   Jouve was a French writer of the time, Masereel was a Belgian artist.

3   In the original German text, Zweig cites this famous quotation from Shakespeare's *Henry V* in English.

4   Hernán Cortez, Spanish explorer of Mexico in the early part of the sixteenth century, burnt his ships on landing to prevent any mutiny among his men.

5   *Ulysses* is obviously the work to which Zweig refers.

GOING HOME TO AUSTRIA

.

F ROM THE LOGICAL POINT OF VIEW the most foolish thing I could have done after the defeat of Germany and Austria was to go back to what was now only a grey, lifeless shadow of the old Austro-Hungarian Monarchy. Its new outline on the map was uncertain. The Czechs, Poles, Italians and Slovenians had taken back their lands, leaving a mutilated torso bleeding from all its arteries. Of the six or seven million inhabitants who were now required to describe themselves as German Austrians, two million freezing, hungry people crowded into the capital. The factories that used to bring wealth to the country were now in foreign territory, the railway network was a mere remnant of its former self, the national bank's reserves of gold had been seized, and it still had to pay off the huge burden of the war loan. The frontiers were not yet finally drawn because the peace conference had hardly begun and Austrian liabilities had not been fixed. There was no bread, no coal, no oil. Revolution or some other catastrophic outcome appeared inevitable. For all practical purposes, it looked as if the country could not exist independently in its new form, artificially imposed on it by the victorious states, and it did not want to be independent either. So said all the parties with one accord, Socialist, Clerical, and National. As far as I know, this paradoxical situation was unique of its kind: a country forced to be independent when it bitterly rejected the whole idea. Austria wanted either to be reunited with its old neighbour states, or to unite with Germany, whose people were of the same origin. It did not want to be reduced to the humiliating condition of beggary

305

in its new, truncated form. The neighbour states, however, were not anxious for any economic alliance with Austria as it now was, partly because it was so poverty-stricken, partly for fear that the Habsburgs might return. Meanwhile the Allies would not hear of union with Germany in case that strengthened their defeated German enemy. So it was decreed that the German-Austrian Republic must stay as it was. A country that did not want to exist was told—for the first time in the course of history!—that it must.

Today I myself can hardly explain what made me go back there of my own free will, at the worst time a country ever knew. But we of the pre-war period had grown up, despite everything and anything, with a strong sense of duty. We thought that now more than ever, in this hour of its greatest need, we should be in our native land and with our families. It somehow seemed to me cowardly to avoid the tragedy now brewing at home for the sake of comfort, and—especially as the author of *Jeremiah*—I felt that I had a responsibility to be there and put my writing to the service of overcoming national defeat. I had not been needed in Austria during the war, but now the war was lost it seemed to me the right place to be, and in addition my opposition to the prolongation of hostilities had given me a certain moral authority, especially among the young. And even if there was nothing I could do, at least I would have the satisfaction of sharing in the general suffering that was foretold.

A journey to Austria at that time called for the kind of preparations you would make for an expedition to the Arctic. You had to equip yourself with warm clothing and woollen underwear, because everyone knew there was no coal on the Austrian side of the border—and winter was coming. You had your shoes soled; once across the border the only footwear available was wooden clogs. You took as much food and chocolate with you as Switzerland would allow you to take out of the country, to keep from starving until you were issued with your first ration cards for bread and fats. Baggage had to be insured for as high a sum as possible, because most of the baggage vans were looted, and every shoe or item of clothing was irreplaceable. Only when I went to Russia ten years later did I make similar preparations. For a moment I hesitated as I stood on the platform of the border station at Buchs, where I had been so happy to arrive more than a year earlier, wondering whether to turn back at the last minute after all. I felt that this was a crucial moment in my life. But finally I decided to do the difficult thing, with all that it entailed, and I boarded the train.

On my arrival a year before, reaching that Swiss border station of Buchs had been an uplifting experience. Now, on the return journey, I was to have a equally memorable experience in Feldkirch. Even as I got out of the Swiss train I noticed that the border officials and police officers seemed curiously expectant. They took no special notice of us, and just glanced casually at our papers; obviously they were waiting for something more important. At last I heard the bell announcing that a train was coming from the Austrian side of the border. The policemen stood to attention, all the border officials came out of their shelters, and their wives, who had obviously been told something in advance, crowded together on the platform. I particularly noticed an old lady in black with her two daughters among the waiting crowd. Judging by her bearing and her dress, she must be a member of the aristocracy. She was visibly moved, and kept dabbing her eyes with a handkerchief.

Slowly, I might almost say majestically, the train rolled into the station—a special train, not the usual shabby, rain-washed passenger train but a train of broad, black saloon cars. The locomotive stopped. A perceptible movement ran through the watching ranks, but I still had no idea why. Then, behind the plate glass window of the train, I recognised Emperor Karl standing very erect beside his black-clad wife Empress Zita. It gave me a shock—the last emperor of Austria, heir to the

Habsburg dynasty that had ruled the land for seven hundred years, was leaving his domains! Although he had refused to abdicate formally, the Republic had allowed him—or rather, forced him—to leave the country with all due honour. Now he stood at the window of the train, a tall, grave man, looking for the last time at the mountains, the buildings and the people of his land. I was witnessing a historic moment—and it was doubly shattering for a man who had grown up in the tradition of the empire. The first thing I had sung in school was the national anthem, and later I had taken a military oath promising "obedience on land, at sea and in the air" to the man in civilian clothing who was now looking out of the train, grave and thoughtful. I had seen the old emperor many times in the now legendary magnificence of the great festive occasions, I had seen him on the wide flight of steps outside Schönbrunn Palace, surrounded by his family and the glittering uniforms of his generals, receiving the homage of eighty thousand Viennese schoolchildren standing on the huge green expanse of grass, their reedy voices rising movingly in chorus as they sang Haydn's *Gott erhalte*.[1] I had seen him in his magnificent uniform at the court ball, attending performances at the Théâtre Paré, and again in Ischl, off hunting in a green Styrian hat. I had seen him, head devoutly bowed, walking in the Corpus Christi procession to St Stephen's Cathedral—and on his catafalque on the misty, wet winter's day in the middle of the war when the old man was laid to rest in the Capuchin vault. To us, the word 'Emperor' had been the quintessence of all power and riches, the symbol of an enduring Austria, and from childhood we learnt to speak it with veneration. And now here was the old man's heir, the last Austrian Emperor, an exile leaving the country. The celebrated Habsburg dynasty that, century after century, had passed on the imperial orb and crown from hand to hand ended with this man. All of us there felt that we were witnessing a tragic moment in history. The police and the soldiers seemed

308

to be in some difficulty and looked away in embarrassment, unsure whether or not to give him the old salute of honour, the women dared not look up, no one said a word, and so we suddenly heard the quiet sobbing of the old lady in mourning, who had come Heaven knows how far to see 'her' emperor for the last time. Finally the engine driver gave his signal. Everyone instinctively jumped, and the moment that would never return had come. The locomotive started with a laboured jolt, as if it too had to summon up its strength, and slowly the train moved away. The officials respectfully watched it go. Then, with that touch of awkwardness you see at funerals, they turned back to the shelters where they transacted their business. At that moment the Austrian Monarchy that had lasted for nearly a thousand years came to its real end. I knew that I was going back to another Austria, another world.

As soon as the train had disappeared into the distance, we were told to change from the neat, clean Swiss carriages into their Austrian counterparts. You only had to set eyes on those carriages to know in advance what had become of the country. The conductors showing us to our seats looked thin, hungry and shabbily clothed. Their worn-out uniforms hung loose on their stooped shoulders. The leather straps for pulling the windows up and down had been cut off; every scrap of leather was valuable. Bayonets or sharp knives had been hacking at the seats as well, and whole chunks of upholstery had been ruthlessly cut away by some unscrupulous person who, anxious to get his shoes mended, was carrying off any leather he could find. The ashtrays had been stolen as well for the sake of their small nickel and copper content. Soot and cinders from the poor-quality brown coal used to heat engines these days were blown in through the broken windows by the late autumn wind, leaving black marks on the floor and walls of the compartment, but at least the stink of it took the edge off the sharp smell of iodoform that reminded me how many sick and wounded

309

men must have travelled in these skeletal carriages during the
war. The mere fact that the train was on the move at all was a
miracle, if a tedious one. Whenever the wheels, which needed
lubricating, screeched a little less shrilly we were afraid that the
worn-out engine was giving up the ghost. It took four or five
hours to travel a distance that used to be covered in an hour,
and once twilight came on it was pitch dark inside the train.
The light bulbs had been smashed or stolen, so if you were
searching for anything you had to grope about with the aid of
matches, and the only thing that kept you from freezing was
the fact that six to eight people had been sitting close together
from the start of the journey. But further passengers crowded
in at the very first station, and then more and more, all tired
already after waiting for hours. The corridors were crammed
full, people even perched on the steps up to the carriages, and
in addition they were all anxiously clutching their luggage and
their food parcels. No one dared let go of anything for as much
as a minute in the dark. In the middle of peacetime I had gone
back to what I had thought were the past horrors of war.

Outside Innsbruck the train's stertorous breathing suddenly
faltered, and for all its huffing and puffing it could not get up
a slight incline. The railwaymen anxiously ran up and down
in the dark with their smoking lanterns. It was an hour before
an auxiliary engine came puffing up, so that in all it took us
seventeen hours instead of seven to get to Salzburg. There
were no porters at the station, and finally a few ragged soldiers
offered help in carrying my baggage to a cab, but the cab horse
was so old and undernourished that it seemed to be leaning
on the shafts for support rather than pulling the vehicle along
between them. I could not find it in my heart to ask this poor
ghost of a creature to do yet more by adding the weight of
my baggage to the cab, and deposited it in the station's left
luggage office, though with many misgivings. Would I ever see
it again?

I had bought a house in Salzburg during the war; my alienation from my old friends because of our very different attitudes to the hostilities had put me off the idea of living in large, crowded cities. Later, too, I found that wherever I went a secluded way of life was good for my work. The geographical position of Salzburg and the surrounding landscape made it seem the best of all small Austrian cities for my purposes. It was near the Austrian border, two and a half hours by rail from Munich, five hours from Vienna, ten hours from Zurich and Venice, and twenty from Paris, so it was a good point of departure for Europe in general. At the time, of course, its Festival had not yet made it both famous and a popular summer resort for the great and the good—and the snobbish—or I would not have chosen it as a place to work in. It was still a sleepy, old-fashioned, romantic little city on the slopes where the Alps fell gently away to the plain among low mountains and foothills. The small wooded hill on which I lived was like the last wave of the mighty mountain range rolling in. Inaccessible by car—you could reach it only by an arduous climb up a path with over a hundred steps in it—it repaid you for your trouble with an enchanting view from the terrace of the house over the rooftops, gables and many towers of Salzburg. Beyond that I could gaze at the panorama of the beautiful Alpine chain—and also, admittedly, at the Salzberg near Berchtesgaden, where a then entirely unknown man by the name of Adolf Hitler was soon going to take up residence opposite me. The house itself proved to be as romantic as it was impractical. Built in the seventeenth century as an archbishop's hunting lodge, and adjoining a mighty fortified wall, it had had two rooms added to it at the end of the eighteenth century, one on the right and one on the left. There was wonderful old wallpaper, and a painted ball, one of a set, which Emperor Franz had rolled down the long corridor of this house of ours[2] during a game of bowls when he visited Salzburg in 1807. Several old documents on

311

parchment conveying the property rights to various owners bore visible witness to its distinguished past.

Our guests were enchanted later by the fact that this little castle—its long façade did make it look rather grand, although there were only nine rooms because it had no depth—was a curiosity from the old days, but at the time its historical origin presented problems. We found our home almost uninhabitable. Rain was dripping happily away into the rooms, every time it snowed the corridors were flooded, and it was impossible to get the roof properly repaired because carpenters had no timber for rafters and plumbers no lead for gutters. We laboriously covered the worst holes with roofing felt, and when more snow fell there was nothing for it but for me to climb on the roof myself and shovel it away before it came through. The telephone gave trouble; the engineers had had to use iron instead of copper wire for the connection. As no one delivered goods up there, we had to bring the least little thing up the hillside ourselves. But worst of all was the cold, because there was no coal available for miles around. Wood from the garden was too green, hissed like a snake instead of giving any heat, and spat and crackled rather than burning properly. As a makeshift we used peat, which at least provided an appearance of warmth, but for three months I did most of my work in bed, writing with fingers blue with cold, and after each sheet of paper that I filled I had to put my hands back under the covers to warm them. However, even this inhospitable dwelling had to be defended, for as well as the general shortages of food and fuel, housing was short in that disastrous year. No new buildings had been erected in Austria for four years, many houses were in a dilapidated state, and now suddenly countless demobilised soldiers and prisoners of war were streaming back and had nowhere to go, so that a family had to be accommodated in every available room. Officials from committees came to see us, but we had voluntarily given up two of our rooms already, and the inhospitable chill of our house which at first had seemed so hostile now came in useful. No one else wanted to climb those hundred steps of the path just to freeze up here.

Every foray down to the city was a distressing experience at the time. For the first time I saw, in the yellow, dangerous eyes of the starving, what famine really looks like. Bread was nothing but black crumbs tasting of pitch and glue, coffee was a decoction of roast barley, beer was yellow water, chocolate a sandy substance coloured brown. The potatoes were frozen. Most people trapped rabbits so as not to forget the taste of meat entirely. A young lad shot squirrels for Sunday lunch in our garden, and well-nourished cats and dogs seldom came back if they wandered far from home. The only fabric on sale was treated paper, a substitute for a substitute. Almost all the men went around dressed in old uniforms, even Russian uniforms, collected from a depot or a hospital, clothing in which several people had died already. You often saw trousers made of old sacks. Every step you took along the streets, where the shop windows were as empty as if they had been looted, mortar was crumbling away like scabs from the ruinous buildings, and obviously undernourished people dragged themselves to work with difficulty. It was deeply upsetting. Country people on the plain were better off for food. The general breakdown of morale meant that no farmer would dream of selling his butter, eggs and milk at the legally fixed 'maximum prices'. He kept what he could in store and waited for buyers to come and make him a better offer. Soon there was a new profession— hoarding. Unemployed men would and go from farm to farm with a couple of rucksacks, even taking the train to particularly productive areas, and bought up food at illegal prices. They then sold it on in cities for four or five times what they had paid. At first the farmers were happy with all the paper money coming in for their butter and eggs, and they in turn hoarded the banknotes. But as soon as they took their fat wallets to town to buy things for themselves, they discovered, to their discomfiture, that they had asked only five times the price for their food they sold, but meanwhile the price of the scythes, hammers and pots and pans they wanted to buy had risen by twenty or fifty times. After that they tried direct exchange for manufactured objects, bartering in kind. Humanity had already cheerfully reverted to the cave-dwelling age in trench warfare, and was now rejecting thousands of years of conventional financial transactions and going back to primitive exchange. A grotesque style of trading spread through the whole of Austria. Town-dwellers took what they could spare out into the country, Chinese porcelain vases, carpets, swords and guns, cameras and books, lamps and ornaments. If you walked into a farmhouse near Salzburg, you might see, to your surprise, an Indian statue of the Buddha staring at you, or a rococo bookcase containing leather-bound books in French of which the new owners were inordinately proud. "Genuine leather! France!" they would boast with a broad grin. Real goods were in demand, not money. Many people had to get rid of their wedding rings or their leather belts just to keep body and soul together.

Finally the authorities intervened to put an end to this under-the-counter trading, which did no one any good except those who were well off already. Cordons were set up in province after province, and goods were confiscated from the hoarders transporting them by rail or bicycle and handed over to the rationing offices in urban areas. The hoarders struck back by organising a Wild-West kind of nocturnal transport, or bribing the officials in charge of the confiscations, who had hungry children at home themselves. Sometimes there were actual battles with knives and revolvers, which after four years at the front these men could handle expertly, just as they knew the fieldcraft of taking cover when in flight. The chaos grew worse by the week, and the population more and more agitated, for financial devaluation was more obvious every day. The neighbour states had replaced the old Austrian banknotes with their own currencies, leaving tiny Austria with almost the entire burden of redeeming the old crown. As the first sign of distrust among the people, coinage disappeared, for a small copper or nickel coin still represented something more real than mere printed paper. The state might crank up the printing presses to create as much artificial money as possible, in line with the precepts of Mephistopheles,[3] but it could not keep pace with inflation, and so every town and city and finally every village began printing its own 'emergency currency', which would not be accepted in the neighbouring village, and later on, when it was recognised, correctly, that it had no intrinsic value at all, was usually just thrown away. An economist with a gift for the graphic description of all the phases of the inflation that began in Austria and then spread to Germany would, I think, have been able to write a book far more exciting than any novel, for the chaos took increasingly fantastic forms. Soon no one knew what anything cost. Prices shot up at random; a box of matches could cost twenty times more in a shop that had raised the price early than in another, where a less grasping shopkeeper was still selling his wares at yesterday's prices. His reward for honesty was to see his shop cleared out within the hour, for one customer would tell another, and they all came to buy whatever there was to be bought, regardless of whether they needed it or not. Even a goldfish or an old telescope represented 'real value', and everyone wanted real value rather than paper. Most grotesque of all was the discrepancy between other expenses and rents. The government banned any rise in rents in order to protect tenants—who were the majority—but to the detriment of landlords. Soon the rent of a medium-sized apartment in Austria for a whole year cost its tenant less than a single midday meal. In effect, the whole of the country lived more or less rent-free for five to ten years— since even later landlords were not allowed to give their tenants notice. This crazy state of chaos made the situation more absurd and illogical from week to week. A man who had saved for forty years and had also patriotically put money into the war loan became a beggar, while a man who used to be in debt was free of it. Those who had observed propriety in the allocation of food went hungry, those who cheerfully ignored the rules were well fed. If you knew how to hand out bribes you got on well, if you speculated you could make a profit. Those who sold in line with cost price were robbed; those who calculated carefully still lost out. There were no standards or values as money flowed away and evaporated; the only virtue was to be clever, adaptable and unscrupulous, leaping on the back of the runaway horse instead of letting it trample you.

In addition, while the people of Austria lost any idea of financial standards as values plummeted, many foreigners had realised that they could fish profitably in our troubled waters. During the period of galloping inflation, which went on for three years at ever-increasing speed, only one thing had any stable value inside the country, and that was foreign currency. While the Austrian crown was dissolving like jelly in your fingers, everyone wanted Swiss francs and American dollars, and large numbers of foreigners exploited the economic situation to feed on the twitching corpse of the old Austrian currency. Austria was 'discovered', and became disastrously popular with foreign visitors in a parody of the society season. All the hotels in Vienna were crammed full with these vultures; they would buy anything, from toothbrushes to country estates; they cleared out private collections of antiquities and the antique dealers' shops before the owners realised how badly they had been robbed and cheated in their time of need. Hotel receptionists from Switzerland and Dutch shorthand typists stayed in the princely apartments of the Ringstrasse hotels. Incredible as it may seem, I can vouch for it that for a long time the famous, de luxe Hotel de l'Europe in Salzburg was entirely booked by unemployed members of the English proletariat, who could live here more cheaply than in their slums at home, thanks to the generous unemployment benefit they received. Anything that was not nailed down disappeared. Word gradually spread of the cheap living and low prices in Austria. Greedy visitors came from further and further afield, from Sweden, from France, and you heard more Italian, French, Turkish and Romanian than German spoken in the streets of the city centre of Vienna. Even Germany, where the pace of inflation was much slower at first—although later it would be a million times worse than in Austria—took advantage of the falling value of the Austrian crown in relation to its own mark. As Salzburg was on the border I had a good opportunity of observing these raids on us every day. Germans crossed from the neighbouring towns and villages of Bavaria in their hundreds and thousands, pouring into the small city. They had their suits made and their cars repaired here, they went to the pharmacist and the doctor in Salzburg, big firms in Munich sent their letters and telegrams from Austria so as to profit by the difference in postage. Finally, at the urging of the German government, a border checkpoint was set up to prevent German citizens from buying everything cheap in Salzburg, where you could get seventy Austrian crowns for a single German mark, instead of in their shops at home, and all goods coming out of Austria were firmly confiscated by the customs office. However, there was one item that couldn't be confiscated: the beer you had already consumed. And every day the beer-swilling Bavarians worked out, from the rate of exchange, whether the devaluation of the crown enabled them to drink five, six, or even ten litres of beer in and around Salzburg for the price they would pay for a single litre at home. No greater temptation could be imagined, and whole troops of visitors came over the border from nearby Freilassung and Reichenhall, complete with their wives and children, to indulge in the luxury of pouring as much beer down their throats as their bellies would hold. The railway station was in pandemonium every evening, crowded

317

with hordes of intoxicated, bawling, belching and expectorating Germans. Many of them, having overestimated their capacity, had to be wheeled to the carriages on the trolleys generally used to transport baggage before the train took them back to their own country, to the accompaniment of bacchanalian shouting and singing. These cheerful Bavarians, of course, had no idea that a terrible vengeance lay in store for them. For when the crown stabilised, while the fall of the mark assumed astronomical dimensions, the Austrians travelled over from the same station to get drunk on the cheap in their own turn, and the same spectacle was repeated, although in the opposite direction. This beer war in the midst of two inflationary periods is among my strangest memories, because it clearly illustrates in miniature the entire crazy character of those years in perhaps its most graphic and grotesque aspect.

Strangest of all is the fact that today, with the best will in the world, I cannot remember how we managed to keep house in those years, when everyone in Austria had to raise the thousands and tens of thousands of crowns and in Germany the millions of marks they needed every day just to survive, and had to do it again and again. But the mysterious fact was that, somehow, we did manage. We got used to the chaos and adapted to it. Logically, a foreigner who did not see those days at first hand would probably imagine that at a time when an egg cost as much in Austria as the price of a luxury car in the past, and later fetched four billion marks in Germany—roughly the basic value of all the buildings in the Greater Berlin area before inflation—women would be rushing through the streets tearing their hair, shops would be empty because no one could afford to buy anything, and the theatres and other places of entertainment would have no audiences at all. Astonishingly, however, it was just the opposite. The will for life to go on proved stronger than the instability of the currency. In the midst of financial chaos, daily life continued almost unchanged. Individuals, of course, felt a great deal of

318

change—the rich were impoverished when their money in banks and government securities melted away, speculators grew rich. But regardless of individual fates, the flywheel of the mechanism kept on turning in the same old rhythm. Nothing stood still. The baker made bread, the cobbler made boots, the writer wrote books, the farmer cultivated the land, trains ran regularly, the newspaper lay outside your door every morning at the usual time, and the places of entertainment in particular, the bars and the theatres, were full to overflowing. For with the daily loss in value of money, once the most stable aspect of life, people came to appreciate true values such as work, love, friendship, art and nature all the more, and in the midst of disaster the nation as a whole lived more intensely than ever before, strung to a higher pitch. Young men and girls went walking in the mountains and came home tanned brown by the sun, music played in the dance halls until late at night, new factories and businesses were founded everywhere. I myself do not think I ever lived and worked with more intensity and concentration than I did in those years. What had been important to us before mattered even more now. Art was never more popular in Austria than at that time of chaos. Money had let us down; we sensed that what was eternal in us was all that would last.

I will never forget what operatic performances were like in those days of our greatest need. You groped you way through dimly lit streets, for street lighting was feeling the effects of the fuel shortage, you paid for your seat in the gallery with a bundle of banknotes that would once have allowed you to hire a luxurious box for a year. You sat in your overcoat, because the auditorium was unheated, and pressed close to your neighbours for warmth—and the theatre itself, once brilliant with uniforms and expensive gowns, was so dismal and grey! No one knew whether it would still be possible for the opera to keep going next week if money went on falling in value and there were no coal deliveries. Everything seemed doubly desperate in this scene of former luxury and imperial extravagance. The musicians of the Philharmonic sat in the pit, also grey shadows of themselves, emaciated and exhausted by deprivation, and we in the audience looked like ghosts in this now ghostly theatre. But then the conductor raised his baton, the curtains parted, and it was more wonderful than ever before. The singers and musicians gave of their best, for they all felt that this might be the last time they performed in the theatre they loved. And we listened with bated breath, more receptive than ever, knowing that for us, too, this might be the last time. Thousands of us, hundreds of thousands, lived like this. We all strained ourselves to the limit in these weeks and months and years on the brink of downfall. I never felt the will to live in a nation and in myself as strongly as I did then, when the end of everything, life and survival itself, was a stake.

Yet in spite of everything I would find it hard to explain to anyone how our poor, plundered, unhappy country did survive at that time. To our right was Bavaria, where a Communist Republic of People's Councils was now governing, to the left Hungary had turned Bolshevik under Béla Kun,[4] and it still seems to me astonishing that revolution did not also spread to Austria. There was no shortage of explosive material to set it off. Demobilised soldiers walked the streets half-starved, in torn clothes, looking bitterly at the shameless luxury in which war profiteers lived and at the results of inflation; a battalion of Red Guards was already drawn up and armed in the barracks, and there was no well-organised opposition. Two hundred determined men could have seized power over Vienna and the whole of Austria at that time. But nothing too drastic happened. Only once did an ill-disciplined group try a coup, and it was easily countered by four or five dozen armed police officers. So the miraculous became reality—this impoverished country, cut off from its former factories, coal mines and oilfields, its now worthless paper currency falling like an avalanche, asserted itself. Perhaps that was even due to its weakness, because the people were too enfeebled and hungry to fight for anything, or perhaps it was because of the characteristic, secret strength of the Austrians, their innate tendency to be conciliating. For in this darkest hour, and in spite of their deep differences, the two main political parties, Social Democrats and Christian Socialists, came together in a coalition government. Each made concessions to the other to prevent a catastrophe that would have carried all Europe away with it. Slowly, conditions began to consolidate, some kind of order imposed itself, and to our own surprise an incredible thing happened—the mutilated state went on existing, and later was even ready to defend its independence when Hitler came to carry off the soul of this loyal nation, ready as it had bravely been to make sacrifices in its time of deprivation.

But radical upheaval was averted only outwardly and in the political sense; in the minds of the people a huge revolution took place in those first post-war years. Something had been crushed along with the armies—a belief in the infallibility of those authorities to which my generation had been brought up to be so subservient in our youth. But how could the Germans go on admiring their Kaiser, a man who had sworn to fight "to the last breath drawn by man and horse", and then escaped over the border under cover of night and fog? Or their army commanders and politicians, or the writers who kept writing their patriotic verses, still rhyming *Not* with *Tod* and *Krieg* with *Sieg*?[5] Only now, as the gunpowder smoke over the country dispersed, was the full terrible extent of the devastation inflicted by the war visible. How could moral commandments be considered still in force, when for four years murder and robbery had been committed in the name of heroism and the necessity of requisitions? How could a nation believe the promises of a state that simply annulled all its duty to its citizens when it liked? And now the same people, the same clique of old, allegedly

321

experienced men, had outdone themselves, compounding the folly of the war by patching up a botched peace. Everyone knows now—and a few of us knew at the time—that the peace following the Great War had presented one of the greatest moral opportunities of history, if not *the* greatest. Wilson had known it. With far-ranging vision, he had sketched out a plan for true and enduring international understanding. But the old generals, the old statesmen, the old interests had mangled his great idea, tearing it into little scraps of paper. The great and sacred promise made to millions that this was the war to end wars, the one thing that had brought the soldiers, desperate, half-exhausted and already half-disillusioned, to draw on their last reserves of strength, was cynically sacrificed to the interests of the munitions manufacturers and the gambling of politicians, who triumphantly rescued their old, fateful tactics of secret treaties and negotiations behind closed doors from Wilson's wise and humane demands. In so far as the eyes of the world were open, it saw that it had been betrayed. The mothers who had sacrificed their children were betrayed, so were the soldiers who came home as beggars, all those who had patriotically contributed to the war loan, everyone who had believed in the promises of the state. All of us who had dreamt of a new and better world, and now saw the old game, on which our lives, our happiness, our time and our possessions were staked, about to begin again, played by the same gamblers or new ones—we had all been betrayed. No wonder a whole young generation looked bitterly and scornfully at their fathers, who had allowed themselves to be deprived first of victory and then of peace, who had done everything wrong, had foreseen nothing, and had made the wrong calculations in every respect. Was it not understandable for the new generation to feel no respect whatsoever for their elders? None of these young people believed their parents, the politicians or their teachers. Every state decree or proclamation was read with distrust. The post-war generation emancipated itself, with a sudden, violent reaction, from all that had previously been accepted. It turned its back on all tradition, determined to take its fate into its own hands, moving forcefully away from the old past and on into the future. An entirely new world, a different order, was to begin with these young people in every area of life, and of course it all started with wild exaggeration. Anyone or anything not their own age was finished, out-of-date, done for. Instead of going away on holiday with their parents, children of eleven and twelve went hiking through the countryside in the *Wandervögel* [6] groups—organised and well-instructed in sexual matters— reaching Italy and the North Sea. Schools councils on the Russian model were set up, with young people keeping a sharp eye on the teachers and making their own changes to the curriculum, because children wanted to learn only what they liked. There was rebellion, purely for the fun of rebelling against everything once accepted, even against the natural order and the eternal difference between the sexes. Girls had their hair cut in such short bobs that they could not be told from boys; young men shaved off their beards to look more like girls. Homosexuality and lesbianism were very much in fashion, not a result of a young person's instinctive drives but in protest against all the old traditional, legal and moral kinds of love. Every form of expression, of course including art, tried to be as radical and revolutionary as possible. The new painters declared everything done by Rembrandt, Holbein and Velázquez out of date, and embarked on the wildest of Cubist and Surrealist experiments. In every field, what could be understood was poorly esteemed— melody in music, a good likeness in portraiture, clarity in language. The definite article was omitted, sentence structure reversed, everything was written in abbreviated, telegraphese style, with excitable exclamations—and in addition all literature that was not 'activist', meaning based on political theory, was thrown on the garbage heap. Music persistently strove

323

for a new tonality, splitting up the notes; architecture turned buildings inside out; in dance, Cuban and black American rhythms replaced the waltz; fashion, emphasising nudity, came up with more and more absurdities; *Hamlet* was acted in modern dress and tried to express explosive drama. A period of wild experimentation began in all fields of art, in an attempt to overtake all that had ever been done in the past in a single mighty bound. The younger you were and the less you had learnt, the more your freedom from tradition was welcomed—ultimately, this was youth triumphantly working off its grudge against the parental generation. But in the midst of this hectic carnival, nothing seemed to me a more tragi-comic spectacle than the way many intellectuals of the older generation, panic-stricken at the idea of being outstripped and considered out-dated, aped an artificial wildness with desperate haste, trying to limp along and keep up with the most obvious deviations from the norm. Staid, grey-haired professors at the art academies added symbolic cubes and dice to their now unsaleable still lifes, because young curators—you had to be young now, the younger the better—were clearing all other pictures out of the galleries and putting them into store, on the grounds that they were too neoclassical. Authors who had written in good, clear German for years chopped up their sentences and went to extremes of 'activism'; stout Prussians proudly bearing the honorary title of Privy Councillor lectured on Karl Marx; former court ballerinas danced half-naked with strange contortions to Beethoven's *Appassionata* sonata or Schönberg's *Verklärte Nacht.* Everywhere, old age frantically pursued the latest fashion. Suddenly all that mattered was your desire to be young, promptly following up yesterday's latest topical trend with one even more topical, more radical and unprecedented.

What a wild, anarchic, improbable time were those years when, with the dwindling value of money, all other values in Austria and Germany began to slide! An era of frenzied ecstasy

324

and chaotic deception, a unique mixture of impatience and fanaticism. This was the golden age of all that was extravagant and uncontrolled—theosophy, occultism, spiritualism, somnambulism, anthroposophy, palm-reading, graphology, the teachings of Indian yoga and Paracelsian mysticism. Everything that promised an extreme, unheard-of experience, every form of narcotic—morphine, cocaine, heroin—sold like hot cakes, in the theatre incest and patricide featured in plays, the extremes of communism and fascism were the only subjects of conversation in politics. Any kind of normality and moderation was rejected. But I would not like to have missed experiencing that chaotic time, for the sake of either my own experience or the development of art. Advancing, like all intellectual revolutions, with orgiastic energy in its first fine frenzy, it cleared the air of musty traditions, discharging the tensions of many years, and in spite of everything its audacious experiments produced some valuable ideas that would last. Uneasy as we felt with its exaggerations, we sensed that we had no right to condemn and reject them arrogantly, for at heart this new generation was trying—if too heatedly and too impatiently— to make good our own generation's sins of omission when we cautiously stood aloof. Their fundamental feeling that the post-war time must be different from the period before the war was right. A new time, a better world—wasn't that just what we, their elders, had wanted before and during the war? It was true that even after the war we older people had only recently proved unable to counter the dangerous re-politicisation of the world with an supranational organisation at the right time. Even during the peace negotiations Henri Barbusse, who had acquired international stature with his novel *Le Feu*, had tried to set up a union of all European intellectuals with a view to reconciliation. This group was to be called Clarté—Clarity—an association of people who thought clearly, and it was to unite the writers and artists of all nations in a vow to oppose any future

325

encouragement of inflammatory popular feeling. Barbusse had asked me and René Schickele to head the German-language section of the association, thus giving us the more difficult part of the work, for bitterness over the Treaty of Versailles still smouldered in Germany. There were few prospects of winning over prominent German figures to an intellectual supranationalism as long as the Rhineland, the Saar and the Mainz bridgehead were still occupied by foreign troops. All the same, we might have succeeded in setting up an organisation such as Galsworthy founded later in the PEN Club, if Barbusse had not then let us down. Fatally, a journey to Russia and his enthusiastic reception there by large crowds had convinced him that bourgeois states and democracies could never usher in true fraternity between nations; he thought international fraternity was conceivable only under communism. By imperceptible degrees, he was trying to make Clarté a weapon in the class struggle. We declined to commit ourselves to a radicalism that was inevitably sure to weaken our ranks. So this project too, in itself a major one, fell through. Once again, valuing our own freedom and independence too highly, we had failed in the struggle for intellectual freedom.

So there was only one thing for it—we must get on with our own work quietly and in seclusion. In the eyes of the Expressionists and the Excessionists—if I may coin a term—at the age of thirty-six I had already reverted to the older, defunct generation through refusing to adapt to the new generation by aping it. I did not like my own earlier work any more; I would not let new editions of any of the books of my 'aesthetic' period be brought out. That meant beginning again, waiting for the impatiently rolling wave of all these 'isms' to ebb away, and here my lack of personal ambition came in useful. I began to write my series of *Baumeister der Welt*[7] deliberately, in the knowledge that it would certainly occupy me for years. I also wrote novellas like *Amok* and *Letter from an Unknown Woman* in a far from 'activist' spirit of composure. The country and the world around me gradually began returning to a state of order, so I myself could no longer hold back. The time for deceiving myself into thinking that everything I began was just a temporary expedient was over. I had reached the middle of life; I was beyond the age of mere promise. It was time to show that something had come of that promise, and either prove myself or give up the attempt.

NOTES

1   The first words of the old Austrian national anthem, *Gott erhalte Franz den Kaiser*—God Save Emperor Franz. When Joseph Haydn wrote the melody, Franz II was Emperor of Austria. Haydn also included it in his *Emperor Quartet*, and the tune is now in use as the national anthem of Germany. It is known in the English-speaking world as the melody of the hymn *Glorious Things of Thee Are Spoken*.

2   Although Zweig keeps personal details of his private life out of his account, this first use of the first person plural shows that by now he was married to his first wife Friderike. It was her own second marriage.

3   In Goethe's *Faust, Part II*, the demonic figure of Mephistopheles advises an emperor of the Middle Ages to extricate himself from his difficulties by printing paper money.

4   Béla Kun, 1886-1938, headed the Soviet Republic of Hungary, which lasted for only six months in 1919.

5   See above, page 252.

6   Literally meaning 'migratory birds', these groups began as a non-political form of organisation, but later took on nationalistic colouring.

7   This, translated into English as *Master Builders*, was the general title that Stefan Zweig gave to his long series of biographies of famous figures such as Tolstoy, Casanova, Stendhal, Dickens and a number of others.

OUT INTO THE WORLD AGAIN

I SPENT 1919, 1920 AND 1921, the three worst post-war years in Austria, buried in Salzburg, almost giving up hope of ever seeing the wider world again. Taken together, the effects of the post-war collapse, hatred in other countries of anyone German or writing in German, and the devaluation of our currency were so catastrophic that we had already reconciled ourselves to the prospect of staying within the narrow borders of our own country for life. But everything was better now. There was enough to eat again. I could sit at my desk undisturbed. There had been no looting, no revolution. I was alive and conscious of my powers. Why shouldn't I revisit the pleasures of my youth and travel abroad?

A long journey was out of the question. But Italy was close, only eight or ten hours away. Why not make the venture? The Italians considered Austrians their arch-enemies, but I myself had never felt that. Must I accept the likelihood of a hostile reception and feel obliged to ignore my old friends in case I embarrassed them? No, I *would* try it, and at noon one day I crossed the border into Italy.

I arrived in Verona that evening and went to a hotel. The receptionist handed me the registration form, I filled it in. He read what I had entered, and was astonished when, under the heading of 'Nationality' he saw the word, '*Austriaco*'. "*Lei è Austriaco?*"—You are Austrian? he asked. Was he going to show me the door, I wondered. But when I said yes, he was positively delighted. "*Ah, che piacere! Finalmente!*"—Oh, what a pleasure! At last. That was my welcome to Italy, and further confirmation of

329

the impression I had gained in the war that all the propaganda and incitement to hatred had caused only a short fit of feverish mental illness, but fundamentally had never touched the great majority of Europeans. A quarter-of-an-hour later the friendly receptionist came up to my room to make sure everything was all right. He praised my Italian enthusiastically, and we shook hands warmly when we parted.

Next day I was in Milan, where I saw the cathedral and wandered through the Galleria.[1] It was good to hear the musical sound of the Italian language I loved so much again, to find my way so confidently around all the streets, and enjoy my familiarity with this foreign city. In passing, I saw the words *Corriere della Sera* on one of the large buildings. It suddenly struck me that my old friend G A Borgese held a top post in the editorial offices of that newspaper—Borgese, in whose company I, Count Keyserling, and Benno Geiger had spent many lively evenings in Berlin and Vienna. One of Italy's best and most impassioned writers, a man with enormous influence on the younger generation, he had adopted a firm stance of opposition to Germany and Austria in the war, even though he had translated Goethe's *The Sorrows of Young Werther* and was fanatically enthusiastic about German philosophy. Standing shoulder to shoulder with Mussolini (they fell out later), he had urged the country to fight. All through the war it had been strange for me to think of an old friend as an interventionist on the other side. I wanted to see my 'enemy' all the more now. However, I didn't want to run the risk of a cold dismissal, so I left my card for him, writing the address of my hotel on it. I wasn't even down the steps when someone came running after me, his lively face beaming with pleasure—it was Borgese himself. Within five minutes we were on the same friendly terms as before, perhaps even friendlier. He too had learnt lessons from the war, and from our respective sides of the conflict we had come closer than ever to each other.

It was the same everywhere. In Florence, my old friend the painter Albert Stringa came up to me in the street to fling his arms around me so suddenly and vigorously that my wife, who was with me and didn't know him, thought this bearded stranger was planning to assassinate me. Everything was just as it had been, or even better. I breathed a sigh of relief—the war was buried. The war was over.

But it was not over. We just didn't know it. In our innocent gullibility, we were all deceived, confusing our personal friendly feelings with those of the world. Not that there was any need for us to be ashamed of our mistake, since the politicians, economists and bankers were equally deceived. In those years they, too, thought that deceptive upward trends denoted real recovery and sheer exhaustion was actually satisfaction. In reality the struggle had merely shifted from the national to the social sphere, and in my first few days abroad I witnessed a scene the full significance of which I understood only later. All we knew in Austria about Italian politics at this time was that, with the disappointment of the post-war period, strong socialist and even Bolshevik tendencies had spread. You could see "*Viva Lenin*" scrawled clumsily with charcoal or chalk on every wall. We had also heard that a Socialist leader called Mussolini had left the party during the war and organised some kind of opposition group. But we listened to such news with indifference. What could a small group like that mean? There were similar cliques in every country at the time; irregulars on the move in the Baltic, separatist groups forming in the Rhineland and Bavaria, there were demonstrations and coups everywhere, but they were almost always put down. And it did not occur to anyone to see these 'Fascists', who wore black shirts instead of the red shirts of Garibaldi's old movement, as a significant factor in the future development of Europe.

In Venice, however, the term 'Fascist' suddenly assumed real significance for me. It was afternoon, and I was on my way from Milan to my beloved city of lagoons. There was no porter in sight when I arrived, no gondola. Workmen and railwaymen stood around idle with their hands ostentatiously in their pockets. I was carrying two quite heavy suitcases, so I looked around for help and asked an elderly gentleman where I could find a porter. "You've picked a bad day," he said regretfully. "But we get days like this quite often. There's another general strike on." I didn't know the cause of this strike, but asked no more questions. We were used to these things in Austria, where the Social Democrats, much to their own disadvantage, only too often resorted to that strongest of threats without making effective use of it. So I went on laboriously carrying my cases until at last I saw a gondolier quickly bringing his boat towards me out of a minor canal and giving me a surreptitious wave. He took me and my two suitcases on board. In half-an-hour, after passing several men shaking their fists at strike-breakers, we were at my hotel. It was the most natural thing in the world, an old habit of mine, to go straight to the Piazza San Marco. It looked remarkably deserted. The shutters were down over most of the shop-fronts, there was no one sitting in the cafés, only a large crowd of workers standing under the arcades in isolated groups, as if waiting for something out of the ordinary. I waited with them. And then, suddenly, it came. Out of a side street marched or rather strode, rapidly but keeping in step, a group of young men in good order, singing a well-rehearsed song with words that I didn't know. Later, I discovered that it was the *Giovinezza*.[2] And soon they had passed at their swift pace, swinging batons, before the hundreds of men waiting for them in far superior numbers had time to make a move against their enemy. The audacious and genuinely brave march staged by this small, organised group was all over so quickly that the waiting crowd were aware of the provocation only when there was no chance for them to get to grips with their adversaries. Angrily, they crowded together, clenching their fists, but it was too late. They could not catch up with the little storm troop.

Visual impressions are always particularly convincing. For the first time, I realised that the now legendary Fascist movement, hardly known to me at all at the time, was something real, very well led, and fanatically supported by determined, bold young men. After that experience, I could not agree with my older friends in Florence and Rome who dismissed these young men as a hired gang, and laughed at their 'Fra Diavolo'.[3] Out of curiosity, I bought several issues of the *Popolo d'Italia,* and from the Latinate brevity of Mussolini's sharp, graphic style of writing I gained the same impression of determination as I had from those young men briskly marching across the Piazza San Marco. Naturally I could not guess the dimensions this struggle was to assume only a year later. But from then on I was aware that a struggle did lie ahead, here and everywhere, and that the peace of the time was not real peace at all.

To me, that was the first warning that there were dangerous undercurrents beneath the apparently calm surface of Europe. I did not have to wait long for the second. Now that my pleasure in travelling had been revived, I had decided to go to Westerland on the German North Sea coast that summer. At the time it was still good for morale to visit Germany. So far, the German mark had stood its ground well by comparison with the decline of the Austrian crown, and recovery seemed to be going full speed ahead. The trains ran punctually; the hotels shone with cleanliness; you saw new houses and new factories rising on both sides of the railway tracks. The immaculate, silent, well-disciplined order of Germany was back—we had hated it in the pre-war period, and learnt to value it again in the chaos of war. Yes, there was a certain tension in the air, because the whole country was waiting to find out whether, as it hoped, the negotiations in Genoa and Rapallo, the first in which Germany took part on equal terms with the former enemy powers, would bring any relief from the full burden of war reparations, or at least some small gesture of reconciliation. Heading the German negotiating team on this memorable occasion was my old friend Rathenau. His brilliant organisational instinct had shown to very good effect during the war; right at the start he had identified the weakest spot in the German economy, the place where it later suffered a mortal blow—the supply of raw materials. Ahead of his time as usual, he had organised the entire economy centrally at just the right moment. After the war, when a man who was the equal of the cleverest and most experienced diplomats among the enemy nations had to be found, to put the country's case as German Foreign Minister, he was the obvious choice.

I telephoned him in Berlin, but with some hesitation. How could I intrude on a man while he was deciding on the course of current events? "Yes, it's difficult," he said on the phone. "I even have to sacrifice friendship to duty these days." But with his extraordinary ability to use every minute to the full, he immediately found a way for us to meet. He had to leave a few visiting cards at various embassies, he said, and as that meant he would have to spend half-an-hour travelling by car from Grunewald, it would be the simplest thing if I came to him and we talked during his half-hour's drive around the city. His power of intellectual concentration and the astonishing ease with which he switched from one subject to another were so prodigious that he could talk in a car or train at any time as profoundly and incisively as if he were in his own room. I didn't want to waste the opportunity, and I think it did him good as well to talk to someone who had been a friend of his for years but was not involved in politics. It was a long conversation, and I can vouch for it that Rathenau, who was by no means free of personal vanity, had not accepted his appointment as Foreign Minister lightly, still less with any impatient greed for office. He knew in advance that his task was impossible for the time being, and at best he would be able to bring home only a token of success, a few minor concessions. A genuine peace, a generous meeting of minds, was too much to hope for just yet. "In ten years' time, maybe," he said to me, "always supposing that everyone else is in difficulties as well, not just us. First the older generation must leave the diplomatic path open, and the generals must keep their mouths shut, like monuments in a public square." He was well aware of the double responsibility he bore, having the added disadvantage of being a Jew. I think that seldom in history can so sceptical a man with so many private reservations have undertaken a task which he knew only time could solve, and he also knew how personally dangerous it was. Since the assassination of Erzberger,[4] who had taken on the thankless task of negotiating the armistice—which Ludendorff avoided by going abroad—he had no doubt that a similar fate lay in wait for him, as another champion of rapprochement. But unmarried and childless as he was, and a loner at heart, he did not shrink from the danger. I did not feel bold enough to urge him to be cautious. It is now seen as a historical fact that Rathenau carried out his mission in Rapallo as well as possible in the circumstances. His brilliant talent for seizing every favourable moment, his sophistication and his personal prestige were never used to better effect. But already certain groups were gaining ground in the country, knowing that they would recruit supporters only if they kept assuring defeated Germany that it had not been defeated after all, and all negotiations and concessions were treasonous. There were already secret associations (with strong homosexual leanings) wielding greater power than was suspected by the new republic's leaders, whose own ideas of liberty led them to allow all kinds of developments that would have done away with true liberty in Germany for ever.

I said goodbye to him in the city, outside the Ministry, never guessing that it was for the last time. Later, I saw from press photographs that the street down which we had been driving together was the one where, shortly afterwards, his assassins lay in wait for the same car. It was pure chance that I had not witnessed that historically fateful scene myself, a fact that left me more deeply impressed and emotionally aware than ever of the tragic episode with which the misfortune of Germany and indeed of all Europe began.

I was already in Westerland that day, where hundreds upon hundreds of visitors to the spa resort were on the beach, happily bathing. Once again a band was playing, like the band in Baden on the day when news came of Franz Ferdinand's assassination. The musicians was entertaining a carefree audience enjoying their summer holiday when newspaper vendors came running along the promenade like a flock of stormy petrels, shouting,: "Walther Rathenau assassinated!" Panic broke out, shaking the entire Reich.[5] The mark dropped sharply, and there was no stopping it until it fell to fantastic, crazy numbers running into billions. Only now did a real witches' sabbath of inflation begin, and by comparison our Austrian figures of fifteen thousand crowns falling to the value of one looked like a mere children's game. I would need a whole book to describe it in all its incredible detail, and that book would sound like a fairy tale to modern readers. There were days when I had to pay fifty thousand marks for a newspaper in the morning and a hundred thousand in the evening; anyone who had to exchange foreign currency did it piecemeal, by the hour, because at four o'clock he would get many more marks than at three, and at five o'clock many more again than sixty minutes earlier. I sent my publisher a manuscript that I had been working on for a year, and I thought I could safely request an immediate advance payment for what ten thousand copies of the book would earn me. Once the sum was transferred to my account, it hardly covered the postage for the parcel a week before. You paid your tram fare in millions of marks, trucks carted paper money from the central Reichsbank to the commercial banks, and two weeks later you could find banknotes to the value of a hundred thousand marks lying in the gutter, contemptuously tossed aside by a beggar. A shoelace cost more than a shoe in the past, more than a luxury shop with a stock of two thousand pairs of shoes; repairing a broken window was more expensive than building the whole house had once been, while a book cost more than a printing works with hundred of presses before inflation. You could buy whole rows of six-storey buildings on the Kurfürstendamm for a hundred dollars. Convert the sums of money, and factories cost the same as a wheelbarrow in the past. Teenage boys who had found a crate of bars of soap forgotten on the docks drove around in cars and lived like princes for months on end by selling one bar of soap a day, while their parents, who had once been rich, were now reduced to beggary. Deliverymen founded banking houses and speculated in all kinds of foreign currency. Above them all rose the towering figure of the plutocrat Stinnes[6] as he made money on the grand scale. Extending his credit by exploiting the fall in the value of the mark, he bought everything there was to be bought, coal mines and ships, factories, blocks of stocks and shares, castles and country estates, in effect paying nothing for them, because no agreement amounted to anything, nor did any debt. Soon a quarter of Germany was in his hands, and strangely enough the Germans, always intoxicated by visible success, hailed him as a genius. Meanwhile, the unemployed stood around in their thousands, shaking their fists at the black-marketeers and foreigners in their flashy cars who would buy up a whole street like a box of matches. Even the barely literate were dealing and speculating now, earning money with the secret feeling that they were all deceiving themselves and being deceived by some hidden hand, cleverly staging a scene of chaos in order to free the state from its debts and obligations. I think I have a fairly good knowledge of history, and never, so far as I know, has madness of such gigantic dimensions been seen. All values were changed, and not just material

337

values; state decrees were laughed out of court, manners and morals were thrown overboard, Berlin was the worst sink of iniquity in the world. Bars, amusement arcades and shady dives sprang up like mushrooms. What we had seen in Austria was only a mild and gentle prelude to this witches' sabbath, for the Germans now turned their methodical methods to the cause of perversions. Youths in wasp-waisted coats, their faces made up, promenaded along the Kurfürstendamm, and not all of them were professional rent boys; every grammar-school student wanted to earn something, and state secretaries and prominent financiers could be seen sitting in darkened bars shamelessly courting the favour of drunken sailors. Even the Rome of Suetonius never knew such orgies as those at the transvestites' balls in Berlin, where hundreds of men in women's clothing and women dressed like men danced under the benevolent gaze of the police. Amidst the headlong fall of all values, a kind of madness took hold of the bourgeois circles that had so far resisted any change to their well-ordered society. Young girls boasted proudly of perversities; to be suspected of still being a virgin at the age of sixteen would have been thought a disgrace in any Berlin school. Every girl wanted to be able to boast of her adventures, and the more exotic they were the better. But the outstanding feature of this pathetic eroticism was that it was all pretence. At heart, the orgiastic mood that broke out in Germany with inflation was merely feverish imitation; you could tell that these girls from good middle-class families would rather have been wearing their hair neatly parted than slicked back into a masculine style, and would have been happier eating apple cake with whipped cream than drinking spirits. It was impossible not to notice that the whole country was unhappy with this overheated atmosphere, this daily torture on the rack of inflation, nerves stretched to breaking point, or that all the entire war-weary nation really wanted was peace and quiet, good order and a little security. And secretly it hated the new

German Republic, not because the government might suppress some of this wild freedom but, on the contrary, because it held the reins too loosely.

Anyone who lived through those apocalyptic months and years, repelled and embittered, also felt that there must be some reaction, a terrible backlash. And there, waiting in the wings with a smile, stopwatches in their hands, were the very people responsible for bringing Germany to this plight. "The worse things are in the country, the better for us!" was their motto. They knew that their hour would come. Counter-revolutionaries were already openly gathering around Ludendorff—not Hitler yet; he had little power at the time. The officers whose epaulettes had been torn off organised themselves into secret societies, members of the lower middle class, seeing themselves cheated of their savings, quietly closed ranks and placed themselves in advance at the disposal of any regime ready to promise law and order. Nothing was so disastrous for the German Republic as its idealistic attempt to leave the people and even its enemies their liberty. The orderly German nation did not know what to do with its liberty, and was already looking impatiently for someone to take it away again.

The day in 1923 that marked the end of German inflation could have been a turning-point in history. When the bell tolled for every crazy, dizzying million marks, now to be redeemed by a single new mark, a norm had been set. And indeed, the murky tide soon ebbed, taking all its dirt and debris with it. The bars and dives disappeared, conditions reverted to normality. Now everyone could calculate what he had won and what he had lost. Most people, the great majority, were losers. But the men who were to blame for the war were not held responsible; instead, feeling turned against those who, in a spirit of self-sacrifice, had taken on the thankless burden of reconstruction.

Nothing, as we have to keep reminding ourselves, made the German people so bitter, so mad with hatred, so ripe for Hitler as the inflation. For the war, murderous as it had turned out, had provided hours of jubilation at the start, with the ringing of bells and victorious fanfares. And as an incurably militaristic nation, Germany considered that its pride had been bolstered by the occasional victory in the war, while it felt only soiled, deceived and humiliated by inflation. A whole generation never forgot or forgave the German Republic for those years, preferring to summon their own murderers again. But that was still in the distant future. To all outward appearance, the whole wild phantasmagoria seemed to be over like a dance of will-o'-the-wisps. Day had dawned again, you could see the way ahead. And already we saw and welcomed the return of order as the beginning of a lasting period of peace and quiet. Hopeless fools that we had always been, we thought yet again that war was defeated. However, that fatal delusion at least gave us a decade of work, of hope, even of security.

Seen from today's viewpoint, in spite of everything, those years from 1924 to 1933—in fact just short of a decade—from the end of German inflation to the moment when Hitler came to power, represent a pause in the succession of catastrophes that our generation had witnessed and suffered since 1914. Not that there was any shortage of individual instances of tension, agitation and crisis—more particularly the economic crisis of 1929—but within that decade peace seemed to prevail in Europe, and that in itself meant a great deal. Germany had been received into the League of Nations on honourable terms, and loans had encouraged its economic reconstruction, although in point of fact that really meant secret rearmament. Britain had disarmed. In Italy, Mussolini had undertaken to protect Austria. The world seemed to want to rebuild itself. Paris, Vienna,

Berlin, New York, Rome—the victorious and the defeated cities alike were more attractive than ever; aeroplanes speeded up travel, passport restrictions were relaxed. Fluctuation between currencies was over; you knew how much you had coming in and how much you could spend. Your attention was no longer so anxiously fixed on outside problems. You could work again, collect your thoughts, think of intellectual matters. You could even dream again and hope for a united Europe. For those ten years—for a brief moment in the history of the world—it seemed as if our sorely tried generation could live a normal life once more.

The most notable event in my personal life during those years was the arrival in my house of a guest who settled benevolently in, a guest I had never expected—success. Understandably, I feel uncomfortable about mentioning the success my books enjoyed in the outside world, and in a normal situation I would have left out even a fleeting mention that might be interpreted as self-satisfaction or boastfulness. But I have a particular right, even a duty, not to hush up this part of the story of my life, for that success has become a thing of the past in the last seven years, since the advent of Hitler. Not one of the hundreds of thousands, even millions of copies of my works, books that had secured their place in bookshops and countless private houses, can be bought in Germany today. Anyone who still has a copy of one of them keeps it carefully concealed. They are consigned to the 'poison cupboard' of public libraries, kept there for the few who want to study them, by special permission of the authorities, for research purposes, meaning mainly for the purpose of denunciation. It is a long time since the readers and friends who write to me have dared to put my reprehensible name on an envelope. And as if that were not enough, in France, Italy, and all the countries now reduced to servitude, where my books used to be widely read in translation, they are also banned today by Hitler's orders. I am now a writer

341

who, as Grillparzer[7] said, "walks behind his corpse in his own
lifetime". Everything, or almost everything, that I built up over
forty years in the international arena has been smashed by that
one fist. So in mentioning my own 'success' I am not speaking
of something that is really mine, but something that once was
mine, like my house, my native land, my self-confidence, my
freedom, my lack of inhibition. I cannot illustrate the depths
to which I and countless other innocent people sank later in
all their depth and their full extent without mentioning, first,
the height from which we fell, or the unique consequences of
this elimination of our entire literary generation. I really cannot
think of any similar example in history.

Success did not arrive suddenly, storming into my house;
it came slowly and discreetly, but it proved a faithful friend,
and stayed with me until Hitler drove it away with the lash
of his decrees. It grew year by year. The very first work I
published after *Jeremiah*, the first volume in my *Master Builders*
series, a study of three writers,[8] paved the way for me. The
Expressionists, the activists and other experimental writers
had had their day, and other writers who had waited patiently
had access to readers again. My novellas *Amok* and *Letter from
an Unknown Woman* enjoyed the popularity usually reserved for
novels, and were dramatised, read in public and filmed. A small
book of historical miniatures, *Sternstunden der Menschheit*[9]—read
in every school, and published in the Insel-Bücherei series—
sold 250,000 copies in a very short time. Within a few years I
had acquired what, to my mind, is the most valuable kind of
success a writer can have—a faithful following, a reliable group
of readers who looked forward to every new book and bought
it, who trusted me, and whose trust I must not disappoint. My
success grew slowly greater, until every time I published a book
twenty thousand copies were sold in Germany in the first few
days after it came out, even before any advertisement had
appeared in the papers. Sometimes I deliberately tried to keep

out of the way of my own success, but it followed me around with remarkable persistence. For instance, I had written a book for my own personal pleasure, my biography of Fouché, and when I sent it to my publisher he wrote to say he was going to print ten thousand copies immediately. I urged him, by return of post, not to print so many of this particular title. Fouché was not an attractive character, the book contained not a hint of any love interest, and was never going to appeal to a wide circle of readers. I said I thought he had better print just five thousand for a start. After a year fifty thousand copies had been sold in Germany alone—the same Germany where no one is allowed to read a line of my work today. My almost pathological self-distrust made me doubtful of my version of Ben Jonson's *Volpone*. I intended to produce a verse adaptation, and in nine days I sketched out the course of the action quickly and freely in prose. It so happened that the Dresden Court Theatre, to which I felt a moral obligation because it had staged the premiere of my first play *Thersites*, had just been asking whether I had any plans to write another drama, and I sent them the prose version, saying apologetically that it was only a sketch for my planned adaptation in verse. However, the theatre telegraphed back at once, telling me for Heaven's sake not to change anything. And sure enough, the play was produced all over the world in that form (in New York by the Theatre Guild, with Alfred Lunt starring). Whatever I did in those years, my success and an ever-growing number of German readers remained faithful to me.

When I was writing biographies or essays, I always felt an urge to explore the motives, or lack of motives, that made my subjects act as they did in the context of their own time. So sometimes, when I was in a thoughtful mood, I could not help wondering what exactly it was that made my books so unexpectedly popular. In the last resort, I think it arose from a personal flaw in me—I am an impatient, temperamental reader. Anything long-winded, high-flown or gushing irritates me, so does everything that is

vague and indistinct, in fact anything that unnecessarily holds
the reader up, whether in a novel, a biography or an intellectual
argument. A book really satisfies me only if it maintains its pace
page after page, carrying readers breathlessly along to the end.
Nine-tenths of the books that come my way seem to be padded
out with unnecessary descriptions, too much loquacious dialogue
and superfluous minor characters; they are just not dynamic and
exciting enough. I get impatient with many arid, slow-moving
passages even in the most famous classic masterpieces, and I
have often suggested a bold idea of mine to publishers—why not
bring out a series of the great works of international literature,
from Homer through Balzac and Dostoevsky to Mann's *The
Magic Mountain*, with the unnecessary parts cut? Then all those
undoubtedly immortal works would gain a new lease of life in
our own time.

This dislike of mine for anything tediously long-winded must
have transferred itself from my reading of other authors' works
to the writing of my own, making me train myself to be especially
alert for such passages. I naturally write easily and fluently, and in
the first draft of a book I let my pen run on as it pleases, setting
down anything that comes into my head. Similarly, when I am
writing a biography I study all the factual material available. For
my biography of Marie-Antoinette, for instance, I looked at all
the details of her financial accounts to find out what her personal
expenses were, I studied all the contemporary newspapers and
pamphlets, I ploughed my way through the case files of her trial
to the very last line. But none of that will be found in the final
printed version, because I have hardly finished writing the first
rough draft of a book before I begin on what to me is the real work,
condensing my material and finding the right way to put it. I go
on working tirelessly like this from draft to draft. I am constantly
throwing ballast overboard, intensifying and clarifying a book's
inner architecture. Most writers cannot bring themselves to leave
anything out, and having fallen rather in love with their subject

hope to display a greater breadth and depth of knowledge than they really possess in every well-turned line, whereas my own ambition is always to know more than shows on the outside.

Later, at the proof stages, I then repeat this process of intensifying and thus enhancing the dramatic effect once, twice or three times. In the end I find myself enjoying a kind of hunt for another sentence, or just a word, which can be cut without affecting my precise meaning and at the same time might speed up the tempo. I really get my greatest satisfaction in my work from leaving things out. I remember that once, when I rose from my desk feeling pleased with what I had done, my wife said I seemed to be in a cheerful mood today. "Yes," I replied proudly, "I've managed to cut a whole paragraph and make the action move faster." So if my books are sometimes praised for sweeping readers along at a swift pace, it does not come from any natural heated or agitated approach to the work of writing, but is entirely the result of my system of always cutting unnecessarily slack passages—anything at all that, like radio interference, might distract the reader's attention. If I have mastered any kind of art, it is the art of leaving things out. I do not mind throwing eight hundred of a thousand written pages into the waste-paper basket, leaving me with only two hundred to convey what I have sifted out as the essence of the work. So if anything at least partly accounts for the success of my books, it is my strict discipline in preferring to confine myself to short works of literature, concentrating on the heart of the matter. Since my ideas have always been European and not nationalist, it was a great pleasure for me when I heard of publishers from other countries wanting to bring out my works in French, Bulgarian, Armenian, Portuguese, the Spanish of Argentina, Norwegian, Latvian, Finnish and Chinese. Soon I had to buy a large cupboard to house all the different copies of my foreign editions, and one day, in the statistics of the *Co-opération Intellectuelle* published by the League of Nations in Geneva, I saw that I was the most translated writer in the world—although true to my usual form, I thought this report was probably mistaken. Another day a letter came from my Russian publisher, saying he wanted to bring out a collected edition of all my books in Russian, and asking if I would agree to having an introduction written by Maxim Gorky. Would I agree! As a schoolboy, I had surreptitiously read Gorky's stories under my desk; I had loved and admired him for years. But I would never have imagined that he had ever heard my name, let alone read anything of mine, and certainly not that my work could seem important enough to such a great master for him to write a foreword to it. On another occasion an American publisher turned up at my house in Salzburg with a recommendation—as if I would have needed that!—proposing to take on my entire work and publish it book by book. This was Benjamin Huebsch of Viking Press, who has been my most reliable friend and adviser ever since. Now that my original homeland has been crushed underfoot by Hitler's jackboots, he has made sure that I still have a literary home even though my real German and European one is lost to me.

Public success of that kind was dangerously likely to confuse a man who, until then, had believed more in his good intentions than his skill and the influence his work might have. In itself all publicity disturbs a man's natural equilibrium. In normal circumstances your name means no more than the band on a cigar—a means of recognition, an outward object of little importance that is only loosely linked to the real subject, the Self. But in the case of success that name, so to speak, swells to a larger dimension. It frees itself from the man who bears it and becomes a power, a force, something independent, a commodity, capital. And then, with a violent backlash, it turns in on its bearer as a force that begins to influence, dominate and change him. Happy, self-confident natures unconsciously start identifying themselves with the influence they exert. A title, a position, a medal or decoration, and the publicity that now goes with their names can enhance their self-confidence, tempting them to feel that special recognition is their right in contemporary society and their country, and they instinctively puff themselves up to make themselves personally influential in the outside world. However, a man who naturally distrusts himself tends to feel that outward success of any kind makes it his duty, in what to him is a difficult situation, to change as little as possible.

I do not mean to say that I didn't enjoy my success. On the contrary; it pleased me a great deal, but only in so far as it confined itself to what was separate from myself—my books and the mere letters of my name traced on them. Once, when I happened to be in a bookshop in Germany, I was touched to see a schoolboy who came in, did not recognise me, asked for a copy of *The Tide of Fortune* and paid for it out of his meagre pocket-money. It gratified my vanity when the conductor who asked for my passport in the sleeping car of the train treated me respectfully once he had seen my name, or an Italian customs officer, realising that he had read a book of mine, kindly refrained from treating my baggage roughly as he checked through it. And there is something seductive for an author in the mere quantitative effect his work has on the world around him. By chance I was travelling to Leipzig on the same day as a new book of mine was on its way out of that city for delivery. I felt remarkably excited to see how much human labour I had kept busy, without knowing it, on something that I had spent three or four months setting down on three hundred sheets of paper. Workmen were packing the copies of the book into huge crates, others were groaning under the weight as they took them down to the trucks, to be loaded on to the freight cars of the trains that would transport them to all four quarters of the compass. Dozens of girls had collated the pages in the printing works, the typesetters, binders, shippers and wholesale booksellers had been at work from morning to night, and I calculated that

347

these books, stacked up like piles of bricks, might almost be enough to build a handsome street. I never arrogantly despised the material side of success. In the early years of my career I had never dared to think that I would earn real money with my books, let alone being able to base a whole lifestyle on them. Now they were suddenly bringing in large and ever-increasing sums of money, and it seemed—and who could foresee the future in our times?—as if they would relieve me of all anxiety. I could indulge my youthful passion for collecting autograph manuscripts, and many of the finest and most valuable of those wonderful relics found their way into my possession, where I cared for them lovingly. In return for what, by comparison, must be called my own rather ephemeral books, I could acquire manuscripts of immortal works, manuscript documents by Mozart and Bach and Beethoven, Goethe and Balzac. I would be putting on ridiculous airs if I were to say I was indifferent to my unexpected success, or even disliked it.

But I am being honest when I say that I enjoyed success only as long as it related to my books and my literary name. When it was transferred to my physical presence it was a nuisance. Nothing in me has been stronger since my early youth than an instinctive wish to stay free and independent. And I felt that anyone's personal freedom suffers from misrepresentation by photographic publicity. However, the work on which I had embarked simply out of inclination threatened to become not just a career but a business. Mail arrived by every post, stacks of letters, invitations, requests, questions, and all these missives had to be answered. If I went away for a month, I had to spend two or three days when I came back making my way through the accumulated mass and disposing of it before I could get the 'business' running smoothly again. Without my wanting it, the marketability of my work had made my books into a kind of industry that called for order, supervision, punctuality and skill if it was going to be run successfully—all of those being admirable virtues, but unfortunately alien to my nature, and they threatened to disturb my mind and my dreams in the most dangerous way. The more I was asked to take part in literary events, give readings, appear at official occasions, the more reluctant I felt to agree. I have never overcome this near-pathological dislike of letting my person stand in for my reputation. Today I instinctively still sit in the last, most inconspicuous row of seats in a large hall, at a concert or a theatrical performance, and I hate nothing so much as having to show my face on a platform or some other public place. I feel a deep need for anonymity in all areas of life. Even as a boy, I could never understand those writers and artists of an earlier generation who liked to attract attention in the street with their velvet jackets and heads of waving hair, locks dangling down over their foreheads, like my dear friends Arthur Schnitzler and Hermann Bahr, or who sported showy beards and whiskers or extravagant clothes. I feel sure that making his own likeness widely known must unconsciously tempt anyone to feel, in Werfel's phrase, like a "mirror man", assuming a certain style not natural to him in everything he does, and with this change in his outward attitude he generally loses his warmth of heart, sense of liberty, and inner freedom from care. If I could begin again today, I would make sure to have my works published under another name, a pseudonym, and then I could enjoy those two happy conditions, literary success and personal anonymity, at the same time. Life in itself is so attractive and full of surprises—why not lead a double life?

NOTES

1   The Galleria Vittorio Emanuele II, a huge covered arcade built in Milan in the latter part of the 19th century.

2   The song of the Italian Fascist party. Mussolini had commissioned new lyrics to be set to an older melody.

3   Probably not referring to Auber's opera of that name, but the character on which it was based, an early nineteenth-century guerrilla regarded as a Robin Hood character who adopted the nickname Fra Diavolo—Brother Devil. The emergent Fascists may have seen themselves as modern versions of this hero of the people.

4   Matthias Erzberger, 1875-1921, a centrist politician, handled negotiations on the German side in November 1918. He was murdered by right-wing extremists in 1921.

5   We know this period of German history today as the Weimar Republic, but although it was a republic it also retained the older German term Reich, to be adopted later on by Hitler in the Third Reich.

6   Hugo Stinnes, 1870-1924, German industrialist and tycoon, who as Zweig describes it here took advantage of the galloping inflation in Germany to do some clever deals involving foreign currency.

7   Franz Grillparzer, 1791-1872, Austrian dramatist.

8   Balzac, Dickens and Dostoevsky; see above, page 326.

9   Literally *Great Moments of Mankind*; it was translated into English as *The Tide of Fortune*.

THE SETTING SUN

F OR EUROPE, AS I SHALL ALWAYS remember gratefully, that decade from 1924 to 1933 before one man destroyed our world was a relatively peaceful time. Simply because our generation had suffered so much, we regarded this period of relative calm as an unexpected gift. We all had a sense that we must catch up with everything that the terrible years of the war and its immediate aftermath had stolen from our lives—happiness, freedom, the chance to concentrate on things of the mind. We worked harder, yet with a sense of relief; we moved freely, we experimented, we discovered Europe all over again. There was never so much travelling as in those years—was it the impatience of the young to make up for what they had missed when countries were cut off from each other? Or was it, perhaps, a dark foreboding, a sense that we must take our chance to break out of confinement before the barriers began coming down again?

I travelled a great deal myself at that time, but my travels were not the same as in my younger days. I was no longer a stranger when I went abroad; everywhere I went I had friends, publishers and readers; I was travelling as the author of my books, not as an interested but anonymous tourist. That meant a number of advantages. I could give more forceful and effective support to the idea of the intellectual union of Europe that had dominated my life for years. With that in mind, I delivered lectures in Switzerland and the Netherlands, I spoke in French at the Palais des Arts in Brussels, in Italian in the historic Sala dei Dugento in Florence, which Michelangelo and Leonardo had known in their time, I spoke English in America on a lecture tour taking me from the Atlantic to the Pacific Ocean. This was a different kind of travelling; wherever I went, I met the most distinguished men of every nation without having to seek them out. While I had looked up to these figures with veneration in my youth, I would never have dared to write them a line, but now they were my friends. I moved in circles that usually haughtily excluded foreigners; I saw the palaces of the Faubourg St Germain, the *palazzi* of Italy, all the private collections. I no longer had to wait at the book-borrowing counters of public libraries to ask for a volume; head librarians personally showed me their carefully guarded treasures. I was a guest of antiquarian booksellers like Dr Rosenbach of Philadelphia, men who sold to the dollar millionaires and whose shops I had timidly passed by when I was only a collector in a small way. For the first time I had a glimpse of life in the higher echelons of society, and with it the pleasant, comfortable feeling that I did not have to ask anyone's permission to gain entry; everything came to me of its own accord. But was this really a better way of seeing the world? I found myself thinking nostalgically of the travels of my young days, when no one was expecting me, and everything seemed more interestingly mysterious because I was on my own. I did not want to abandon my old way of travelling. When I went to Paris I made sure not to let even my best friends, like Roger Martin du Gard, Jules Romains, Duhamel and Masereel, know I was there on the very first day. First I wanted to wander through the streets as I had in my student days, at liberty and with no appointment to meet anyone. I sought out the old cafés and little restaurants that I used to frequent; I played at being back in my youth. Similarly, when I wanted to work I went to some unexpected, even unlikely places, small provincial towns like Boulogne or Tirano or Dijon. It was wonderful to be unknown, staying in small hotels after establishments that were too luxurious for my liking, alternating between them, choosing light or shade as I liked. And in spite of all that Hitler took from me later, even he was unable to spoil or destroy my pleasant awareness that I had lived a truly European life as a free man, exactly as I liked, for another decade.

One of those journeys was particularly exciting and instructive—it took me to the new Russia. I had been planning to go there in 1914, just before the war, when I was working on my book about Dostoevsky. Then the bloodstained scythe of war had cut me off from my plan, and since then certain reservations had held me back. For thinking men, the Bolshevik revolution had made Russia the most fascinating country of the post-war period, either enthusiastically admired or fanatically hated by those who knew nothing much about it. Thanks to propaganda and counter-propaganda, both of them equally ferocious, no one knew for certain what was going on there. But we did know that an experiment was being made with something entirely new, and it could determine the future shape of the world for better or worse. Shaw, Wells, Barbusse, the Romanian Istrati, Gide and many others had gone there, some coming home enthusiastic, others disappointed, and I would not have been a man with a mind ready to accept innovation if I too had not felt tempted to form an idea of Russia from the evidence of my own eyes. My books had been very widely distributed there, not just in the complete edition with Maxim Gorky's introduction but also in small, cheap editions costing only a few copecks that reached the general public, so I could be sure of a welcome. What kept me from going, however, was that at the time travelling to Russia meant adopting some kind of partisan stance, forcing a visitor to endorse or condemn the new Russian society publicly. I had a deep dislike of anything dogmatically political, and I did not want to feel obliged to pass judgement on a vast country and a problem still unsolved after a brief survey of only a few weeks. In spite of my burning curiosity, I could not make up my mind to go to Soviet Russia.

Then, in the early summer of 1928, I was invited to go to Moscow as a delegate representing Austrian writers on the centenary of Leo Tolstoy's birth, and to speak in his honour at the evening of the festive celebrations. There was no reason for me to avoid such an occasion, since its non-partisan nature would mean there was nothing in the least political about my visit. Tolstoy, the apostle of non-violence, could hardly be presented as a Bolshevik, and I had an obvious right to speak on him as a writer—thousands of copies of my book on him had been distributed. It also seemed to me an important demonstration of European unity for writers of all nations to come together in paying a joint tribute to the greatest among them. So I accepted the invitation, and I had no cause to regret my decision. The journey to Russia through Poland was an experience in itself. I saw how quickly, these days, time can heal self-inflicted wounds. The same Galician towns that I had seen in ruins in 1915 now looked bright and new. I realised, yet again, that ten years are a good part of an individual human being's life, but no more than the blink of an eye in the life of a nation. In Warsaw, there was no visible sign that armies, either victorious or defeated, had passed through the city twice, three, four times. The presence of elegant women made the cafés sparkle. The officers promenading down the streets, slender and well-groomed, looked more like expert actors playing soldiers in some court theatre than the genuine article. You felt a spirit of enterprise and confidence everywhere, together with legitimate pride that the new, strong Polish Republic was rising from the detritus of centuries. Our journey went on from Warsaw to the Russian border. The land was flat now and the soil sandy; the entire population of every village had assembled in colourful traditional costume at every station, for at the time only a single passenger train a day passed through Poland to the forbidden country over the border and sealed off from all others, so the sight of the shining carriages of an express train, linking the world of the East with the world of the West, was a great event. Finally we reached the border station of

354

Nyegorolye. A banner the colour of blood was stretched above the tracks, with an inscription in the Cyrillic alphabet which I could not read. Someone translated it for me: "Workers of the world, unite!" In passing under that banner we had entered a new world, the empire of the proletariat, the Soviet Republic. As a matter of fact, the train in which we were travelling was far from proletarian. It turned out to be a sleeper train from the Tsarist period, more comfortable even than the de luxe trains of Europe because it was broader and its pace was more leisurely. I was passing through the Russian countryside for the first time, and oddly enough it did not seem strange to me. In fact everything appeared remarkably familiar—the wide, empty steppes with their slightly melancholy aura; the little huts; the small towns with their onion domes; the men half-peasant, half-prophet with their long beards, greeting us with wide, friendly smiles; the women in brightly coloured headscarves and white aprons selling kvass, eggs and cucumbers. How did I know all this? Solely from the masterpieces of Russian literature, from Tolstoy, Dostoevsky, Aksakov and Gorky, who had given us such wonderfully realistic descriptions of the lives of these people. Although I did not know the language, I thought I could understand what these Russians were saying—the simple men—touchingly simple—who stood foursquare, legs apart, wearing voluminous shirts; the young workers on the train playing chess, reading or arguing, their restless, active minds stimulated by the call to exert all their powers. Was it Tolstoy and Dostoevsky's love of the people that acted like a memory in me? However that may be, I was overwhelmed, even on the train, by an instinctive sympathy for the childish, touching simplicity of these Russians, whose minds were untaught but acute.

I passed the two weeks I spent in Soviet Russia in a constant state of heightened tension. I observed and listened; I marvelled at the country, I was repelled, fascinated, intrigued; my feelings swung between hot and cold. Moscow itself was a city of contradictions—here was magnificent Red Square with its great walls and onion domes, wonderfully Tatar and oriental, Byzantine, redolent of old Russia. Next door to it, like a foreign horde of American giants, stood ultra-modern highrise buildings. Nothing quite went together—the old smokeblackened icons and bejewelled altars of the saints drowsed only a hundred yards from Lenin's corpse in his glass casket, clad in a black suit and freshly made up, whether in our honour or not I have no idea. Close to a few shiny new motor cars, bearded, dirty *izvoshiks* whipped their thin little horses on, clicking their tongues. The grand opera house where we writers spoke was a brilliant sight in the fine old Tsarist style, with a proletarian audience present, and crumbling buildings stood in the suburbs like grubby, desperate old men leaning against each other for support. Everything had been old, lethargic and rusty for too long. Now, putting on a sudden spurt, it wanted to be modern, indeed ultra-modern, right up to date with the latest technology. This haste made Moscow seem over-full, overpopulated, and as if it were living in a state of frantic confusion. There were crowds of people everywhere, in all the shops, outside the theatres, and they all had to wait. Everything was over-organised and so failed to work properly. The new bureaucracy, which was supposed to impose order, was still enjoying itself writing memos and making out permits, and everything was delayed. On the great evening of the Tolstoy celebrations, which were supposed to begin at six, nothing got under way until half-past nine, and when I left the opera house feeling exhausted, the other speakers were still holding forth at length. Western Europeans were sure to arrive an hour early for every reception and appointment. Time ran away through your fingers, yet every second was filled with observation and discussion, all of it at fevered pace, and you felt gradually infected by the mysterious Russian inflammation of the intellect, with its wild desire to unburden itself of feelings and ideas in the heat of the moment. Without quite knowing why, you felt mildly excited yourself. It was something to do with the new, restless atmosphere; maybe you were developing a Russian soul.

Much of what I saw was magnificent, in particular Leningrad, a city planned by princes with audacious minds, a place of broad avenues and mighty palaces—yet at the same time still the oppressive St Petersburg of the *White Nights*, and known to Raskolnikov.[1] The Hermitage museum was truly impressive, and I shall never forget the sight of troops of workmen, soldiers and peasants, hats reverently held in their hands just as they would have taken them off respectfully before icons in the old days, tramping with their heavy shoes through former imperial halls and looking at the pictures with secret pride, as if saying—all this is ours now, and we will learn to understand it. Teachers led round-cheeked children through the halls, art commissars explained Rembrandt and Titian to peasants who listened rather self-consciously, looking timidly up from under their heavy eyelids when details were pointed out. Here, as elsewhere, there was a touch of absurdity in this honest and well-meant effort to turn 'the people' overnight from illiterates into connoisseurs able to appreciate Beethoven and Vermeer—but the effort made by one party to the transaction to convey an instant idea of the highest artistic values, and by the other to understand them, gave rise to some impatience on both sides. Children at school were allowed to paint the wildest, most extravagant pictures; girls of twelve had the works of Hegel and Sorel,[2] whom I myself did not know at this time, on the desks in front of them. Cabbies who could hardly read had books in their hands, just because they *were* books and books meant education, so it was an honour and a duty for the new proletariat to get educated. We often found ourselves smiling when we were shown round perfectly ordinary factories and were expected to gaze in wonderment, as if we had never seen such marvels in Europe and America. "Look, electric!" one worker told me proudly, pointing to a sewing machine and obviously expecting me to break into exclamations of astonishment. Because the Russian people were seeing these technical things for the first time, they humbly thought they had all been thought up and invented by the Revolution and Little Fathers Lenin and Trotsky. So although we were secretly amused, we smiled and admired everything. This new Russia, we thought, resembled a large, wonderfully talented and good-natured child, and we wondered—will it really learn such wide-ranging lessons as quickly as it thinks? Will the great plan go on developing, or will it fail and relapse into the old Russian apathy of Oblomov?[3] Sometimes you felt confident that all would be well, sometimes you doubted it. The more I saw of Russia the less sure I could feel.

But was I the one in a state of indecision, or was it something in the Russian nature, even in the mind of Tolstoy, whom we had come to celebrate? On the train journey to his estate of Yasnaya Polyana I discussed him with Lunacharsky. "Yes, what was he really?" Lunacharsky said to me. "A revolutionary or a reactionary? Did he himself know? Like a real Russian, he wanted everything too quickly; after thousands of years he wanted to change the whole world in the twinkling of an eye. Just like us now," he added, smiling, "and with a single prescription, again just like us. It's a mistake to think of us Russians as patient. Our bodies are patient, and so even are our souls. But we think more impatiently than any other nation, we want to know every truth, we want to know *the* truth, and we want to know it now. How that old man tormented himself in search of it!" And indeed, as I walked round Tolstoy's house at Yasnaya Polyana, I kept thinking the same thing—how that great old man had tormented himself! I saw the desk where he sat to write his immortal works, and he had left it to make shoes—not very good shoes, either—in the unassuming room next door. I saw the door and the staircase through which he had tried to escape this house and his indecision. There was the gun with which Tolstoy, an enemy of all war, had killed enemies in war. The entire problem of his existence forced itself upon me graphically in that low-built white manor house. But the aura of tragedy was dispelled by our walk to his last resting place.

I saw nothing finer or more moving in Russia than Tolstoy's grave. That illustrious place of pilgrimage lies out of the way, alone in the middle of the woods. A narrow footpath leads to the mound, nothing but a rectangle of soil raised above ground level, with no one guarding or keeping watch on it, only two huge trees casting their shade. Leo Tolstoy planted those trees himself, so his granddaughter told me beside his grave. When he and his brother Nikolai were boys, they had heard one of the village women say that a place where you planted trees would be a happy one. So they planted two saplings, partly as a kind of game. Only later did the old man remember that promise of happiness, and then he expressed a wish to be buried under the trees he had planted. And his wish was carried out. In its heart-rending simplicity, his grave is the most impressive place of burial in the world. Just a small rectangular mound in the woods ⌁ with trees overhead, no cross, no tombstone, no inscription. The great man who suffered more than anyone from his own famous name and reputation lies buried there, nameless, like a vagabond who happened to be found nearby or an unknown soldier. No one is forbidden to visit his last resting place; the flimsy wooden fence around it is not kept locked. Nothing guards that restless man's final rest but human respect for him. While curious sightseers usually throng around the magnificence of a tomb, the compelling simplicity of this place banishes any desire to gape. The wind rushes like the word of God over the nameless grave, and no other voice is heard. You could pass the place without knowing any more than that someone is buried here, a Russian lying in Russian earth. Napoleon's tomb beneath the marble dome of Les Invalides, Goethe's in the grand-ducal vault

359

at Weimar, the tombs in Westminster Abbey are none of them as moving as this silent and movingly anonymous grave somewhere in the woods, with only the wind whispering around it, uttering no word or message of its own.

I had been in Russia for fourteen days, and I still felt the same inner tension, a slight daze of intellectual intoxication. What actually moved me so much? I soon worked it out—it was the people and their impulsive goodwill. All of them, from the first to the last, were convinced that they were participating in a great endeavour for the good of all humanity; they all felt sure that while they might have to put up with deprivations and restrictions, it was all in the service of a higher cause. The old Russian sense of inferiority to the rest of Europe had turned to an ecstasy of pride in being ahead, in advance of everyone else. "*Ex oriente lux*"[4]—they were bringing salvation from the East. They honestly and genuinely thought that they had seen the one true light, and it was given to them to do what others only dreamt of. When they showed you the least little thing their eyes shone: "We made that." And the whole nation identified itself with that "we". The cabbies who drove you around would point their whips at some new building, grinning broadly: "We built that." The Tatar and Mongol students in the lecture halls came out to meet us, proudly showing off their books. "Darwin!" one proclaimed. "Marx!" said another. They were as proud as if they had written the works of Marx and Darwin themselves. They all wanted to show us something, explain it to us, they were so glad that someone had come to see their work. All of them—this was years before Stalin—had boundless faith in a European. They looked at you with trust in their eyes, and shook your hand in hearty, fraternal fashion. But at the same time even the least among them made it clear that while they might like you, there was no special reason to show anyone respect, for we were all brothers, to be addressed as *tovarish*, comrade. It was the same among the writers. We were all gathered in

360

the house that had once belonged to Alexander Herzen, not just Europeans and Russians but also Tungus, Georgian and Caucasian writers; every Soviet state had sent its delegate to the Tolstoy centenary. It was impossible to converse with most of them, but we understood each other all the same. One of them would get to his feet, come over to me, mention the title of one of my books and indicate his heart, meaning that he liked it very much. Then he would take my hand and shake it as if to show his approval by dislocating all my joints. Even more touchingly, they all had presents to give. The economy was still in a very bad way; they had nothing valuable left, but everyone found something to give a visitor as a memento—a worthless old engraving, a book that I couldn't read, a piece of peasant carving. It was easier for me, of course, since I could respond with precious items that hadn't been seen in Russia for years—a Gillette razor blade, a fountain pen, a few sheets of good white notepaper, a pair of soft leather slippers—so that I travelled very light on my way home. The tongue-tied but impulsive reception they gave us, with a depth and warmth unknown at home, was overwhelming. Back in Europe, a writer never really came into contact with all classes of society, and spending time with these people was an irresistible temptation to many of the foreign writers visiting Russia, where they were acclaimed. They had never been hailed in quite that way by the vast majority at home, so they thought they had to respond in kind by praising the regime under which their books were read and they were so popular. It is only human nature, after all, to answer generosity with generosity, exuberance with exuberance. I must admit that while I was in Russia I myself was often close to bursting into paeans of praise and becoming an enthusiastic admirer of the Russians' own enthusiasm.

I owe my resistance to that intoxicating frenzy not so much to my own strength of mind as to a stranger whose name I still do not know, and never will. It happened after a party where

some students were present. They surrounded me, embraced
me, shook my hand. Their enthusiasm was heart-warming, and
I looked with pleasure at their lively faces. A little company of
four or five of them escorted me home, with the girl student who
was acting as my interpreter translating everything they said for
me. Only when I had closed the door of my hotel room behind
me was I really alone, for the first time in twelve days, because
foreigners were always accompanied, carefully guarded, carried
along on warm waves of emotion. I began undressing and took
off my coat. As I did so I felt something crackle inside it. I put
my hand in my pocket. It was a letter. A letter in French, but
it had not arrived by post. Someone in the crowd must have
slipped it into my pocket during all those embraces.

It was an unsigned letter, very clever and humane, not written
by a White Russian but bitterly critical of the ever-increasing
curtailment of liberties in Russia over recent years. "Don't believe
everything they tell you," wrote my unknown correspondent.
"Whatever you are shown, never forget that they're not letting
you see much. Remember that the people who talk to you are
not usually saying what they want to say, only what they are
allowed to tell you. We are all under surveillance, you too. Your
interpreter passes on everything you say. Your telephone is
bugged, they watch every step you take." He added a whole
list of examples and details. I was not in a position to check
those, but I burnt his letter as he asked—"Don't just tear this
up, please, because the separate scraps would be retrieved from
your waste-paper basket and fitted together." And for the first
time I began to think about it soberly. It was indeed a fact that in
the midst of all this honest warmth and delightful comradeship,
I had never once had a chance of talking frankly to anyone tête-
à-tête. My ignorance of the language had prevented me from
really getting into touch with ordinary people. Then again,
what a tiny part of this vast country I had seen in these two
weeks! If I were to be honest with myself and others, I had

362

to admit that my impression, moving and inspiring as it had been in many ways, could not be objective. And that accounts for the fact that while almost all other European writers who came back from Russia at the time immediately published a book either enthusiastically endorsing the regime or strongly condemning it, I wrote only a couple of articles. I did well to keep my distance, because three months later much in Russia was not the way I had seen it, and a year later, thanks to rapid change, the facts would have given the lie to every word I might have written earlier. All the same, at almost no other time and place in my life did I feel the current of contemporary events flowing more strongly than I did in Russia.

My suitcases were fairly empty when I left Moscow. I had given away what I could spare, and the only acquisitions of my own that I brought back were two icons that hung in my room for a long time. But the most valuable thing I took home was my friendship with Maxim Gorky, whom I had met in person for the first time in Moscow. I saw him again him two or three years later in Sorrento, where he was staying for the sake of his frail health, and spent three unforgettable days in his house there.

This first meeting of ours in Russia was really a very strange affair. Gorky knew no foreign languages, I knew no Russian. By all the dictates of logic we should have been condemned to face one another in silence, or keeping a conversation going only through the skills of our mutual and much-esteemed friend Maria, Baroness Budberg, who acted as interpreter. But not for nothing was Gorky one of the most brilliant storytellers in the history of literature—narrative was not only an artistic form of expression for him, it was a function of his entire nature. When he was telling a story he lived in the narrative, was transformed into the narrative, and without understanding what he was saying I understood him through the activity of his mobile

363

face. In himself he simply looked—well, I would have to say 'Russian'. There was nothing striking about his features; you could have taken this tall, thin man with yellow, straw-coloured hair and broad cheekbones for a peasant in the fields, a driver in his cab, a cobbler in a small way of business, an unkempt vagabond—he was nothing but one of the common people, the concentrated quintessence of Russian humanity. You would have passed him without a second thought in the street, never noticing anything special about him. Only when you sat facing him and he began to tell a story did you realise who and what he really was, because he spontaneously *became* the person he was portraying. I remember his description—I understood it even before it was translated—of a hunchbacked, weary little old man he had once met in his wanderings. He instinctively bowed his head, his shoulders slumped, his eyes, bright blue and shining when he had begun to speak, grew dark and tired, his voice faltered; without knowing it he had turned into the old hunchback. And if he had a funny story to tell he burst out laughing, leant back in a relaxed attitude, with a glint in his eyes. It was indescribably delightful to listen to him as he presented the setting and people around him with sweeping, graphic gestures. Everything about him was simple and natural—his way of walking, sitting, listening, his exuberant high spirits. One evening he dressed up as a boyar, buckled on a sword, and at once majesty came into his eyes. His eyebrows arched commandingly, he strode energetically up and down the room as if he planned to proclaim some grim ukase, and next moment, after taking off his fancy dress, he was laughing as childishly as a peasant boy. His vitality was miraculous; one of his lungs was in such a bad way that he kept alive in defiance of all the laws of medicine, but an extraordinary will to live and an iron sense of duty kept him going. He worked on his great novel every morning, writing in his classic calligraphic hand, he answered hundreds of questions sent by young writers and workers from his native Russia. To

364

me, being in his company meant meeting Russia—not Bolshevik Russia, not the Russia of the past or of today, but the great, strong, dark soul of the eternal Russian people. Privately, he had not quite made up his mind which way to go in those years. As a former revolutionary, he wanted society to change and had been a personal friend of Lenin, but he still hesitated to commit himself entirely to the Party, "to be a priest or pope", as he put it. Yet his conscience pricked him for not being with the Russian people in the years when every week called for new decisions.

At the time I happened to witness an incident characteristic of the new Russia, one that revealed Gorky's entire dilemma to me. For the first time, a Russian warship had anchored off Naples on a training exercise. The young sailors, who had never been in an international metropolis before, sauntered down the Via Toledo, gazed at all the novelties they saw with their wide, curious peasant eyes, and couldn't get enough of it. Next day a group of them decided to come over to Sorrento to visit 'their' writer. They did not give advance notice of their arrival; in their Russian notion of fraternity they took it for granted that their writer would always have time to see them. Suddenly there they were outside his house, and they had been right—Gorky didn't keep them waiting, but invited them straight in. However—Gorky himself told this story with a smile next day—these young men, in whose minds the cause of Communism reigned supreme, started by addressing him sternly. "What are you doing here?" they asked as soon as they were in his attractive, comfortable villa. "You're living a bourgeois life! Why don't you come back to Russia?" Gorky had to explain to them as best he could. But the well-intentioned young men didn't really mean to rebuke him. They had just wanted to show that they were not going to kowtow to a famous man, they wanted to find out his real opinions. They sat down at their ease, drank tea, talked, and when they left they embraced him each in turn. Gorky told this story with wonderful verve, delighted by the free and easy manners of the new generation, and not in the least

365

upset by their strictures. "How different *we* were in our youth,"
he kept saying, "either cowed or indignant, but never so sure
of ourselves." His eyes shone all evening. And when I said to
him, "I think you'd really have liked to go home with them,"
he paused and looked at me keenly. "Now how did you know
that? To be honest, right up to the last moment I was wondering
whether to just leave everything here, my books and papers, my
work, and sail off into the blue for a couple of weeks with those
young sailors on their ship. I would have seen Russia again. You
forget the best of yourself when you're abroad. None of us has
yet done any good work in exile."

But Gorky was wrong to call Sorrento exile. After all, he could
go home any day, and indeed he did. He was not banished with
his books into personal exile, as Merezhkovsky was—I met that
tragically embittered man in Paris—or as we are today, those of
us who can say, with Grillparzer, that we have "two foreign homes
and yet no native land",[5] not at home in borrowed languages,
driven where the wind wills. On the other hand, I visited a real
exile in Naples during the next few days—Benedetto Croce. For
decades he had been the intellectual mentor of the young, his
country's honours had been heaped on him as a senator and
government minister, until his opposition to Fascism brought
him into conflict with Mussolini. He resigned from office and
withdrew into seclusion, but that did not satisfy his intransigent
enemies. They wanted to break his spirit and if necessary even
discipline him. A band of students, who in contrast to the old
days are now the storm-troops of reaction everywhere, attacked
his house and broke the windows. But that stocky little man,
who looked like a comfortable bourgeois with his clever eyes and
little pointed beard, was not to be intimidated. He did not leave
the country, he stayed in his house behind the rampart of his
books, although he had had invitations to go to American and

other foreign universities. He went on editing his journal *Critica* in the same spirit as before, he continued to publish his books, and so great was his authority that censorship, imposed on Mussolini's orders and usually implacable, stopped short at him, although it affected all his pupils and like-minded colleagues. It took particular courage for an Italian and even a foreigner to visit him, since the authorities knew perfectly well that he spoke frankly and without dissimulation in the citadel of his book-lined rooms. He was living, as it were, in an airtight space like a kind of sealed gas bottle, in the middle of his forty million countrymen. As I saw it, this hermetic isolation of a single man in a city and a country of millions had something both magnificent and ghostly about it. I did not know at the time that this was in fact a considerably milder form of the destructive intellectual violence to be brought to bear against those like us later, and could not help marvelling at the lively mind and intellectual force that this man, already old, preserved in his daily struggles. But he laughed. "Oh, resistance keeps you young. If I were still a senator, my ideas would have turned lazy and slipshod long ago. Nothing is worse for a thinking man than lack of any opposition. Now that I'm on my own, without any young people around me, I'm forced to rejuvenate myself."

But several more years had to pass before I understood that trials are a challenge, and if they do not break your spirit, then persecution fortifies you and isolation enhances your powers. Like all the important aspects of life, we never find out these things from other people's experiences, only our own.

I have never set eyes on Mussolini, the most important man in Italy, because I am always disinclined to approach political figures, even in my small native land of Austria, where it was quite an achievement to have avoided meeting any of the leading statesmen, neither Seipel nor Dollfuss nor Schuschnigg.

367

Yet I ought really have felt in duty bound to see Mussolini who, as I knew from mutual friends, was one of the first and most enthusiastic of my readers in Italy. I should have offered my personal thanks for his spontaneous response to the first request I ever made of a statesman.

It happened like this. One day I had an express letter from a friend in Paris, saying that an Italian lady wanted to visit me in Salzburg on important business, and could I see her at once? She called on me the very next day, and what she had to tell me was indeed shocking. Her husband, a distinguished medical doctor of humble social origin, had been educated at the expense of Matteotti.[6] When Matteotti, leader of the Socialists, was murdered by the Fascists, world opinion, already weary with all the demands on it, had reacted once more against a single crime. All Europe had risen in indignant protest. His loyal friend the doctor had been one of the six brave men who dared to carry Matteotti's coffin openly through the streets of Rome. Soon after that, ostracised and under threat, he had gone into exile. But the fate of Matteotti's family weighed on his mind. In memory of his benefactor, he tried to smuggle Matteotti's children out of Italy to safety abroad. However, in the attempt he himself had fallen foul of spies or agents provocateurs, and had been arrested. As everything calling Matteotti to mind was an embarrassment to Italy, the outcome of a trial on those grounds would not have been too bad for him, but by devious means the public prosecutor had associated his trial with another going on at the same time, and that case was concerned with an attempt to blow up Mussolini with a bomb. So this doctor, who had won the highest honours serving his country on the battlefields of the Great War, was sentenced to ten years' hard labour.

Naturally his young wife was extremely distressed. Something, she said, must be done to overturn the sentence, which her husband could not survive. An appeal must go out to all the literary names in Europe to unite in loud protest, and she was asking me to help her. My immediate reaction was to advise her against trying to get anywhere with protests. I knew how threadbare such demonstrations had worn since the war. I did my best to explain that no country, for reasons of national pride, was going to let outsiders change the decisions of its judiciary, and that European protests in the case of Sacco and Vanzetti[7] in America had had the opposite of the desired effect. I urged her not to do anything of that kind, pointing out that she would only make her husband's situation worse, because Mussolini would never—indeed, could never—recommend leniency if foreign attempts were made to force his hand. But I was genuinely shocked myself, and promised to do my best. It so happened that the next week I was going to Italy, where I had friends in influential positions. Perhaps they could quietly do something to help her husband.

I approached my friends on my very first day in the country. But I could see how fear had already eaten into all minds. As soon as I mentioned the doctor's name everyone looked awkward and said No, he was sorry, but he had no influence, it was impossible to do anything. I went from one to another. I came home feeling ashamed and afraid the man's poor wife might think I hadn't done all I could. Nor, as a matter of fact, had I. There was still one possibility—the direct approach. I would write to the man in whose hands the decision lay, Mussolini himself.

I did that. I sent him a perfectly honest letter. I was not, I wrote, going to begin with flattery, and I ought also to say at once that I did not know the doctor personally or the extent of what he had done. But I had seen his wife, who was certainly innocent of any crime, and she too would suffer the full rigour of the court's sentence if her husband spent all those years in the penitentiary. I did not intend to criticise the verdict in any way, but I could well imagine that it would save the young woman's life if her husband were allowed to serve his sentence not in the penitentiary, but on one of the island penal colonies where wives and children are allowed to live with exiles.

I took the letter, addressed it to His Excellency Benito Mussolini, and put it in the usual Salzburg postbox. Four days later I heard from the Italian Embassy in Vienna. His Excellency, said the Embassy, thanked me for my letter, said that he would do as I asked, and in addition to commuting the doctor's sentence had taken it upon himself to shorten its length. At the same time I had a telegram from Italy confirming that the doctor, as I had asked, had been moved to a penal colony. Mussolini himself had granted my request with a single stroke of his pen, and in fact the convicted doctor soon received a full pardon. No letter in my life has ever given me so much delight and satisfaction, and if I ever think of my own literary success, it is this instance of it that I remember with especial gratitude.

It was good to travel in those years of the last calm before the storm, but it was good to come home as well. Something odd had been quietly going on. A remarkable change had come over the little city of Salzburg, with its 40,000 inhabitants, which I had chosen for the sake of its romantic seclusion. In the summer season it was now the artistic capital not only of Europe but of the whole world. During the worst of the post-war period, and with a view to doing something for the actors and musicians out of work during the summer, Max Reinhardt and Hugo von Hofmannsthal had staged a few works in the Domplatz outside Salzburg Cathedral, including the famous open-air production of *Everyman*. Audiences came from the immediate vicinity at first. Then some operatic productions were added to the programme. They went down very well indeed. Gradually the world began to take notice. The best conductors, singers and actors were eager to come, glad of a chance to perform in front of an international public instead of just their limited home audiences. Suddenly the

Salzburg Festival was a worldwide attraction, amounting to a kind of modern Olympic Games of art in which all nations competed to display their finest achievements. No one wanted to miss these extraordinary productions. Over the last few years kings and princes, American millionaires and glamorous film stars, music-lovers, artists, writers and social snobs had met in Salzburg. Never before in Europe had there been such concentrated thespian and musical perfection as in this little city in little Austria, a country that had been dismissed as unimportant for so long. Salzburg flourished. In summer everyone from Europe and America who sought after the performing arts at their best came there, and you met them in its streets wearing the local traditional costume—short linen trousers and jackets for the men, colourful dirndls for the women. Tiny little Salzburg suddenly dictated world fashion. Visitors competed for hotel rooms, the procession of cars driving to the Festival theatre was as magnificent as the vehicles that used to drive to the Imperial Court Ball, the railway station was always crowded. Other towns and cities tried to divert this profitable stream to themselves, but they all failed. Salzburg was and would remain a place of pilgrimage for European lovers of art during this decade.

So all of a sudden I was living in my home town and at the same time in the middle of Europe. Once again, Fate had granted a wish of mine that I myself had hardly dared to imagine—our house on the Kapuzinerberg became a European meeting-place. Whom did we not entertain there? Our visitors' book would be better evidence than just my memory, but it, the house, and much more besides fell victim to the National Socialists. We spent so many happy hours with all our guests, sitting on the terrace and looking out at the beautiful and peaceful landscape, never guessing that directly opposite, on the mountain in Berchtesgaden, a man lived who would destroy it all. Romain Rolland stayed with us, and Thomas Mann. Among the guests whom we welcomed to our house were H G Wells, Hofmannsthal, Jakob Wassermann, van Loon, James Joyce, Emil Ludwig, Franz Werfel, Georg Brandes, Paul Valéry, Jane Adams, Shalom Asch and Arthur Schnitzler. Musicians included Ravel and Richard Strauss, Alban Berg, Bruno Walter, Bartók, and there were many other guests—painters, actors and scholars from all over the world. We passed many pleasant, cheerful hours in good conversation at our house every summer. One day Arturo Toscanini climbed the steep steps of the path up to the house, and that was the beginning of a friendship that made me love, understand and enjoy music more than ever before. For years I attended his rehearsals, and again and again I saw his impassioned struggle to achieve the perfection that appears both a miracle and entirely natural in his public concerts. (I once wrote an article in which I tried to describe those rehearsals, a model to every artist of the instinctive urge to go on and on until a performance is absolutely faultless.) It was wonderful confirmation that music is not just, as Shakespeare says, the food of love, but nourishment for the soul, and seeing all the arts competing for attention here, I blessed the fate that brought me close to them so often. Those were rich, colourful summer days, when art and the beauty of the landscape complemented each other! And whenever I thought of the little city of Salzburg as it had been immediately after the end of the Great War, dilapidated, dismal and ruinous, and of our own house when we were freezing cold and struggling to keep the rain from coming through the roof, I felt how much these years of blessed peace had done for my life. We were justified in believing in the world and humanity again.

Many welcome and famous guests visited our house in those years, but even in the hours when I was alone I was surrounded by a magic circle of distinguished figures from the past whose shades and whose traces I had gradually managed to summon. I have already mentioned my collection of autograph manuscripts, and it now contained examples in the handwriting of the greatest masters in history. I had started my collection in an amateurish way as a boy of fifteen, and in all these years, thanks to a great deal of experience, more money than when I first began and even greater passion, I had turned a mere assortment of separate items into an organic structure, transforming it, I think it is fair to say, into a genuine work of art in itself. When I began I had set out only, as beginners do, to bring together names—famous names. Then, out of psychological curiosity, I had collected more and more manuscripts, original drafts or fragments of works, which also gave me an insight into the creative methods of a much-loved master. The most profound and mysterious of the countless insoluble riddles of the world is surely the mystery of creation. You cannot eavesdrop on Nature here; she will not show you the final secret of how the earth was created and how a little flower grows, how a poem or a man comes into being. Pitilessly, inflexibly, Nature draws a veil over that last secret. Even the poets and musicians cannot account for the moment of inspiration in retrospect. Once the act of creation is complete, the creative artist does not know where it came from or how it grew to fruition. Artists can never, or almost never, explain how, in their heightened state of consciousness, words come together to form a verse, or single notes to make a melody that will echo through the centuries. Nothing can give an idea of the incomprehensible process of creation except, to some slight extent, handwritten pages, particularly those that are covered with corrections and not yet ready to go to press, and the still tentative first drafts from which the final form of a work will emerge. The second and more knowledgeable stage in my collecting activities was to bring together such autograph pages and corrected versions by all the great writers, philosophers and musicians, evidence of their creative struggles in their work. It was a pleasure to hunt them up at auctions, and a labour of love to track them down in the most remote hiding-places. At the same time there was a kind of science in it, for as well as my collection of autograph manuscripts I had gradually made another, comprising all the books that had ever been written on the subject, all the catalogues of autograph manuscripts that had ever been printed, over four thousand in all, an unparalleled library of manuals, for even dealers in antiquities and manuscripts cannot spend so much time and love on a single specialised branch of the subject. I think I am justified in saying—as I would never venture to say of my achievements in literature or any other sphere of life—that in my thirty or forty years of collecting I had become the leading authority in the field of autograph manuscripts, and knew where every important autograph page now was, who owned it, and how it had come into the owner's hands. I had become a true expert who could tell at first glance if a manuscript sheet was genuine, with more experience in assessing such autographs than most professionals.

But after a while my ambitions as a collector went further. I felt it was no longer enough to have just a gallery of autograph manuscript pages of great literature and music, a reflection of a thousand creative methods. Simply enlarging my collection did not tempt me any more. In my last ten years as a collector I set out to refine it. While it had once been enough for me to own manuscript sheets showing writers or musicians in the process of creation, my efforts now went into finding autographs that would illustrate their work at their most inspired and successful creative moments. So I looked not just for the manuscript of any of a writer's poems, but for one of his finest, if possible one of those works that begin to form when inspiration first finds earthly expression on the page in ink or pencil, and then go on and on into eternity. Bold and presumptuous it may have been, but I wanted to have those manuscripts—relics of the immortals illustrating what made them immortal in the first place.

So the collection was really in constant flux; I removed from it, sold or exchanged all the autograph pages that did not quite come up to the highest standards as soon as I had succeeded in finding a more significant and characteristic example, one that—how shall I put it?—had a touch of eternity about it. And strange to say, in many cases I succeeded, because there were very few other collectors trying to acquire these important items as persistently and with as much expert knowledge as I did. So first I had a portfolio and finally a whole display case, fitted with metal and asbestos to ward off the depredations of time, containing the original manuscripts of works, or extracts from works, that are part of the enduring manifesto of creative mankind. I now have to live a nomadic life, and I do not have the catalogue of that collection, dispersed long ago, here with me, so I can enumerate only at random the items in it showing how earthly genius became immortal.

I had a page from Leonardo's sketch book, with his comments on his drawings in mirror writing beside them; Napoleon's army orders to his soldiers at Rivoli, jotted down on four pages in a barely legible hand; I had an entire proof copy of a novel by Balzac, every sheet of it a battlefield of corrections, illustrating with extraordinary clarity his titanic struggle for perfection from change to change—fortunately there is a photocopy of it kept safely in an American university. There was a first and previously unknown draft of Nietzsche's *The Birth of Tragedy*, on which he worked for a long time before presenting it to his beloved Cosima Wagner, a Bach cantata, an aria from Gluck's *Alceste*, and one from Handel, whose music manuscripts are the rarest of all. I always looked for a writer's or musician's most characteristic works, and I usually found them—Brahms's *Zigeunerlieder*, Chopin's *Barcarole*, Schubert's immortal *An die Musik*, the imperishable melody of the Austrian national anthem from Haydn's *Emperor Quartet*. In some cases I even managed to expand an isolated creative illustration into an entire picture of the range of an individual artist's creativity. I had, for instance, not just a sheet clumsily written by Mozart at the age of eleven, but also evidence of his mature composition of lieder in the immortal *Veilchen*, a setting of Goethe, and to illustrate his dance music the manuscript of the minuet paraphrased by Figaro in *Non più andrai*. From *Le Nozze di Figaro* itself I had Cherubino's aria—and another aspect of Mozart in his delightfully indecent letters to his girl cousin, never then printed in full for public consumption, as well as a scabrous canon, and finally an aria from *La Clemenza di Tito*, written just before Mozart's death. My picture of Goethe ranged just as widely. I had the first page of a translation from Latin that he had done at the age of nine, the last of a poem written in his eighty-second year not long before his death, and in between a fine illustration of the poet at the height of his powers—a double folio sheet from *Faust*—as well as a manuscript on the natural sciences, many poems, and drawings from various periods of his life. Those fifteen manuscript pages added up to a survey of Goethe's entire career. With Beethoven, whom I revere most of all, I could not, admittedly, manage to build up such a complete and rounded picture. As with Goethe, my publisher Professor Kippenberg, my adversary who outbid me here, one of the richest men in Switzerland, was the collector of an unparalleled treasury of Beethoven works. But apart from his youthful notebook, the song *Der Kuss*, and fragments of the incidental music to *Egmont*, I did succeed in visually presenting at least one moment in his life, the most tragic of all, more completely than any museum on earth can do. Through a lucky chance, I was able to acquire all the furniture left in his room and auctioned after his death, when it was bought by Councillor Breuning. The outstanding item was his huge desk, complete with pictures in the desk drawers of the two women he had loved, Countess Giulietta Guicciardi and Countess Erdödy, the money box that he kept beside his bed to the last, the small portable desk on which he wrote his last letters and compositions in bed, a white lock of his hair, cut off on his

death, the invitation to his funeral, the last laundry list he had
written in a shaky hand, the inventory of his house contents for
the auction sale, and the subscription got up by his Viennese
friends to provide for his cook Sali, who was left without any
means of financial support. And since chance is always kind
enough to play into the hands of a true collector, soon after I
had acquired all these things from the room where he died I
also had an opportunity to buy the drawings done of him on
his deathbed. From contemporary accounts of these drawings
I knew that a young painter who was a friend of Schubert's,
Josef Teltscher by name, had tried to draw Beethoven on 26th
March 1827 when he was in his death throes, but had been
asked to leave by Breuning, who felt that such a thing was
inappropriate. The drawings were lost for a hundred years until,
at a small auction sale in Brünn, several dozen sketchbooks by
this minor artist were being sold off cheap, and the sketches of
Beethoven were suddenly found in them. Coincidence tends
to follow coincidence, and one day a dealer called me to ask
if I was interested in the original of the death-bed drawing of
Beethoven. I said that as a matter of fact it was already in my
hands, but then it turned out that the new drawing being offered
to me was the original on which Danhauser's famous lithograph
of Beethoven on his deathbed was based. And so now I had
everything recording that final memorable and truly immortal
last moment of the composer's life.

Of course I never considered myself the owner of these
things, only their custodian for a certain time. I was not tempted
by a sense of possession, of having them for myself, but I was
intrigued by the idea of bringing them together, making a
collection into a work of art. I was aware that in this collection
I had created something that in itself was worthier to last than
my own works. In spite of many offers, I hesitated to draw up
a catalogue of my collection, because I was still in the middle
of extending it, and the final structure needed many more

names and items to bring it to perfection. I had thought carefully, and intended to leave my unique collection on my death to an institution that would agree to my condition, which was to spend a certain sum of money every year to continue adding to it along the lines I had devised. Then it would not have been a dead thing, but a living organism refining and adding to itself for fifty or a hundred years after my own lifetime, becoming an increasingly beautiful whole.

But it is not granted to our much-tried generation to make such plans for the future. When the Hitler period began and I left my house, my pleasure in collecting was gone, and so was any certainty that something of what I had done would last. For a while I kept parts of the collection in safes and at friends' houses, but then, remembering Goethe's warning that museums and collections will ossify if they do not go on developing, I decided that instead, since I could not devote my own efforts to perfecting my collection, I would say goodbye to it. I gave part of it to the Viennese National Library when I left, mainly those items that I myself had been given as presents by friends and contemporaries. Part of it I sold, and what happened or is now happening to the rest of it does not weigh on my mind any more. I had enjoyed creating the collection more than I enjoyed the collection itself. So I do not mourn for what I have lost. For if there is one new art that we have had to learn, those of us who have been hunted down and forced into exile at a time hostile to all art and all collections, then it is the art of saying goodbye to everything that was once our pride and joy.

So the years passed in work and travel, learning, reading, collecting, and the enjoyment of those pleasures. One November day in 1931, I woke up and I was fifty years old. That day was a hard one for our good white-headed Salzburg postman. Since the civilised custom of celebrating a writer's fiftieth birthday at length in the papers was still practised in Germany and Austria, the old postman had a considerable number of letters and telegrams to haul up that steep path with all its steps. Before opening and reading them, I thought what this day meant to me. Your fiftieth year is a turning point; you look back uneasily to see how much of your path you have already trodden, and ask yourself privately if it still leads upward. I thought of the time I had lived through; I looked back at those fifty years as I looked from my house at the Alpine range and the valley gently falling away, and I had to admit that it would be perverse of me not to feel grateful. After all, I had been given far, far more than I had hoped or expected. My wish to develop and express myself through writing works of some literary merit had been granted beyond my wildest childhood dreams. Before me, printed by Insel Verlag as a fiftieth birthday present, was a bibliography of my published books in all their languages of translation, and it was a book in itself. No important language was missing, they were all there, Bulgarian and Finnish, Portuguese and Armenian, Chinese and Marathi. My words and ideas had reached readers in Braille, in shorthand symbols, in all kinds of exotic characters and idioms. My existence had had immeasurable influence beyond the confines of my own life. I had made friends with many of the finest people of our time; I had seen and enjoyed wonderful artistic performances, immortal cities and pictures, and the most beautiful landscapes in the world. I had remained free, independent of any official position or career, my work was a pleasure to me, and even better, it had given pleasure to others! What could go wrong? Here were my books, and who could do away with them? (Or so I asked myself at the time, innocent of any presentiment.) Here was my house, and who could drive me out of it? There were my friends—could I ever lose them? I thought without fear of death and illness, but not the faintest inkling came into my mind of what still lay ahead of me. I had no idea that I would be driven out of my own home, a hunted exile who must wander from land to

land, over sea after sea, or that my books would be burnt, banned
and despised, my name pilloried in Germany like a criminal's,
or that the same friends whose letters and telegrams lay on the
table before me would turn pale if they happened to meet me by
chance. I did not know that everything I had achieved by hard
work for thirty or forty years could be extinguished without trace,
that my whole life, firmly constructed on sound foundations at it
seemed to be, could collapse in ruins, and after nearly reaching
the summit I would be forced to begin again from the beginning,
with my powers already weary and my mind disturbed. It was
not, to be sure, a day for me to think of anything so absurd and
nonsensical. I could be happy; I loved my work and so I loved life.
I was free of care; even if I never wrote another line my books
would provide for me. I seemed to have achieved a good deal; I
had tamed Fate. By my own efforts, I had won back the security
I had known in my parental home as a child, and then lost in the
war. What did I have left to wish for?

Strange to say, the very fact that I could think of nothing left
to wish for at that moment made me feel mysteriously uneasy.
Would it really be a good thing, some impulse in me asked—
not really my conscious self—for life to go on like this, so calm,
well-regulated, financially profitable and comfortable, without
any more tensions or trials? Isn't it, I asked myself, wrong for
your real self to be living this secure, privileged life? I walked
thoughtfully around my house. Over the years it had become
a beautiful place, just what I had wanted. But all the same, was
I always going to live here, sitting at the same desk and writing
books, one book and then another, earning royalties and yet
more royalties, gradually becoming a dignified gentleman who
has to think of his name and his work with decorous propriety,
leaving behind everything that comes by chance, all tensions and
dangers? Was I always to go on like this until I was sixty and
then seventy, following a straight, smooth track? Wouldn't it be
better for me—so I went on daydreaming—if something else

happened, something new, something that would make me feel more restless, younger, bringing new tension by challenging me to a new and perhaps more dangerous battle? There is always a mysterious conflict in every artist; if life treats him roughly he longs for peace and calm, but if he comes into safe harbour he longs to be back in the turmoil. On that fiftieth birthday of mine, then, I had in my heart only the perverse wish for something to happen that would tear me away from all that security and comfort again, would force me not just to go on as I was, but to start again. Was it fear of growing old, weary and apathetic? Or was it a mysterious foreboding that made me wish on that day for a harder life, for the sake of my further development? I don't know.

I don't know. For what rose from the twilight of the unconscious mind at that strange hour was not a clearly expressed wish, certainly nothing to do with my conscious will, just a fleeting idea that brushed past me, perhaps not even my own idea but one rising from depths of which I knew nothing. But the dark power presiding over my life, an intangible power that had already done so much more for me than I would ever have had the audacity to wish for, must have sensed it. And that power was already obediently preparing to smash my life to its foundations, forcing me to reconstruct a harsher, harder life from its ruins and rebuild it from the ground up.

NOTES

1   The references are to works by Dostoevsky. *White Nights* is one of his short stories, and Raskolnikov the central character of *Crime and Punishment*, both set in St Petersburg.

2   Georges Sorel, 1847-1922, French philosopher and revolutionary theorist.

3   The central character of a novel by Ivan Goncharov 1812-1891, Oblomov can never make up his mind, take a decision or rouse himself from lethargy.

4   *Out of the East comes light.*

5   A line of verse by Grillparzer, see note above.

6   Giacomo Matteotti, 1865-1924, of a wealthy family, was a prominent Socialist politician.

7   Two anarchists of Italian extraction, found guilty of robbery and murder and executed in 1927. There was considerable doubt of their guilt—it was suspected that anti-immigrant prejudice had played a part at their trial—and mass demonstrations took place in Europe.

INCIPIT HITLER[1]

I T IS AN IRON LAW OF HISTORY that those who will be caught up in the great movements determining the course of their own times always fail to recognise them in their early stages. So I cannot remember when I first heard the name of Adolf Hitler, one that for years now we have been bound to speak or call to mind in some connection every day, almost every second. It is the name of the man who has brought more misfortune on the world than anyone else in our time. However, I must have heard it quite early, because Salzburg could be described as a near neighbour of Munich, only two-and-a-half hours' journey away by rail, so that we soon became familiar with its purely local affairs. All I know is that one day—I can't now recollect the exact date—an acquaintance from Munich who was visiting us complained that there was trouble there again. In particular, he said, a violent agitator by the name of Hitler was holding meetings that became wild brawls, and was abusing the Republic and stirring up anti-Jewish feeling in very vulgar language.

The name meant nothing in particular to me, and I thought no more about it. In the insecure German state of the time, the names of many agitators calling for a *putsch* kept emerging, only to disappear quickly from public attention, and they are now long forgotten. There was Captain Ehrhardt with his Baltic Brigade, there was Wolfgang Kapp, there were the Vehmic murderers, the Bavarian Communists, the Rhineland separatists, the leaders of the various bands known as Freikorps.[2] Hundreds of these little bubbles of discontent were bobbing about in the general fermentation of the time, leaving nothing behind when they burst but a bad smell which clearly showed how Germany's still open wounds were festering and rotting. At some point the newsletter of the new National Socialist movement was among those that came into my hands. It was the *Miesbacher Anzeiger*, later to become the *Völkischer Beobachter*.[3] But Miesbach was only a little village, and the newsletter was very badly written. Who would bother with that kind of thing?

Then, however, bands of young men suddenly turned up in the neighbouring border towns of Reichenhall and Berchtesgaden, places that I visited almost every week. These gangs were small at first, and then grew larger and larger. The young men wore jackboots and brown shirts, and each sported a garishly coloured armband with a swastika on it. They marched and held meetings, they paraded through the streets, singing songs and chanting in chorus, they stuck up huge posters and defaced the walls with swastikas. For the first time, I realised that there must be financial and other influential forces behind the sudden appearance of these gangs. Hitler was still delivering his speeches exclusively in Bavarian beer cellars at the time, and he alone could not have fitted out these thousands of young men with such expensive equipment. Stronger hands must be helping to propel the new movement forwards. For the uniforms were sparkling neat and clean, and in a time of poverty when genuine army veterans were still going around in their shabby old uniforms, the 'storm troops' sent from town to town and city to city could draw on a remarkably large pool of brand new cars, motorbikes and trucks for transport. It was also obvious that these young men were getting tactical training from military leaders—were being drilled, in fact, as paramilitaries—and also that the regular German army itself, the Reichswehr, for whose secret service Hitler had acted as a spy, was providing regular technical instruction in the use of equipment readily supplied to it. It so happened that I had an opportunity of observing

one of these combat training exercises. Four trucks suddenly
roared into one of the border villages where a perfectly
peaceful meeting of Social Democrats was being held. All the
trucks were full of young National Socialists armed with rubber
truncheons, and they overwhelmed the meeting, which was not
expecting them, by dint of sheer speed. I had seen just the same
thing in the Piazza San Marco in Venice. It was a method they
had learnt from the Fascists, but they executed it with much
greater military precision, systematically carrying it out down
to the last detail, as you might expect of the Germans. A whistle
gave the signal, and the SA[4] men jumped swiftly out of their
trucks, bringing rubber truncheons down on anyone who got in
their way. Before the police could intervene, or the workers at
the meeting could group together, they had jumped back into
the trucks and were racing away. What surprised me was the
practised way in which they jumped out of the vehicles and
back in again, both times following a single sharp whistle signal
from their leader. You could see that the muscles and nerves of
every one of these young men had been trained in advance, so
that he knew how to move and over which wheel of the vehicle
he must jump out to avoid getting in the way of the man behind
him and thus endangering the whole manoeuvre. It was not a
matter of personal skills. Each of those movements had had
to be practised in advance, dozens or even hundreds of times,
in barracks and on parade grounds. From the first, as anyone
could see at a glance, this gang had been trained in methods of
attack, violence and terrorism.

Soon we heard more about these underground manoeuvres
in Bavaria. When everyone else was asleep, the young men stole
out of their houses and assembled for nocturnal 'field exercises'.
Army officers either still serving or demobilised from the
Reichswehr, paid by the state or by the mysterious figures who
financed the Nazi Party, drilled the troops. The authorities paid
little attention to these strange nocturnal manoeuvres. Were

they really asleep or turning a blind eye? Were they indifferent to the movement, or actually encouraging it in secret? In any case, even those who surreptitiously supported National Socialism were first surprised, then shocked by the brutality and speed with which it suddenly asserted itself. One morning the authorities woke up to find Munich in Hitler's hands, all the government offices closed, the newspapers forced at gunpoint to hail, in triumphant tones the revolution that had taken place. Like a deus ex machina coming down from the clouds to which the unsuspecting Republic was vaguely looking up, General Ludendorff appeared, the first of many who though they could outwit Hitler and whom he outwitted instead. The famous *putsch*[5] that was supposed to conquer Germany began in the morning and, as we all know, had been put down by midday (I am not setting out to write a book about international history here). Hitler fled, and was quickly arrested. That seemed to be the end of his movement, In that year, 1923, the swastikas, storm troops, and the name of Adolf Hitler almost lapsed into oblivion. No one thought of him as a potential political force any more.

It was a few years before he surfaced again, and this time the growing wave of discontent quickly raised him on its crest. Inflation, unemployment, political crises and not least the folly of the outside world had aroused the ire of the German people. A great desire for order was felt in all quarters of a nation to which good order had always seemed more important than liberty and justice. And a man promising order—Goethe himself had said that he hated disorder even worse than injustice—had hundreds of thousands of supporters behind him from the first.

But we still did not notice the danger. Those few writers who had really gone to the trouble of reading Hitler's book did not look seriously at his programme, but laughed at his pompous prose style instead. The great national newspapers, instead of warning us, kept soothing their readers daily by assuring them that National Socialism, which could finance its agitation only with money provided by heavy industry and by audaciously running up debts, must inevitably collapse tomorrow or the next day. And perhaps the outside world never understood the real reason why Germany underestimated and made light of Hitler and his increasing power in all those years—not only has Germany always been a class-conscious country, but within its ideal class hierarchy it has suffered from a tendency to overrate and idolise the values of higher education. Apart from a few generals, the high offices of state were filled exclusively by men who had been to university. While Lloyd George in Britain, Garibaldi and Mussolini in Italy and Briand in France had risen to their offices from the ranks of the common people, it was unthinkable for the Germans to contemplate a man who, like Hitler, had not even left school with any qualifications, let alone attended any university, who had slept rough in men's hostels, living a rather shady and still mysterious life at that time, could aspire to the kind of position that had been held by Freiherr von Stein, Bismarck and Prince Bülow. More than anything, it was the high value they set on education that led German intellectuals to go on thinking of Hitler as a mere beer-hall agitator who could never really be dangerous. By now, however, thanks to those who were invisibly pulling strings for him, he had long ago recruited powerful assistants in many different quarters. Even when he had become Chancellor on that January day in 1933, the vast majority, including some who had helped him to rise to that position, still thought that he was just a stopgap and National Socialism would be only a transient episode.

It was now that Hitler's cynically brilliant technique first revealed itself on the grand scale. He had been making promises to all and sundry for years, and gained important supporters in all the political parties, each of whom thought that he could exploit the mysterious powers of this 'unknown soldier' for his own ends. But the same technique that Hitler later used in international politics, when he swore alliances and the loyalty of Germany on oath to the very powers that he intended to annihilate utterly, triumphed for the first time. He was such a master of the art of deceit by making promises to all sides that, on the day he came to power, there was rejoicing in totally opposite camps. The monarchists in Doorn[6] thought he was going to prepare the way for the Kaiser's return, but equally happy were the Wittelsbach[7] monarchists in Munich, believing that Hitler was their man. The German Nationalists hoped he would do their work for them—their leader Hugenberg[8] had concluded an agreement which guaranteed him the most important office in Hitler's cabinet, and thought that had given him a foot in the door of power, but of course he was forced to resign after the first few weeks in spite of the sworn agreement. The captains of heavy industry felt that Hitler would provide relief from the Bolshevik threat; the man they had been secretly financing for years was now in power. At the same time the impoverished lower middle class, to whom he had promised, at hundreds of meetings, relief from their state of serfdom to interest payments, drew a great breath of enthusiasm. Small shopkeepers remembered his undertaking to close down the big department stores, their most dangerous competitors— a promise that never came to anything—and Hitler was particularly welcome to the army, because his thinking was militaristic and he abused pacifism. Even the Social Democrats regarded his ascent in a friendlier way than might have been expected, hoping that he would eliminate their arch-enemies, the Communists now coming up so uncomfortably close behind them. The most varied parties, holding diametrically opposite opinions, regarded this unknown soldier who had promised the earth to every class, every party, every tendency as their friend—even the Jews of Germany were not especially uneasy. They reasoned that a *ministre jacobin* was by definition not a real Jacobin any more, and a Chancellor of the German

Reich would of course divest himself of the vulgarities of an anti-Semitic agitator. After all, what violent actions could he carry out in a state where the law was firmly established, the parliamentary majority was against him, and every citizen was assured of his liberty and equal rights by the solemn wording of the constitution?

Then came the Reichstag fire,[9] parliament vanished from the scene, Goering let his wolf pack off the leash, and all at once the rule of law in Germany was over. We were horrified to hear that concentration camps were being set up in the middle of peacetime, and secret cells where innocent people were murdered without the formality of a trial had been built in the barracks. This could only be an initial outburst of senseless rage as the new regime took power, we told ourselves, such things cannot last long in the twentieth century. But it was only the beginning. The world began to pay attention, and at first would not believe anything so incredible. However, it was in those days that I saw the first refugees arriving in Austria. They had climbed over the Salzburg mountains by night, or swum the river marking the border. Starving, ragged and distressed, they stared at us, and with them a panic flight from inhumanity had begun. Refugees were to spread over the whole earth. But still I did not guess, when I saw these exiles, that their pale faces heralded my own fate, and we would all be victims of this one man's raging lust for power.

It is difficult to rid yourself, in only a few weeks, of thirty or forty years of private belief that the world is a good place. With our rooted ideas of justice, we believed in the existence of a German, a European, an international conscience, and we were convinced that a certain degree of inhumanity is sure to self-destruct in the face of humane standards. I am trying to be as honest as possible here, so I must admit that in 1933 and 1934, none of us in Germany and Austria would have contemplated the possibility of one hundredth part, one thousandth part of what was about to break over us a little later. However, it was obvious from the first that those of us who were freelance, independent writers must expect a certain amount of unpleasantness in the way of difficulties and hostility. Immediately after the Reichstag fire I told my publisher that the end of any future for my books in Germany was imminent. I shall never forget his astonishment. "But who on earth would ban your books?" he asked, baffled. This was early in 1933. "You've never written a word criticising Germany, you've never dabbled in politics." Obviously, a week after Hitler had come to power the idea of monstrous events such as the burning and public execration of books, to become fact a few months later, was still beyond the comprehension of broad-minded people. National Socialism, with its unscrupulous methods of deception, took care not to show how radical its aims were until the world was inured to them. So it tried out its technique cautiously—one dose at a time, with a short pause after administering it. One pill at a time, then a moment of waiting to see if it had been too strong, if the conscience of the world could swallow that particular pill. And as the conscience of Europe—to the detriment and shame of our civilisation—was quick to say that it was not taking sides, because all these violent acts were perpetrated within the borders of Germany, the doses administered were stronger and stronger, until at last all Europe fell victim to them. Hitler never had a more brilliant idea than this tactical approach—gradually sounding out opinion and then putting more and more pressure on Europe, where increasing moral weakness was soon to be military weakness as well. He had privately decided long before on an operation to eliminate all free speech and every independent book from Germany, and he did it by the same means, feeling his way forward first. No law was immediately passed banning our books—that came two years later. Instead,

390

he quietly tested the waters to see how far he could go, leaving the first attack to a group not officially responsible, the National Socialist students. Just as "public anger" was cited as the reason for implementing the boycott of Jews, a measure on which Hitler had decided long before, a quiet hint was dropped that the students might like to hold a public demonstration to express their "indignation" at the existence of our books. And the German students, glad of any chance to display their reactionary attitudes, obediently banded together at every university, seized copies of our books from the bookshops, and marched with this loot, banners waving, to an open square. Here the books were either literally pilloried, publicly nailed to a wooden post in the medieval manner—medieval customs were back in fashion, and I have a copy of one of my books through which a nail was driven at the time, retrieved after its execution by a student friend who gave it to me—or as the burning of human beings was not, unfortunately, allowed, they were burnt to ashes on huge pyres while the students chanted patriotic slogans. It is true that at the last minute Goebbels as Minister of Propaganda had decided, after long hesitation, to bestow his blessing on the book-burning, but it was still only semi-official, and nothing shows more clearly how little as yet Germany identified itself with such actions than the fact that the general public drew no conclusions at all from the burning and ostracism of the books. Although booksellers were warned not to display any of our works in their windows, and hardly any newspaper would mention them now, none of it had any effect on the genuine reading public. As long as no threat of being imprisoned or sent to a concentration camp faced readers, my books sold almost as many copies in 1933 and 1934 as before, in spite of all the difficulties and harassment. Hitler's great scheme for "protecting the German people" by declaring the printing, sale and distribution of our books a crime against the state had yet to become law. When it did, its object was to alienate us

391

by force from the hundreds of thousands, indeed millions of Germans who are still happier to read us than the writers of *Blut und Boden*[10] literature who have now come to prominence. Our readers would have liked to stay loyal to us.

I felt that it was more of an honour than a disgrace to share the fate of total literary annihilation in Germany with such eminent contemporaries, including Thomas Mann, Heinrich Mann, Werfel, Freud and Einstein, and many others whose work I regard as far more important than my own. And I dislike putting on airs of martyrdom so much that I mention my inclusion in our common destiny only with reluctance. But strangely enough, it was given to me to place the National Socialists, even Adolf Hitler in person, in a particularly awkward situation. Of all the literary names now cast into outer darkness, mine was to be the frequent subject of great agitation and endless debates in high places, indeed the highest, the company at the Berchtesgaden villa. So I can count, among the most pleasing moments of my life, the modest satisfaction of having caused great annoyance to Adolf Hitler, the most powerful man of the modern age.

In the first days of the new regime I had already, although innocently, been responsible for a certain amount of uproar. At the time a film based on my novella *Burning Secret*, and bearing the same title, was being shown all over Germany. No one took the faintest offence. However, on the day after the Reichstag fire, for which the National Socialists tried, unsuccessfully, to blame the Communists, people gathered in front of the cinema posters and advertising for *Burning Secret*, nudging one another, winking and laughing. Soon the Gestapo discovered the reason for their mirth. The same evening, policemen raced around on motorbikes, further showings of the film were banned, and by next day the title of my novella *Burning Secret* had vanished without trace from all newspaper advertisements and all the advertising pillars where posters went up. Of course it was easy enough for the National Socialists to ban a single word that

392

offended them, even to burn and destroy all our books, but in one particular instance they could not attack me without also injuring a man who was vitally necessary to their international prestige at this critical moment, the greatest and most famous musician in Germany, Richard Strauss, with whom I had just been collaborating on an opera.

It was the first time I had worked with Richard Strauss. Hugo von Hofmannsthal had been his regular librettist ever since he wrote the texts for *Elektra* and *Der Rosenkavalier*, and I had never met Richard Strauss personally. After Hofmannsthal's death, however, he got in touch with me through my publishers, saying he wanted to begin a new opera and asking if I would be willing to write the libretto. I was very well aware of the honour of such a commission. Music and musicians had been part of my life ever since Max Reger had set my early poems. Busoni, Toscanini, Bruno Walter and Alban Berg were close friends of mine. But there was no creative musician of our time whom I would more willingly have served than Richard Strauss, last of the great line of German composers of genius running from Handel and Bach, by way of Beethoven and Brahms, and so to our own day. I agreed at once, and at our first meeting I suggested that Ben Jonson's *The Silent Woman* would make a good subject for an opera. It was a pleasant surprise to see how quickly and perceptively Strauss agreed to all my suggestions. I had not expected him to show such a ready understanding of literature, and his knowledge of the theatre was amazing. Even as I was outlining the course of the action, he saw it in dramatic terms and immediately adapted it to suit the limits of his own powers, which he understood with almost uncanny clarity. I have met many great artists in my life, but never before one who looked at himself with such impersonal and unswerving objectivity. At that first meeting Strauss frankly confessed that he knew a musician of seventy no longer had his former youthful powers of inspiration. He did not think, he said, that he could

393

write symphonic works like *Till Eulenspiegel* and *Tod und Verklärung* today, for pure music needs a very high degree of creative freshness. But written text still inspired him. Given a subject in verbal form, he could illustrate it to the full dramatically, because he found that musical themes spontaneously developed from situations and words, so in his later years he had turned exclusively to opera. He knew that opera as an art form was played out, he added. Wagner represented such a mighty mountain peak that no one could rise any higher. "However," he added with a broad Bavarian smile, "I found a solution by going around the mountain instead."

After we had worked out the basic structure he gave me a few more small directions. He would leave me absolute freedom, he said, because he was never inspired by a libretto made to measure in advance, in the manner of Verdi's operas, only by a genuine work of literature. But he would be glad if I could provide places for a few complex musical forms that would enable the musical colouring to develop in a certain way. "I'm not thinking of long melodies such as you can find in Mozart. I manage short themes best. But I can vary and paraphrase such themes, get everything possible out of them. In fact I think I do that better than anyone else today." Again, I was amazed by the frank way he spoke, because it is true that Strauss's melodies hardly ever go beyond a few bars, but the way those few bars are worked up into a fugal structure—think of the *Rosenkavalier* waltz—gives them fully rounded perfection.

Not just at this first meeting but at all our others I was astonished, over and over again, by the objectivity and certainty that the old master brought to the relation between himself and his works. Once I was alone with him at a private rehearsal of *Die ägyptische Helena* in the Salzburg Festival Theatre. There was no one else in the auditorium, and we sat in the dark. He was listening. Suddenly I noticed him drumming his fingers slightly but impatiently on the arm of his seat. Then he whispered to me, "Poor! Oh, very poor. I obviously couldn't think of anything better!" And after a minute or so he added, "If only I could cut that! Oh God, oh God, it means nothing and it goes on too long, much too long." But after another few minutes: "Ah, there—now, you see, that's good!" He assessed his own work in as matter-of-fact a way as if he were hearing the music for the first time, and it had been written by some other composer entirely unknown to him. That extraordinary awareness of his own capabilities never left him. He always knew exactly who he was and what he could do. He did not seem very interested in how much or how little other composers meant by comparison to him, or in what he meant to them. It was the work of composition itself that he liked.

With Strauss, that work is a remarkable process. There is nothing daemonic about it, none of the artist's fine, careless rapture, or the depression and desperation we know from accounts of the lives of Beethoven and Wagner. Strauss works coolly and objectively, he composes—like Johann Sebastian Bach and all those other sublime musical craftsmen—calmly and with regularity. He sits down at his desk at nine in the morning, and goes on composing exactly where he left off the day before, regularly writing the first sketch in pencil, the piano score in ink, and going on without a break until twelve or one o'clock. He plays Skat[11] in the afternoon, transfers two or three pages of his composition to the full score, and then may have to go to the theatre to conduct in the evening. He is never nervous in any way, and his artist's intellect is bright and clear by day and night alike. When a servant knocks on his door to bring him the tailcoat he wears for conducting he leaves his work, drives to the theatre, and conducts music with the same sure touch and air of calm as when he was playing cards in the afternoon, and inspiration returns to him at exactly the right place next morning. For, to borrow a term from Goethe, Strauss is "in command" of his ideas. To him art means ability, even all-embracing ability. As he has said, amusingly, "Anyone who wants to be a real musician must be able to set a restaurant menu to music." Difficulties do not deter him; his creative intellect sees them as a game. I like to remember how his little blue eyes twinkled as he told me triumphantly, when the musicians reached a certain passage: "I gave the singer quite a problem to solve there! Let her puzzle away at it until she works out the answer!" In such rare moments of amusement, you feel that something daemonic does in fact lie buried in the mind of this remarkable man, although you may have doubted it at first because of the meticulous, methodical, reliable craftsmanship of his working method and the apparent absence of any nervous strain. In the same way his face initially looks rather ordinary—plump, childlike cheeks, rather commonplace fleshy features, and his forehead is not domed but recedes slightly. However, one glance at his clear, blue, beaming eyes, and you instantly feel some kind of special magical force behind the everyday bourgeois façade. I think they are the most watchful eyes I ever saw in any musician—if not daemonic then far-seeing, the eyes of a man who knows his art inside out.

Back in Salzburg after this invigorating meeting with Strauss, I set to work at once. Wondering what he would make of my verses, I dispatched the first act to him only two weeks later. By return of post, he sent me a postcard with a quotation from *Die Meistersinger* on it: *The opening was good.* The second act brought me an even warmer comment in the shape of the opening bars of his own song: *How glad I am I found you, my dear child!*[2] This pleasure, even delight of his made the rest of my work a true delight as well. Richard Strauss did not change a single line of the entire libretto, and only once asked me to add thee or four lines so that he could bring in another voice. A very friendly relationship developed between us; he came to our house and I visited him in Garmisch, where little by little he played me the entire opera from the sketch of the score, his long, thin fingers moving over the piano keys. Without any written contract, we agreed to take it for granted that when this opera was finished we would start on another one at once. He had already approved of its general outline in advance.

In January 1933, when Adolf Hitler came to power, the piano score of our opera *Die schweigsame Frau*—The Silent Woman— was as good as finished, and Strauss had completed the orchestration of most of the first act. A few weeks later came the decree strictly banning from the German stage works by non-Aryans, and even those in which a Jew had been involved in any way at all. This sweeping prohibition extended to the dead, and Mendelssohn's statue was removed from its place outside the Leipzig Gewandhaus, an outrage bitterly resented by all music-lovers. It looked to me as if the ban sealed the fate of our opera, and I assumed that Richard Strauss would naturally give up any idea of further collaboration with me and begin again with a new librettist. Instead he wrote me letter after letter, asking what on earth I was thinking of—on the contrary, he said, now that he was busy orchestrating *Die schweigsame Frau* he would like me to start preparing the libretto for his next opera. He had no intention of letting anyone forbid him to collaborate with me, and I must acknowledge freely that in the course of the entire affair he maintained his loyal friendship with me as long as possible. At the same time, I have to admit, he did take certain precautions that I found less attractive—he moved closer to the men who wielded power, he was often seen in the company of Hitler, Goering and Goebbels, and he let himself be appointed President of the Reich Chamber of Music at a time when even Furtwängler[13] was still declining to support the National Socialists.

To have Strauss openly on their side was enormously important to the National Socialists at this moment. Infuriatingly, not only the best writers but also the outstanding musicians of the time had rejected their ideas outright, and the few who did agree with them, or went over to them, were not widely known. To win the support of the most famous musician in Germany at such a delicate moment would be extremely profitable, in a purely decorative sense, to Goebbels and Hitler. Hitler, who during his vagrant years in Vienna, as Strauss told me, had somehow scraped up the money to go to Graz for the premiere of *Salome*, paid ostentatious tribute to him. The only music performed at evening parties at Berchtesgaden, apart from Wagner's, consisted of Strauss lieder. Strauss himself had ulterior motives for siding with the National Socialists. He always freely and coolly admitted that, with the egotism of an artist, he was indifferent at heart to any political regime. He had served the Kaiser as his Kapellmeister, and had made instrumental arrangements of military marches for him. Then he had gone to Vienna to be Court Kapellmeister to the Austrian Emperor, but subsequently was *persona gratissima* in both the Austrian and the German Republics. Obliging the National Socialists was also of vital importance to him, because he had put himself morally in the wrong by Nazi standards—his son's wife was Jewish, and he feared that his grandchildren, whom he loved dearly, would be excluded from school; the librettos of his earlier operas had been by Hugo von Hofmannsthal, who was not a 'pure Aryan'; and his publisher was a Jew. So it seemed to him particularly advisable to gain support, and he went about it with great persistence. He conducted anywhere the new masters of Germany asked him to, and set an anthem to music for the Olympic Games in Berlin. At the same time he was writing me extraordinarily candid letters, and he mentioned that commission with little enthusiasm. With the *sacro egoismo* of the artist, his only real concern was to safeguard his work, and most of all to see the new opera, which was especially close to his heart, go into production.

Naturally making concessions of this kind to the National Socialists was bound to be very awkward for me. It could easily

398

give the impression that I was secretly on the same side, or just agreeing that a single exception to the disgraceful boycott of Jewish artists might be made in my own special case. My friends kept pressing me to protest publicly in Nazi Germany. But for one thing I hate emotional public gestures on principle, and for another I was not inclined to put difficulties in the way of a genius of the stature of Richard Strauss. After all, Strauss was the greatest living musician and was seventy years old; he had spent three years writing this work, and all that time he had shown friendship for me, had behaved perfectly correctly, and had even shown courage. So I thought the right thing for me to do was keep quiet and let things run their course. I also knew that complete passivity was my best way of making life more difficult for the present custodians of German culture. The Reich Chamber of Literature and the Ministry of Propaganda were just looking for a good pretext, one that would hold water, for imposing a ban on their greatest composer in this affair. How convenient it would have been if *Die schweigsame Frau* had contained a risqué situation, like the scene in *Der Rosenkavalier* when a young man comes out of a married woman's bedroom! Then they could have claimed that they must protect German morality. But to their disappointment, there was no immorality in my libretto. Then they searched any number of Gestapo files and read my earlier books. But again, they could find no evidence that I had ever said a disparaging word about Germany—or indeed about any other nation on earth—or had been politically active. Whatever they did, whatever they tried, the decision was still going to be theirs alone. Were they going to deny the old master, whom incidentally they themselves had appointed to carry the banner of National Socialist music, the right to have his new opera performed, and do it before the eyes of the whole world, or was the name of Stefan Zweig, on whose mention as his librettist Richard Strauss expressly insisted, to contaminate German theatrical programmes as it had so often done before? What a shameful day that would be! I quietly relished their anxieties and their painful dilemma. I guessed that if I simply did nothing, or rather refrained from helping or hindering the affair in any way, this musical comedy was bound to degenerate into party-political caterwauling.

The Nazi Party hummed and hawed over its decision as long as it possibly could. But early in 1934 it finally had to decide whether it was going to break its own law or oppose the greatest musician of the time. The day of decision could not be put off any longer. The score, the piano score, the libretto had all been printed long ago. In the Dresden Court Theatre, costumes had been ordered, the cast list decided, and the singers had even begun learning their parts. And still the various authorities, Goering and Goebbels, the Reich Chamber of Literature and the Cultural Council, the Ministry of Education and Streicher's associates could not agree. Idiotic as all this may seem, the production of *Die schweigsame Frau* finally became a hotly debated affair of state. None of those authorities would venture to take full responsibility for giving the go-ahead to the straight Yes or No that would resolve the dilemma. So there was nothing for it but to leave the matter to the personal decision of the master of Germany and the Nazi Party, Adolf Hitler. My books had now had the honour of being read at length by National Socialists, and it was *Fouché* in particular that they had studied and discussed because its subject was a man without political scruples. But I really had never expected that, after Goebbels and Goering had read it, Adolf Hitler himself would have to go to the trouble of studying the three acts of my verse libretto *ex officio*. He evidently did not find the decision easy. As I found out later, from accounts reaching me by devious ways, there was then another endless series of conferences. Finally Richard Strauss was called before these almighty powers, and Hitler in person told him that in this exceptional case he would allow the performance of his opera, although it was an offence against all

400

the laws of the new German Reich. It was a decision that he probably made as unwillingly—and dishonestly—as when he decided to sign his treaty with Stalin and Molotov.

It was a dark day for Nazi Germany when an opera was produced, once again, with the unmentionable name of Stefan Zweig displayed on all the programmes. I was not at the first night myself, of course, knowing that the auditorium would be bristling with brown uniforms. Even Hitler himself was expected to attend a later performance. The opera was a great success, and I must mention that, much to the credit of the music critics, nine out of ten of them seized with enthusiasm on this chance to show their private opposition to the racist Nazi stance by praising my libretto in the kindest of terms. All the German opera houses—Berlin, Hamburg, Frankfurt, Munich—immediately announced that they would be including productions of the work in their next season.

Then, after the second performance, a lightning bolt suddenly descended from the blue. Everything was cancelled, the opera was banned in Dresden and the whole of Germany overnight. Even more astonishing, the papers said that Richard Strauss had resigned as President of the Reich Chamber of Music. Everyone knew that something extraordinary must have happened. But it was some time before I discovered the whole truth. Strauss had written me another letter urging me to start on the libretto of his next opera soon, and expressing his personal opinions rather too freely. His letter had fallen into the hands of the Gestapo. It was placed before Strauss, who consequently had to resign from his position, and the opera was banned. Since then it has been staged in German only in neutral Switzerland and in Prague, later in Italian at La Scala, Milan, by special agreement with Mussolini, who had not yet fallen in line with the racist standpoint. But the German people have never again been allowed to hear a note of this sometimes enchanting opera of their greatest musician's old age.

While this affair was going on, attended by a considerable amount of uproar, I was living abroad. I could tell that the unrest in Austria was going to make it impossible for me to work in peace. My house in Salzburg was close enough to the border for me to see, with the naked eye, the mountain where Adolf Hitler's own Berchtesgaden house stood. Having Hitler as a neighbour was an unedifying and extremely disturbing situation. My proximity to the border with the German Reich, however, meant that I could assess the threat to Austria better than my friends in Vienna. The Viennese who frequented the cafés, even the men in the Ministries, thought of National Socialism as something that was going on 'over there', and couldn't have anything to do with Austria. The well-organised Social Democratic party was in power here, after all, with almost half the population backing it. Even the Clerical party, with strong Catholic support, went along with it in passionate opposition to Hitler's "German Christians", who were now openly persecuting the Christian religion and calling their Führer literally "greater than Christ himself" in public. Surely France, Britain and the League of Nations were our friends and would look after us? Hadn't Mussolini expressly undertaken to protect Austria, going so far as to guarantee the country's independence? Even the Jews were not anxious, and behaved as if Jewish doctors, lawyers, scholars and actors were being deprived of their civil liberties in China, instead of just three hours' journey away in the same German-speaking part of the world. They took their ease at home and drove around in their cars. And the comforting phrase, "This can't last long" was on all lips. But I remembered a conversation with my former publisher in Leningrad during my brief visit to Russia. He told me how he had once been a rich man; he told me about the beautiful pictures he had owned, and I had asked why, in that case, he didn't do as so many others had done and emigrate as soon as the Revolution broke out. "Oh, well," he said, "who'd have thought at the time that a republic consisting of workers' councils and the army would last more than two weeks?" Here we had the same delusion, arising from the same propensity for self-deception.

In Salzburg, of course, close to the border, you saw things more clearly. For a start, there was constant coming and going over the narrow river that marked the border. Young people slipped across it by night and were given training; agitators crossed the border in cars or with their alpenstocks looking like ordinary tourists and organised themselves into cells in all classes of society. They began recruiting supporters, while threatening that those who did not accept the one true faith at the right time would be sorry for it later. The police and the civil servants were intimidated. More and more clearly, I began to detect a certain insecurity in people's behaviour as they started to waver. Your own small personal experiences of life are always more persuasive than anything else. A friend of my youth lived in Salzburg, a very well-known writer with whom I had been in close and cordial contact for thirty years. We were on first-name terms, we had dedicated books to each other, we met every week. One day I saw my old friend walking along the street with a gentleman I didn't know, and noticed that he immediately stopped in front of a display window that could hardly mean much to him, pointing something in it out to this gentleman with an air of uncommon interest, while he kept his back turned to me. How odd, I thought; he must have seen me. But it could be just coincidence. Next day he suddenly phoned me—could he come round to my home for a chat that afternoon? I said yes, rather surprised, for in the usual way we always met at the coffee house. It turned out that he had nothing particular to say, in spite of this hasty arrangement to visit me. I immediately realised that although he wanted to keep up his friendship with me, in future he would rather not appear too familiar with me in this small city, in case he was suspected of being a friend to Jews. That put me on my guard, and I soon noticed that a number of acquaintances who often used to visit me had stayed away lately. They were in a dangerous position.

I was not thinking of leaving Salzburg for ever at this time, but I did make up my mind more readily than usual to spend the winter abroad, so that I could avoid all these little tensions. But I had no idea that when I left my pleasant house in October 1933 that I was already, in a way, saying goodbye to it.

I had meant to spend the next January and February working in France. I loved that beautiful and intellectual country as a home from home, and I never felt like a foreigner there. Valéry, Romain Rolland, Jules Romains, André Gide, Roger Martin du Gard, Duhamel, Vildrac, Jean-Richard Bloch—these leading lights of literature were my old friends. My books had almost as many readers in France as in Germany; no one thought of me as a foreign writer, a stranger. I loved the people, I loved the country, I loved the city of Paris and was so familiar with it that every time my train came into the Gare du Nord I felt I was coming home. This time, however, I had travelled earlier than usual because of the special circumstances, and I did not really want to be in Paris until after Christmas. Where should I go in the meantime? Then it occurred to me that I had not been in England for almost quarter-of-a-century, not since my student days. Why always Paris, I asked myself? Why not ten days to two weeks in London, seeing the museums, the city, the country again with new eyes? So I took the express train to Calais instead of Paris, and got out at Victoria Station on an appropriately foggy November day, thirty years after my last visit, and was quite surprised, on my arrival, to be driving to my hotel in a car instead of a horse-drawn cab. The cool, soft grey fog was the same as ever. I hadn't set eyes on the city itself yet, but even over three decades my sense of smell had recognised that curiously acrid, dense, damp atmosphere that wraps itself around you when you come close.

I brought no great amount of luggage with me, and no great expectations either. I had hardly any close friends in London, and in literary terms there was little contact between us Continental writers and our British counterparts. They led a rather carefully demarcated life of their own, having its own sphere of influence within a tradition not accessible to the rest of us—of all the many books from all over the world that found their way to my desk at home, I cannot remember ever feeling that a book by an English author was like a present from a colleague. I had once met Shaw at Hellerau, Wells had visited my house in Salzburg, and my own books had all been translated into English but were little known there. Britain had always been the country where they made the least impression. And while I was on terms of personal friendship with my American, French, Italian and Russian publishers, I had never met anyone from the firm that published my books in Britain. So I was prepared to feel as much a stranger there as thirty years ago.

But I was wrong. After a few days I felt extraordinarily well at ease in London. Not that the city itself had changed very much, but I myself had changed. I was thirty years older, and after the years of the Great War, and then the post-war years of ever-increasing tension, I longed to live a quiet life again and hear nothing about politics. Of course there were political parties in Britain too. As successors to the old Whigs and Tories, there were the Conservative, Liberal and Labour Parties, but their discussions were nothing to do with me. I am sure various groups and trends also existed in literary life, controversies and covert rivalries, but I was outside all that. The real advantage was that at last I felt I was in a civil, courteous, calm and friendly society again. Nothing had poisoned my life in recent years so much as the sense of hostility and tension around me at home, in country and city alike, feeling forced to defend myself all the time, constantly drawn into arguments. The British were not in the same state of agitation, there was a greater degree of decent, law-abiding behaviour in public life than in our Continental countries, where morality itself had been impaired

405

by the great fraud practised on us by inflation. The British lived more quietly, were more content, thought more about their gardens and their little hobbies than about their neighbours. You could breathe, think and reflect here. But what really kept me going was a new book.

It came about like this. My *Marie Antoinette* had just been published, and I was reading the proofs of my book on Erasmus, in which I tried to paint an intellectual portrait of the humanist who, although he understood the absurdity of his times more clearly than those who made it their business to set the world to rights, was tragically unable to do anything about it in spite of his fine mind. After finishing this book, which presented my own views in veiled form through the person of Erasmus, I meant to write a novel that I had been planning for a long time. I had had enough of biographies. But then, on only my third day in London, I was in the British Museum, attracted to the place by my old passion for autograph manuscripts and looking at those on public display. They included the handwritten account of the execution of Mary Queen of Scots. Instinctively I found myself wondering what Mary Stuart was really like. Had she or had she not been implicated in the murder of her second husband? As I had nothing to read in the evening, I bought a book about her. It was a paean of praise, defending her as a saint. The book was shallow and foolish. Next day my incurable curiosity led me to buy another book, which claimed almost exactly the opposite. The case was beginning to interest me. I asked for the title of a really authoritative work on Mary. No one could recommend one, and so by diligent searching and making my own enquiries I was involuntarily drawn into making comparisons. Without really knowing it, I had begun a book about Mary Stuart that kept me in libraries for weeks on end. When I returned to Austria early in 1934, I had decided to go back to London, a city that I had grown to love, to finish the book in peace and quiet there.

Back in Austria, it took me only two or three days to see how the situation had deteriorated in my few months away. Returning from the quiet, secure atmosphere of England to a country shaken by fevered conflicts was like being in New York on a hot July day, and suddenly stepping out of an air-conditioned room into the sultry heat. National Socialist pressure was beginning to wear down the nerves of those in religious and bourgeois circles. They felt the economic thumbscrews turn, while subversive German influence was exerted more and more harshly. The Dollfuss government, trying to keep Austria independent and preserve the country from Hitler, sought with increasing desperation for some last kind of support. France and Britain were too far away, and at heart too indifferent to Austria; Czechoslovakia was still full of old rancour and rivalries with Vienna—only Italy was left. At the time Italy was trying to establish an economic and political protectorate over Austria, so as to secure itself the Alpine passes and Trieste. But Mussolini asked a high price for that protection. Austria was to accept the Fascist line, there must be an end of the Austrian parliament, and with it Austrian democracy. That was going to be impossible without the elimination or disenfranchisement of the Social Democrats, the strongest and best-organised political party in Austria. The only way to break it was by brutal violence.

Dollfuss's predecessor, Ignaz Seipel, had already set up an organisation, known as the Heimwehr,[14] to carry out this terrorist operation, At first glance the Heimwehr was the least impressive body imaginable, its members being small provincial lawyers, demobilised army officers, shady characters of various kinds, unemployed engineers—all of them mediocrities who had suffered disappointment in life and hated one another heartily. Finally a leader was found for them in the shape of young Prince Starhemberg, who had once sat at the feet of Hitler and denounced the Republic and democracy. Now he featured as Hitler's antagonist, strutting about with his paramilitaries and promising that heads would roll. What exactly the Heimwehr proposed to do on the positive side was not at all clear. In fact its only aim was to get its snout in the trough, and the only power behind it was Mussolini's strong fist propelling it forward. Claiming to be patriotic Austrians, its members failed to notice that in accepting the bayonets supplied by Italy, it was sawing off the branch it was sitting on.

The Social Democratic party had a better idea of where the real danger lay. It did not really have any reason to fear open conflict. It had its own weapons—if it called a general strike it could cripple all the railways, the waterworks and the electricity plants. But it also knew that Hitler was just waiting for what he could call a Red Revolution, because that would give him a pretext for moving into Austria as its 'saviour'. So the Social Democrats preferred to sacrifice a large part of their civil rights and even the Austrian parliament in order to come to a reasonable compromise. In view of the predicament in which Austria found itself in the looming shadow of Hitler, all sensible people supported such an arrangement. Even Dollfuss himself, a glib and ambitious but very realistic man, seemed inclined to accept the agreement. Young Starhemberg, however, with his friend Major Fey, who played a notable part in the assassination of Dollfuss, insisted that the Schutzbund[15] must hand in its weapons, and every trace of democratic and bourgeois freedom must be annihilated. The Social Democrats opposed these demands, and threats passed back and forth between the two camps. It could be sensed that a decision was in the air now, and in this mood of general tension I could not help thinking apprehensively of Shakespeare's words: "So foul a sky clears not without a storm."[16]

I was in Salzburg for only a few days, and soon went on to Vienna. And it was in those first days of February that the storm broke. The Heimwehr had attacked the municipal building in Linz where the workers had their headquarters, to seize the weapons that they assumed were stored there. The workers responded with a general strike, and Dollfuss in his own turn by calling for this artificially contrived 'revolution' to be put down by armed force. So the regular army closed in on the workers' municipal buildings in Vienna with machine guns and artillery. There was bitter house-to-house fighting for three days, with democracy defending itself against Fascism for the last time until the Spanish Civil War. The workers held out for three days until falling to the superior technological force of their opponents.

I was in Vienna during those three days, which makes me a first-hand witness of this deciding battle and with it the suicide of Austrian independence. But as I would like to be a truthful witness, I must paradoxically begin by admitting that I myself saw nothing at all of this revolution. A writer setting out to give as honest and graphic a picture as possible of the time in which he lives must also be brave enough to disappoint romantic expectations. And nothing strikes me as more characteristic of the form taken by revolutions today, and the methods they employ, than the fact that within the huge area of a modern metropolis they take place only in a very few parts of the city, and most of its population never sees anything. Strange as it may seem, I was in Vienna during those historic February days of 1934, and saw none of the crucial incidents going on there, nor did I know the least thing about them while they were in progress. Artillery was fired, buildings were occupied, hundreds of dead were carried away—and I never saw a single body. Every newspaper reader in New York, London and Paris knew more about what was really going on than those of us apparently well placed to witness it. And I later found more and more confirmation of the remarkable phenomenon whereby, in our days, you may be ten streets away from the scene of events

409

which will have wide repercussions, and yet know less about them than people thousands of kilometres away. A few months later, when Dollfuss was assassinated in Vienna one day at twelve noon, I saw the news vendors' placards in the streets of London at five-thirty that afternoon. I tried telephoning to Vienna at once; to my astonishment I was put through immediately, and discovered to my even greater amazement that in Vienna itself, five streets away from the Foreign Office, far less was known about the assassination than you could read on every street corner in London. So I can present only the negative, so to speak, of my experience of the Vienna revolution, by showing how little contemporaries see today of events that will change the face of the world and their own lives if they do not happen to be on the spot at the time. All I knew about it was this—I had an appointment to meet the choreographer of the Opera House, Margarethe Wallmann, in one of the cafés on the Ringstrasse. So I walked to the Ringstrasse, and thinking nothing of it was going to cross the road. A few men in makeshift old uniforms, carrying firearms, came up to me and asked where I was going. When I explained that I was on my way to the Café J, they let me pass. I had no idea why there were suddenly guardsmen in the street, or what they were actually planning to do there. In fact there had been bitter fighting with many shots fired in the suburbs for several hours that day, but no one in the city centre had any idea of it. Only when I got back to my hotel in the evening and went to pay my bill, because I was planning to travel back to Salzburg in the morning, did I hear from the clerk at the reception desk that he was afraid I wouldn't be able to do that. The railways were on strike, he said, and there was trouble of some kind in the suburbs.

Next day the newspapers published rather vague reports of a Social Democrat riot, adding that it had been more or less put down. The facts were that the fighting was at its worst that day, and the government decided to back up the machine guns already in use by bringing in artillery against the workers' municipal headquarters. But I never heard the cannon either. If all Austria had been occupied at the time, whether by the Socialists, the National Socialists or the Communists, I would have known as little about it as the population of Munich did when they woke up that morning in the past to discover from the *Münchener Neueste Nachtrichten* that their city was in Hitler's hands. At the heart of the city everything went on as calmly and regularly as usual, while battle raged in the suburbs, and we foolishly believed the official bulletins telling us that the dispute had been settled and was now over. I had to go and look something up in the National Library, where the students were reading and studying as usual; all the shops were open, no one was in a state of agitation. Only on the third day, when it really was all over, did the truth begin to come out bit by bit. On the morning of the fourth day, as soon as the trains were running again, I went back to Salzburg, where two or three acquaintances whom I met in the street immediately bombarded me with questions about what had been going on in Vienna. And I, a 'first-hand witness' of the revolution, had to tell them honestly: "I'm afraid I don't know. You'd better buy a foreign newspaper."

As it happened, I came to a decision about my own life next day, in connection with the following events. When I arrived back from Vienna that afternoon, I went home to my house in Salzburg, found stacks of proofs and letters waiting for me there, and worked until late into the night to catch up with them. I was still lying in bed next morning when there was a knock on the bedroom door. Our good old manservant, who would never usually wake me if I had not expressly asked him to do so at a certain hour, appeared with an expression of dismay on his face. Would I come downstairs, please, he said; there were some gentlemen from the police who wanted to speak to me. I was rather surprised, but I put on my dressing gown and went down to the ground floor. There stood four policemen

411

in plain clothes, who told me they had a warrant to search the place, and I was to hand over all the weapons of the Republican Schutzbund that were hidden in the house.

I must confess that I was taken too much aback at first to say anything. Weapons of the Republican Schutzbund in my house? It was absurd. I had never belonged to any party or bothered with politics at all. I had been away from Salzburg for months, and apart from all that, it would have been utterly ridiculous to set up a weapons depot in this particular house, which was outside the city and on top of a mountain, so that anyone carrying rifles or other firearms could easily be observed on his way up. So all I said, in cool tones, was: "Do by all means look around." The four detectives went through the house, opened several cupboards, tapped some of the walls, but it was instantly obvious to me from their casual search that it was just for form's sake, and none of them seriously thought there was a weapons depot there. After half-an-hour they told me their search was over, and left.

I am afraid that the reason why this farce annoyed me so much calls for an explanatory historical note. In the last few decades, Europe and the world had almost forgotten how sacred personal rights and civil liberties used to be. Since 1933 searches, arbitrary arrests, the confiscation of property, forced exile from a man's hearth and home, deportations and every other form of humiliation imaginable had become almost everyday events to be taken for granted. I know hardly any of my European friends who have not gone through something of the sort. But at the time, early in 1934, having your house searched was still a monstrous affront in Austria. There must be some reason why a man like me, who kept his distance from all politics and had not even exercised his right to vote for years, should have been singled out, and in fact this was a typically Austrian affair. The Salzburg Chief of Police had been obliged to take severe action against the National Socialists, who were disturbing the population with bombs and explosives night after night, and stern control of this kind showed courage on his part, because even then the Nazi Party was employing its terrorist technique. Government offices received threatening letters every day, saying that if they went on "persecuting" National Socialists they were going to pay for it, and sure enough—for when it came to exacting revenge, the Nazis always kept their word one hundred per cent—the most loyal Austrian civil servants were taken off to concentration camps the day after Hitler's invasion. So the idea of searching my house was a way of showing publicly that they did not shrink from taking such security measures in the case of anyone at all. However, behind this intrinsically insignificant little episode I sensed the present gravity of the state of affairs in Austria, and saw what enormous pressure Germany was putting on us. I did not like my house any more after that official visit, and a certain presentiment told me that such episodes were only the tentative prelude to much farther-reaching measures. That same evening I began packing my most important papers, determined to live only abroad from now on, and departure meant more than leaving my house and property because my family loved the house as they loved their native land. But to me, personal liberty was the most important thing on earth. Without telling any of my friends or acquaintances what I was going to do, I travelled back to London two days later. The first thing I did there was to inform the Salzburg authority responsible that I had given up residence in that city for good. It was the first step towards cutting the link between me and my native Austria. But I had known, since those few days in Vienna, that Austria was a lost cause, although I did not yet guess how much I myself was losing.

NOTES

1 *Here begins Hitler.*

2 All of these were names of persons or movements of various political colours agitating or planning insurrection in Germany at the time. Most notable in this context are probably the Freikorps. By the terms of the Treaty of Versailles after the Great War, the numbers of Germany's army were greatly reduced. Many small groups, such as the Baltic Brigade mentioned above, also known as the II Marine Brigade, formed what amounted to small freelance armies. These were known as the Freikorps—free corps—and were right-wing nationalist. Many of them later became part of the National Socialist movement and were incorporated into the SA and SS.

3 The *Völkischer Beobachter*—People's Observer. Notorious as the regular Nazi newspaper, published from the 1920s until the defeat of Nazi Germany in 1945.

4 Short for *Sturmabteilung*, the Storm Section, or storm troopers, of the brownshirts.

5 Generally known as the Beer Hall Putsch, and at this first attempt Hitler did not succeed in his aims.

6 The town in the Netherlands where Kaiser Wilhelm lived in exile after being forced to abdicate at the end of the Great War.

7 The Wittelsbachs had been the rulers of the royal house of Bavaria. The last king of Bavaria, Ludwig III, was deposed at the end of the Great War.

8 Alfred Hugenberg, leader of the right-wing German National People's Party, dissolved soon after Hitler came to power.

9 An act of arson that burnt down the German parliamentary building in February 1933, after which many civil liberties were suspended.

10 *Blut und Boden*—Blood and the Soil—was a genre of usually sentimental fiction extolling patriotism and attachment to the land, and it came to be associated with Nazi ideology.

11 Skat is a popular trick-taking German card game.

12 *Ach, dass ich dich gefunden, liebes Kind.*

13 The conductor Wilhelm Furtwängler—like Richard Strauss himself, as Zweig records it—tried to tread a middle way between expressing

open hostility to the Nazis and incurring their wrath. He defended himself in front of a denazification tribunal after the Second World War, and was finally cleared. A slight shadow still hangs, however, over his name and that of Strauss.

14 Home Guard, or Home Defence.

15 'Protection League', the Austrian Social Democratic Party's own paramilitary organisation.

16 From *King John*.

THE DEATH THROES OF PEACE

The sun of Rome is set. Our day is gone.
Clouds, dews and daggers come; our deeds are done.

Shakespeare *Julius Caesar*

I N THOSE FIRST YEARS, England did not really mean exile for me any more than Gorky had been in exile in Sorrento. Austria still existed, even after the so-called revolution and the attempt made by the National Socialists soon afterwards to take control of the country by mounting a surprise attack following the assassination of Dollfuss. The death throes of my homeland were to last another four years. I could go home any time I liked, I was not formally exiled or outlawed. My books stood untouched in my house in Salzburg, I still carried an Austrian passport, Austria was my country and I had full rights as an Austrian citizen. I was not yet in the cruel condition of a stateless expatriate, a condition hard to explain to anyone who has not known it himself. It is a nerve-racking sense of teetering on the brink, wide awake and staring into nothing, knowing that wherever you find a foothold you can be thrust back into the void at any moment. I was still only at the start of the process. But this time, in late February 1934, I felt a difference when I arrived in London and got out of the train at Victoria Station. When you have decided to live in a city, it is not the same as a city that you are only visiting; you see it in a different way. I didn't know how long I would be staying in London. All that mattered was to be able to get on with my own work, defending my private and public liberty. Property meant tying myself down, so I didn't want to buy a house. Instead I

417

rented a little flat, just large enough to take a desk and the few books I had not wanted to leave behind, fitting them into two wall cupboards. That gave me everything that a man who works with his mind needs. There was no room for me to entertain company, but I preferred to live in a small space and be able to travel freely from time to time. Subconsciously, I had already switched my life to a temporary rather than a permanent mode.

On my first evening—it was already getting dark and the walls were blurred in the twilight—I walked into the tiny flat, which was ready for me at last, and had a shock. It was just as if I had walked into that other small apartment, the place I had furnished for myself in Vienna almost thirty years ago where the rooms were just as small; the only welcome came from those same books along the walls, and I had a hallucinatory feeling that I was being observed by the eyes of Blake's King John, the drawing that went everywhere with me. It really took me a moment to gather my wits; I hadn't thought of that first apartment of mine for years and years. Was this a sign that my life, after ranging so widely for so long, was retreating into the past, and I was only a shadow of myself? When I had chosen my apartment in Vienna thirty years before, it was a beginning. I had not done anything yet, or nothing much, my books were still unwritten and my name still unknown in my country. Now the situation, curiously enough, was the reverse—my books had disappeared from their original language, and what I wrote from now on would be unknown in Germany and Austria. My friends were far away, my old circle of acquaintances scattered, the house with its collections and pictures and books was lost to me. I was in a strange place again, just as I had been then. Everything I had tried, done, learnt and enjoyed in the interim seemed to have been drifted away on the wind, and now, at the age of fifty, I faced another beginning. Once more I was a student who would sit at his desk and go off to the library in the morning, but I was not as trustful as before. There was a touch of grey in my hair and a faint, twilight despondency weighing on my weary mind.

I hesitate to say much about those years I spent in England from 1934 to 1940, because I am already coming close to the present time, and we have all been through that to much the same extent, feeling the same fears aroused by the radio and newspapers, the same hopes and cares. We are none of us very proud of our political blindness at that time, and we are horrified to see where it has brought us. Anyone trying to explain it would have to level accusations, and which of us has any right to do so? There is also the fact that I kept myself very much to myself while I was living in England. I had inhibitions, and foolish as I knew my inability to overcome them was, in all those years of semi-exile and then full exile I kept away from outspoken company, feeling mistakenly that I had no right to join in discussions of the present situation when I was in a foreign land. In Austria I had been unable to do anything about folly in high places, so how could I try it here? I felt that I was a guest in this hospitable island and that if—with my clear and well-informed knowledge gleaned in Europe—I pointed out the danger Hitler represented, it might be taken as personal prejudice. In fact it was sometimes difficult to keep my mouth shut when I heard views that were obviously mistaken. It was painful to see how the greatest virtue of the British, their loyalty and their honest wish to think well of everyone in the absence of evidence to the contrary, was abused by brilliantly staged propaganda. I kept hearing that all Hitler meant to do was bring the ethnic Germans from outlying areas into the German fold, and then he would be satisfied and show his gratitude by rooting out Bolshevism. The hook was skilfully baited. Hitler had only to utter the word 'peace' in a speech, and the newspapers broke into impassioned jubilation, forgetting all the crimes that had been committed and never asking why Germany was rearming. Tourists coming home from Berlin, where they had been carefully shown around and flattered, praised the orderly regime of the country and its new master, and the English were coming to think that his claims to a Greater Germany might be justified. No one here realised that Austria was the vital keystone, and as soon as it was broken out of the wall Europe would come tumbling down. As for the naivety, the high-minded trustfulness with which the British in general and their leaders let themselves be beguiled, I observed it with the burning eyes of a man who, at home, had seen the faces of the storm troopers at close quarters and had heard them chanting: "Germany is ours today, tomorrow the whole world." The greater the political tension, the more I avoided conversation and anything else meant for public consumption. Britain is the only Old World country where I never published an article on current events in a newspaper or contributed to radio talks or public discussions. I lived anonymously in my little flat, just as I had lived in my small apartment in Vienna in my student days. So I have no right to describe Britain as if I were an expert on the subject, especially since I did not admit until later that, before the war, I never really appreciated the country's real, deep-seated strength, which emerges and unfolds only at the hour of utmost danger.

I did not see many British writers either. The two to whom I had begun to feel close, John Drinkwater and Hugh Walpole, died prematurely, and I did not often meet younger writers, since I avoided going to clubs, dinners and public occasions out of the tiresome sense of insecurity that weighed on me because I was a foreigner. However, I did once have the special, truly memorable pleasure of seeing the two keenest minds of their time, Bernard Shaw and H G Wells, in a dispute which beneath the surface was highly charged, but to all outward appearances was both brilliantly and civilly conducted. It was at a small lunch given by Shaw, and I was in the half-intriguing, half-embarrassing position of not knowing beforehand the real cause of the subliminal tensions that could be felt flying between the two Grand Old Men of English Literature like sparks of electricity from the first, when they greeted each other with a familiarity slightly tinged with irony. They must have had some difference of opinion on matters of principle, a quarrel that had only just been settled, or perhaps was to be settled at this lunch. Half-a-century earlier the two great men, both of them famous representatives of their country, had fought shoulder to shoulder as members of the Fabian Society in the cause of Socialism, itself still young at the time. Since then, in keeping with their very pronounced and different characters, they had moved progressively further apart, with Wells standing by his active idealism and still tirelessly building on his vision of the future of humanity, while Shaw increasingly contemplated both the future and the past with sceptical irony, exercising his mordant wit on them. Over the years they had also become opposites in their physical appearance. Shaw, an improbably sprightly eighty-year-old who nibbled only nuts and fruits for lunch, was tall, thin, always highly strung, with a wry smile playing around the corners of his loquacious mouth, more enamoured than ever of his own firework display of paradoxes; Wells, in his seventies, was still full of zest for life and appreciative of its good things. He was increasingly comfortable in appearance, small and rosy-cheeked, but relentlessly serious behind his occasional show of merriment. Shaw's aggressive manner was dazzling as he swiftly changed from one attacking standpoint to another; Wells was tactically strong in defence and as always stood firmly by his own convictions. My impression was that he had not just come to this lunch for friendly conversation, but for a confrontation on principles. Unaware of the background to this conflict of ideas, I sensed the atmosphere all the more strongly. Pugnacity, often high-spirited but perfectly serious, was evident in every gesture, glance and word of the two combatants; they were like two fencers trying out their agility with small, exploratory feints before launching into a serious attack. Shaw's mind worked faster, and his intellect flashed in his eyes beneath those beetling brows when he answered or parried a thrust. The pleasure he took in wit and wordplay, honed to virtuoso perfection over sixty years, was intensified to the point of exuberance. His bushy white beard sometimes shook with his soft, sardonic laughter, and as he tilted his head slightly to one side he seemed to be watching the flight of his arrow, to see if it had hit the mark. Wells, of the red cheeks and calm, hooded eyes, was keener and more straightforward in attack; he too had a remarkably quick mind, but it did not strike such a dazzling shower of sparks. He preferred to thrust less fiercely, but with easy self-confidence. The strokes went swiftly back and forth, blades flashing as they fenced, parry and thrust, thrust and parry, always apparently just in play. A neutral spectator could admire all this, enjoying the cut and thrust of their sparkling swordplay to his heart's content. But behind this swift exchange of dialogue, conducted on the highest level, there was a kind of intellectual anger tamed, in the civilised British way, to take a dialectically urbane form. There was a serious note in their playfulness and a playful note in their gravity; that was what made the discussion so fascinating—a keenly fought conflict between two characters who were poles apart, superficially sparked off by some down-to-earth matter, but really conducted from behind lines immutably drawn for hidden reasons of which I had no idea. However, I had seen the two finest minds in England at one of their finest moments, and the polemics which continued in print in the *New Statesman and Nation*[1] over the next few weeks did not give me one-hundredth of the pleasure I had felt in their scintillating conversation, because the arguments in the pages of the journal were abstract, and a reader did not see the nature of the living writers who had produced them so clearly. In fact I have seldom relished the sparks struck off one intellect by another as much, and never before or since have I seen, in a comedy on any stage, such a dazzling display of the art of dialogue as at that lunch, where it was all performed on the spur of the moment, without theatrical artifice, and in the most high-minded spirit.

But I spent those years in England only in the sense that I was physically there, not with my whole heart and mind. Nerve-racking anxiety about the fate of Europe induced me to travel a great deal in those years between Hitler's rise to power and the outbreak of the Second World War, even crossing the Atlantic Ocean twice. Perhaps I was driven by a presentiment that as long as the world was still open, and ships could navigate the seas in peace, I ought to gather as many impressions and experiences as the heart could hold, to be stored up for darker days, or perhaps it was a desire to know that, while distrust and discord were tearing our old world to pieces, another was in construction. Perhaps it was even a vague premonition that our future, including my own, lay outside Europe. A lecture tour taking me all over the United States was a welcome opportunity to see that great country, unified as it essentially is in spite of its wide variety, travelling through it from east to west and north to south. Even stronger, if anything, was the impression made on me by South America when I happily accepted an invitation to attend the International PEN Club Congress there. I had never felt it more important to show support for the idea of intellectual solidarity between all lands and all languages. The last hours I spent in Europe before setting out on this journey gave me plenty to think about on the way. The Spanish Civil War had broken out in the summer of 1936. On the surface, it was only an internal dispute in that beautiful and tragic country, but it really represented the preparatory manoeuvring of two ideological groups in their struggle for power. I had sailed from Southampton on a British ship, and expected that the steamer would avoid putting in at Vigo, usually its first port of call, in order to avoid the war zone. To my surprise, however, we did come into harbour there, and passengers were even allowed to go ashore for a few hours. At the time Vigo was in the hands of the Francoists, and was some way from the real theatre of war. All the same, I saw something in those few hours that would have caused anyone unhappy reflections. Outside the Town Hall where Franco's flag was hoisted, young men in rustic clothing, in parties usually led by priests and obviously brought in from the surrounding villages, were standing lined up in rows. At first I didn't understand what they were there for. Were they labourers being recruited for some kind of emergency service, or the unemployed who had come for a distribution of food? But fifteen minutes later I saw the same young men coming out of the Town Hall again transformed. They wore neat brand-new uniforms, and were carrying rifles and bayonets. Under the supervision of officers, they were loaded into equally brand-new motor vehicles and driven through the streets and out of town. It was a shock. Where had I seen that before? First in Italy, then in Germany! Those immaculate new uniforms, new vehicles and new machine guns had suddenly materialised in both countries. And once again I asked myself: "Who is supplying those uniforms, who is paying for them, who is organising these obviously indigent young rustics to go and fight their own legally elected representative body, the parliament in power?" I knew that the state treasury and the arsenals were in the hands of the legal government. These vehicles and guns must therefore have come from abroad, no doubt brought in over the border with neighbouring Portugal. But who had supplied and paid for them? There was a new power here aiming to seize government in the country, and the same power was already at work in other places, a power that was not averse to violence, actively called for violence, and regarded all the ideas we valued and for which we lived, such as peace, humanity, reconciliation, as outmoded weakness. There were mysterious groups hiding under cover in offices and industries that cynically exploited the naive idealism of youth for their own ends, to promote their own will to power.

It was a desire for violence using a new, more subtle technique to bring down the old barbarism of war on our unhappy continent of Europe again. Something that you may have seen just once, but with your own eyes, is always more forceful than a thousand newspaper reports and pamphlets. I never felt that more strongly than when I saw those innocent young men, provided with guns by mysterious figures pulling strings behind the scenes, going off to fight equally innocent young men who were also their own countrymen. I was overwhelmed by a presentiment of what lay ahead—ahead of us and of Europe. When the ship sailed after several hours in port, I went straight down to my cabin. I would have found it too painful to take another look at that beautiful country, fallen victim to terrible devastation through no fault of its own. I felt that Europe, in its state of derangement, had passed its own death sentence—our sacred home of Europe, both the cradle and the Parthenon of Western civilisation.

The sight of Argentina was all the more delightful. Here was Spain again, its old culture preserved and kept safe in a new, wider land not yet fertilised with blood and poisoned by hatred. There was plenty of food, enough and to spare, and plenty of land to ensure food in the future. I felt a sense of great happiness, and a kind of new confidence. After all, cultures had emigrated from land to land for thousands of years, and when the axe had felled the tree its seeds had been saved to provide new blossom and new fruit. What generations had done before us was never entirely lost. You just had to learn to think in larger dimensions, to expect everything to be on a larger scale. I told myself that we ought not to think solely in terms of Europe, but begin looking further afield, not burying ourselves in a dying past but participating in its rebirth. From the warm welcome given to our Congress by the whole population of this new city of millions of inhabitants, I could tell that we were not really strangers here, a place where the belief in intellectual unity to which we had devoted the best part of our lives was still alive and well—in these days of new, faster transport, even the ocean did not separate us. A new task lay ahead instead of the old one—to build the sense of community we had always dreamt of, but on a larger scale and to a bolder concept. If I had given up Europe for lost with that last glimpse of the coming war, I began to have faith and hope again under the Southern Cross.

I gained an equally powerful and no less promising impression of Brazil, a country on which Nature had lavished gifts and boasting the most beautiful city on earth, a country of such vast extent that it still cannot be crossed entirely by rail or road, and only just by air. The past was more carefully preserved here than in Europe itself; the brutalisation that followed in the wake of the First World War had not yet infected manners and morals this side of the ocean. People lived together more peacefully and with more courtesy here, and relations between different ethnic groups were not as hostile as we are used to in Europe. Man was not separated by man on the grounds of absurd theories of blood, race and origins. I felt, with a curious premonition, that I could live in peace in Brazil, a country with untold space for future development, whereas in Europe states fought and politicians argued fiercely over every little scrap of territory. Here the land was still waiting for people to come and live in it, make use of it, fill it with their presence. Here the civilisation created in Europe could continue and develop in new and different forms. My eyes, delighted by the vast variety of the beauties of this new nature, had a glimpse of the future.

But travelling, even as far as to other worlds under other stars, did not allow me to escape Europe and my anxieties. It seems almost like Nature's fierce revenge on mankind that all the achievements of technology through which we have taken her mysterious forces into our own hands simultaneously destroy the soul. The greatest curse brought down on us by technology is that it prevents us from escaping the present even for a brief time.

Previous generations could retreat into solitude and seclusion when disaster struck; it was our fate to be aware of everything catastrophic happening anywhere in the world at the hour and the second when it happened. However far I went from Europe, its fate came with me. Landing in Pernambuco by night, with the Southern Cross overhead and dark-skinned people around me in the street, I saw a newspaper placard with news of the bombing of Barcelona and the shooting of a Spanish friend of mine with whom I had spent several pleasant hours a few months before. Sitting in a Pullman car passing through Texas, between Houston and another oil town, I suddenly heard a voice shouting furiously in German. A fellow passenger, thinking nothing of it, had tuned the train radio to a German wavelength, and as the train rolled on through the Texas plain I had to listen to one of Hitler's harangues. There was no getting away from it by day or night; I was forced to keep thinking with terrible anxiety about Europe, and within Europe about Austria. It may seem like petty patriotism that, considering the entire vast complex of danger extending from China to the Ebro and Manzanilla, I should be concerned with the fate of Austria in particular. But I knew that the fate of all Europe was linked to the fate of the little country that just happened to be my native land. Looking back, if I try to pick out the political mistakes made after the Great War, I would say that the worst of them was the refusal of European and American politicians alike to adopt Wilson's clear, simple plan, hacking it about instead. His idea had been to grant the smaller nations liberty and independence, but he had correctly seen that such liberty and independence could be maintained only within an organisation of states both large and small linked under a supreme authority. Failure to create that supreme authority—which would have been a genuine League of Nations—implementing only the part of his plan that guaranteed small states their independence, meant not peace but constant tension, for nothing is more dangerous than the

craving of small countries for prestige, and as soon as the first
of those small states were created they began intriguing against
each other, quarrelling over tiny areas of territory, Poles against
Czechs, Hungarians against Romanians, Bulgarians against
Serbs, and the weakest of all in this rivalry was tiny Austria
facing the mighty power of Germany. A country whose rulers
had once governed Europe, now partitioned and mutilated,
Austria was, I repeat, the keystone in the wall. I knew something
that the millions of people around me in the British capital
could not see—with Austria, Czechoslovakia would be bound
to fall, and then the Balkans would be open to Hitler. Thanks
to the particular situation of Vienna, National Socialism would
have in its hands a lever enabling it to take the whole of Europe
apart. Only we Austrians knew how much ambition fuelled by
resentment was driving Hitler on to Vienna. The city had seen
him at his lowest point, and now he wanted to march into it
in triumph. Whenever I had paid a quick visit to Austria and
then went away again over the border, I breathed a sigh of
relief, thinking: "Not yet." And then I looked back as if for the
last time. I could see disaster inevitably coming. Hundreds of
times, every morning in all those years while others confidently
picked up the newspaper, I was afraid of seeing a headline
announcing the fall of Austria. How deluded I had been when
I thought I had detached myself from its fate long ago! From
a distance, I still suffered every day as I witnessed its fevered,
long-drawn-out death agony—I suffered more than my friends
still in the country who were deceiving themselves with patriotic
demonstrations, assuring one another every day: "France and
Britain won't let Austria down, and anyway Mussolini would
never let it happen." They believed in the League of Nations
and the peace treaties just as the sick believe in medicine with
a pretty label. They lived happy and carefree, while I saw the
situation more clearly, and my heart misgave me.

My last journey to Austria had been for the sole reason that

I felt one of those spontaneous fits of fear as the catastrophe came closer and closer. I had been in Vienna in the autumn of 1937 to visit my old mother, and a few weeks later—it must have been towards the end of November—I was walking home down Regent Street and bought a copy of the *Evening Standard* in passing. That was the day when Lord Halifax flew to Berlin to try negotiating personally with Hitler for the first time. The front page of that edition of the *Evening Standard*—I can still see it in my mind's eye, with the text to the right of the page in big black letters—set out the various points on which Halifax hoped to come to an agreement. Among them was a paragraph on Austria. Reading between the lines I saw, or thought I saw, that Austria was soon to be handed over, because what else could a discussion of that subject mean? We Austrians knew that Hitler would never give way on that point. Oddly enough, this programmatic enumeration of points for discussion was printed only in the midday edition of the paper that I had bought, and had vanished without trace from all the subsequent afternoon editions. (I later heard a rumour that the Italian Embassy had leaked it to the paper, because there was nothing Italy feared more in 1937 than an agreement behind its back between Germany and Britain.) I don't know how much of the content of the report—which probably went unnoticed by the vast majority—in that one edition of the newspaper was fact and how much was not. All I know is that I was shocked by the idea of negotiations over Austria already being conducted by Hitler and Britain. I am not ashamed to say that my hands shook as they held the paper. True or false, that news agitated me more than any news item for years, because I could see that if even a fraction of it proved true it was the beginning of the end, the stone would come out of the wall and the wall would collapse. I turned round at once, boarded the next bus going to Victoria Station, and went to the Imperial Airways counter to ask if there was a seat available on a flight to Austria next morning. I wanted to see my old mother, my family and my homeland again. I was able to buy a ticket, and I quickly flung a few things into a case and flew to Vienna.

My friends were surprised to see me back so suddenly and so soon. How they laughed when I told them my fears! Still the same old Jeremiah, they said sarcastically. Didn't I know that the entire population of Austria was now one hundred per cent behind Schuschnigg? They talked at length about the great demonstrations by the Fatherland Front.[2] But in Salzburg I had already seen that while most of those demonstrators wore the regulation party badge on the collars of their jackets for show, so as not to endanger their position, they had long ago hedged their bets by joining the National Socialists in Munich. I had read and indeed written too many stories not to know that the vast majority always go straight over to whichever side holds the balance of power at a given moment. I knew that the voices calling "Heil Schuschnigg!" today would be bellowing "Heil Hitler!" tomorrow. But everyone I spoke to in Vienna genuinely appeared not to have a care in the world. They invited each other to parties where evening dress was *de rigueur*, never guessing that they would soon be wearing the convict garb of the concentration camps; they crowded into the shops to do Christmas shopping for their attractive homes, with no idea that a few months later those homes would be confiscated and looted. For the first time I was distressed by the eternally light-hearted attitude of old Vienna, which I always used to love so much—I suppose I will dream of it all my life—a freedom from care once summed up by the Viennese writer Anzengruber[3] in a line in Viennese dialect, "*Es kann dir nix g'schehn*—nothing can go wrong for you". But perhaps in the last resort all my friends in Vienna were wiser than me, because they did not start suffering in earnest until disaster struck, whereas my own imagination had been through it all in advance, and then had to suffer it a second time in reality. None the less, I did not understand them and could not get them to

430

understand me. After the second day I stopped warning anyone. Why upset people who didn't want to be upset?

However, it is not a retrospective flourish but the plain truth when I say that on those last two days in Vienna, I looked at every one of the familiar streets, every church, every park and garden, every old nook and cranny of the city where I had been born with a desperate, silent farewell in my mind—"Never again." I embraced my mother with the same secret knowledge that it was for the last time. I turned that farewell glance on everything I saw in the city and the country, knowing that it was goodbye for ever. I passed Salzburg, where the house in which I had worked for twenty years stood, without even getting out of the train. I could have seen my house on the hill, with all its memories of past years, from the carriage window, but I didn't look. What was the point? I would never live there again. And as the train crossed the border I knew, like the patriarch Lot in the Bible, that all behind me was dust and ashes, the past transformed into a pillar of bitter salt.

I thought I had anticipated all the terrible things that could happen when Hitler's hate-fuelled dream came true and he made his triumphant entry into Vienna, the city that had rejected him as a poverty-stricken failure in his youth. But my ideas, indeed any imaginable human ideas, lagged far behind the inhumanity that discharged itself on 13th March 1938, the day when Austria fell victim to naked violence, and with Austria all Europe. The mask came off. Now that the other states had openly shown they were afraid, there was no need for any show of moral scruples to inhibit the regime's brutality. What did Britain, France and the rest of the world matter? The Nazis no longer resorted to hypocritical pretexts about the urgency of opposing and eliminating Marxism. They did not just rob and steal, they gave free rein to every kind of private vengeful instinct. University professors were forced to scrub the streets with their bare hands; devout, white-bearded Jews were hauled into the synagogues by young men bawling with glee, and made to perform knee-bends while shouting "Heil Hitler!" in chorus. They rounded up innocent citizens in the streets like rabbits and dragged them away to sweep the steps of the SA barracks. All the sick, perverted fantasies they had thought up over many nights of sadistic imaginings were now put into practice in broad daylight. They broke into apartments and tore the jewels out of the ears of trembling women—it was the kind of thing that might have happened when cities were plundered hundreds of years ago in medieval wars, but the shameless pleasure they took in the public infliction of pain, psychological torture and all the refinements of humiliation was something new. All this has been described not by one victim but by thousands, and a more peaceful age, not morally exhausted like our own, will shudder some day to read what horrors were inflicted on that cultured city in the twentieth century by a single half-deranged man. For in the midst of his military and political victories, that was Hitler's most diabolical triumph—one man succeeded in deadening every idea of what is just and right by the constant attrition of excess. Before this 'New Order' was ushered in, the world would have been horrified if a single human being had been murdered for no reason, and without recourse to the law. Torture had been considered unthinkable in the twentieth century, and expropriation was called, in plain language, robbery and theft. However, after a whole series of St Bartholomew's Eve Massacres,[4] of prisoners tortured to death in SA cells and behind the barbed wire of concentration camps, what was still considered wrong, what did earthly suffering mean? After the annexation of Austria in 1938, our world became inured to inhumanity, injustice and brutality as never before in hundreds of years. Once what happened in the unfortunate city of Vienna alone would have been internationally condemned, but in 1938

432

the conscience of the world kept quiet, or murmured just a little before forgetting and forgiving.

Those days, when appeals for help cried out from our native land, when you knew your close friends were being taken away, tortured and humiliated, and you trembled for every helpless soul you loved, were among the most terrible of my life. And I am not ashamed to say—for a time like that perverts our hearts so much—that I was not horrified or plunged into grief when news came of the death of my old mother, who had been left behind in Vienna. On the contrary, I even felt a kind of relief to know that now she was safe from any suffering and danger. Aged eighty-four, almost stone deaf, she had been living in an apartment that was part of our family home, so that for the time being she could not be dislodged from it even under the new Aryan laws, and we had hoped to be able to bring her out of Austria in some way or other after a while. One of the first decrees issued for Vienna had hit her hard. At eighty-four she was not good on her legs, and when she took her little daily constitutional, after five or ten minutes' walking with some difficulty she used to sit down and rest on a bench beside the Ringstrasse or in the park. Hitler had not been master of the city for a week before brutal orders were given that no Jew must sit on any public bench—one of those prohibitions obviously and exclusively designed for the sadistic purpose of maliciously tormenting people. For there was some kind of logic and perceptible point in robbing Jews, since the Nazis could feed their own forces and pay their hangers-on with the proceeds of the loot they had taken from factories, dwelling houses, villas, and other places now vacated. After all, Goering's picture gallery owes its splendours mainly to that practice, in his case exerted on the grand scale. But forbidding an old lady or an exhausted elderly gentleman to rest for a couple of minutes on

433

a bench was an idea reserved for the twentieth century and the man adored by millions as the greatest of his age.

Fortunately my mother was spared long experience of such brutal humiliation. She died a few months after the occupation of Vienna, and I cannot refrain from recording an incident connected with her death. It seems to me important to mention such details for the benefit of posterity, who will surely consider these things impossible. My mother, aged eighty-four, was found unconscious one morning. The doctor who was called in said at once that she was unlikely to live through the next night, and found a nurse, a woman of about forty, to stay beside her deathbed. Neither my brother nor I, her only children, were in the city, and of course we couldn't come back; even returning to see our dying mother would have been considered a crime by the representatives of German culture. A cousin said he would spend the evening there, so that at least one of the family was with her when she died. This cousin of ours was a man of sixty at the time, not in good health himself, and in fact he died a year later. When he began improvising himself a bed for the night in the next room, the nurse came in and said—to her credit, looking ashamed of it—that under the new German laws she was afraid that meant she couldn't stay with her patient overnight. My cousin was Jewish, and as a woman under fifty she wasn't allowed to spend a night under the same roof as a Jew, even to care for a dying woman. By the standards of the Streicher mentality, any Jew's first thought was bound to be to commit an act of 'racial disgrace' with her.[5] Of course, she said, this prohibition was terribly embarrassing to her, but she was obliged to obey the law. So my sixty-year-old cousin had to leave the apartment that evening, just to enable the nurse to stay with my dying mother. It will perhaps be understandable that I thought my mother lucky not to have to live among such people any longer.

The fall of Austria brought a change in my private life which at first seemed to me entirely unimportant, a mere formality. I lost my Austrian passport and had to apply to the British authorities for a white substitute document, a passport for a stateless person. In my cosmopolitan reveries I had often secretly thought what a fine thing it would be, how very much in accordance with my own feelings, to be stateless, owing no obligation to any country and for that very reason belonging to them all without distinction. But yet again I was forced to recognise how inadequate the human imagination is, since we understand our strongest feelings only when we have suffered them in person. Ten years earlier, when I happened to meet Dmitri Merezhkovsky in Paris and he was bewailing the fact that his books were banned in Russia, I had tried to console him—rather thoughtlessly, given my own inexperience—by making light of that fact, which was as nothing compared to their distribution all over the world. I understood his grief that his words could now appear only in translation, in a changed and diluted medium, much better when my own books disappeared from the German language. And only at the moment when, after some time spent in the applicants' waiting room, I was admitted to the British office dealing with these matters, did I really understand what exchanging my passport for a document describing me as an alien meant. I had had a right to my Austrian passport. It had been the duty of every Austrian consular official or police officer to issue it to me as an Austrian citizen with full civil rights. But I had had to ask for the favour of receiving this English document issued to me as an alien, and it was a favour that could be withdrawn at any time. Overnight I had gone down another step in the social scale. Yesterday I had still been a foreign guest with something of the status of a gentleman, spending his internationally earned money here and paying his taxes, but now I was an emigrant, a refugee. I had been placed in a lower although not dishonourable category. From now on

I also had to ask specially for every foreign visa stamped on that sheet of white paper, since all countries were suspicious of the kind of person I had suddenly become, without rights or a native land, someone who could be turned out at will and deported back to his birthplace if he was a nuisance or outstayed his welcome. I kept thinking of something a Russian exile had said to me years before: "A man used to have only a body and a soul. Now he needs a passport too, or he won't be treated as a man."

And indeed, perhaps nothing more graphically illustrates the monstrous relapse the world suffered after the First World War than the restrictions on personal freedom of movement and civil rights. Before 1914 the earth belonged to the entire human race. Everyone could go where he wanted and stay there as long as he liked. No permits or visas were necessary, and I am always enchanted by the amazement of young people when I tell them that before 1914 I travelled to India and America without a passport. Indeed, I had never set eyes on a passport. You boarded your means of transport and got off it again, without asking or being asked any questions; you didn't have to fill in a single one of the hundred forms required today. No permits, no visas, nothing to give you trouble; the borders that today, thanks to the pathological distrust felt by everyone for everyone else, are a tangled fence of red tape were then nothing but symbolic lines on the map, and you crossed them as unthinkingly as you can cross the meridian in Greenwich. It was not until after the war that National Socialism began destroying the world, and the first visible symptom of that intellectual epidemic of the present century was xenophobia—hatred or at least fear of foreigners. People were defending themselves against foreigners everywhere; they were kept out of everywhere. All the humiliations previously devised solely for criminals were now inflicted on every traveller before and during a journey. You had to be photographed from right and left, in profile and full face, hair cut short enough to show your ears; you had to have fingerprints taken—first just your thumbs, then all ten digits; you had to be able to show certificates—of general health and inoculations—papers issued by the police certifying that you had no criminal record; you had to be able to produce documentary proof of recommendations and invitations, with addresses of relatives; you had to have other documents guaranteeing that you were of good moral and financial repute; you had to fill in and sign forms in triplicate or quadruplicate, and if just one of this great stack of pieces of paper was missing you were done for.

All this seems petty, and at first glance it may seem petty of me to mention it at all. But this pointless pettiness has cost our generation a great deal of valuable and irretrievable time. When I work out how many forms I have filled in over the last few years—declarations before making any journey, tax returns, certificates of foreign exchange, forms made out for crossing borders, applications for permits to stay in a country and travel out of it, registration forms for arrival and departure—when I think how many hours I have spent in the waiting rooms of consulates and government offices, facing officials friendly and unfriendly, bored or over-stressed; when I think of the time taken being searched and questioned at border crossing points, only then do I realise how much human dignity has been lost in this century. When we were young we dreamt of it trustingly as a century of liberty and the advent of an era of international citizenship. So much of our productivity, creativity and thought has been wasted by this unproductive and simultaneously soul-destroying fretfulness! Every single one of us has studied more official regulations than books to nurture the mind in these years. Your introduction to a foreign city or a foreign country was no longer, as it used to be, by way of its museums or its scenery, but through getting a permit at a consulate or police station. When we were together—and by 'we' I mean those of us who used to discuss the poetry of Baudelaire and hold

437

impassioned conversations on intellectual problems—we found ourselves talking about affidavits and permits, and whether to apply for a long-term visa or a tourist visa. In the last decade, knowing a girl who works in a consulate and can cut the waiting time short has been more crucially important than the friendship of someone like Toscanini or Rolland. We have been constantly made to feel that we might have been born free, but we were now regarded as objects, not subjects, and nothing was our right but was merely a favour granted by the authorities. We have been repeatedly questioned, registered, issued with numbers, searched, rubber-stamped, and today, incorrigible representative of a freer age that I am, the would-be citizen of a world republic, I regard every one of those rubber stamps in my passport as a brand, all those questionings and searches as demeaning. Yes, all these things are petty, mere pettiness, I know it, pettiness in a time when the value of human life has fallen even faster than the value of currencies. But only if we record these little symptoms will a later world be able to make a correct diagnosis of the circumstances and intellectual devastation of the world we knew between the two world wars.

Perhaps I had been over-indulged in the old days. Perhaps my sensitivity was gradually over-exacerbated by the abrupt reversals of the last few years. Every form of emigration inevitably, of its nature, tends to upset your equilibrium. You lose—and this too has to be experienced to be understood—you lose something of your upright bearing if you no longer have the soil of your own land beneath your feet; you feel less confident, more distrustful of yourself. And I do not hesitate to confess that since the day when I first had to live with papers or passports essentially foreign to me, I have not felt that I entirely belong to myself any more. Something of my natural identity has been destroyed for ever with my original, real self. I have become less outgoing than really suits me, and today I—the former cosmopolitan—keep feeling as if I had to offer special thanks for every breath of air that I take in a foreign country, thus depriving its own people of its benefit. If I think about it clearly, of course I know that is absurd, but when has reason ever had the upper hand of your own feelings? It has not been any help that for almost half-a-century I trained my heart to beat as the heart of a citizen of the world. On the day I lost my Austrian passport I discovered, at the age of fifty-eight, that when you lose your native land you are losing more than a patch of territory within set borders.

But I was not alone in this sense of insecurity. Unrest gradually began spreading all over Europe. The political horizon had been dark since the day Hitler marched into Austria, and those in Britain who had secretly prepared the way for him, hoping that would buy peace for their own country, began having second thoughts. From 1938 onwards every conversation in London, Paris, Rome, Brussels, in any town or village, far removed as it might initially seem from the subject, led to the inevitable question of whether and how war could be avoided or at least postponed. Looking back at all those months of the constant and growing fear of war in Europe, I remember only two or three days of real confidence, two or three days when I felt once more, and for the last time, that the clouds would pass over, and we would be able to breathe freely and in peace again. Perversely, those two or three days were the very ones that are now described as the most fateful in recent history—the days when Chamberlain and Hitler met in Munich.

I know that no one now likes to be reminded of that meeting, when Chamberlain and Daladier, with their backs to the wall and helpless, caved in to Hitler and Mussolini. But as I am trying to present the facts of the matter here, I must admit that everyone who lived through those three days in England felt that they were wonderful while they lasted. The situation

439

at the end of September 1938 was dire. Chamberlain was just back from his second flight to see Hitler, and a few days later we knew what had happened. He had gone to Godesberg to grant Hitler, without reservation, everything that Hitler had previously demanded of him in Berchtesgaden. But what had seemed adequate to Hitler a few weeks earlier was no longer enough to satisfy his hysterical lust for power. The policy of appeasement and the principle of 'try, try and try again' had failed miserably; the epoch of trust and confidence came to an end in Britain overnight. Britain, France, Czechoslovakia, Europe as a whole had to choose between bowing to Hitler's will for power or taking up arms against him, with no other option. Britain seemed determined to fight. The country's rearmament was not being hushed up any longer, but was shown openly, even ostentatiously. Workmen suddenly appeared and began digging in the London parks—Hyde Park, Regent's Park, right opposite the German Embassy—building shelters for the air raids that were expected. The navy was mobilised; officers of the general staff kept flying between Paris and London to ensure that France and Britain coordinated their final preparations. Ships bound for America were besieged by foreigners wanting to get to safety in good time. Britain had not been so much on the alert since 1914. People were visibly more serious and thoughtful. You looked at the buildings and the crowded railway stations wondering, secretly, whether bombs would be dropping on them next day. And Londoners stood and sat behind closed doors to listen to the radio news. Invisibly, yet perceptibly in everyone at every moment, there was great tension throughout the country.

Then came the historic session of Parliament when Chamberlain told the House of Commons that he had made another attempt to come to an agreement with Hitler, and yet again, for the third time, had proposed visiting him in Germany at any place he chose in the hope of lifting the threat of war. No answer had yet come. But in the middle of the meeting of Parliament—with timing that was only too dramatic—a telegram arrived to say that Hitler and Mussolini would agree to a conference in Munich. At that moment the Parliament of Britain ran wild—an almost unprecedented event in the country's history. MPs leapt to their feet, shouting and applauding. The galleries echoed with jubilation. The honourable old House had not been in the grip of such an outburst of elation for years and years as it was at that moment. In human terms, it was a wonderful sight to see how genuine enthusiasm for the thought that peace could be preserved overcame the reserved, stiff-upper-lip attitude generally displayed by the British with such virtuoso skill. Politically, however, that outburst was a serious mistake, for the wild rejoicing in Parliament showed how much the country hated the thought of war, and how ready it was to make any sacrifice for the sake of peace, giving up its own interests and even its own prestige. The result meant that from the first Chamberlain was marked out as a man going to Munich not to fight for peace but to beg for it. But still no one guessed what kind of capitulation lay ahead. Everyone thought—I thought myself—that Chamberlain was going to Munich to negotiate, not to surrender. Then there were another two or three days of waiting on tenterhooks, days when the whole world seemed to hold its breath. Digging went on in the parks, work went on in the munitions factories, anti-aircraft guns were put in place, gas masks were handed out, the evacuation of children from London was considered and mysterious preparations made. No one really understood them, but everyone knew what they were for. Morning, noon, evening and night were passed again in waiting for the newspaper and listening to the radio. That terrible waiting for a Yes or No, with nerves torn to shreds, was like those moments in July 1914 all over again.

And then, suddenly, the oppressive storm clouds cleared as if blown away by a mighty gust of wind, hearts cast off their burden, minds were easy again. News came that Hitler and Chamberlain, Daladier and Mussolini had come to a complete understanding, and even better, that Chamberlain had succeeded in concluding an agreement with Germany which guaranteed the peaceful resolution of all possible future conflicts between the two countries. It seemed like a decisive victory for the persistent desire for peace shown by a Prime Minister who, in himself, was a dry-as-dust, insignificant statesman, and all hearts beat in gratitude to him at that first moment. The message of "peace for our time"[6] was first heard on the radio, and it told our much-tried generation that we could live in peace and free of care once more and go on helping to construct a new and better world. Anyone who tries to deny in retrospect that he was bewitched by those magic words is a liar. Who could believe that a man coming home defeated would stage a triumphal procession? That morning, if the vast majority of Londoners had known precisely when Chamberlain would be arriving back from Munich, hundreds of thousands would have been waiting at the airfield in Croydon to welcome and applaud him as the man who, so we all thought at the time, had saved the peace of Europe and the honour of Britain. Then came the newspapers. They showed the photograph of Chamberlain, whose harsh-featured face usually bore an unfortunate similarity to the head of an angry bird, standing in the doorway of the aeroplane, proud and laughing, waving that historic piece of paper announcing "peace for our time", bringing it home to his people like the most precious of gifts. By evening the cinemas were already showing the scene on newsreels. Audiences jumped up from their seats, shouting and cheering—almost embracing in the spirit of the new fraternity now expected to spread all over the world. Everyone in Britain and particularly London at the time found that an unforgettable day, a day to lift the heart.

I like to walk about the streets on such historic days so as to get an even stronger and more immediate idea of the atmosphere, literally breathing the air of the time. The workmen had stopped digging in the parks, and people stood around them laughing and talking, because the message of "peace for our time" had rendered the air-raid shelters superfluous. I heard two young men making fun of the shelters in the purest cockney, expressing a hope that they could be converted into underground public conveniences, since London didn't have nearly enough of those. Everyone joined in the laughter, all the people there seemed refreshed, livelier, like plants after a heavy storm. They walked more erect than the day before, their shoulders were straight again, and there was a cheerful light in those usually cool English eyes. The buildings seemed less dismal now that the threat of bombs was gone, the buses looked smarter, the sun brighter, the spirits of thousands upon thousands were raised and strengthened by that one intoxicating phrase. I felt elated myself. I walked on without tiring, faster and faster, more relaxed. I too was borne up more strongly and cheerfully by the new wave of confidence. On the corner of Piccadilly I suddenly saw someone hastily coming towards me. He was a British civil servant whom I knew, but only slightly, and he was naturally a reserved and unemotional man. In normal circumstances we would just have passed the time of day politely, and it would never have occurred to him to accost me. Now, however, he came right up to me, eyes shining. "Well, what about Chamberlain, then?" he said, beaming with delight. "Nobody believed him, but he was right all along. He never gave way, and he's saved peace."

That was how everyone felt, and so did I that day. The next day too was a happy one. The newspapers all rejoiced, rates shot up on the Stock Exchange, friendly messages came from Germany for the first time in years. There was some idea in France of putting up a monument to Chamberlain. But that was only the flame flaring brightly for the last time before it finally went out. Over the next few days, the depressing details seeped through—how complete capitulation to Hitler had been, how shamefully Czechoslovakia, which had been promised help and support, had been abandoned to its fate, and in the next week it was already obvious that capitulation to Hitler had not been enough. Even before the ink of the signatures on the agreement was dry, it was being breached in every point. Goebbels was shouting it to the rooftops that Britain had been up against the wall in Munich. The bright light of hope had gone out. But it had shone for a day or so, warming our hearts. I cannot forget those days, and would not wish to.

Although I was in England, paradoxically enough, from the moment when we realised what had actually happened in Munich I mingled with few of my English acquaintances. It was my fault for avoiding them, or rather avoiding conversation with them, although I found myself admiring them more than ever. They were generous to the refugees who came flooding over now, and gave evidence of great helpfulness and sympathy. But a kind of wall grew up between them and us, keeping us on separate sides. We had been through what was coming on an earlier occasion, and they had not. We understood what had happened and would happen—but they refused to understand it, to some extent against their better judgement. In spite of everything they tried to persist in the delusion that a man's word was his bond, a treaty was a treaty, and they could negotiate with Hitler if they were only reasonable and talked to him on a human level. Pledged to keep the law by hundreds of years of their democratic tradition, leading circles in British society could not or would not see that a new technique of deliberate and cynical amorality was being built up next door, and the new Germany was breaking all the rules of the game usual in dialogue between law-fearing nations as soon as those rules got in their way. To the clear-thinking and far-sighted British, who

444

had given up ideas of adventure long ago, it seemed unlikely that a man like Hitler who had risen to such a high position so fast would go to extremes. They persisted in hoping and thinking that he would turn against other enemies first, preferably Russia, and in the interim period some kind of agreement with him could be reached. We, on the other hand, knew that terrible things were to be expected as a matter of course. We all had the image of a murdered friend or a tortured comrade in our minds, and so our eyes were colder, sharper, more unsparing. We had been cast out, hunted, deprived of our rights; we knew that no pretext was too ridiculous or mendacious when it came to robbery and violence. So we spoke different languages, those who had gone through trials and those who had been spared them, the emigrants and the British. I don't think I am exaggerating if I say that apart from a vanishingly small number of English people, we were alone in the country at that time in cherishing no illusions about the extent of the danger. As in Austria in the past, in England now I was fated to look ahead with painful clarity, torment in my heart, and see the inevitable approaching, except that here it was not for me, as a foreigner and a guest suffered to stay in the country, to issue warnings.

So those of us already branded with the mark of war had only ourselves to talk to when the bitter foretaste of what was coming seared our lips, and our hearts were tormented by anxiety for the country that had taken us in like brothers. However, the friendly hours I spent with Sigmund Freud in those last months before the catastrophe showed me, memorably, how even in the darkest days a conversation with an intellectual man of the highest moral standards can bring immeasurable comfort and strength to the mind. For months the idea that Freud, then eighty-three years old and unwell, was still in Hitler's Vienna weighed on me, until that wonderful woman Princess Maria Bonaparte,[7] his most faithful pupil, managed to get him out of the city now reduced to servitude and bring him to London. It was a happy day in my life when I read in the newspaper that he was in the British Isles, and I saw the most revered of my friends, whom I had already thought lost, return from the realm of Hades.

I had known Sigmund Freud—the great, stern figure who deepened and expanded our knowledge of the human mind like no one else of our time—in Vienna when he was still considered a dogged and awkward loner. Fanatical in his pursuit of truth, but also well aware that every truth has its limitations—he once said: "Nothing is one hundred percent true, just as there's no one hundred per cent proof alcohol!"—he had alienated himself from the academic caution of the University by his tenacity in venturing into areas of the conscious and unconscious mind hitherto unexplored, indeed avoided fearfully, for the subject was in a sphere that, at the time, was decidedly taboo. The optimistically liberal world somehow sensed that this man of uncompromising intellect, with his theories of depth psychology, was implacably undermining its own belief in the gradual suppression of instinctive drives through reason and progress, and his pitiless technique of revelation would endanger its way of ignoring what was uncomfortable. However, not only did the University and the coterie of old-fashioned neurologists band together against this inconvenient outsider—so did the whole world, or the whole of the old world, the old way of thinking, moral conventions, the entire epoch that feared him as a man who would reveal secrets. Gradually a medical boycott formed against him, he lost his practice, and since it was impossible to provide scientific refutation of his theses and even the boldest of the problems he formulated, attempts were made to deal with his theories of the meaning of dreams in the typical Viennese way by treating them ironically or turning them into a joke, a comical parlour game. Only a small circle of faithful friends and students assembled around the solitary man for the weekly discussion evenings in which the new science of psychoanalysis first took form. Long before I myself was aware of the extent of the intellectual revolution slowly gathering pace as a result of the first works of Freud, which laid the foundations of psychoanalysis, that extraordinary man's strong, morally unshakeable attitude had won me over. Here at last was the kind of man of science who was the ideal model for a young man, cautious in every statement he made until he had final proof of it and was absolutely certain, but not to be moved by the opposition of the whole world once he felt that a hypothesis was a valid certainty. He was a modest man himself, but would fight firmly for every point in his doctrines, and faithful until his death to the inherent truth that he defended in his scientific findings. I can think of no man more intellectually fearless. Freud would never shrink from saying what he thought, even if he knew that his clear, implacable approach was going to disturb and upset others. He never tried to make the least concession—even a formal one— to ease his difficult position. I am certain that Freud would have been able to express four-fifths of his theories without encountering any academic resistance if he had been prepared to put them in a more discreetly veiled form, to say 'eroticism' instead of 'sexuality', 'Eros' instead of 'the libido', and if he had not always insisted on setting out all his conclusions clearly but had just hinted at them. However, where his ideas and the truth were concerned, he was intransigent; the more resistance he met the more firmly determined he was. If I look around for an example of moral courage—the only form of heroism on earth that does not ask other people to make sacrifices—I always see before me the handsome, virile clarity of Freud's face, with his calm dark eyes looking straight at you.

The man who had fled to London from his native land, to which he had brought fame all over the world and for all time, was old and had been severely ill for some while. But he was not a bowed, exhausted figure. I had been secretly a little afraid of finding Freud embittered or with his mind disturbed when I saw him again, after all the terrible trials he must have endured in Vienna, but I found him more at ease and happier than ever. He took me out into the garden of his suburban London house. "Did I ever live better anywhere?" he asked, with a bright smile playing around the corners of his once severe mouth. He showed me his beloved Egyptian statuettes, which Maria Bonaparte had rescued for him. "I'm home again, as you see." The big folio pages of the manuscript on which he was working lay open on his desk. At eighty-three he still wrote every day in the same clear, round hand, and his mind was as lucid and untiring as in his prime. His strong will had overcome everything—sickness, old age, exile, and for the first time the kindliness stored up in his nature during the long years of conflict flowed freely. Age had only made him milder, and the trials he had undergone more understanding. He sometimes indulged in affectionate gestures in a way I had never seen in him before, because he was a reserved man. He would put an arm around my shoulders, and there was a warmer expression in his eyes behind his flashing glasses. In all those years, a conversation with Freud had always been one of my greatest intellectual pleasures. You were learning from him and admiring him at the same time; you felt, with every word he spoke, that you were understood by that great mind, which never condemned anyone, and could not be shocked by any confession or thrown off balance by anything anyone said. To him, his will to see others clearly and help them to understand their own feelings equally clearly had long ago become the instinctive purpose of his life. But I never felt how irreplaceable those long conversations were, or felt it more gratefully, than in that dark year, the last of his life. As soon as you entered his room, it was as if the lunacy of the outside world had vanished. All that was particularly cruel became abstract, confusions were clarified, the present meekly took its place in the great cyclical phases of transient time. I truly felt, at last, that I really knew that genuinely wise man who rose above himself, regarding pain and death not as a personal experience but an impersonal subject for study and observation. His death was no less of a great moral achievement than his life. Freud was very ill at the time with the disease that was soon to take him from us. It was obviously hard for him to talk with the plate he wore in his mouth, and you felt ashamed of receiving every word he spoke because articulating it was such a strain. But he never let one word go unspoken. It meant much to his steel-hard mind to show his friends that his will was still stronger than the lesser torments his body gave him. Mouth distorted with pain, he wrote at his desk until the very last few days, and even when his sufferings kept him from sleeping at night—and his wonderfully deep, healthy sleep had been the source of his strength for eighty years—he refused sleeping pills or pain-killing injections. He did not want the clarity of his mind to be impaired for a single hour by such palliatives, he prefered to suffer and stay fully conscious, he would rather think while in pain than not think at all. His was a heroic mind to the very last moment. His death was a terrible struggle, and the longer it lasted the more uplifting it was. As time went by, death cast its shadow more and more clearly over his face. Death hollowed his cheek, chiselled the line of his temples beside his brow, twisted his mouth sharply, silenced his lips. But Death the dark strangler could not prevail over his eyes and the impregnable watchtower from which his heroic spirit looked out at the world. Eyes and mind remained clear to the last. Once, on one of my last visits to him, I took Salvador Dalí, in my view the most talented painter of the new generation, who venerated Freud. While I was talking to Freud, Dalí did a sketch of him. I never dared show it to Freud, because Dalí had prophetically shown death in his face.

That struggle by the strongest will and most penetrating mind of our time against its downfall grew more and more cruel. Only when he himself clearly recognised—he, to whom clarity had always been the prime virtue of thought—that he would not be able to write or think any more did he act as a Roman hero would, and allow the doctor to put an end to his pain. It was a fine conclusion to a fine life, a memorable death even among the many deaths of that murderous time. And when we, his friends, lowered his coffin into English earth, we knew that we had given that earth the best of our own native land.

I often mentioned the horrors of Hitler's world and the war in those conversations with Freud. As a humane man, he was deeply distressed by that terrible outbreak of bestiality, but as a thinker he was not at all surprised. He had always been considered a pessimist, he said, because he denied the supremacy of culture over our instinctive drives, and current events confirmed in the most dreadful way—not that he was proud of it—his opinion that it is impossible to root the elemental, barbaric destructive drive out of the human psyche. Perhaps, he said, some means of at least suppressing such instincts in the communal life of nations might be found in centuries yet to come, but they would remain ineradicable forces in daily life and fundamental human nature, and maybe they were necessary to maintain a vital tension. In those last days of his life he was even more concerned with the problem of Jewish identity and the present tragedy. The scientist in him had nothing to suggest here, and his lucid mind knew no answer to the problem. He had recently published his study of Moses, presenting Moses himself as a non-Jew, an Egyptian, and by placing him in that category, a theory that would be hard to substantiate, he had offended devout Jews as much as the nationalists. He was sorry now, he said, that he had published the book in the middle of the most terrible hour in Jewish history— "Now that everything is being taken away from the Jews I come

along and take away their great man as well." I had to agree with
him that every Jew had now become seven times more sensitive,
for even in the middle of international tragedy they were the
real victims, the victims everywhere because they had already
been stricken before this blow fell, and wherever they went they
knew that all evils would affect them first and to a greater degree,
and that Hitler, a man more rabid with hatred than any other in
history, was intent on humiliating them and would hunt them to
the ends of the earth until they were underground. More and
more refugees kept arriving week after week, month after month,
and every week in more poverty and distress than the refugees
who had arrived the week before. The first to leave Germany and
Austria in haste had been able to save their clothes, their baggage,
their household goods, and many of them even brought some
money out. But the longer they had believed in Germany, the
harder it was for them to tear themselves away from the country
they loved and the worse it had been for them. First the Jews had
been forbidden to work in their professions, to go to the theatre,
the cinema, museums, and academics had been banned from
visiting the libraries. They had stayed on out of either apathy
or a sense of loyalty, timidity or pride. They would rather, they
thought, be humiliated at home than lower themselves to the
status of beggars abroad. Then they had been deprived of their
domestic servants; radios and telephones had been removed from
their homes, then those homes themselves had been confiscated,
and they had been forced to wear the Star of David, so that
everyone would avoid them in the street like lepers and they
would be recognised as outcasts, to be avoided and abused. All
their rights were cancelled, they suffered all kinds of mental and
physical violence, inflicted on them with playful relish, and every
Jew found that the old Russian proverb—"No one is safe from the
beggar's bag or from prison"—had suddenly come horribly true
for them. Those who were left were thrown into concentration
camps, where German discipline broke the spirit of even the

proudest, robbed them of everything and expelled them from the
country with only the clothes they wore and ten marks in their
pockets. On reaching the border they had to beg at consulates
for shelter in their lands, usually in vain, because what country
wanted to take in destitute beggars who had lost everything?
I will never forget the sight I saw one day in a London travel
agency. It was full of refugees, nearly all of them Jewish, and
they all wanted to go somewhere, anywhere. It didn't matter
what country, they would have gone to the ice of the North Pole
or the blazing sands of the Sahara just to get away, move on,
because their permits to stay where they were had run out and
they *had* to move on with their wives and children, under strange
stars, in a world where foreign languages were spoken, among
people whom they didn't know and who didn't want to know
them. I came upon a man there who had once been a very rich
Viennese industrialist and also one of our most intelligent art
collectors. I didn't recognise him at first, he looked so old, grey
and tired as he clung faintly to a table with both hands. I asked
where he wanted to go. "I don't know," he said. "Who bothers
about what we want these days? You go wherever they'll still let
you. Someone told me it might be possible to get a visa for Haiti
or San Domingo here." It wrung my heart—an old, exhausted
man with children and grandchildren, trembling with the hope
of moving to a country he could hardly even have located on
the map, just so that he could go on begging his way there, a
stranger without any real aim left in life! Near us, someone else
was asking with desperate eagerness how you got to Shanghai.
He had heard that the Chinese would still let refugees in. They
were all crowded together there, former university professors,
bankers, businessmen, property-owners, musicians, all of them
prepared to go anywhere, over land and sea, with the pitiful
ruins of their lives, to do anything and put up with anything
just to get away from Europe. They were like a company of
ghosts. But what shook me most was the thought that these fifty

tormented people represented only a tiny advance guard of the vast, scattered army of five, eight, perhaps as many as ten million Jews already setting out in their wake, millions of people who had been robbed and then crushed in the war, waiting for donations from charities, for permission from the authorities, *&* for money to travel, a gigantic crowd, cruelly expelled and fleeing in panic from the forest fire started by Hitler, thronging the railway stations on all European borders, an entire disenfranchised nation forbidden to be a nation, but a nation all the same, wanting nothing so much, after two thousand years, *¶* as not to be made to go on wandering, to find quiet, peaceful ground on which they could venture to rest their feet.

But the most tragic part of this Jewish tragedy of the twentieth century was that those who were its victims could not see what the point of it was, and knew they were not to blame. When their ancestors had been cast out in medieval times, at least they had known what they were suffering for—their faith and their *¶* law. As a talisman for their souls, they still had what today's Jews lost long ago, an inviolable faith in their God. They lived—and suffered—in the proud delusion that, as Chosen People of the creator of the world and mankind, they were marked out for a great destiny and a special mission, and the promise of the word of the Bible was their commandment and law. When they were burnt at the stake, they held the holy scripture to their breasts, and the inner fire it gave them made the murderous flames seem less fierce. When they were hunted down all over the world they still had one last refuge in the Lord their God, and no earthly power, no emperor, king or Inquisition could drive them out of it. As long as their religion held them together they were still a community, and so a force to be reckoned with; when they were exiled and persecuted they thought they were atoning for their fault in deliberately cutting themselves off from all other nations on earth by their religion and their customs. However, the Jews of the twentieth century were not a community any more, nor had they been for a long time. They had no faith in common with each other, they felt their Jewish identity was a burden rather than a source of pride, and they were not aware of having any mission. They lived at several removes from the commandments of the books that had once been sacred to them, and they did not want to speak the old language they used to share. They were increasingly impatient to integrate with the lives of the peoples around them and become part of their communities, dispersing into society in general, if only to have some relief from persecution and rest instead of moving on. As a result they no longer understood each other, having become part of those other nations—they were more French, German, British and Russian than they were Jews. Only now, when they were all lumped together, swept up in the streets like dirt, bankers from their grand homes in Berlin, synagogue servers from the Orthodox communities, Parisian professors of philosophy, Romanian cabbies, layers-out of the dead and Nobel prize-winners, operatic divas, women hired as mourners at funerals, writers and distillers, men of property and men of none, the great and the small, observant Jews and followers of the Enlightenment, moneylenders and wise men, Zionists and those who had assimilated, Ashkenazi and Sephardic Jews, the just and the unjust, and behind them the frantic crowd of all those who thought they had escaped the curse long ago, converts to Christianity and half-Jews. Only now were Jews forced, for the first time in centuries, to be a single community again. It was a long time since they had felt like that, a community of outcasts driven out again and again since the exile from Egypt. But why was this their recurrent fate and theirs alone? What was the reason for this pointless persecution, what was its aim? They were driven out of the lands where they had lived, but never given any land of their own. They were told: "Don't live here with us", but no one told them where they *were* to live. They were blamed for transgressions but offered no means of atonement.

454

And so they looked at one another with burning eyes as they fled. Why me? Why you? Why you and I together when I don't know you, I don't understand your language, I don't grasp your way of thinking, when we have nothing in common? Why all of us? No one could answer that question. Even Freud, with the most lucid intellect of the time, to whom I talked a great deal at the time, could see no sense in this nonsense and no way out of it. But perhaps it is the ultimate point of the existence of the Jews that, through their mysterious persistence in living on, they raise Job's eternal question to God again and again, to keep that question ⤴ from being quite forgotten.

Nothing is quite such an eerie sensation as when something you thought long dead and buried suddenly approaches you again in its old form and figure. It was the summer of 1939, Munich with its brief delusion that we might have "peace for our time" was long gone, Hitler had already broken his sworn oath and attacked mutilated Czechoslovakia, Memel[8] was occupied, the German press was whipping up feeling and vociferously calling for the annexation of Danzig and the Polish corridor. The awakening of Britain from its blind trust had been a bitter one. Even simple, uneducated people whose horror of war was purely instinctive were beginning to express great displeasure. All the English would speak to you of their own accord, although they are usually so reserved—the porter in our block of flats, the lift boy, our parlour maid as she did the housework. None of them had any clear idea of what had happened, but they all remembered one thing, obvious and undeniable—Chamberlain, as Prime Minister of Britain, had flown to Germany twice to safeguard peace, and no amount of concessions had been enough for Hitler. Harsher voices were suddenly being raised in Parliament, demanding: "Stop aggression!" You could sense preparations being made for—or rather, I should say against—the war that was on its way. Once again the pale barrage balloons went up, still looking as innocent as grey toy elephants—to hover over London, once again air-raid shelters were dug, and the gas masks already distributed were carefully checked. The situation now was just as tense as it had been a year ago, perhaps even more so, because this time the government had a determined and embittered population behind it, a nation that was not naive and innocent any more.

During those months I had been out of London, and had gone out into the country, to Bath. I had never in my life felt more painfully aware of mankind's helplessness in the face of world events. There was I, an alert, thinking human being, remote from anything political, dedicated to my work, quietly and persistently toiling away to give form and meaning to my years of life in my books. And there, somewhere out of sight, were a dozen other people entirely unknown to me, on whom I had never set eyes, a few men in Wilhelmstrasse in Berlin, at the Quai d'Orsay in Paris, in the Palazzo Venezia in Rome, in Downing Street in London, and those ten or twenty people, few of whom had ever shown any evidence of particular intelligence or skill, were talking and writing and telephoning and coming to agreements that the rest of us knew nothing about. They made decisions in which we took no part—we never did come to know the details of them—and in the end they determined the course of my own life and the lives of every one else in Europe. My fate was in their hands, not my own. They destroyed us or spared us, powerless as we were, left us our liberty or forced us into servitude; they decided, for millions, whether it would be war or peace. And there I sat, like everyone else, in my own room, defenceless as a fly, powerless as a snail, while matters of life and death were at stake along with my own private person and my future, the ideas developing in my brain, my plans already made or yet to be made, my waking and sleeping, my will, my possessions, my entire being. There I sat staring

into space like a condemned man in his cell, walled in, chained
up in this senseless, powerless waiting and waiting, while my
fellow prisoners to right and left asked questions, consulted each
other, chattered, as if any of us knew or could know what was
going to happen to us and why. The telephone rang; it was a
friend calling to ask what I thought. The newspaper came, and
confused me even more. There was talking on the radio, one
voice contradicting another. I went out into the street, and the
first person I met asked me whether I thought there was going
to be war or not, although I had no more idea than he did. And
I myself asked other people questions, and talked and chattered
as well, although I knew perfectly well that all the knowledge
and experience I had gathered over the years, all the foresight
I had acquired, was nothing by comparison with the decision
of those dozen or so strangers. I knew that for the second time
within twenty-five years I faced my fate powerless, and there
was nothing I could do of my own free will. Pointless ideas
came into my aching head. In the end I couldn't bear being in
the big city any more, because the posters up on every street
corner with the shrill words on them leapt at me like fierce dogs,
and because I found I was trying to guess the opinions of every
one of the thousands of people passing by simply from looking
at them. But we were all thinking the same—we were thinking
purely in terms of Yes or No, Black or Red, in this crucial game
on which my whole life was staked, the last years still before me,
the books I had not yet written, everything that I had felt until
now was my task in life and gave meaning to life itself.

But the ball on the roulette wheel of diplomacy went on rolling
this way and that, at a slow and nerve-racking pace. This way
and that, back and forth, black and red, red and black. Hope
and disappointment, good news and bad news, and still there
was never a final outcome. Forget it all, I told myself, escape into
your mind and your work, into the place where you are only your
living, breathing self, not a citizen of any state, not a stake in that

infernal game, the place where only what reason you have can still work to some reasonable effect in a world gone mad.

I had a task ready to hand. For years I had been steadily accumulating material in preparation for a major, two-volume account of Balzac and his work. However, I had never found the courage to get down to such a huge, long-term project. Now my lack of courage in facing current events gave me the courage to start it. I went to Bath—Bath because that city, where much of England's glorious literature, above all the works of Fielding, was written, soothes the eye more reliably than any other city in England, giving the illusion of reflecting another and more peaceful age, the eighteenth century. But what a painful contrast there was between the landscape around it, blessed with gentle beauty, and the growing turmoil of the world and my thoughts! Just as the month of July had been more beautiful in Austria in 1914 than any I can remember, that August of 1939 in England was glorious. Once again the soft, silken blue sky was like God's blessing over us, once again warm sunlight shone on the woods and meadows, which were full of a wonderful wealth of flowers—there was the same sense that all was at peace on earth while its people armed for war. And once again, such madness seemed incredible in the face of those meadows flowering on in luxuriant bloom, the peace that the valleys around Bath breathed as if enjoying it themselves. The delightful scene was mysteriously reminiscent of the landscape of Baden in 1914.

And once again I would not believe it. I prepared, as I had before, for a summer trip abroad. The PEN Club Congress was to be held in Stockholm in the first week of September 1939, and my Swedish friends had invited me as an honorary guest, since I no longer represented any nation. My kind hosts had a timetable planned ahead for me which would occupy every midday, every evening, every hour in the next couple of weeks. I had booked a passage by sea long ago. And then the threatening announcements of imminent mobilisation came thick and fast. By all the dictates of reason, I ought at this point to have packed up my books and manuscripts in a hurry before leaving Britain, a country likely to be at war, because as a foreigner in England I was likely to be seen as an enemy alien if war came, and then I would be threatened by every imaginable curtailment of my freedom. But something odd in me refused to obey the dictates of reason and save myself. It was half defiance—I was not going to take to flight again and again, since Fate looked like following me everywhere—and half just weariness. "We'll meet the time as it meets us," I said to myself, quoting Shakespeare. And if it does want to meet you, I told myself, then don't resist. Close as you are to your sixtieth year, it can't get at the best part of your life anyway, the part you have already lived. I stuck to that decision. There was also something else I wanted to do as soon as possible, to put my life in order. I was going to marry for the second time,[9] and I did not want to lose a moment, in case I was separated from my future wife over a long period by internment or some other unpredictable measure. So that morning—it was 1st September, a public holiday—I went to the registry office in Bath to apply for a marriage licence. The registrar looked at our papers, was very friendly and efficient, and like everyone else at that time he understood our wish to marry as quickly as possible. The ceremony was set for next day, and he picked up his pen and began writing our names in the register in handsome, rounded characters.

At this moment—it must have been about eleven o'clock— the door of the next room was flung open. A young civil servant hurried in, flinging his coat on at the same time. "The Germans have invaded Poland. This means war!" he cried out loud in the quiet room. The word fell on my heart like a hammer blow. But the hearts of our generation are used to blows of all kinds. "It doesn't *have* to be war, not yet," I said, with genuine conviction. The young man's reply sounded almost bitter. "No!" he shouted forcefully. "We've had enough! We can't let this start all over again every six months! There has to be an end to it now."

Meanwhile the other civil servant, the registrar who had begun writing out our marriage licence, thoughtfully put down his pen. After all, he said, we were foreigners, and in the case of war that automatically made us enemy aliens. He didn't know whether it was still all right for him to marry us in such circumstances. He was sorry, but he would have to get instructions from London. Then came two days of waiting, hoping and fearing, two days of the most anxious suspense. On Sunday morning news came over the radio—Britain had declared war on Germany.

It was a strange morning. We retreated in silence from the radio that had thrown the bombshell of that message into the room. A message that would outlast centuries, that was going to change our world entirely for ever, and with it the lives of every one of us. A message meaning death for thousands who heard it in silence, meaning mourning and unhappiness, despair and a threat to us all. It might be years and years before any creative impulses could return. War was here again, a war more terrible and far-reaching than any conflict had ever been on earth before. Once again an era had come to an end, and a new era was beginning. We stood in silence in the room, which was suddenly deathly quiet, and avoided looking at each other. Carefree birdsong came in from outside, the sound of the birds' casual love-play carried to us on the mild wind, and the trees swayed in the golden light as if their leaves wanted to touch tenderly like lips. Our ancient Mother Nature, as usual, knew nothing of her children's troubles.

I went into my room and packed my things in a small suit-case. If what a highly placed friend had told me was true, we Austrians living in England would be seen in the same light as Germans and must expect the same restrictions on our movements. I might not be able to sleep in my own bed tonight. I had gone yet another step down in the social scale. For the last hour I had been not just a foreigner in this country but an enemy alien, forcibly banished to some place that did not appeal at all to my anxious heart. For a man who had been exiled from his home long ago by a Germany that branded him anti-German because of his racial origins and his ideas, could there be any situation more absurd than to be forcibly classified now, in another country and on the grounds of a bureaucratic decree, as a member of a community to which, as an Austrian, he had never belonged anyway? With a single stroke of the pen, the meaning of a whole life was turned upside down and meant nothing. I still wrote and thought in German, but all my ideas, every wish I had, belonged to the countries now in arms to fight for the freedom of the world. All other links, all that had been and was now past, everything was torn apart, broken to pieces, and I knew that I would have to begin again—yet again!—after this war was over. For the personal cause to which I had lent the force of my convictions for forty years, the peaceful union of Europe, had been wrecked. What I feared more than my own death, war waged by everyone against everyone else, had been unleashed for the second time. And a man whose impassioned efforts had gone into promoting human and intellectual reconciliation was made, at this moment which of all moments called for a steadfast joint stand, to feel useless and alone as never in his life before, suddenly thrust into outer darkness.

Once again I walked down to the city of Bath for a last look at peace. It lay quiet in the noonday sunlight and seemed just the same as ever. People went their usual way, walking with their usual gait. They were in no haste, they did not gather together in excited talk. They looked casual and composed, in proper Sunday mood, and for a moment I wondered: "Don't they know what has happened yet?" But they were English, they were used to concealing their feelings. They didn't need drums and banners, noise and music, to fortify them in their tough and unemotional resolution. How different it had been in

461

those July days of 1914 in Austria, but then again, how different I myself had been at the time, young and inexperienced, not the man I was today, weighed down by memories! I knew what war meant, and as I looked at the crowded, shining shops I saw a sudden vision of the shops I had seen in 1918, cleared of their goods, cleaned out, empty windows looking back at you wide-eyed. I saw, as if in a waking dream, the long lines of careworn women waiting outside food shops, the grieving mothers, the wounded and crippled men, all the mighty horrors of the past came back to haunt me like a ghost in the radiant midday light. I remembered our old soldiers, weary and ragged, coming away from the battlefield; my heart, beating fast, felt all of that past war in the war that was beginning today, and as yet kept its horrors hidden from view. And I knew that yet again all the past was over, all achievements were as nothing—our own native Europe, for which we had lived, was destroyed, and the destruction would last long after our own lives. Something else was beginning, a new time, and who knew how many hells and purgatories we still had to go through to reach it?

The sunlight was full and strong. As I walked home, I suddenly saw my own shadow going ahead of me, just as I had seen the shadow of the last war behind this one. That shadow had never left me all this time, it lay over my mind day and night. Perhaps its dark outline also lies over the pages of this book. But in the last resort, every shadow is also the child of light, and only those who have known the light and the dark, have seen war and peace, rise and fall, have truly lived their lives.

NOTES

1   This weekly periodical became simply the *New Statesman* in 1964.

2   *Vaterländische Front*, a fascist party founded by Dollfuss, Kurt Schuschnigg's predecessor as Chancellor of Austria, in his attempt to keep the country independent.

3   Ludwig Anzengruber, 1839-1889, dramatist and novelist.

4   Referring to the massacre in Paris in 1572 of the French Protestant Huguenots by Catholics. It began on St Bartholomew's Eve, 23rd August, but in fact went on for weeks and spread from Paris to other parts of the country.

5   *Rassenschande*, racial disgrace, meant sexual relations between a Jew and an Aryan.

6   Frequently misquoted as "peace in our time". But Zweig, who quotes it in English in his original text, got it right.

7   Maria or Marie Bonaparte, a great-great-niece of the Emperor Napoleon, 1881-1962, married the second son of the king of Greece. She was interested in psychology, consulted Freud and became friendly with him. It was to her that he put his famous question, "What does a woman want?"

8   This city in Eastern Prussia, once the most northerly in Germany, had with the surrounding territory been separated from the rest of the country by the Treaty of Versailles, and was to be administered for the time being by the League of Nations. This area was one of the first territories to be annexed by Hitler.

9   As mentioned earlier, Zweig keeps his private life strictly out of his memoirs. When he left Salzburg for the last time, however, his first wife Friderike went on living in the house on top of the mountain, with her daughters by a previous marriage. She and Zweig corresponded, and she sent him the books he asked for when he was in Britain and for his voyage to the American continent. However, during these years they grew apart, and Zweig was becoming emotionally close to his secretary in London, Lotte Altmann. He and Friderike divorced—it seems to have been a fairly amicable arrangement for the most part—and he married Lotte, who died with him in their suicide pact in 1942.

INDEX OF NAMES

$24.95

6/14